Adobe InDesign Masterclass

A comprehensive guide to taking your digital design skills from beginner to professional

Mohammed Jogie

Adobe InDesign Masterclass

Copyright © 2024 Packt Publishing

All rights reserved. No part of this book may be reproduced, stored in a retrieval system, or transmitted in any form or by any means, without the prior written permission of the publisher, except in the case of brief quotations embedded in critical articles or reviews.

Every effort has been made in the preparation of this book to ensure the accuracy of the information presented. However, the information contained in this book is sold without warranty, either express or implied. Neither the author, nor Packt Publishing or its dealers and distributors, will be held liable for any damages caused or alleged to have been caused directly or indirectly by this book.

Packt Publishing has endeavored to provide trademark information about all of the companies and products mentioned in this book by the appropriate use of capitals. However, Packt Publishing cannot guarantee the accuracy of this information.

Group Product Manager: Rohit Rajkumar
Publishing Product Manager: Nitin Nainani
Book Project Manager: Sonam Pandey
Senior Editor: Debolina Acharyya
Technical Editor: Reenish Kulshrestha
Copy Editor: Safis Editing
Indexer: Hemangini Bari
Production Designer: Joshua Misquitta
DevRel Marketing Coordinator: Anamika Singh and Nivedita Pandey

First published: October 2024

Production reference: 1060924

Published by Packt Publishing Ltd.
Grosvenor House
11 St Paul's Square
Birmingham
B3 1RB, UK

ISBN 978-1-80324-744-1

www.packtpub.com

This book is dedicated to all the people who have made me a better person. In memory of my gran, Amina, and adoptive uncle and aunt. To my dear mentors for life, Rehana, Raees, and Nasreen, thank you for your support and love. I extend my gratitude to Professor Don Ryun and Felix for your very kind forewords. To Ken and Joseph, thank you for keeping me honest with your insightful technical reviews. To all my teachers, mentors, colleagues, students, friends, fellow artists, designers, and dreamers, I wish I could mention each of you by name. Suffice it to say, a personal thank you to every single one of you.

I also wish to extend my gratitude to my publisher, Packt, and the amazing team of professionals I've had the distinct pleasure of working with on this project. You are my second family. To Rohit, Nitin, Sonam, Debolina, Reenish, Safi, Joshua, Aparna, Hemangini, Anamika, Nivedita, Naved, all the support staff, and contributors (Keagan, Aamir, Joseph) who are no longer part of the team, a heartfelt thank you.

Finally, I wish to extend my gratitude to you, dear reader, for purchasing this book. Your support of fellow designers helps to build a thriving global creative community founded on shared experience and mutual care.

Mohammed Jogie

Forewords

As a professor deeply involved in branding, design, and interdisciplinary media, I recognize the profound impact mastering a versatile tool like Adobe InDesign can have on a designer's professional trajectory. *Adobe InDesign Masterclass*, expertly compiled by my esteemed colleague Mohammed Jogie, who is a worldly recognized Adobe Creative Ambassador and served with me as a board member for the **International Council of Design (Ico-D)**, is a critical resource for educators, publishers, artists, seasoned professionals, young designers, and students eager to augment their creative potential and elevate their capabilities set in today's digitally driven design media environment.

The importance of Adobe InDesign in the design and media industries cannot be overstated. It is more than just a software application; it is an essential framework through which the most compelling and innovative design work can be realized and shared. Under Jogie's guidance, in this book, readers are not only walked through InDesign's vast array of features but also taught how to integrate these features effectively across various media and platforms. This skill is indispensable in a world where print, digital, and online media landscapes are continually evolving and intermingling.

What sets this book apart is its tailored hands-on approach to learning. Designed with the understanding that progressive designers are future pioneers of the media industry, the book offers step-by-step tutorials, practical exercises, and real-world applications that ensure all lessons are both accessible and applicable. The detailed explanations, supported by numerous illustrations and examples, cater to learners at different levels, making complex concepts easy to grasp for future applications.

This guide also addresses the interdisciplinary needs of modern media professionals by demonstrating how InDesign interacts with other tools in the Adobe Creative Suite. Such knowledge is crucial for creating seamless designs that can adapt from print to diverse digital formats and platforms. This blending of skills is what will set future designers apart, enabling them to plan and create work that is not only visually stunning but also strategically optimized for various platforms.

In conclusion, *Adobe InDesign Masterclass* by Mohammed Jogie is more than just a tutorial; it is a gateway to understanding and excelling in the world of professional design. For educators, students, and budding designers, this book is an essential addition to your toolkit as you journey through the exciting landscape of modern media and integration with diverse platforms.

Don Ryun Chang

Adjunct Professor, Yonsei University Underwood International Songdo Campus

As a visual communicator, Adobe InDesign software has been my companion and an indispensable tool throughout my career. However, when I began my design education and career in my home country of Ghana, I had to learn this software through experimentation. If a resource like *Adobe InDesign Masterclass* by Mohammed Jogie had been available back then, it would have significantly eased my learning process.

Mohammed Jogie, popularly known as Mo, is a colleague and a fellow board member of the *Pan Afrikan Design Institute (PADI)*. I have had the pleasure of meeting him several times during our global design activism. Mo is an expert in Adobe InDesign software and is recognized worldwide as an Adobe Creative Ambassador. His expertise and passion for design are evident in his comprehensive guide, which I highly recommend to all creative professionals, educators, and students.

Felix Ofori Dartey

President of Pan Afrikan Design Institute (PADI)

Contributors

About the author

Mohammed Jogie studied fine art and graphic and multimedia design. His post-grad research focuses on circular and regenerative design processes. He has done work for a number of leading multinationals, including Apple, Wacom, HP, Alludo, Pantone, and Adobe. He served as both an EMEA design evangelist and regional manager for Adobe. He is head of strategy and design at the **Institute of Media, Strategy, and Design** (**iMSD**), a specialist practice offering accredited training, strategy, and design consulting. He is also the founder of *Creativeweek*. He has hosted workshops across the globe, making tools like InDesign accessible to a wide variety of audiences.

He is an Adobe Certified Associate, Adobe Certified Expert, Adobe Certified Instructor, and Adobe User Group Manager. He is active on the design scene too. He has served as Vice President of the **International Council of Design** (**Ico-D**), and board member of the South African Graphic Design Council (think), **Design South Africa** (**DSA**), and the **Communications and Advertising Forum for Empowerment** (**Café**).

He is a member of ISTD and Index, and he is a lead on the Mandela poster project collective and 20x20 design democracy initiatives. He currently serves on the boards of the Visual Arts Network of South Africa, the Pan-Afrikan Design Institute, and the Design Education Forum of South Africa.

He is a coordinator for the senior integrated communication design program at the Tshwane University of Technology. He is an accredited assessor and moderator with the **Media, Information, and Communication Technologies** (**MICT**) Sector Education and Training Authority. He is also accredited with the **Fiber, Processing, and Manufacturing** (**FP&M**) Sector Education and Training Authority. He has authored numerous blended e-learning programs, including Photoshop, Illustrator, InDesign, and Acrobat, among others. He has worked with InDesign and the product teams since its inception.

About the reviewer

Ken Leid has over 40 years of experience in the printing and packaging industry. He started his career in pre-press, keeping pace with technology as it migrated from analog to digital. As Executive Director of the Printing Industries Federation of South Africa for 26 years, Ken was responsible for co-authoring learning materials for over 30 occupational qualifications in the pre-press, printing, packaging, signage, and visual communications industry. Now that he's retired, he continues to focus on the development of quality learning and eLearning materials as well as design and business process re-engineering.

Table of Contents

Preface — xv

Part 1: InDesign Fundamentals

1
Exploring InDesign — 3

The Start workspace	4	Core layout concepts and workflows	19
Exploring the InDesign workspace	5	Setting up your document	19
Try it yourself – Exploring the InDesign workspace	6	Try it yourself – setting up a new document	20
The InDesign toolbox	13	Summary	24
Working with panels	16		
Exploring panel menus	18		

2
Working with Text and Shapes — 25

Opening files and accessing resources	26	Working with text	40
		Arranging objects	45
Drawing basic shapes and changing their properties	29	Designing the rear of the card	53
Creating the logo	33	Summary	57

Part 2: Beyond the Basics

3
Designing Social Media Posts — 61

Exploring the completed project and resources	62	Creating a new social media document	63

Adding guides to the document	65
Importing images into InDesign	66
Cropping an image in InDesign	68
Locking objects	69
Creating rounded corner rectangles	70
Working with type	71
Creating reverse type	74
Importing vector graphics	80
Placing multiple objects	81
Generating QR codes	82
Summary	83

4
Designing with Text and Tables — 85

Setting up a presentation document	86
Adding guides to a document	88
Creating placeholder frames	90
Importing multiple images into InDesign	96
Typing and formatting text in InDesign	100
Importing text from Microsoft Word documents	103
Formatting text attributes	107
Working with styles	108
Removing imported Word styles	110
Applying a style selectively	111
Formatting text for a perfect fit	114
Importing Microsoft Excel tables	115
Wrapping text around objects	117
Formatting tables	118
Header and footer rows	121
Adjusting spacing in table cells	122
Changing cell and text color	123
Adjusting the font and weight properties	124
Changing the stroke properties of cells	124
Applying alternating fills to the table	126
Summary	127

5
An Overview of Color Models — 129

Exploring the chapter resources	130
Understanding Color Models	130
CMYK color	131
RGB color	132
Spot colors	134
Summary	137

6
Working with Graphics and Color — 139

Exploring the completed project and resources	141
Getting started	142
Drawing the buttons and notch	144
Importing graphics into InDesign	148
Formatting type	150
Importing a Photoshop image	153
Adjusting object layer options	154
Object transparency and blending modes	155
Duplicating page elements	157

Working with the Direct Selection tool	159	Applying color to objects	167
Adjusting object layer options	160	Importing multiple files	169
Assigning frame content	161	Object hierarchy	170
Creating the status bar	162	**Placing chart objects in InDesign**	**173**
Creating the navigation bar	163	Inline graphics	178
Working with libraries	164	**Summary**	**184**
Drawing a multi-frame grid	165		

7
Transparency and Effects: Part 1 — 185

Exploring the completed project and resources	**187**	**Creating the primary user interface graphic**	**198**
Getting started	**189**	Working with InDesign libraries	200
Setting up guides and grids	190	Adding an Outer Glow effect	201
Setting up midpoint guides	191	Working with object styles	203
Creating the background	**193**	Placing and formatting the world map	204
Drawing and coloring the background	193	Creating the border elements	206
Applying a custom gradient	194	Duplicating and adjusting element properties	208
Duplicating the background	195	Applying multiple feather effects to elements	209
Applying a satin effect	196	Working with ovals and polygons	214
Rearranging objects and applying blend modes	197	**Summary**	**216**

8
Transparency and Effects: Part 2 — 217

Creating borders	**218**	Selecting objects from the Layers panel	236
Using the Eyedropper tool	220	Adjusting object position	238
Combining elements	**221**	Overset text	242
Applying effects to text	**224**	Step and repeat	243
Headlines	224	Applying arrowheads to strokes	250
Applying effects to type	226	Placing the main sequence labels	253
Applying effects to text and text frames	230	Placing the solar system graphic	254
Applying an object stylesheet	233	Placing the corner earth graphic	255
Creating outer glows	234	Using Pathfinder commands	256
		Placing the final design elements	261
		Summary	**262**

Part 3: Advanced Techniques

9
Advanced Typography 269

More on Styles	270	Mapping Word styles to InDesign styles	282
Exploring the completed project and resources	271	Combining paragraph and character styles	295
Getting started with the menu design	273	Placing type along a path	298
		Local overrides	301
Applying paragraph styles	274	Generating QR codes	302
Exploring OpenType	275		
Style mapping from Microsoft Word	278	Summary	304

10
Preparing Documents for Professional Print 305

Setting up Step and Repeat	306	Creating a merged document	317
Preparing artwork for print	308	Creating print-ready PDF files	319
Using scripts in InDesign	309	Color separations	321
Adjusting the document setup	311	Correcting a color mix	325
Using the Step and Repeat command	312	Preflighting	326
Data Merge	314	Summary	330
Preparing the data source	315		

11
Multimedia, Interactivity, and AI 331

Exploring the exported project	332	Adding multimedia elements to InDesign files	348
Getting started with interactive documents	334	Creating interactive multi-state objects	350
Creating hyperlinks	337	Animating elements	355
Testing interactive elements	339	Exporting interactive documents	356
Working with buttons	341	AI in InDesign	363
Animating elements in InDesign	345	Summary	372

12
Help and Troubleshooting — 373

Registering your Packt account	373	Shortcuts for working with text	376
Keyboard shortcuts	374	Summary	378
Shortcuts for tools	375		

Index — 379

Other Books You May Enjoy — 386

Preface

Thank you for purchasing a copy of *Adobe InDesign CC Masterclass* – the most complete guide to taking your digital design skills from a beginner level to a professional level. This book aims to empower you to create high-quality designs for print and online consumption in the shortest possible timeframe. This book covers core concepts, designing projects for online and print consumption, and creating custom award-winning designs. This book has a fresh project-based approach to sharing information.

Who this book is for

This book has been written with all communication professionals in mind. Whether you happen to be a layout artist, book designer, graphic designer, creative director, corporate communication specialist, publisher, art director, writer, design lecturer, or student, there is something for you. If you're looking to improve your InDesign skills or are someone who has tremendous experience with InDesign, this masterclass book is for you. We cover the fundamentals and advanced concepts of InDesign.

What this book covers

Chapter 1, *Exploring InDesign*, is a fundamental-level chapter that covers the basics of InDesign, including the interface and core aspects of the application. Topics include the toolbox, interface optimization, and setting up documents for various communication needs. Get to grips with the basic principles of InDesign and key concepts and terminology used throughout the book.

Chapter 2, *Working with Text and Shapes*, is a fundamental-level chapter that provides a step-by-step guide to designing a business card from the ground up. Learn how to create and format shapes, adjust fill and stroke properties, and modify text elements. We will preview the final design, setting the stage for more comprehensive projects in the next chapter.

Chapter 3, *Designing Social Media Posts*, is an intermediate-level chapter that teaches you how to integrate various elements when designing a social media post. Work with text, images, and vector graphics to create an impactful final design. Create a post that can be used across multiple social media platforms.

Chapter 4, *Designing with Text and Tables*, is an intermediate-level chapter that demonstrates what a text and table-rich design powerhouse InDesign is. It offers gold-standard typographic control, ranging from time-saving stylesheets to powerful OpenType controls. You will learn how to incorporate text from applications such as Microsoft Word and Excel. These text and table formatting skills will help you enhance your efficiency in InDesign.

Chapter 5, An Overview of Color Models, is an intermediate-level chapter that examines the nuances of color, which are crucial in design and publishing. This chapter explores CMYK, RGB, and spot color models. It provides an overview of color used in professional design for screens, print, and bespoke applications. It serves as a primer for understanding color and is a precursor to the more advanced concepts discussed in *Chapter 6*.

Chapter 6, Working with Graphics and Color, is an intermediate-level chapter chapter that focuses on enhancing your projects with color and graphics, building on general notions of various color spaces. Learn how to manage color resources across projects and integrate content from multiple sources into your InDesign workflow.

Chapter 7, Transparency and Effects: Part 1, is an intermediate-level chapter and the first of two chapters to explore transparency, blend modes, and effects within InDesign. It builds on the foundational skills you've learned thus far. We'll create a heads-up display user interface that involves creating multi-element backgrounds, manipulating drawn elements, applying 3D effects, and integrating blending modes and transparency.

Chapter 8, Transparency and Effects: Part 2, is an intermediate-level chapter that continues from the previous one. It focuses on effects applied to attributes of design elements, such as fills, strokes, and text, while ensuring full editability. Learn how to use object styles for consistency and create bespoke custom shapes using the pathfinder.

Chapter 9, Advanced Typography, is an advanced-level chapter that delves into InDesign's comprehensive typographic tools, essential for professional designers. It covers nested styles, GREP styles, OpenType features, variable fonts, style mapping from Microsoft Word, and custom bullet points. Learn how to manage local overrides, type on a path, text variables, and integrate QR codes into your designs.

Chapter 10, Preparing Documents for Professional Print, is an advanced-level chapter that explores the extensive print management features and customizable controls for high-quality output offered by InDesign. We explore how to resolve alerts to potential problems. Learn how to manage crucial factors such as inks, separations, imposition, step and repeat, ISO-aligned PDF/X exports, and soft proofing for optimal print results. Understanding these concepts ensures you master print and avoid costly mistakes.

Chapter 11, Multimedia, Interactivity, and AI, is an advanced-level chapter that focuses on creating and exporting interactive documents and artificial intelligence. InDesign's multimedia and interactive capabilities make it easy to design digital content for on-screen consumption with seamless, code-free interactivity, responsiveness, and navigation. Learn how to design and export a project to popular formats such as Publish Online, ePUB, and interactive PDF. The AI section of the chapter explores InDesign's latest AI features, including AI-powered layout suggestions, intelligent image fitting, and auto styling and text to image generation. It covers how these tools streamline the design process and enhance creativity and efficiency.

Chapter 12, Help and Troubleshooting, is a collection of useful resources, a curated list of default shortcuts, and where to find help.

To get the most out of this book

Adobe InDesign Masterclass is a project-based book. To get the most out of it, follow each chapter sequentially as they build on one another. Advanced users can skip to relevant chapters that may be of interest. Engage actively with the exercises, applying the techniques to your own projects to reinforce learning. Take advantage of the downloadable resources and templates provided. By experimenting with the advanced features and tools discussed, you'll deepen your understanding and proficiency in InDesign, ultimately mastering the software.

Software/hardware covered in the book	Operating system requirements
Adobe InDesign CC 19.5 or later. If you use an earlier version of InDesign, open the files with an .idml extension. This can be used with versions all the way back to CS4. Note, some features discussed may not be available in older versions.	Windows or macOS

Adobe InDesign Masterclass is centered around projects, providing a practical, hands-on approach to mastering the software. Project files and templates are available for download from https://packt.link/a19oQ, allowing you to follow along and apply the techniques directly.

Download the example files

You can download the example files for this book from https://packt.link/a19oQ.

We also have other downloads from our rich catalog of books and videos available at https://github.com/PacktPublishing/. Check them out!

Conventions used

There are a number of text conventions used throughout this book.

Code in text: Indicates code words in text, database table names, folder names, filenames, file extensions, pathnames, dummy URLs, user input, and Twitter handles. Here is an example: "If you have closed it, choose **File** menu | **Open** and reopen it from the Example files folder."

Bold: Indicates a new term, an important word, or words that you see on screen. For instance, words in menus or dialog boxes appear in **bold**. Here is an example: "Click on the eyeball alongside **Cyan**. Then, do the same for **Magenta** and **Yellow**."

> **Tips or important notes**
> Appear like this.

Get in touch

Feedback from our readers is always welcome.

General feedback: If you have questions about any aspect of this book, email us at customercare@packtpub.com and mention the book title in the subject of your message.

Errata: Although we have taken every care to ensure the accuracy of our content, mistakes do happen. If you have found a mistake in this book, we would be grateful if you would report this to us. Please visit www.packtpub.com/support/errata and fill in the form.

Piracy: If you come across any illegal copies of our works in any form on the internet, we would be grateful if you would provide us with the location address or website name. Please contact us at copyright@packt.com with a link to the material.

If you are interested in becoming an author: If there is a topic that you have expertise in and you are interested in either writing or contributing to a book, please visit authors.packtpub.com.

Share your thoughts

Once you've read *Adobe InDesign Masterclass*, we'd love to hear your thoughts! Scan the QR code below to go straight to the Amazon review page for this book and share your feedback.

https://packt.link/r/1803247444

Your review is important to us and the tech community and will help us make sure we're delivering excellent quality content.

Download a free PDF copy of this book

Thanks for purchasing this book!

Do you like to read on the go but are unable to carry your print books everywhere?

Is your eBook purchase not compatible with the device of your choice?

Don't worry, now with every Packt book you get a DRM-free PDF version of that book at no cost.

Read anywhere, any place, on any device. Search, copy, and paste code from your favorite technical books directly into your application.

The perks don't stop there, you can get exclusive access to discounts, newsletters, and great free content in your inbox daily

Follow these simple steps to get the benefits:

1. Scan the QR code or visit the link below

https://packt.link/free-ebook/978-1-80324-744-1

2. Submit your proof of purchase
3. That's it! We'll send your free PDF and other benefits to your email directly

Part 1: InDesign Fundamentals

This part provides a comprehensive introduction to the core aspects of InDesign, ensuring a solid foundation for new and existing users. Learn about the interface, the toolbox, and setting up documents for various communication needs. It also covers essential principles and key terminology. We will design a business card step-by-step. This part focuses on creating and formatting shapes, adjusting fill and stroke properties, and modifying text elements. This part sets the stage for more complex projects in subsequent parts.

This part has the following chapters:

- *Chapter 1, Exploring InDesign*
- *Chapter 2, Working with Text and Shapes*

Level: Fundamentals

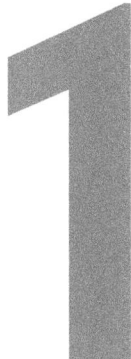

Exploring InDesign

InDesign is a powerful multi-page layout publishing tool for creating dynamic and interactive content across print and digital platforms.

This book is a project-based step-by-step guide to mastering InDesign. You will learn how to create and share professional and impactful visual communications in InDesign. Design with confidence and discover smarter productivity approaches to extract more power from the comprehensive InDesign toolset. You'll learn how to take your designs further by connecting data sources such as Microsoft Word and Excel with the powerful design tools found in InDesign. Craft and enhance your marketing, editorial, and information-based communications with ease.

This book is broken down into three sections. Part one covers the fundamentals of InDesign. Here, we will explore the essentials of the software. We will also work with text, shapes, and the formatting of content. Part two deals with intermediate-level topics. This is where we work with text and tables, graphics and color. We close part two with special effects. Part three looks at advanced features ranging from printing and exporting with confidence, to possibilities with AI-generated and interactive elements in your designs. This book gives you an opportunity to engage with projects relevant to your level of expertise. The book discussess the fundamental features of InDesign and contemporary approaches to design projects. It then moves onto more technically advanced topics including social media, print and electronic publishing, interactive documents, AI, and so much more.

In Chapter 1, we'll explore the interface and familiarize ourselves with the core aspects of the application. This includes the toolbox, setting up rulers, working with panels and menus, and how to correctly set up and control document types for different communication needs. By the end of this chapter, you will be familiar with the fundamental tenets of InDesign. You will also understand some of the key design concepts and terminology used in the field.

The main topics we will cover in this chapter include the following:

- Exploring the InDesign workspace
- The InDesign toolbox
- Panels and panel menus
- Fundamentals of InDesign
- Correct document setup

The Start workspace

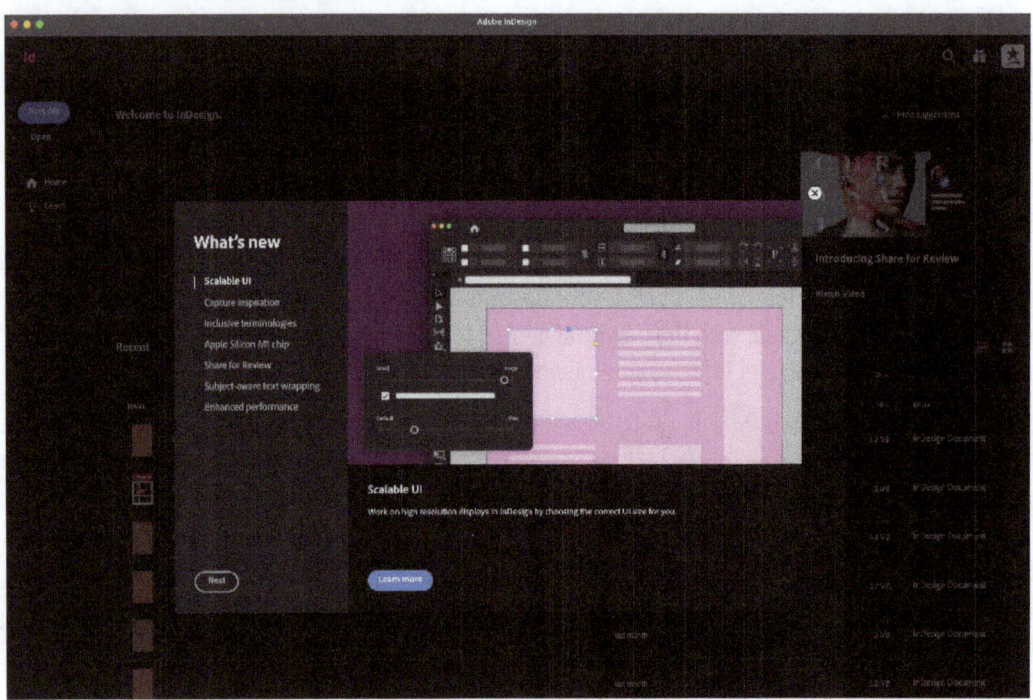

Figure 1.1: The InDesign Start workspace
(The image is intended as a visual reference; the textual information is not essential.)

The Start **Workspace** is the first thing you encounter when you launch InDesign or when you have no documents open. You can invoke the Start workspace at any time by clicking the Home icon . This is a convenient way to open recent documents, access learning resources, create a new document or use an InDesign template.

Exploring the InDesign workspace

InDesign has a rich interface that can appear intimidating to new users. If you are new to InDesign, this chapter will get you up and running in a jiffy. You will have an opportunity to explore it by yourself shortly. A workspace is how the interface elements are arranged. InDesign sports a number of workspaces for different applications, ranging from book design to digital publishing. We'll work primarily with the Essentials workspace in this book. To select this workspace, choose **Window | Workspace | [Essentials]**. We can now explore the InDesign workspace. The numbered screenshot in *Figure 1.2* highlights each component of the interface and is followed by brief descriptions.

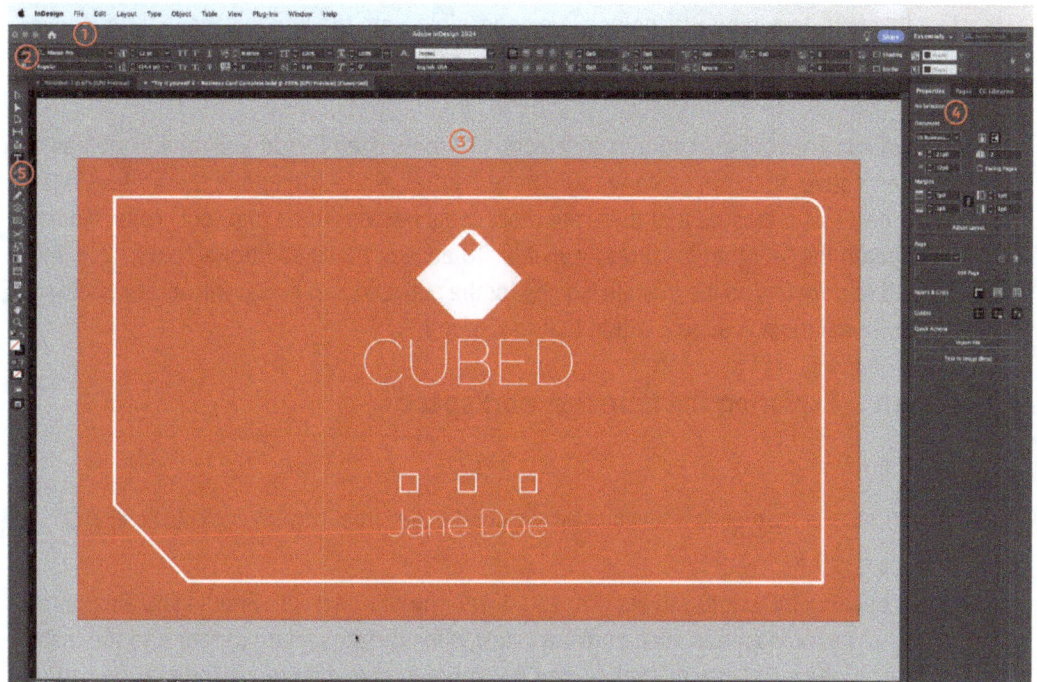

Figure 1.2: The default InDesign interface
(The image is intended as a visual reference; the textual information is not essential.)

1. **Menu Bar**: Found at the very top of the interface, the menu bar includes drop-down options for a wide range of functions, similar to other applications you may be familiar with. Menus include commands for saving files, editing objects, pagination, typographic controls, working with tables, accessing panels, and interface management options.

2. **Control Bar**: This is the context-sensitive horizontal panel found just below the menu bar. The panel presents options and commands depending on the tool or element selected. In other words, panel options are presented relative to the context. For example, text controls will be naturally different from image controls. The control bar offers options that allow for greater control of design elements such as shapes, text, and images.

3. **Document Window**: This is your main work area in InDesign. This is where document composition and layout take place. This area typically hosts document pages and is surrounded by a gray boundary area known as the pasteboard. It is a metaphorical reference to the real-world experience of a page on a desk.

4. **Panels**: Panels provide easy access to important tools and settings for specific tasks. All panels, including the toolbox, are accessible from the **Window** menu. Some have similar functions to the control bar and offer additional controls. Panels are, by default, nested to the right of the InDesign interface.

5. **Toolbox**: The toolbox contains a selection of tools used to add and modify elements in an active document. Many tools have a small white triangle in the bottom-right corner. This indicates that there are more tools nested within that tool group, hidden beneath the tool that is currently visible. To access these additional tools, click and hold your mouse on the triangle icon for the active tool. A popup will appear showing additional tools available within that tool group.

Try it yourself – Exploring the InDesign workspace

> **Note**
> The files referred to in the practical activities can be downloaded from https://packt.link/a19oQ

1. On opening InDesign, you are presented with the Start screen. Should you encounter any pop-up messages such as **What's new**, click the close icon to return to the main Start screen. Be sure to click on the **X** symbol in the white circle to the right of the pop-up message.

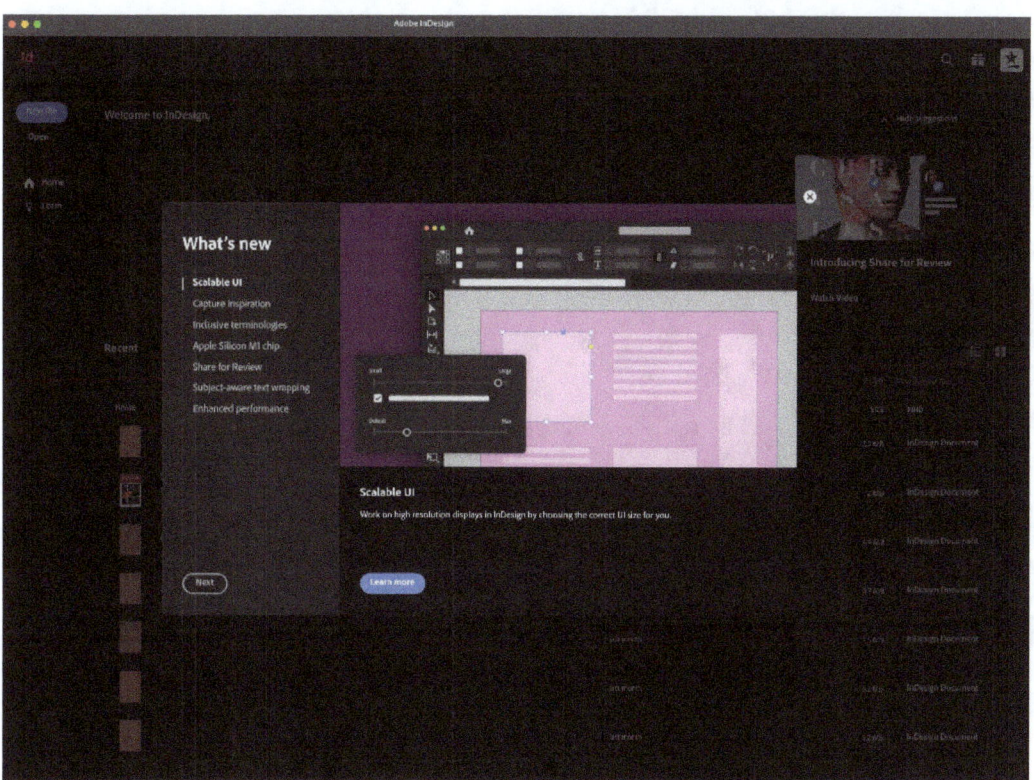

Figure 1.3: The InDesign Start screen
(The image is intended as a visual reference; the textual information is not essential.)

2. To open a file, choose **Open**. Then browse to locate the accompanying downloaded files for this book and choose the file called 01 Exploring the InDesign Workspace.indd from the exercise files.

3. The menu bar is found at the top of your screen, as is the case with the majority of software applications. An important menu is the **Window** menu. This is where you access panels and manage your workspace. Browse through the menus and window options to get a general sense of what is available in the different menus. We will discuss these drop-down menus in detail further on in this book.

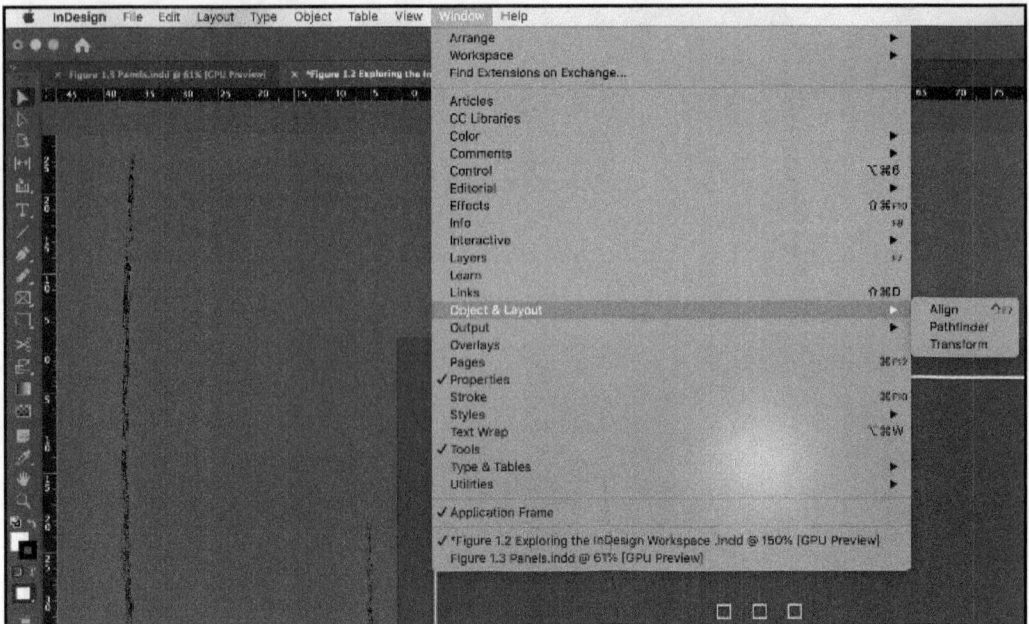

Figure 1.4: The InDesign interface

4. The control bar is found at the top of the interface. If it is not visible, as is the case in *Figure 1.4* above, choose **Window | Control** to make it visible. Let's Explore!. Click on different elements of the artwork, and click on the various tools in the toolbox. Observe the Control bar and **Properties** panel as you do this. Options relevant to the object or tool that you have selected are contextually presented in both panels.

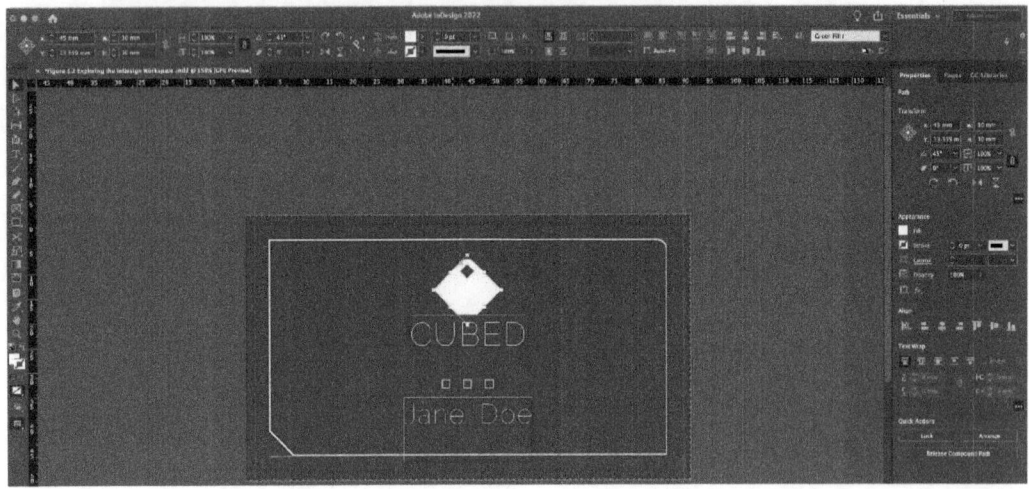

Figure 1.5: The Control bar and Properties panel with a graphic element selected (The image is intended as a visual reference; the textual information is not essential.)

5. Choose the **Type** tool from the Toolbox. The shortcut is the letter *T* on your keyboard. Triple-click the word **CUBED** in the design on the page. The word is highlighted. Note that the options on the Control bar and **Properties** panel have changed to reflect the properties of the selected word while simultaneously offering typographic controls such as font, type size, and so on.

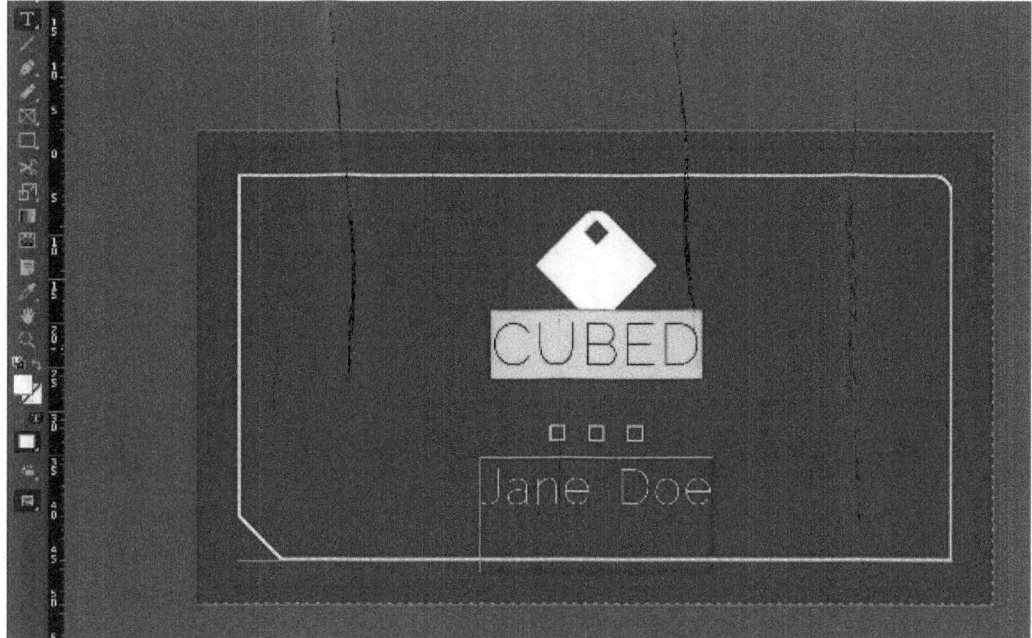

Figure 1.6: The text selected with the Type tool

6. Choose the **Selection** tool from the Toolbox. This is the very first tool found at the very top of the Toolbox on the left side of the workspace. The **Selection** tool shortcut is the letter *V*.

> **Tip**
> If you have the **Type** tool selected, or are typing text in a document, press *Escape* to return to the **Selection** tool.

With the **Selection** tool active, click on the diamond icon (logo) above the word **CUBED**. It will indicate visually that it is selected by way of a series of nodes that appear along the edge of the logo shape. See *Figure 1.7* for a visual of the selected element. Note that the Control bar is displaying a set of controls relevant to the object that is selected.

Figure 1.7: The logo selected with Control bar options

7. Let's change the color of the logo by using a panel. Remember that panels are found to the right of the interface. Click on the **Properties** panel to bring it to the fore. Should you not see the **Properties** panel, choose **Window | Properties**. Under the **Appearance** subset in the **Properties** panel, click on the white swatch alongside the word **Fill**. Then choose **Yellow CMYK** from the flyout menu. The flyout menu is accessed by clicking on the swatch. The logo color should change to yellow.

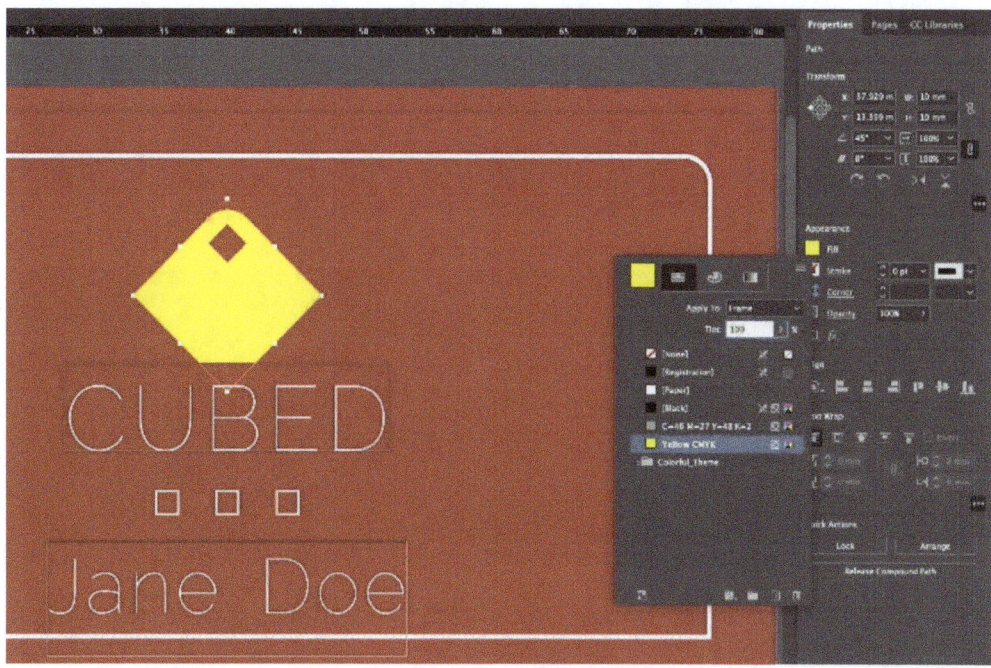

Figure 1.8: The logo with Yellow CMYK applied

8. Let's make the document view slightly smaller, so we have a better overall sense of our change. Making the view smaller or larger is called **zooming**. Right-click on the artwork, then choose **Zoom Out**. You can also choose **View** menu | **Zoom Out** to make the content smaller.

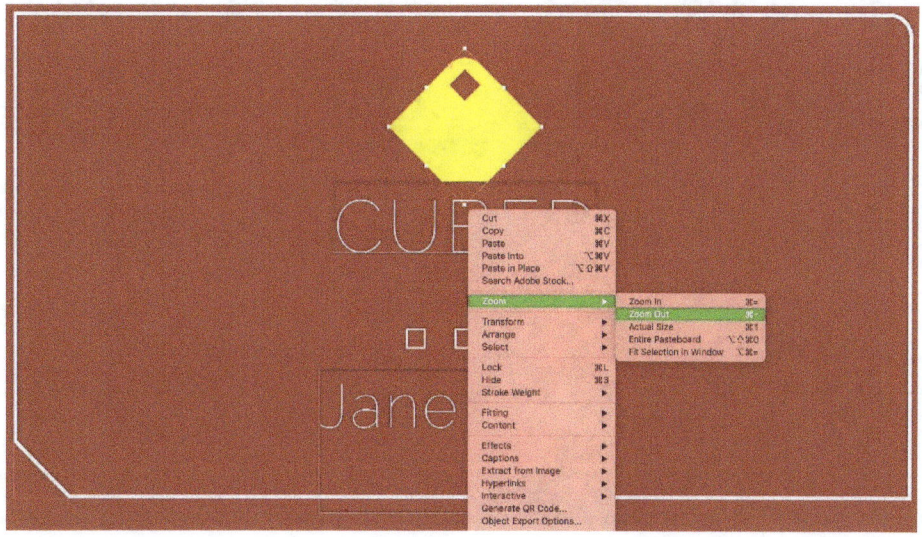

Figure 1.9: Zooming out of the artwork

9. Now choose the **Pages** panel on the right-hand side of the workspace. The panel has two segments. The top section houses **Parent Pages**. We will explore these in a later chapter. The lower segment stores the document pages. You can see, in the following figure, we have two pages in this document numbered 1 and 2. Let's navigate to **Page 2**. Double-click on the icon with the number 2 below it. This will take us to **Page 2**. Let's return to **Page 1**, by double-clicking on the page shown in the panel.

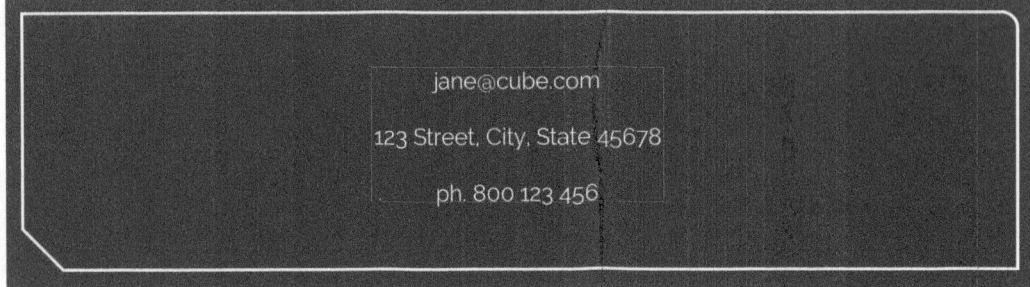

Figure 1.10: The rear of the business card design

10. Well done. You've explored the fundamental tenets of a multi-page design. You should feel a little more comfortable with the InDesign workspace at this stage. Let's close the file. Choose **File | Close**. Choose **Don't Save** in the pop-up box that appears.

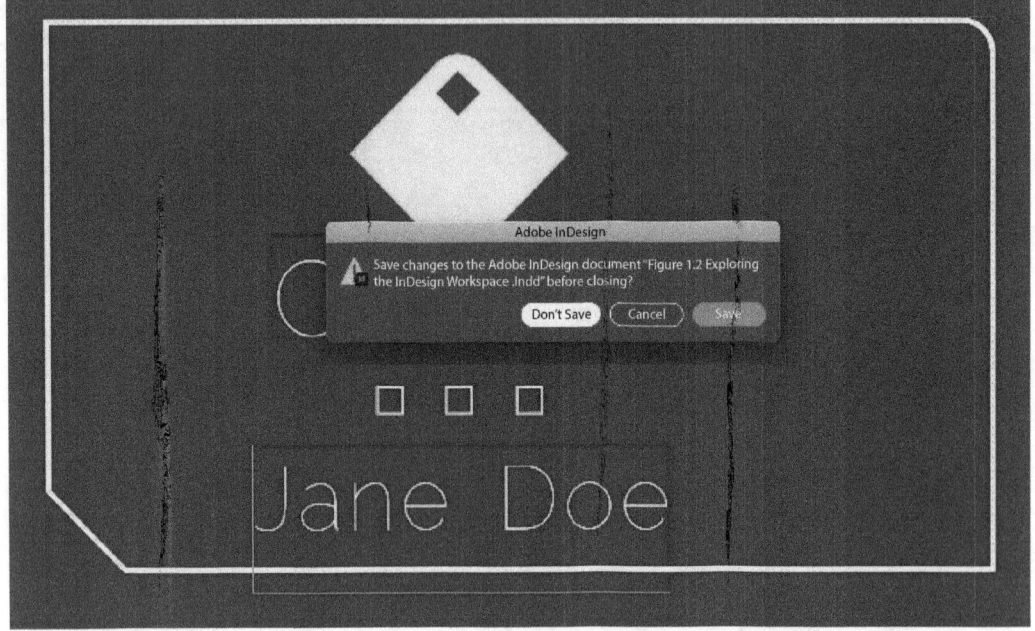

Figure 1.11: Closing the document without saving changes

We now have an understanding of the InDesign interface. In the next section, we'll explore an important panel – the toolbox. We'll look at the individual tools and the options they provide.

The InDesign toolbox

By default, the InDesign toolbox is arranged as a single vertical column of tools to the left of your interface. You can change the toolbox view to a double vertical column or a horizontal row arrangement by clicking on the double arrow  located in the top-left corner of the toolbox. There are tools found in the toolbox that are for specific tasks like selecting, editing, or creating a page. Whether it is type, shapes, lines, or gradients, this is applicable. You can click and drag the top of the toolbox – the vertical lines above the **Selection** tool – to move it to a different location.

Figure 1.12a: The toolbox arranged as a single column

Figure 1.12b: The toolbox set up as double vertical columns

Figure 1.12c: The toolbox arranged in a horizontal row

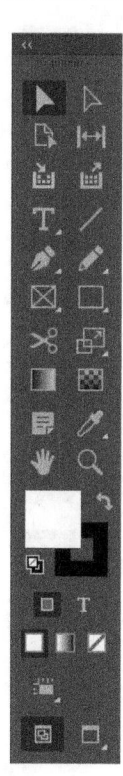

Select a tool from the toolbox by clicking on it. The toolbox also contains several hidden tools related to the visible tools. Hidden tools have tiny arrows that can be accessed by clicking on these arrows found at the bottom right of tool icons in the toolbox. You can select a hidden tool by clicking and holding your mouse on a tool in the toolbox, opening up a set of variations. You can then select the tool that you require from the resulting flyout.

The name of the tool and its keyboard shortcut will appear if you hover it. This is called a tooltip.

The toolbox is organized into six distinct sub-sections (see *Figure 1.13*). Having a general sense of the toolbox arrangement will help speed up your proficiency in InDesign.

Exploring InDesign

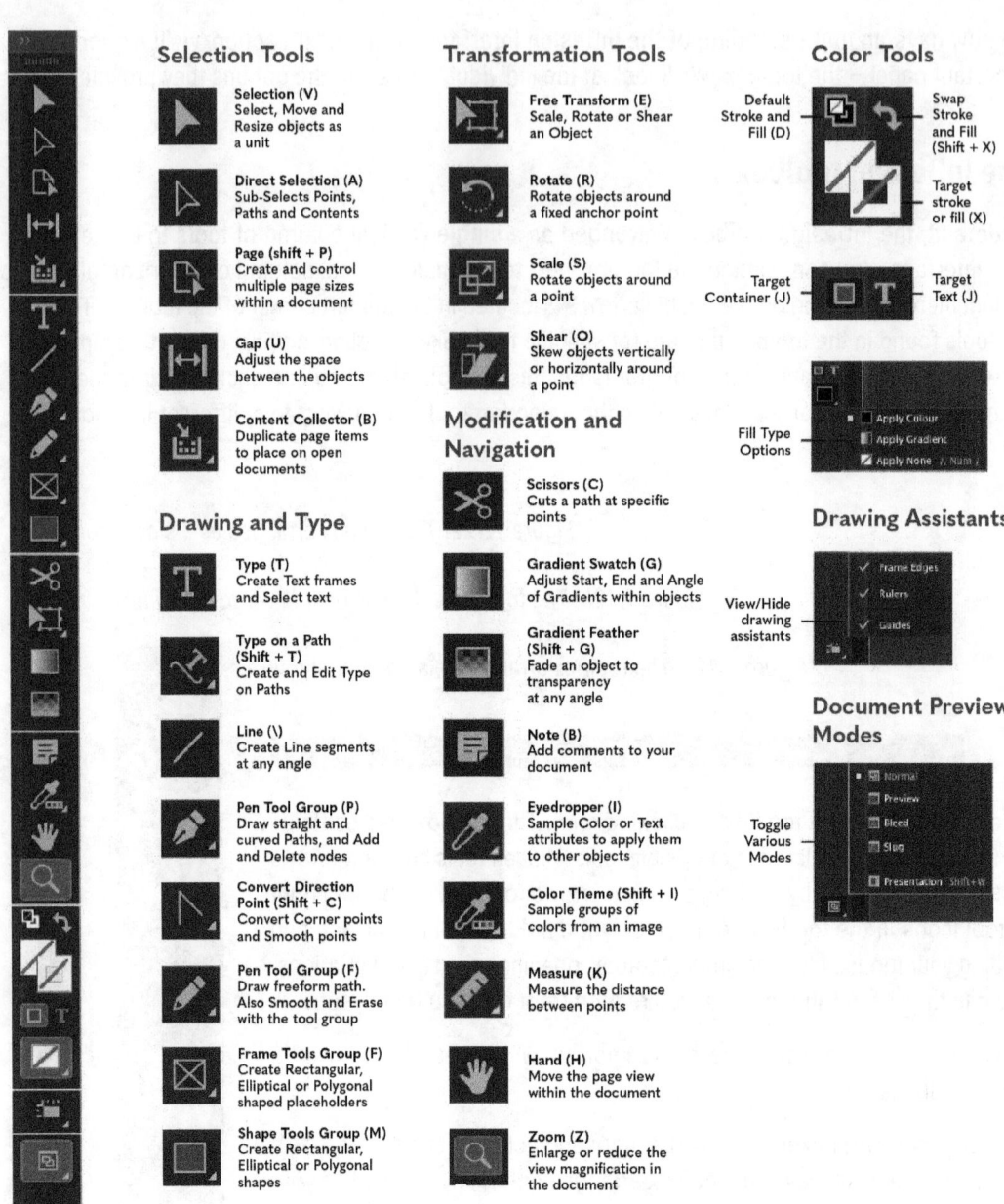

Figure 1.13: An exploded view of the toolbox

- **Selection Tools**: This subset of tools are used to select objects, groups, sub-components of elements, and the page itself.
- **Drawing and Type Tools**: Use these tools to create geometric and freeform shapes, as well as text frames. You can create rectangles, circles, stars, freeform shapes, and open paths. The type tools are used for creating text frames on your page.
- **Transformation Tools**: This collection of tools allow you to rotate, scale, skew and distort content. You can also use them to edit gradients, which are multi-colored fills or strokes that have been applied to objects.
- **Modification and Navigation Tools**: These tools can be used to move around the page and manipulate viewing properties. Additionally, you can magnify or decrease the viewing percentage of your document, measure the properties of objects, and collaborate with fellow InDesign users using notes.
- **Color Tools**: This subset of tools allows you to define the fill and stroke (border) properties for graphic and text objects.
- **Viewing Modes**: You can view a document in multiple ways. Options include hiding and showing non-printing guides and document construction aids. You can also preview the final document as it will appear printed or exported.

This concludes our exploration of the toolbox. Strictly speaking, the InDesign toolbox is a panel. We will discuss panels in greater detail in the next section.

Working with panels

Panels are found to the right of the interface. All panels, including the toolbox, can be accessed from the **Window** menu at the top of the workspace. The beauty of panels is that they afford editing and modification controls for page elements without getting in your way. Panels can be arranged in myriad ways. They can be organized as groups, stacked on top of each other, or collapsed so they are out of your way, yet accessible when you need them. Panels can also be repositioned anywhere in the InDesign interface. Panels not attached to any edge of the InDesign interface are called **floating** panels.

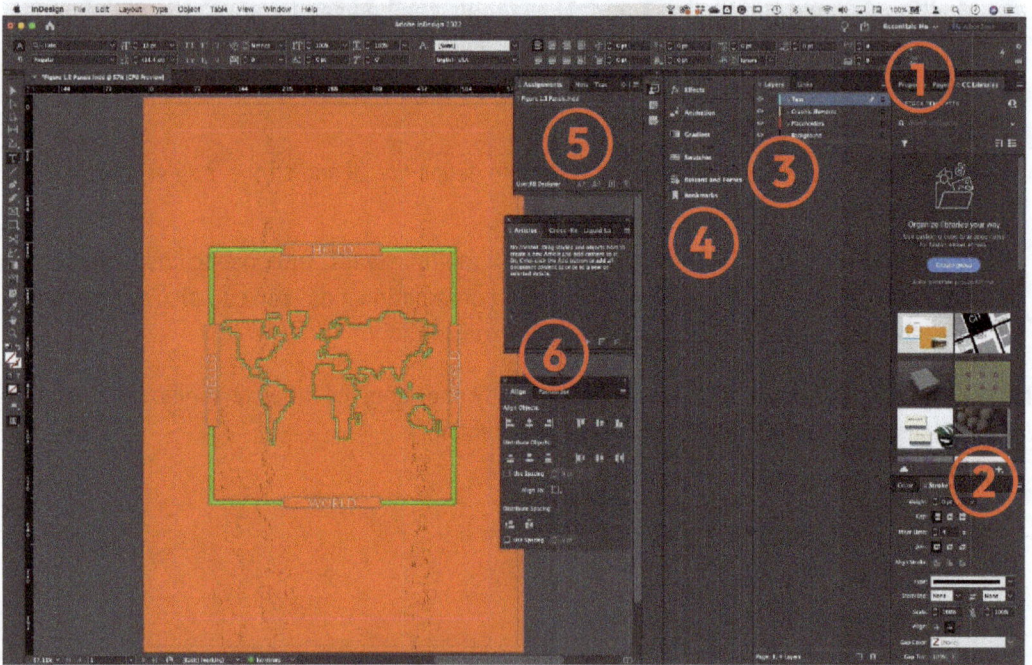

Figure 1.14: InDesign panels in various configurations

Examples of panel configurations can be seen in *Figure 1.14*, which illustrates the various possibilities available to you when customizing the InDesign interface for your unique design requirements. An explanation of each panel arrangement is discussed next:

1. **Panel group**: The **Properties**, **Pages**, and **CC Libraries** panels are arranged in a group. This means that they act as one set.
2. **Stacked**: The **Color** and **Stroke** panels appear in a stack below the layer group. You can stack panels and panel groups in any arrangement you wish.
3. **Expanded with labels**: The **Layers** and **Links** panels are examples of the expanded with labels panel arrangement. They show both an icon and a panel label.

4. **Collapsed with labels**: **Effects**, **Animation**, **Gradient**, and so on are panels that are collapsed with labels. They auto-hide when not in use. They show both an icon and a panel description.

5. **Collapsed – Icons only**: The **Assignments**, **Notes**, and **Track Changes** panels show icons only. They auto-hide when not in use. They are presented as icons only when inactive. They show both an icon and a tooltip when clicked upon.

6. **Floating**: The **Articles**, **Align**, and **Pathfinder** panels are examples of floating panels. They can be placed anywhere in the interface and do not need to be nested against the interface edge.

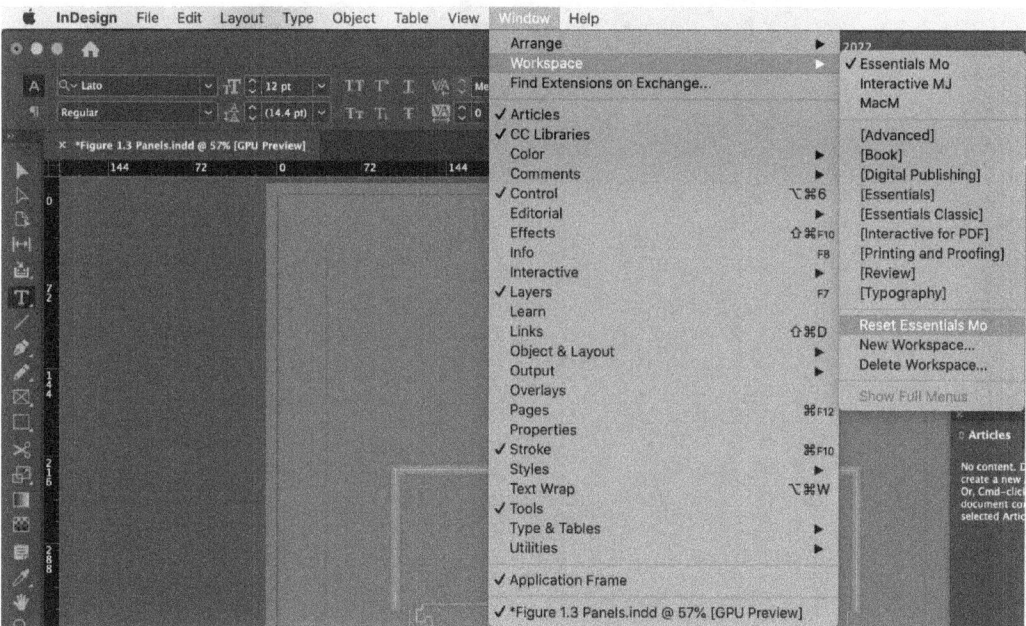

Figure 1.15: Resetting the InDesign interface

You can rearrange, open, and close panels at will to suit the task at hand. Feel free to experiment with different panel arrangements. Should you want to reset the panels to their original workspace configuration, choose **Window | Workspace | Reset…** Ensure that your preferred workspace is selected. Then choose **Reset…**. In the preceding example, the Essentials workspace was chosen. We will be working primarily in this workspace throughout the book. Please choose this workspace when working through the example files.

Now that we've grasped the basic behavior of panels, let's learn about panel menus and additional functions we can access by using them.

Exploring panel menus

Panel menus provide us with additional options and controls. To access panel menus, click on the hamburger icon (≡) found at the top right of any panel.

The menus are contextual and present options for the panel in question. For example, the **Pages** panel menu will present options for pages, including inserting, reordering, and duplicating pages, among a whole host of other options. Take time to familiarize yourself with these additional features.

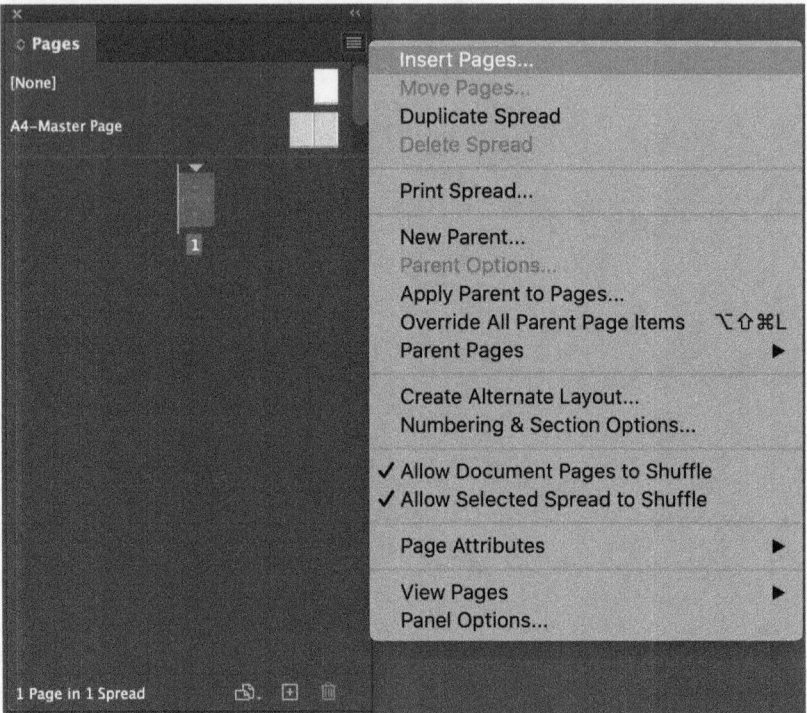

Figure 1.16: The Pages panel menu

Now that we have an understanding of the fundamentals of the InDesign interface, let's look at core concepts and a typical InDesign workflow.

Core layout concepts and workflows

InDesign can be categorized as layout software. It is therefore used to create page designs for both print and digital media. InDesign sports powerful tools for working with text and graphics. It has robust typographical controls and is ideally suited for long documents. Its typographical controls are the gold standard for typesetting in its class. You can prepare interactive and high-quality PDF documents for sharing with audiences and print providers. Some of the projects that InDesign can help you create include books like this one, print and online magazines, ePub documents, and numerous other categories of formats for your design and communication projects.

InDesign works on the metaphor of a page or pages that are attached to a **pasteboard**. This is no different from you placing a piece of paper on a desk. Any elements you place on the page will be printed or exported. Elements that are placed on the pasteboard – the gray area surrounding the page, will not be in the output. You can use the pasteboard as a temporary holding area as you craft your design on the page.

This is a typical InDesign workflow scenario:

1. Import text and tables from Office applications.
2. Place vector and bitmap images from drawing and image editing software.
3. Arrange elements into a pleasing design.
4. Export or print the InDesign file for consumption by relevant target audiences.

The very first step in your InDesign workflow is to set up a new document. In the next section, we will look at the options for setting up and customizing the specifications of our document.

Setting up your document

As with any content creation application you may be familiar with, having an idea of the type of document that you wish to create upfront is helpful. You can use InDesign to create documents for high-end print or online delivery.

Documents can be set up in two ways. You can create a new, empty document by using presets. These documents have predefined dimensions and settings. You can then tweak specific settings to meet your project requirements, for example, the size of the page, the number of columns, or the text margins.

You can also make use of the range of **templates**. These are predesigned InDesign files that you can use as a launchpad for your designs. You can use the templates that are available in-app, or you can search Adobe Stock (Adobe's stock service) for a specific theme that you may require. Some content requires you to pay an additional fee.

Try it yourself – setting up a new document

In this section, we will set up a business card from the ground up. Let's recreate the business card document we opened earlier in the chapter:

1. Launch InDesign. Click the **New file** button on the Start screen. This will open the **New Document** dialog.

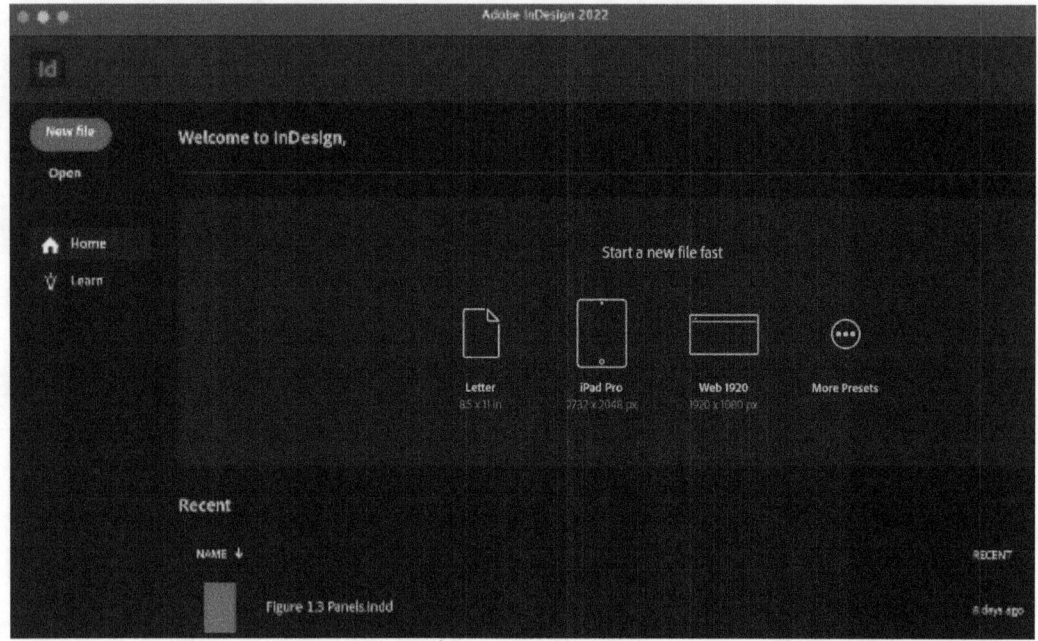

Figure 1.17: The New file button is found at the top left of the Start screen

2. If you use imperial units, complete steps 1 to 4. If you work with the metric system, skip to *step 5*. Click on the **Print** tab. From the list of blank document presets, choose **US Business Card**. Under **PRESET DETAILS** on the right, we'll make the following adjustments:

    A. For **Units**, you can stick with **Picas** or switch to inches. We'll use **Picas** in this exercise.

    B. Uncheck **Facing Pages**. This is primarily used in magazine and book design.

    C. Increase the page count to 2 for the front and the back of the business card.

    D. Change all margin values to **1 pica**.

    E. Add 1 pica **bleed** for all sides. The term bleed in printing refers to the space beyond the trimmed area of the page. It ensures that you have a nice clean edge when the document is trimmed. If page elements touch the outer edge of the format, they should be extended to the bleed guides.

3. Click **Create** to accept the changes.
4. Choose **File | Save**. You can name it anything you wish. You can find a reference file called Try it yourself 2 - Business Card Imperial.indd in the **Chapter 1 - Example Files** folder should you need a visual guide.

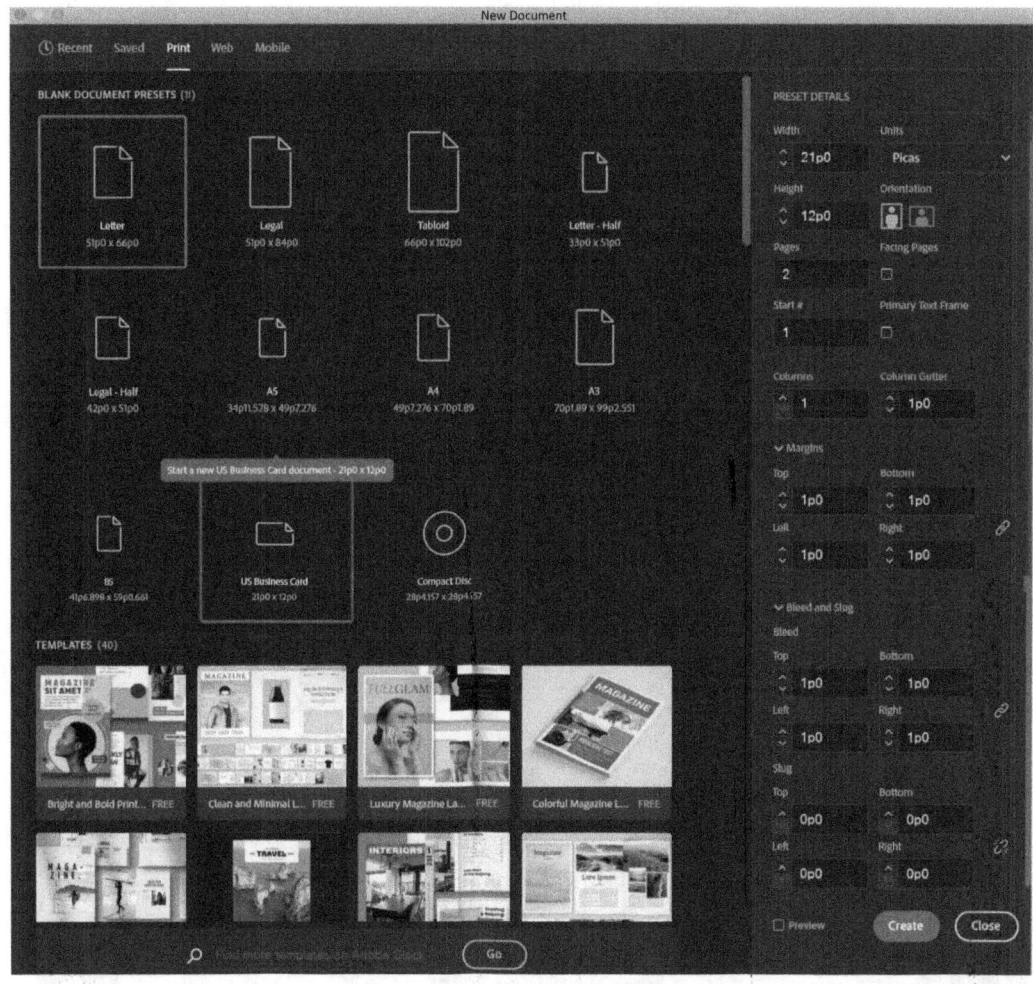

Figure 1.18: Business card setup for imperial units

5. For readers who use the metric system, set up your document as follows. Click on the **Print** tab from the list of blank document presets and choose **US Business Card**. Under **PRESET DETAILS** on the right, let's make the following changes:

   A. For **Units**, choose millimeters.
   B. Change the width to 90mm and the height to 50mm.

C. Uncheck **Facing pages**. This is used in magazine and book design.

D. Increase the page count to 2 for the front and the back of the business card.

E. Change all margin values to 4mm. Click the link icon to make the changes to all margins all at once. The link icon keeps all values identical. If you need to add different values, disable the link option.

F. Add 3 mm bleed for all sides. The term bleed in printing refers to the space beyond the trimmed area of the page. It ensures that we have a nice clean edge if colors or objects run to the edge of the format.

6. Click **Create** to accept the changes and create the document.

7. Choose **File | Save**. You can name it anything you wish. You can find a reference file called Try it yourself 2 - Business Card Metric.indd in the **Chapter 1 - Example Files** folder should you need a visual guide.

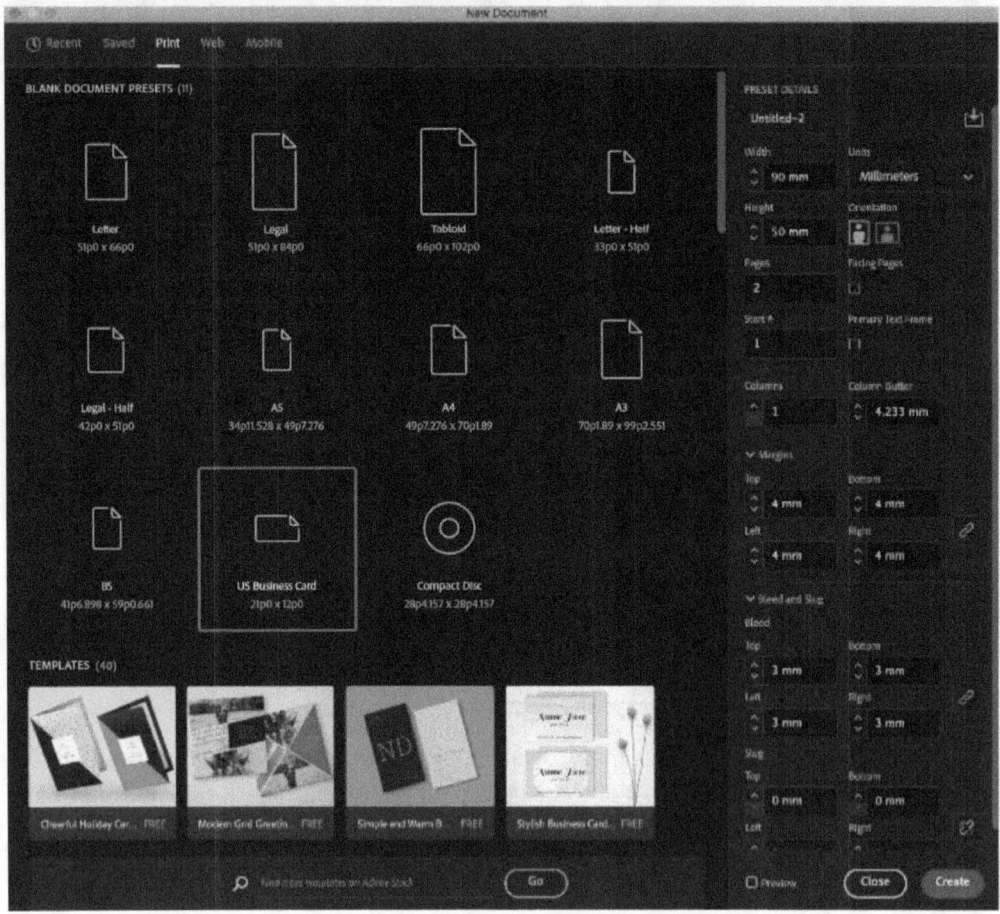

Figure 1.19: Business card setup for metric units

8. InDesign will present a newly created document. Take note of the following in the main viewing window.

9. Your working page is the white area that you see in the middle of the screen.

10. Margins are the pink- and purple-colored lines found inside your page. This is called the text area. These lines do not print or export. The guides are meant to assist you in making sure elements are positioned correctly and accurately on the page.

11. The red lines that fall outside the page are your bleed guides. We extend colors or images to these guides if they touch the format edge. Bleeds are trimmed away by the printer.

Figure 1.20: Your newly created document showing the page, margins, and bleed

12. To navigate between pages, choose the **Pages** panel. Double-click on the thumbnail of the page you would like to navigate to – for example, **Page 2** in the following graphic as shown in *Figure 1.21*. The page you have selected is highlighted.

Figure 1.21: The Pages panel with Page 2 highlighted

Well done. You have successfully set up a multi-page document in InDesign. Save your file at this point. Choose **File** | **Save**. Choose location on your computer where you would like the file to be saved, and choose a filename of your choosing. For example, Business Card Design.indd. We will use this document to add the business card design and text elements to in the next chapter. At this point, you should feel relatively comfortable with the interface and how to get around InDesign. Be sure to revisit any concepts you may feel uncomfortable with. Remember, this book progressively builds on concepts covered in a linear way. It is helpful to understand each concept being discussed before moving on to the next chapter. More experienced users can jump to chapters that you may find relevant.

Summary

In this chapter, we explored various InDesign interface features. We had a look at tools and the toolbox arrangement options available. We familiarized ourselves with the InDesign workspace, panels, and panel menus. We got an understanding of the core tenets of InDesign, and got to grips with the fundamental concepts of the software. Finally, we set up an InDesign document from scratch.

We are well on our way to exploring the next chapter, where we will learn how to work with text and objects in the business card document we have just set up in this chapter.

Level: Fundamentals

Working with Text and Shapes

In this chapter, we'll create the various elements that make up the Cubed business card design document that we set up in the previous chapter. You'll recall we created a blank two-page document for the business card design. We'll add text and graphic elements to create a complete business card design. We'll then format the type and manipulate the properties of graphic elements to meet design objectives. If you did not save the file from the previous lesson, and wish to recreate it, please refer to *Setting up your document* section in *Chapter 1*. Should you wish to continue on, we've saved the starter document for your convenience, with the exercise files for this chapter. Along with other chapters, you can download the files for this chapter from: https://packt.link/a19oQ

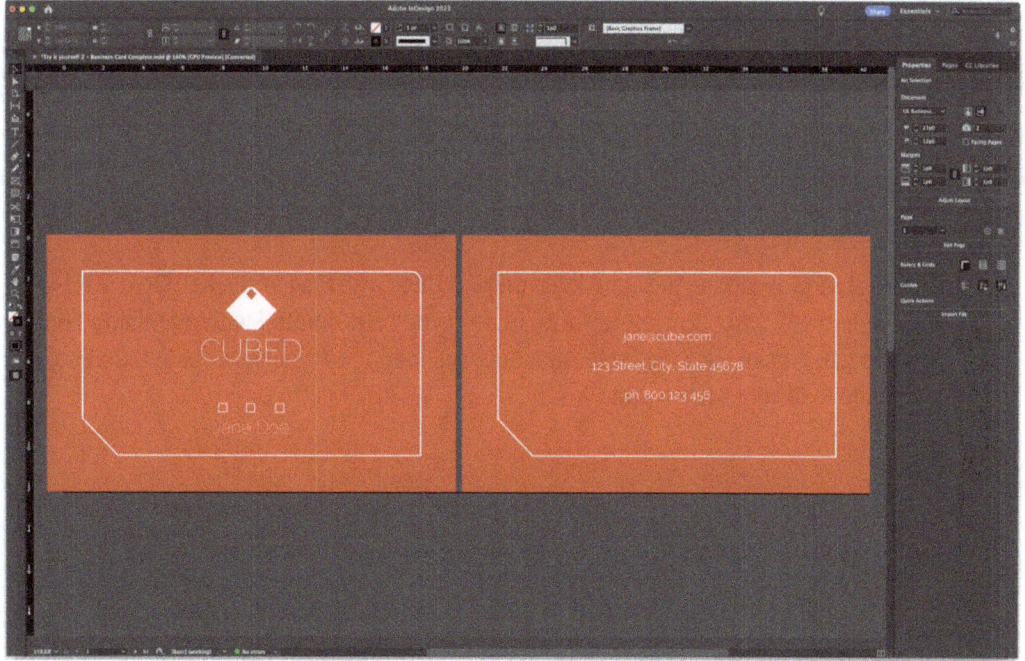

Figure 2.1: The completed project
(The image is intended as a visual reference; the textual information is not essential.)

Figure 2.1 shows the completed project. This is what we will design in this chapter. We will work with several tools and options to complete this project.

Here are the main topics we will cover in this chapter:

- Opening an existing file
- Navigating between pages in a **multi-page** document
- Creating and formatting basic **shape objects**
- Adjusting the **fill** and **stroke** properties of an object
- Creating **text objects**
- Changing the **properties** of text elements
- Previewing the final design

Where appropriate, this book uses picas and points for measurement units. In this way, we can cater to readers that use imperial or metric units. We've done this to accommodate to as many readers as possible, whilst keeping content succinct and easy to follow. For example, a measurement expressed as 21 p0 is equal to 21 picas and 0 points, which in turn translates to 3.5 inches or 90 mm. In the case of the metric mm unit, 89 mm has been rounded up to 90 mm. Please note that this will hold true for documents being prepared for print only. Digital documents will be created using pixels.

Opening files and accessing resources

Let's start by opening the appropriate exercise files. Note that the files referred to in this practical activity can be downloaded from the following link.

https://packt.link/a19oQ

1. We'll start by exploring the completed project. Open with the file labeled Try it yourself 2 - Business Card Complete.indd. Should you be prompted with a **Missing Fonts** message, please click **Activate**. InDesign will load the missing fonts automatically. See the following screenshot.

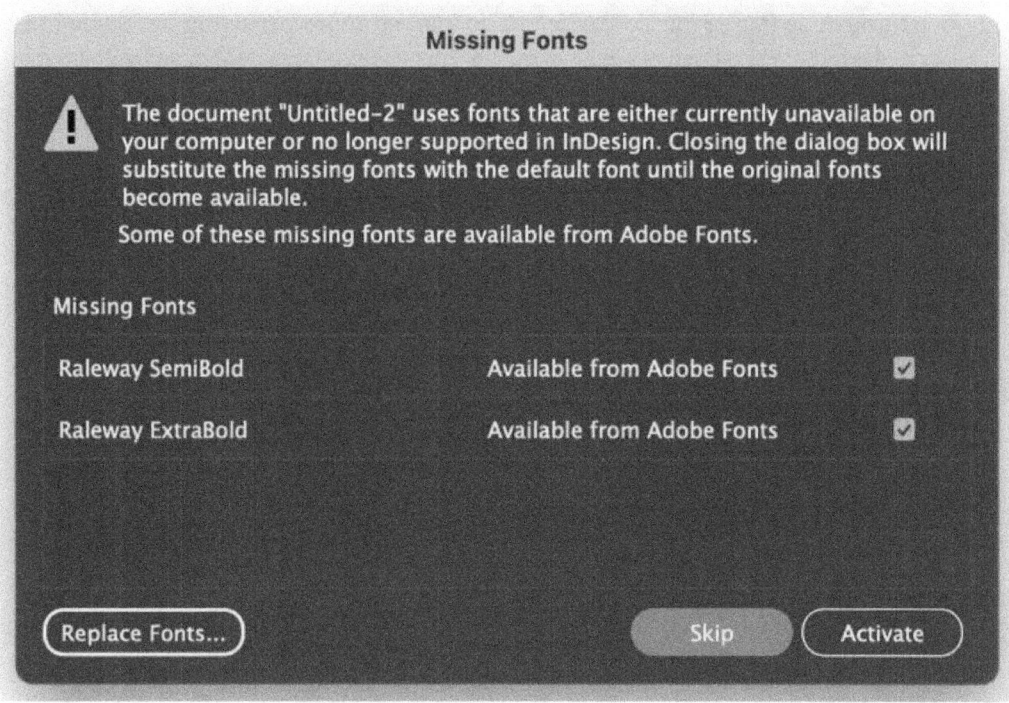

Figure 2.2: The Missing Fonts dialog

2. Choose the **Selection** tool and click on various elements. On **Page 1**, we have a background colored rectangle, a white border, a logo, some cubes, and text.

28 | Working with Text and Shapes

3. Navigate to **Page 2** by double-clicking on it in the **Pages** panel found to the right of the interface. This page has the same background border with personal details. It is the back of the business card design.

4. Close the file when you are done exploring it.

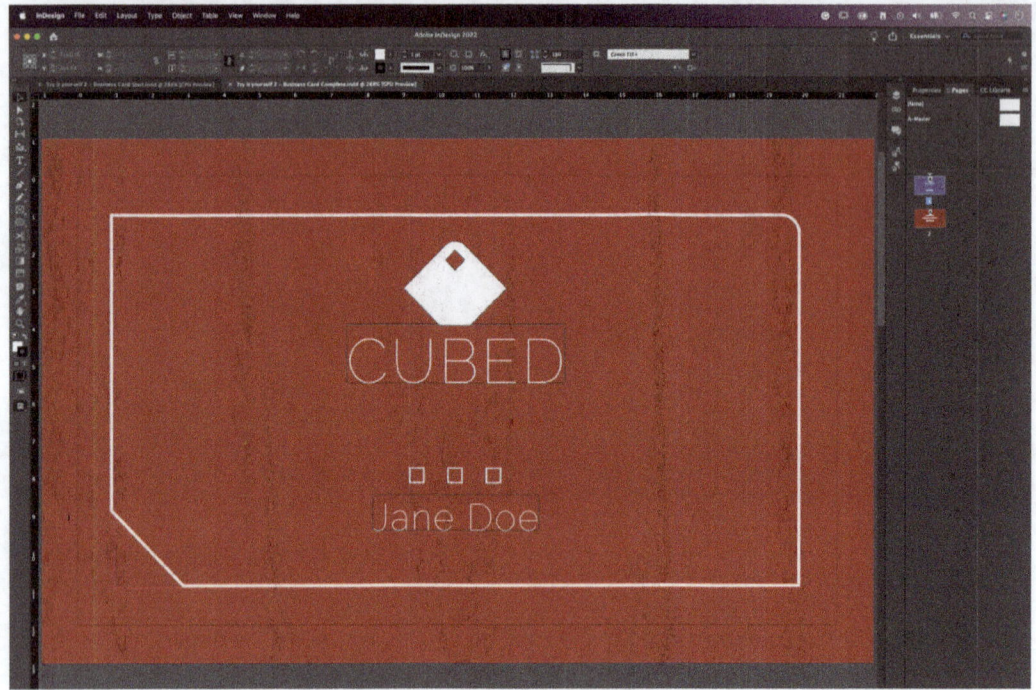

Figure 2.3: The completed project showing Page 1
(The image is intended as a visual reference; the textual information is not essential.)

5. Now, open the file called Try it yourself 2 - Business Card Start.indd. **Ensure that you are on Page 1**. The white frame represents the page, the red lines outside the page are our bleed guides, and the faint blue and pink lines on the page are called margins. They are often referred to as the text area. You can save a copy of your working file by choosing **File | Save as**, and giving the copy any name you wish.

Drawing basic shapes and changing their properties

In this section, we will draw the background rectangle and the white border object. We will apply a fill color to the background and apply a Stroke (outline) to the border.

1. Select the **Rectangle** tool (*M*). Click and drag from the top left of the bleed guides to the bottom right as shown here. Then, choose the **Properties** panel to the right of the interface. The object has a black outline, called a stroke in InDesign. It has no fill and is transparent at this point.

Figure 2.4: The drawn rectangle with no fill and a black stroke
(The image is intended as a visual reference; the textual information is not essential.)

2. Click on the **Fill** swatch under **Appearance** in the **Properties** panel. Then, choose the red color (C=15, M=100, Y=100, K=0). Click on the **Stroke** swatch and choose **None**. That was easy enough, right? Our background is done.

Figure 2.5: The background rectangle with a red fill and no stroke

3. Ensure that you have the **Rectangle** tool selected. Draw a second rectangle from margin edge to margin edge (faint pink and blue lines) as shown here. Then choose the **Stroke** swatch in the **Properties** panel and choose **Paper**. We now have a white border.

Figure 2.6: The white border created with the Rectangle tool

4. Let's change the corners so they resemble the original artwork. Choose the **Selection tool** from the Toolbox (*V* or *Esc*). Ensure that the white border is selected. Click the **Corner** option under **Appearance** in the **Properties** panel. The **Corner Options** dialog will be displayed. Set the corner options as follows:

   - Top left: **0p0 | None**
   - Bottom left: **2p0 | Bevel**
   - Top right: **0p6 | Rounded**
   - Bottom right: **0p0 | None**

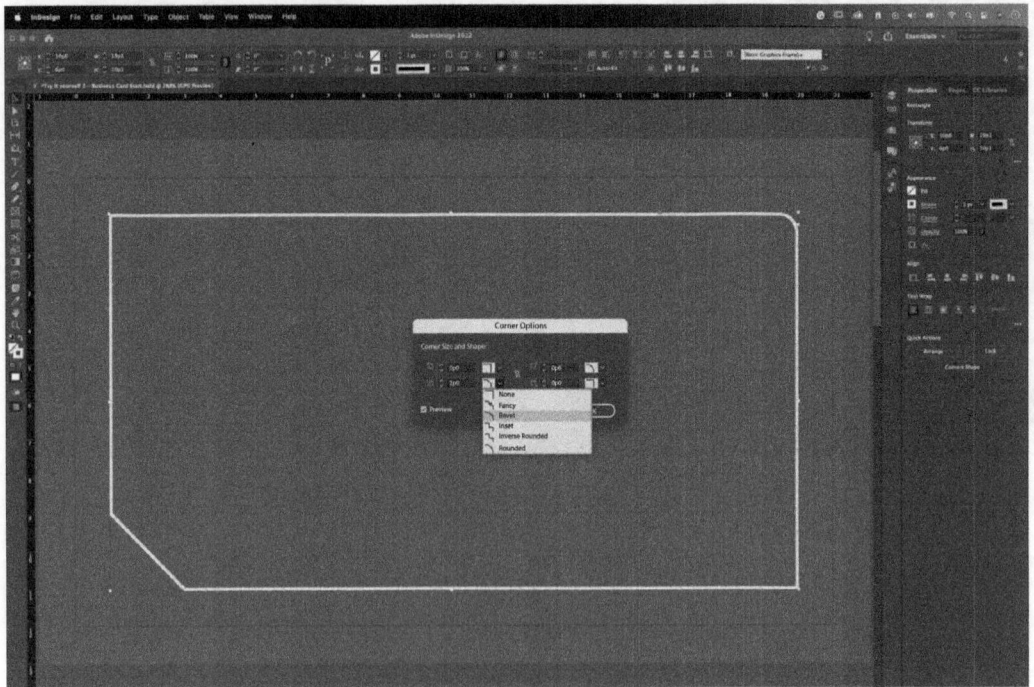

Figure 2.7: Rounded corners applied to the white border
(The image is intended as a visual reference; the textual information is not essential.)

We'll learn how to create the logo in the next section.

Creating the logo

The logo is made up of a series of squares. We'll draw basic shapes and adjust the properties, rotation, and corners of the shapes that make up the logo.

1. Choose the **Rectangle** tool . Double-click on the approximate location at which the logo will appear. This will bring up the **Rectangle** dialog. Key in 2p0 for **Width** and **Height** and click OK.

Figure 2.8: The logo outline drawn using the Rectangle dialog

2. Select the drawn rectangle with the **Selection** tool . Click on the **Corner** control in the **Properties** panel. Disable the **Make all settings have the same** icon , (chainlink). Change the values in the **Corner Options** dialog as follows:

- Top left: **0 | None**
- Bottom left: **0p6 | Bevel**
- Top right: **0p4 | Rounded**
- Bottom right: **0p0 | None**

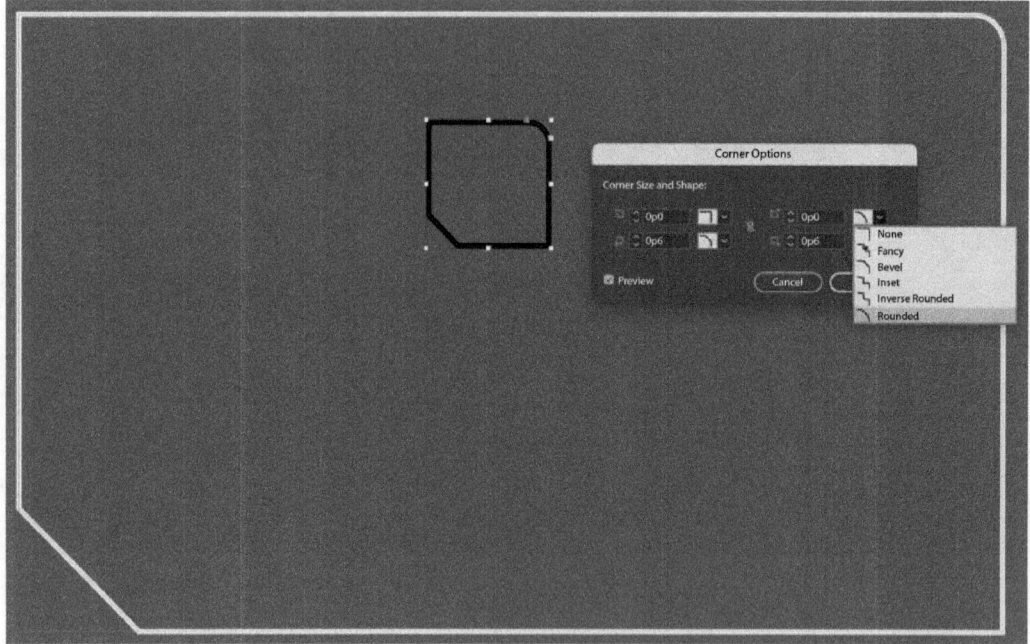

Figure 2.9: The logo corners rounded and beveled

3. In the **Properties** panel, fill the rectangle with **Paper** and set the **Stroke** value to **None**.

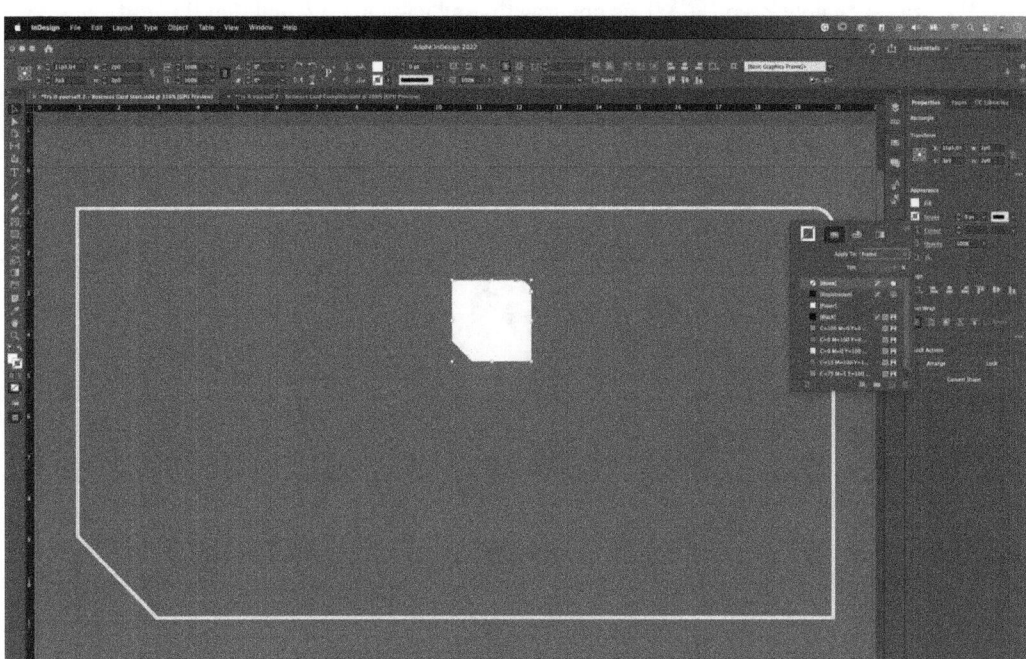

Figure 2.10: The logo with a white (Paper) fill and no stroke
(The image is intended as a visual reference; the textual information is not essential.)

4. We'll now draw in the little rectangle at the top of the logo. Select the rectangle we just drew.
5. Choose **Edit menu Copy.** Then choose **Edit menu Paste in Place**. This places the copy directly on top of the original.

6. Choose the **Corner** option from the **Properties** panel. Click the **Make all settings the same** chainlink icon . This ensures that all values are equal. Set the first value to **0p0**. Enable the **Preview** checkbox found at the bottom of the dialog. Click **OK**.

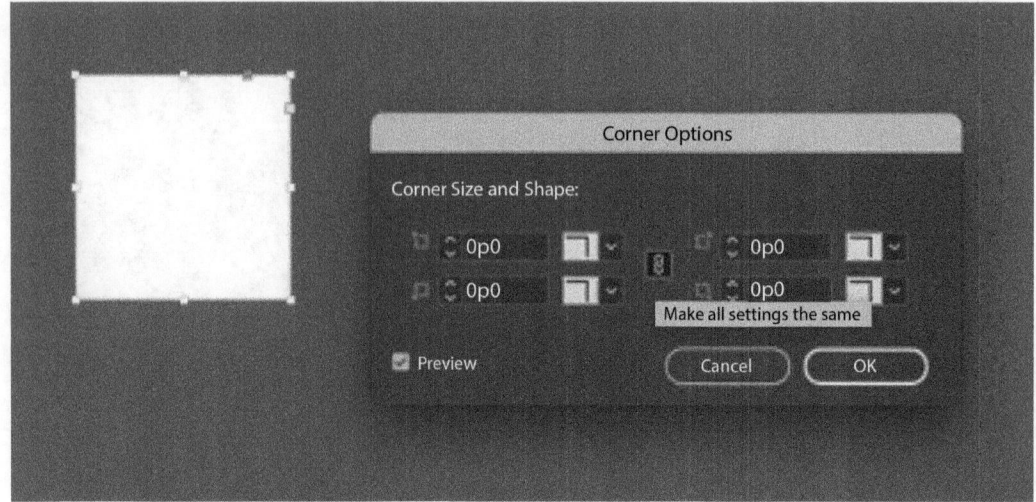

Figure 2.11: The copied rectangle with Corner set to zero

7. Let's now reduce the size of rectangle and change its color. On the **Properties** panel, make the following changes:

   A. Under **Appearance**, click the **Fill** swatch and choose **C**=15 **M**=100 **Y**=100 **K**=0 (Red).

   B. Under **Transform**, choose the top-right reference point. This will lock this point in place.

   C. To the right of the **W** and **H** values, enable the Constrain proportions for width and height chainlink icon .

D. Set the H value to 0p5. The H value will update to the same value

Figure 2.12: The resized smaller rectangle for the inner part of the logo

8. We'll nudge the smaller red rectangle into place using the keyboard arrow keys. Ensure you have the **Selection** tool selected. Then, tap the left arrow key twice and do the same using the down arrow key.

9. We'll now combine these two shapes into a single object. Hold the *Shift* key and click the larger white rectangle of the logo. With both elements selected, choose the **Object** menu | **Paths** | **Make Compound Path**.

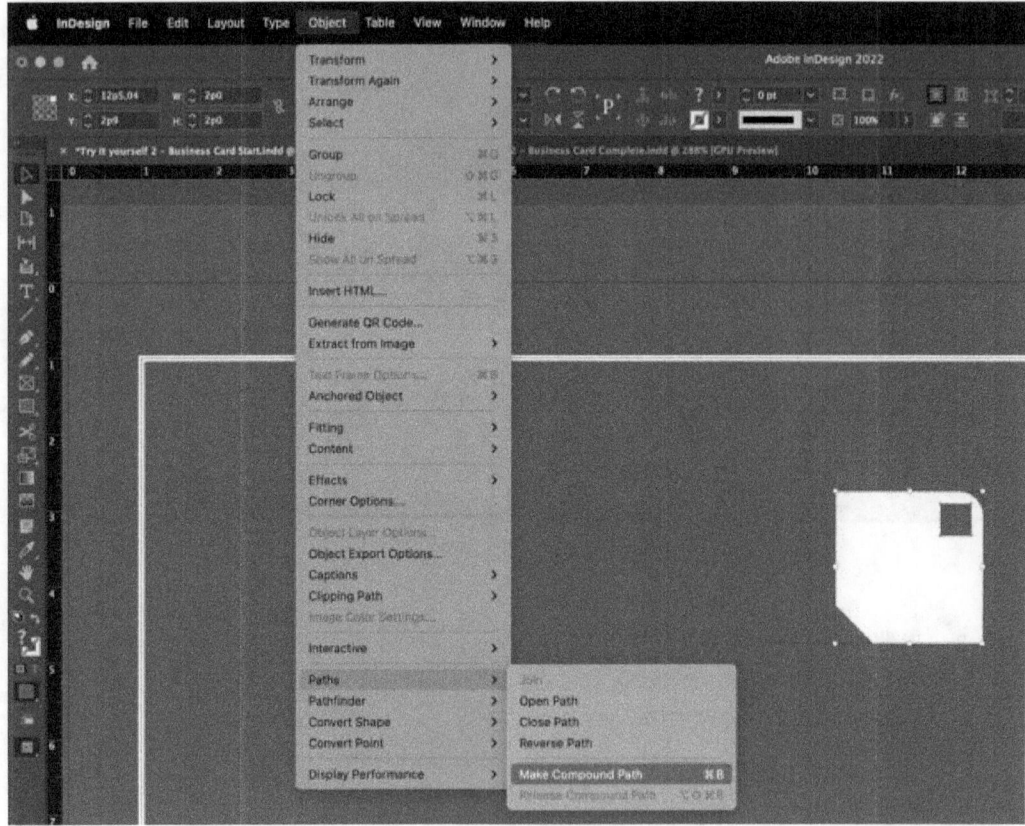

Figure 2.13: The Compound Path is now a single shape

10. Well done so far. We'll now rotate our logo element 45 degrees. Select the object with the **Selection** tool . Then, click the **More Options** ellipsis below the **Transform** controls in the **Properties** panel. Type 45° in **Rotation Angle** input box and press *Return* to accept the change.

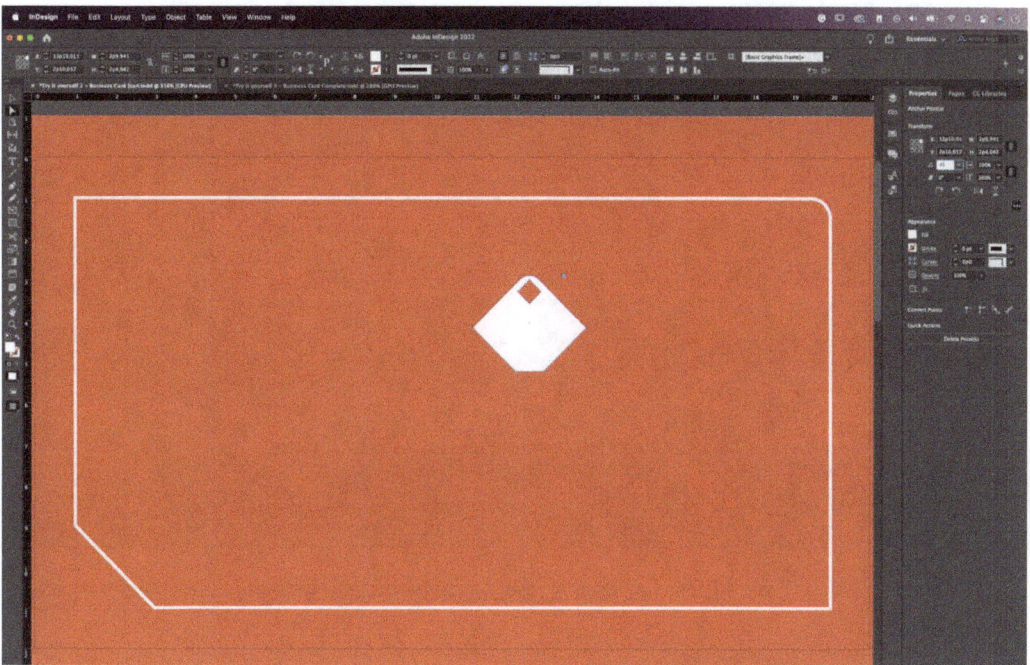

Figure 2.14: The logo with a 45° rotation applied
(The image is intended as a visual reference; the textual information is not essential.)

11. We'll now position the logo. Make the following changes on the **Properties** panel:
    A. Choose the middle reference point for the object
    B. Set the **X** value to 10p6.
    C. Set the **Y** value to 3p0 and press *Return*.

    The object will move to the correct position on the page.

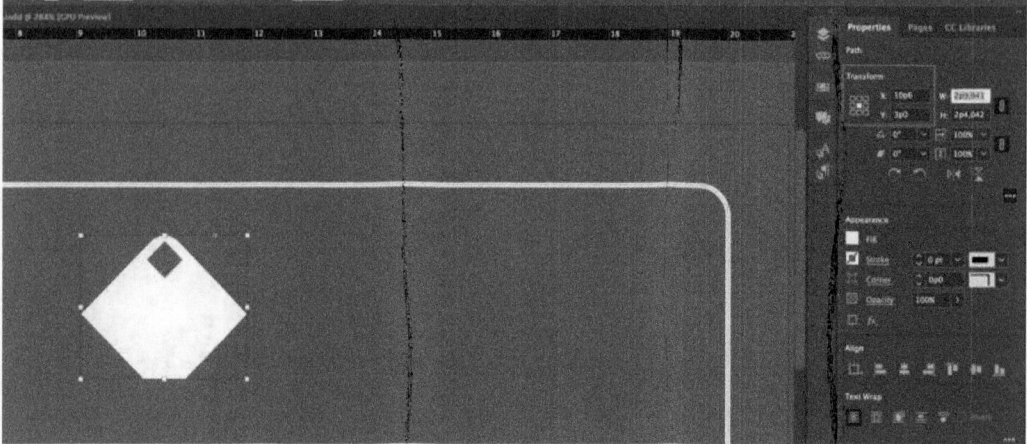

Figure 2.15: The logo is now perfectly aligned with the border and the page

Working with text

We'll now create the text elements on the front of the card. We'll create text frames (containers), type into them, and format the text properties. This will include choosing fonts, adjusting the size, and alignment.

1. Let's start by creating the **CUBED** text below the logo we just designed. Text in InDesign requires a text frame. Visualize this as a text container. If we were to click below the logo, InDesign would assume that we would like to convert the white border into a text frame. We'll avoid this by creating a frame to house our text first. Choose the **Rectangle Frame tool** icon ⊠ from the toolbox. Then, draw a rectangle directly under the logo. It can be any size. We'll resize it later.

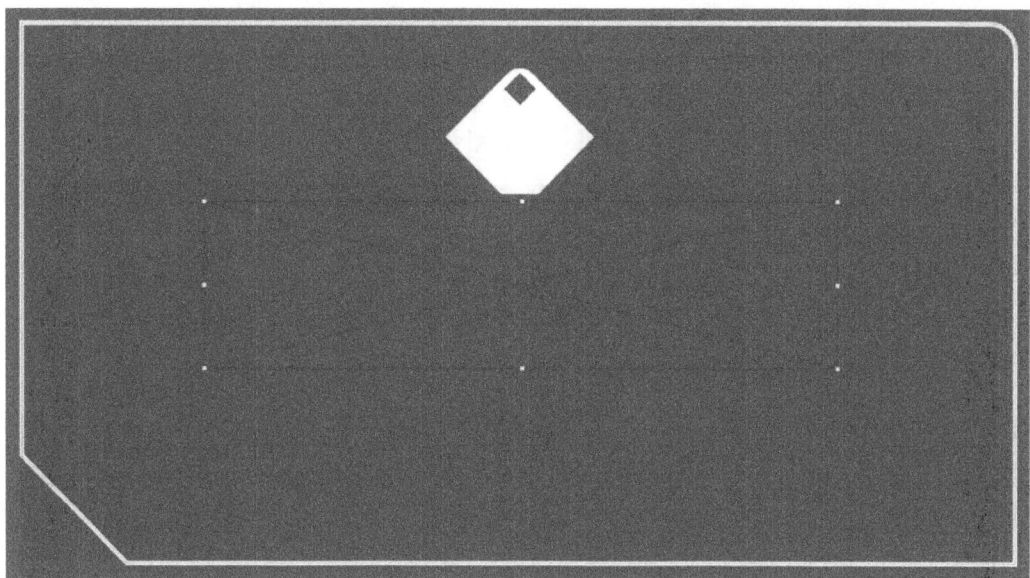

Figure 2.16: Draw a text container with the Rectangle Frame tool

2. Select the **Type** tool from the toolbox. Click on the frame you just drew. Enable Caps Lock on your keyboard, and type CUBED for the company name. The typed text will be black, aligned left, and in the default font. We'll amend these settings next.

Figure 2.17: Type the company name in the text frame container

3. With the **Type** tool icon ![T] still selected, click and drag over the **CUBED** text to select it. We'll make changes to the properties of the text by heading to the **Properties** panel to the right of the interface. Under the **Appearance** section, click on the capital T alongside **Fill**, and choose **Paper** from the resultant popup.

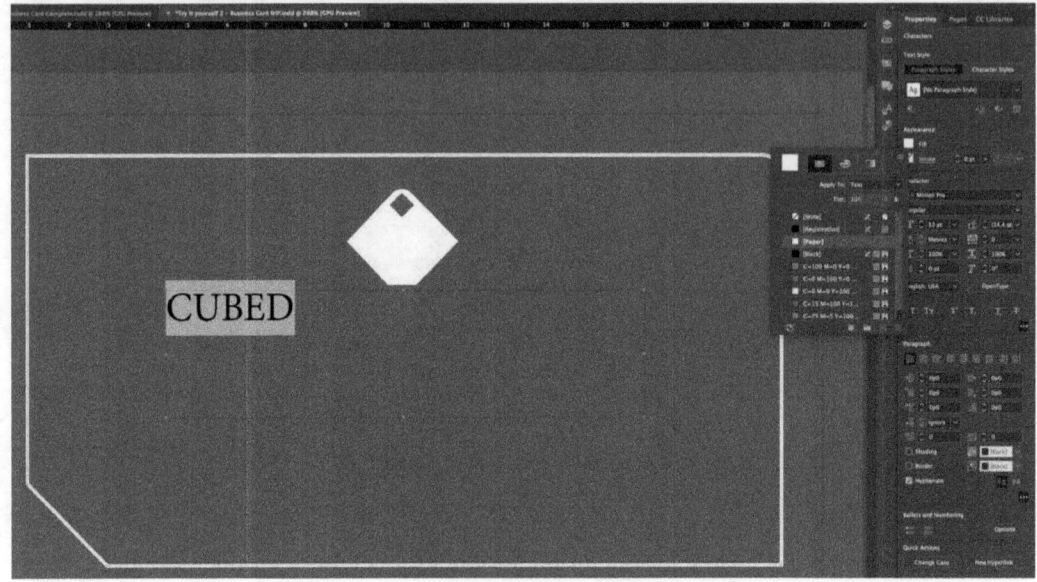

Figure 2.18: Changing the text color to white using the Properties panel

4. Let's change the typeface for our text. Click on the **Character** dropdown on the **Properties** panel and choose **Raleway Thin**. If this font is not available on your system, you can activate the **Raleway** font family via Adobe Fonts (fonts.adobe.com). You are welcome to choose any other typeface if you prefer.

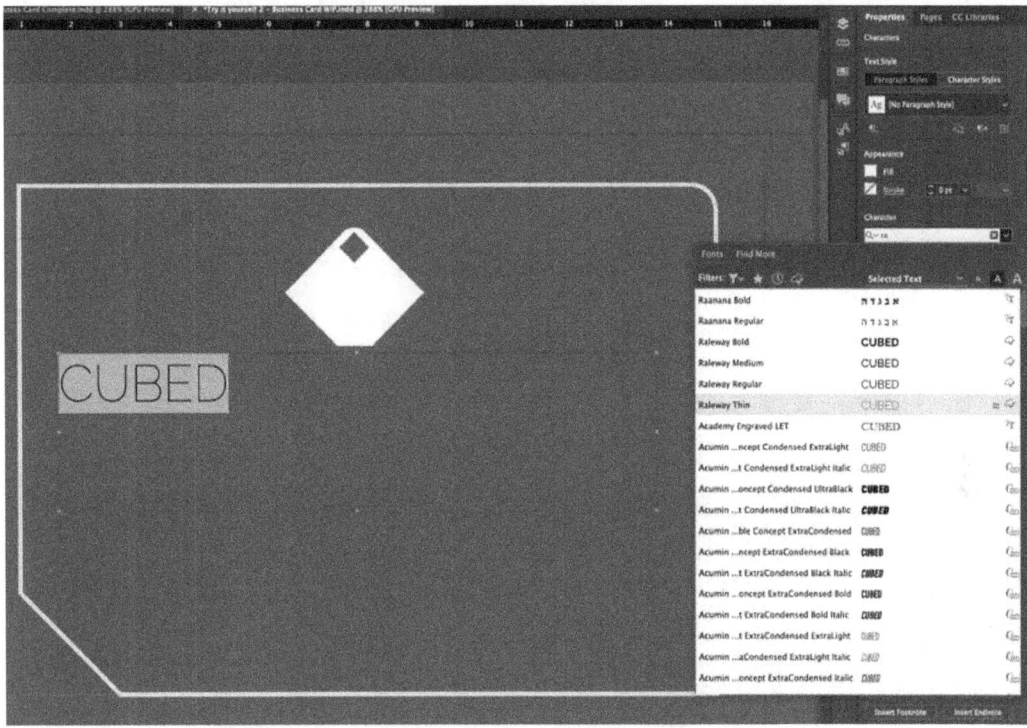

Figure 2.19: Choosing a font for the text

5. Change the font size to 20pt by typing the desired value into the **Font Size** field found under the **Character** subsection in the **Properties** panel.

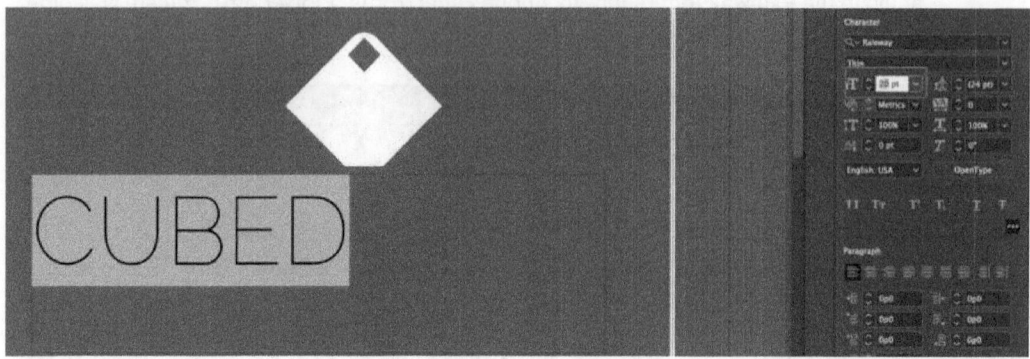

Figure 2.20: Change the text size to 20 pt

6. With the text still selected, let's align the text to the center of the frame. Under **Paragraph** in the **Properties** panel, choose **Align Center** (the second option) to center the text.

Figure 2.21: The text with center alignment applied

Arranging objects

InDesign has powerful tools to help us align objects with other elements in our design. We'll explore this concept by working with various text and graphic elements and arrange them so that they fit perfectly on the page and in relation to one another.

1. Let's resize the container to fit the text. Choose the **Selection** tool . The object frame will show a series of white squares and other widgets along its edge. Hover over the bottom-right control and double-click. This will resize the text frame.

> **Note**
> The text will move because of the resized frame. We'll resolve this in the next step.

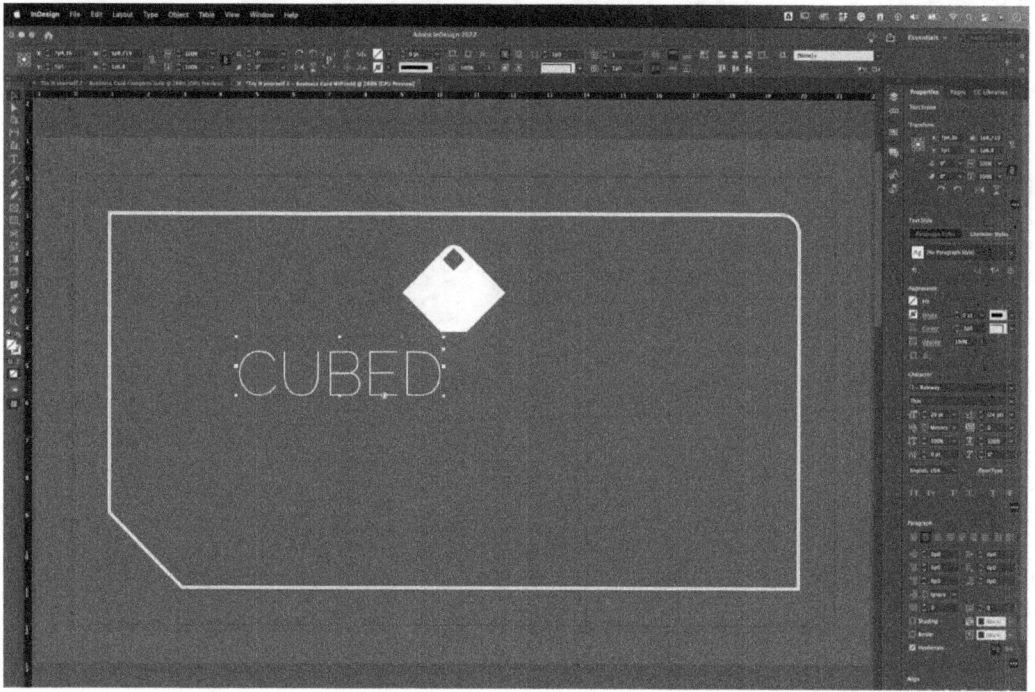

Figure 2.22: The resized text frame fits perfectly around the text
(The image is intended as a visual reference; the textual information is not essential.)

2. We now need to align the text with the logo and ensure they are spaced correctly. Select the text with the **Selection** tool. Then, hold the *Shift* key on your keyboard and click the logo above it. Both objects are now selected. Release the *Shift* key and click a second time on the logo. The selection highlight becomes more pronounced. We have made the logo a **key object**. We'll now align the text with it. Choose the **Align horizontal centers** command from the **Alignment** subsection in the **Properties** panel.

Figure 2.23: The text and logo center-aligned

3. We'll now duplicate the text frame and place it toward the bottom of the card for the person's name. With the **Selection** tool active, click off the artwork to deselect all objects. Then, click once on the text frame once. Click and drag downwards whilst pressing and holding the *Alt* (Win)/*Option* (Mac) and *Shift* keys. This action will create a copy of the text. When the copy appears at the desired location, release the mouse first, then release the keys. *Alt/Option* instructs InDesign to make a copy, while *Shift* keeps the copied object aligned to the original object.

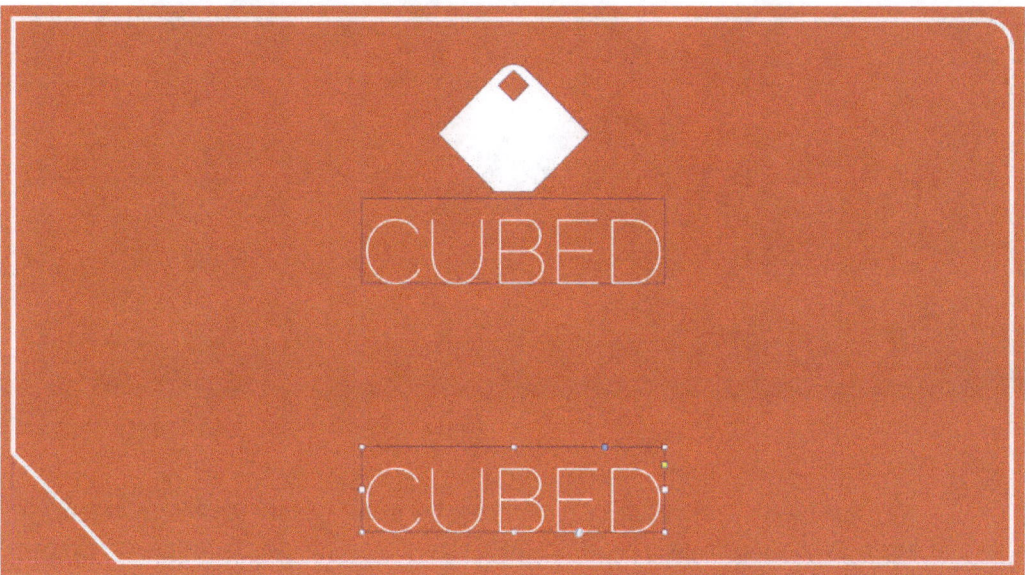

Figure 2.24: The original and copied text frames

4. Let's change the text size to 12 pt and type in a person's name. To change the size of your text, click the text size dropdown under the **Character** subset in the **Properties** panel and choose **12 pt**. Then, type Jane Doe.

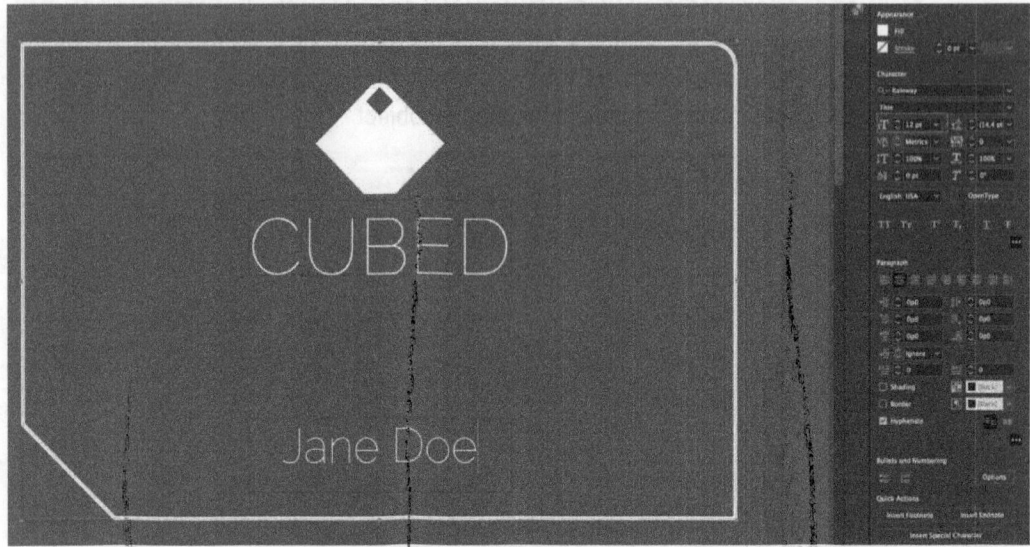

Figure 2.25: The name Jane Doe at 12 pt size

5. We'll now create three squares directly above the name. Choose the **Rectangle** tool again. Draw a rectangle approximately the size of the letter *o* in Jane Doe. Remember to press the *Shift* key so it is a perfect square. Head over to the **Properties** panel and make the following changes to the square you just drew:

   A. Under **Transform**, enable the **Constrain Width and Height** switch (the chainlink icon). Set the values to half a pica (**0p5**).

B. Set **Fill** to None.

C. Set **Stroke** to **Paper**, with a thickness of **0.5 pt**.

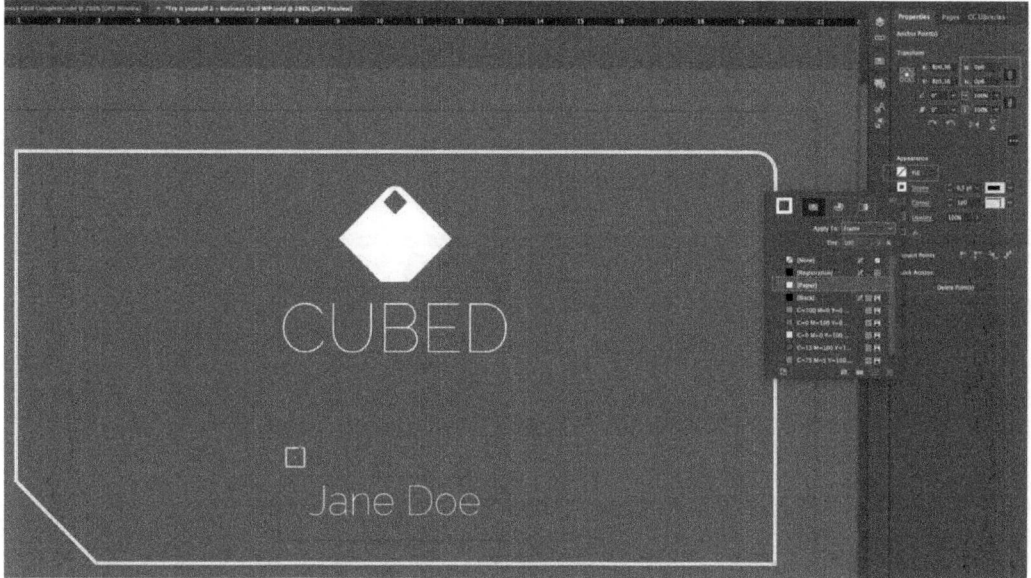

Figure 2.26: The first square with the correct size, fill, and stroke properties

6. We'll make two copies and adjust their spacing. Select the square and choose the **Edit** menu | **Copy**, then choose the **Edit** menu | **Paste in Place**. A copy is placed directly on top of the original. Choose the **Paste in Place** command again. We now have three squares in a stack.

7. Select one copy at a time and move over to the right whilst pressing the *Shift* key. This will constrain the movement to horizontal only. You should now have the three squares in a line. Don't be concerned about the spaces between the squares and their alignment. We'll resolve that next.

Figure 2.27: Copies placed next to the original square

8. Let's align the squares and create equal spacing between them. Select the three squares by clicking the first square the with the **Selection** tool . Then press the *Shift* key and click on the second and thid squares to select them as well. Check **Use Spacing** under the **Distribute** spacing in the **Properties** panel and set the value to 1 pica (**1p0**). Click the **Distribute horizontal space** icon just above the **Us Spacing** input box.

Figure 2.28: The three squares with equal spacing between them

9. The next step is to center the content relative to the **Jane Doe** text below it. First, we'll need to group the squares, so they behave as a single unit. With the three squares still selected, choose **Object** menu | **Group**.

10. *Shift*-select the **Jane Doe** text below to select it as well. Release the *Shift* key, and click on the **Jane Doe** text a second time to make it a key object. Return to the **Properties** panel and choose **Align horizontal centers** (the third icon from left).

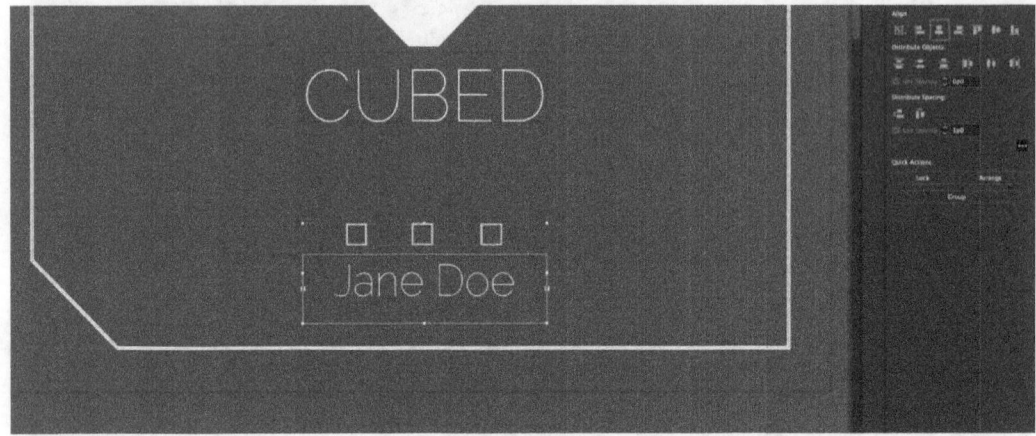

Figure 2.29: Alignment of the square graphics relative to the copy below

Well done! The front of the card is done. We'll now turn our attention to the rear of the card.

Designing the rear of the card

It's time to turn our attention to the rear of the card. In the steps that follow, we'll look at copying and pasting common elements between pages 1 and 2, adding and formatting type, aligning content, and previewing the final design.

1. The red background and white border elements are common to **Page 1** and **Page 2**. We'll copy these elements from **Page 1** and paste them in place on **Page 2**. On **Page 1**, select the white border object by clicking it with the **Selection** tool . Press the *Shift* key and select the red background object to select it as well. Remember to select the red background object by clicking outside of the white border object. This will ensure they are both selected correctly.
2. Choose the **Edit** menu | **Copy**. Then, navigate to **Page 2** on the **Pages** panel. Choose the **Edit** menu | **Paste in Place**. This will place the copied objects on **Page 2** in the exact location it was copied from.

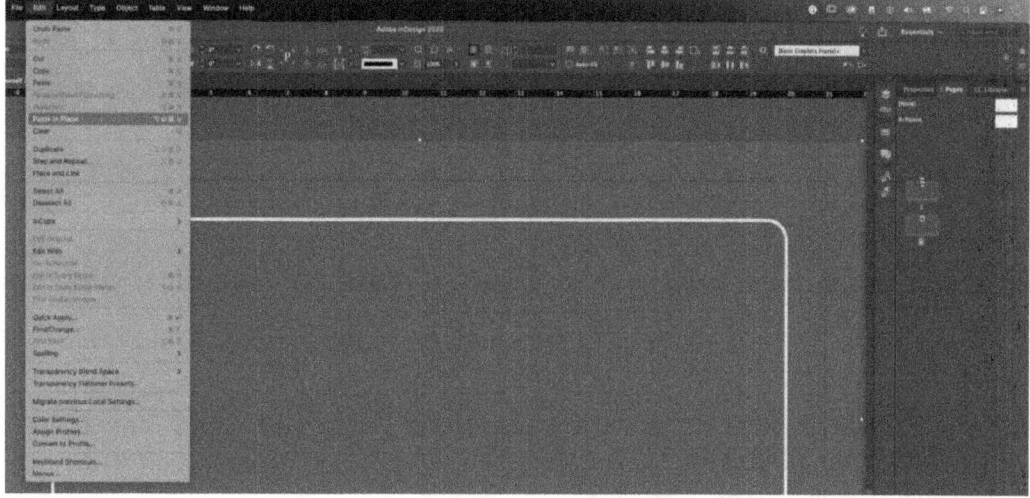

Figure 2.30: The background elements pasted in place on Page 2

3. Draw a frame using the **Rectangular Frame** tool ⊠, as shown in *Figure 2.31*. The size is not important as we will resize it next. Click inside the frame with the **Text** tool T and type the following details:

jane@cube.com

123 Street, City, State 45678

ph. 800 123 456

Figure 2.31: The address details typed onto the rear of the card

4. To format the text, click anywhere in the text frame with the **Type** tool T. Then, choose **Edit** menu | **Select All**. Confirm that all the text is highlighted. Make the following changes in the **Properties** panel:

   A. Under **Appearance**, choose **Paper** for the text **Fill**.
   B. Change the font to *Raleway* and *Regular* from the **Character** category.
   C. Set the size to **8 pt** from the **Character** category.

D. Choose **Align center** (the second icon) under **Paragraph**.

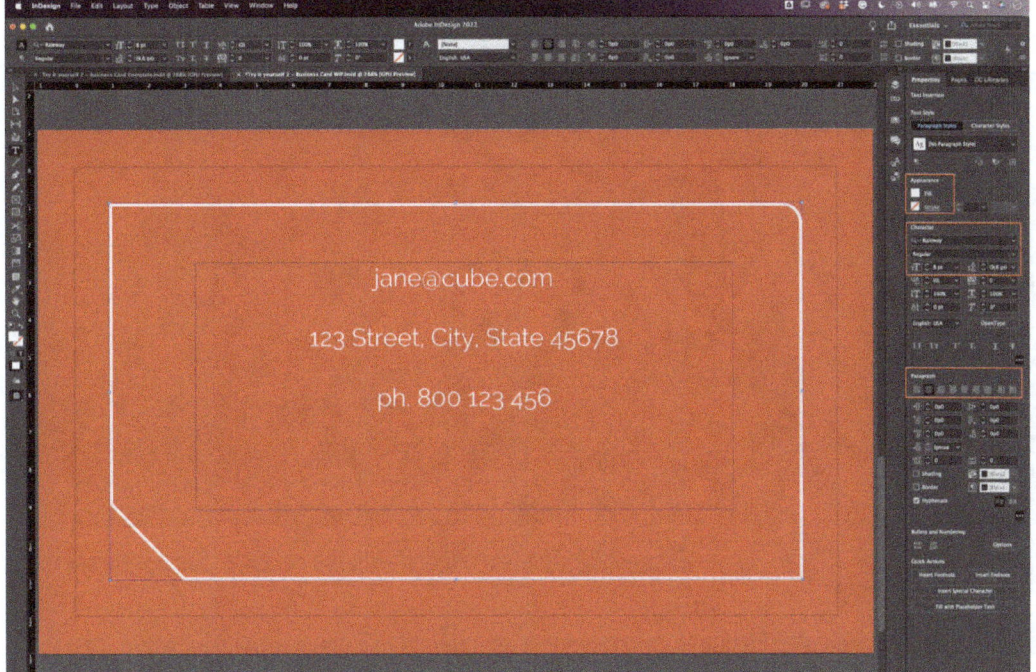

Figure 2.32: The address details formatted correctly onto the rear of the card

5. We'll resize the frame to fit the text and center it on the card relative to the white border. Choose the **Selection** tool . Click on the text object once. The object frame will show a series of white squares and other widgets along its edge. Hover over the bottom right control and double-click. This will resize the text frame.

6. *Shift*-click the white border to select it as well. Release *Shift* and click the border a second time. Now choose **Align horizontal centers** and **Align vertical centers** under the **Align** options in the **Properties** panel.

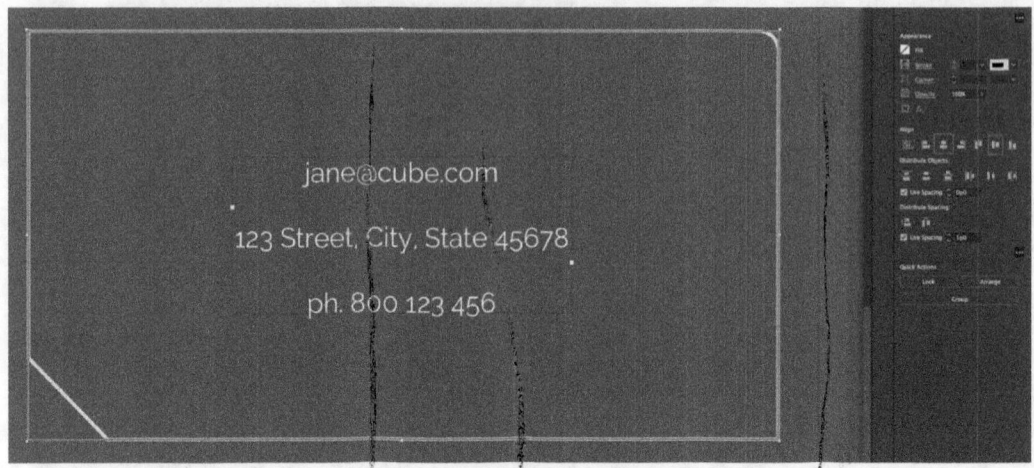

Figure 2.33: The text aligned with the center of the business card

7. Well done. Our business card project is complete. Let's preview the final result. Choose the **View** menu | **Screen Mode** | **Presentation**. The InDesign interface is hidden from view showing the artwork only.

8. Use the arrow keys to navigate between pages. Press the *Esc* key to exit presentation mode. Choose the **File** menu | **Save** as if you wish to save a copy of your completed project.

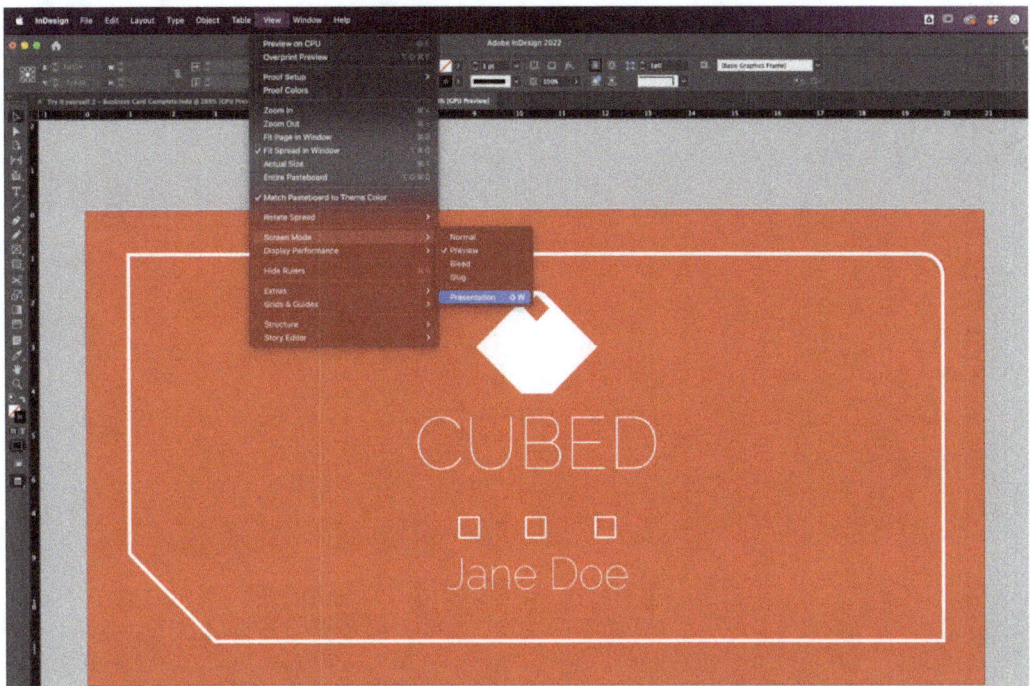

Figure 2.34: Previewing the final design
(The image is intended as a visual reference; the textual information is not essential.)

This brings us to the end of the chapter.

Summary

In this chapter, we designed a business card from the ground up. We learned how to navigate between pages in a multi-page document. We created and formatted basic shape objects, adjusting their **Fill** and **Stroke** properties along the way. We also created text objects and changed the properties of text elements. We previewed the final design as a final step. This knowledge lays the groundwork for the next chapter, in which we will build on what we have learned and design increasingly more complex designs.

Part 2: Beyond the Basics

This part delves deeper into intermediate-level InDesign skills. Learn how to leverage advanced typographic controls and table formatting. Explore and understand the crucial nuances of various color models, providing a foundational understanding of color used in professional cross-media design. You'll learn how to use transparency, blend modes, and effects to create compelling designs for any use case.

This part has the following chapters:

- *Chapter 3, Designing Social Media Posts*
- *Chapter 4, Designing with Text and Tables*
- *Chapter 5, An Overview of Color Models*
- *Chapter 6, Working with Graphics and Color*
- *Chapter 7, Transparency and Effects: Part 1*
- *Chapter 8, Transparency and Effects: Part 2*

Level: Intermediate

Designing Social Media Posts

In this chapter, we will bring together various elements into a social media design. We'll work with text and graphics. We'll also work with images, and vector graphics, which would typically be designed in an application such as Illustrator. The elements will be organized in the layout to create a pleasing, impactful final design. We will create a square post that can be used on multiple social media platforms. Please visit https://packt.link/a19oQ to download the relevant exercise files for this chapter. The folder's name is: Chapter 3 - Designing Social Media Posts Example Files. The following screenshot shows our completed project.

Figure 3.1: The completed social media project showing elements on the Layers panel (The image is intended as a visual reference; the textual information is not essential.)

This is what we will aim to achieve in this chapter. We will build on what we learned in *Chapter 2, Working with Text and Shapes*, to complete this project. The areas we will focus on are listed below.

The main topics we will cover in this chapter are as follows:

- Open an existing file
- Arrange objects and explore object hierarchies on the **Layers** panel
- Set up a document for social media
- Adjust the **fill** and **stroke** properties of objects
- Work with **rounded corners**
- Create **text** objects
- Change the **properties** of text elements
- **Align and distribute** objects in the artwork
- **Create a compound path object**
- **Preview** the final design

When creating digital media, this book uses **pixels**. This is a universal unit of measurement for digital assets. Remember that pixels are not appropriate when creating print documents.

Exploring the completed project and resources

This book is written in a practical, hands-on way. We'll start by exploring the completed project file to help orient ourselves. Download the files referred to in this project and follow along with us. These example files can be downloaded here: https://packt.link/a19oQ

1. Open the completed project by choosing **File menu | Open**. Navigate to the Chapter 3 - Designing Social Media Posts Example Files folder. Open the file named Try it yourself 3 – Social Media Post Complete.indd. If you are presented with a missing font warning, please click **Activate**. InDesign will automatically install any missing fonts.

2. Access the **Layers** panel from the **Window** menu. Choose the **Selection** tool from the **Toolbox**. Click on the individual elements on the page. As you do so, the object will be highlighted in the **Layers** panel. This is a good way of working through a document you may have received from a colleague or fellow designer.

3. Let's identify the various elements in our design, as can be seen in *Figure 3.1* above. There is an image in the background, with a rounded corner border. We have some text elements in various configurations. A logo, QR code, and social media icons that finish off the design. All relevant elements files have been created for you and can be found in the Chapter 3 - Designing Social Media Posts Example Files folder.

4. Close the file when you are done exploring. It is advisable not to save any changes you made. In this way, you always have a clean version of the file to reference as you work through the chapter.

Now that we've explored the design, we are ready to create it from the ground up. We'll start by setting up a new document and working our way through to the completed social media post.

Creating a new social media document

In this section, we will create a new document. We'll then adjust the parameters to suit our desired outcome by setting the size and units of measurement.

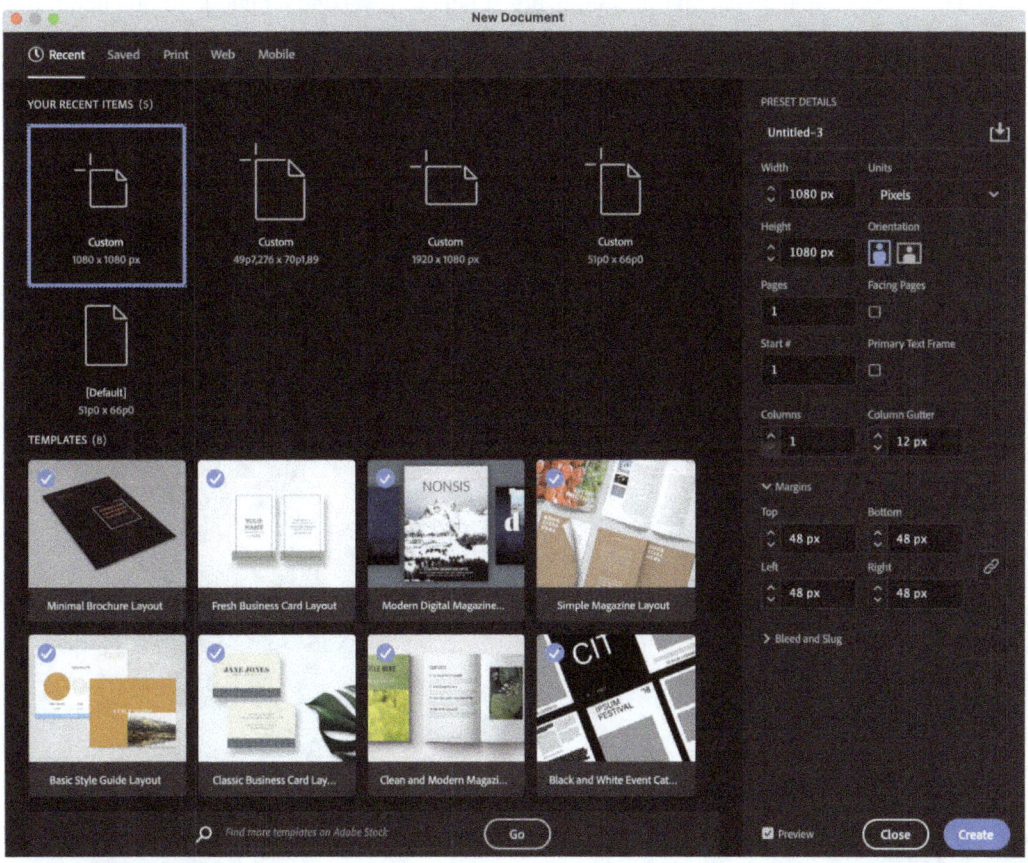

*Figure 3.2: Setting up the new social media document
(The image is intended as a visual reference; the textual information is not essential.)*

1. Click the **New File** button on the InDesign home screen. In the resultant **New Document** dialog, choose the **Web** subset. Then make the following changes to the document settings:

   A. Set **Units** to **Pixels**.
   B. Type 1080 for the **Width** and **Height** values.
   C. Type **1** in the **Pages** field.
   D. Disable **Facing Pages** as this only applies to multi-page documents.
   E. Type 1 in the **Columns** field. The **Column Gutter** value is irrelevant as there is only one column in our design.
   F. Ensure that the chain-link icon is unbroken under the **Margins** subcategory. By doing so, all margin values are connected. Making a change to one updates all of them. Set this value to 48 pixels.
   G. **Bleed and Slug** can be ignored as these are settings for printed documents.

2. Enable the **Preview** checkbox. InDesign will present the document to you in real time so that you can confirm that your settings are correct.

3. Click the **Create** button. You will be presented with the working document as seen in *Figure 3.3*.

Figure 3.3: The page with margins visible
(The image is intended as a visual reference; the textual information is not essential.)

Good work! The document is set up for our social media design. It has the appropriate margins, units of measurement, and page settings for us to lay down some guides to help with the positioning of elements.

Adding guides to the document

Guides help in positioning and aligning content in a design. By working with guides, you can easily create consistency and balance in your projects. We'll create a grid made up of three columns and three rows, resulting in nine design units on the page. This will help us arrange objects on our page with greater precision. This type of grid is called a Rule of Thirds grid.

1. Choose **Layout** menu | **Create Guides**. In the **Create Guides** dialog, tick the **Preview** switch.
2. Type a value of 3 for both the **Columns** and **Rows** fields. A gutter of 12 px is perfect. **Gutter** refers to the spacing between columns.
3. Under **Options**, enable the **Margins** radio button to have the guides drawn between the page margins we set up when creating the document. Click **OK** to confirm our margin values:

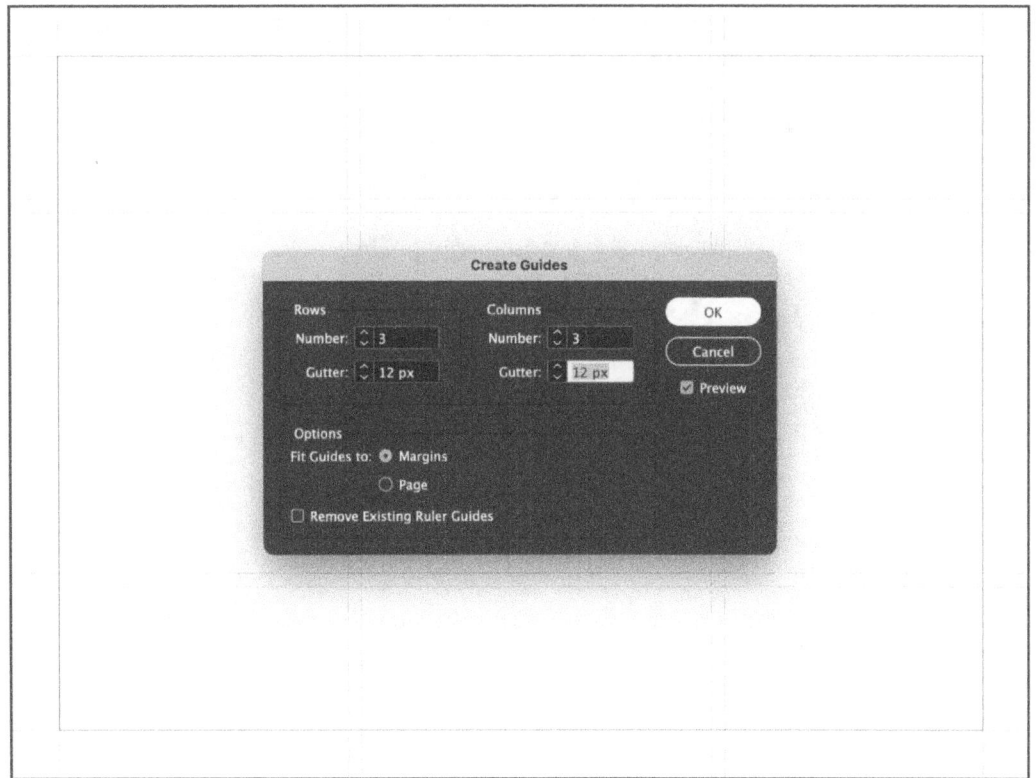

Figure 3.4: Column and row margins applied to the design

Setting up guidelines, as we just did, is an extremely useful way of dividing the format into design units. In the next section, we'll import the image that forms the background to our design.

Importing images into InDesign

Now that we've set up our social media document, we're able to import content into it. InDesign allows for a large variety of content to be imported into your designs. These can range from images and text, all the way through to interactive objects. Our design requires us to import a background image, which can be found in the Chapter 3 - Designing Social Media Posts Example Files folder. The ubiquitous command in almost all Adobe applications is the Place command. To do this, follow these steps:

1. Choose the **Selection** tool (*V* or *Esc*). Choose **File** menu | **Place**. Navigate to the Chapter 3 - Designing Social Media Posts Example Files folder. **Choose the image file named** 03 Park Image.jpg. **Click Open**. The mouse icon changes. This new icon is called a **Place Gun**. Click anywhere on the page. Remember to click and release the mouse. Do not click and drag, as this will change the size and resolution of the image.

Figure 3.5: The image placed on the page

2. Access the **Properties** panel. Under the **Transform** subset, enable the chain-link icon alongside the **W** and **H** input fields. This will constrain the width and height values. Change the **H** value to 1080. By doing so, the frame that is hosting the image will change to the required size.

3. To have the image fit the new dimensions, click the very first icon (**Fill Frame Proportionally**) under the **Frame Fitting** options toward the bottom of the **Properties** panel. The image should now fill the frame.

4. To center the image on the page, choose the following options on the **Properties** panel:

    A. Under the **Align** category, click on the first icon which is a drop-down list. Choose **Align to Page** from the options available. Then, click the **Align Horizontal Centers** and **Align Vertical Centers** icons to position the image to the center of the page.

5. Let's save our file at this point. Choose **File | Save**. Choose a filename and location where you would like to save your file and click the **Save** button. You can see the **Transform**, **Align**, and **Frame Fitting** values in the following screenshot.

Figure 3.6: The scale, fill, and align controls are highlighted

Cropping an image in InDesign

Cropping is the command that hides areas of an image you do not wish to have visible. You'll recall that all content within InDesign is placed inside a **frame**. Imagine frames as content holders or containers. A frame was automatically created when we placed the background image. We now simply need to change its width to match the page to initiate our crop. Follow these steps:

1. Choose the **Selection** tool and click on the image once. A single click is important as it will select the image and its container frame. Disable the chain-link icon alongside the **W** and **H** values to allow for a non-proportional scale. Type in 1080 for the **W** value. This will change the width of the image to match the width of the page. You should now have an image that fits the page dimensions perfectly.

Figure 3.7: The image cropped to fit the page

Well done! You now know how to place image files into InDesign, place them in a location that works for the design at hand, and crop unwanted areas of the image. We'll explore how to lock this background image next to prevent unwanted edits.

Locking objects

InDesign provides you the ability to selectively show, hide, and lock objects. It's worth noting that content is stacked one on top of another. The object that is was created or imported last appears on the top of the object stack, while the first object appears at the bottom. This hierarchy can be changed at will. In our example, we will ensure that the background image is at the bottom of the object stack. We will lock the background image so we don't inadvertently move or edit it as we create objects above it. These objects will include borders, graphics, and text. To lock the background image we just placed, follow these steps:

1. Choose the **Selection** tool and click on the object to make it active.
2. Choose the **Layers** panel. If it is not visible, select it from the **Window** menu.
3. Click on the **Twirldown** arrow to the left of **Layer 1**. You will see our image is labeled **<03 Park Image.jpg>**.
4. Click the box between the eyeball and the layer color (blue by default). A lock icon appears where you click in that box. This indicates the object is locked. If you try to select or move the object on the page, it should not be possible.

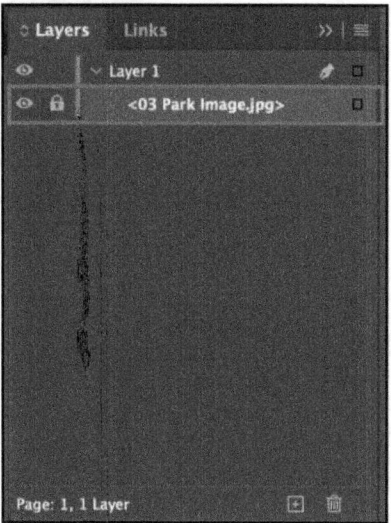

Figure 3.8: The Layers panel showing the image has been locked

Awesome job! The image background is locked and loaded! We'll now turn our attention to the various graphic elements that sit above this background image, starting with the white rounded corner rectangle that frames the design.

Creating rounded corner rectangles

Now that we have our background in place, we can turn our attention to the graphic elements. To create a white rectangular border along the edge of the artwork, we'll use the **Rectangle** tool. We'll round the corners of the rectangle after having drawn it.

1. Choose the **Rectangle** tool. Click and drag from the top-left margin to the bottom right margin. InDesign, by default, will snap your cursor into these guides.
2. Head over to the **Properties** panel.
   A. Under the **Appearance** subset of controls, ensure that the object has no fill, and **Paper** as its stroke color.
   B. Set the **Stroke** thickness to **8 pt**.
   C. To round off the corners, click on the corner type drop-down list arrow to the right of the word **Corner**. This option appears directly below the **Stroke** property on the **Properties** panel. Choose the very last option, which is **Rounded**. Increase the roundness value to 48 pixels. Lock this object too by choosing **Object** menu | **Lock**

Figure 3.9: The border with a white stroke and rounded corners

The design is starting to take shape. The background image and rounded corner border have been completed. We learned how to draw objects on the page, manipulate stroke and fill properties, and adjust the size to a high degree of accuracy. We can now turn our attention to the typographic components of the design.

Working with type

It is time for us to introduce the type elements to our design. InDesign offers multiple ways to work with type. For this design, we will create different frames for our type and create shapes to create reverse type as well.

1. Choose the **Type** tool (*T*). Click and drag a textframe in the top quadrant of the middle column. Enable *Caps Lock* on your keyboard and type FUN RUN. Highlight the text with the **Type** tool . Under **Character** on the **Properties** panel, set the following properties:

    A. Choose **Bebas Neue** for the font.

    B. Set the weight to **Bold** from the drop-down list just below the font name.

    C. Set the size to **200 pt**.

    D. With the text still selected, change the **Fill** color to **Paper**. This option is found on the **Properties** panel just above the **Character** controls.

    E. Choose **Align Center** from the **Paragraph** controls on the **Properties** panel.

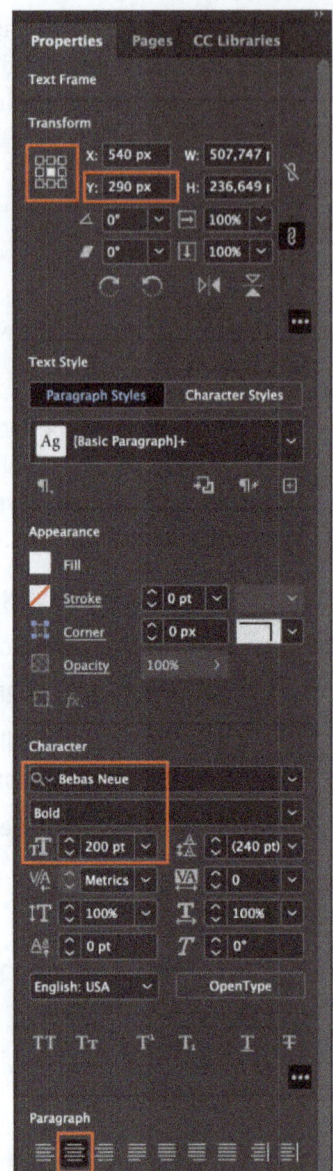

Figure 3.10: The Properties panel with the changes above highlighted in red

2. If the text frame is too small to accommodate the text. Choose the **Zoom** tool (*Z*) and click and drag on the word **FUN** to zoom into the artwork. Click the text object once with the **Selection** tool. Double-click on the little white square at the bottom-right of the textbox (see *Figure 3.11*). This can be found just below the overset text control, denoted by a red square with a plus in it. This will resize the text frame optimally to accommodate the text.

Figure 3.11: The resize text frameresize text frame control

3. Let's align the object dead center on the page. Ensure the text object is selected with the **Selection** tool . Under the **Align** controls on the **Properties** panel, click the first icon and choose **Align to Page** from the resultant dropdown list. Then, click the **Align horizontal centers** icon (third from left).

4. Set the **Y** value to 245 px under the **Transform** controls on the **Properties** panel. Ensure that the center reference point is selected on the proxy (See *Figure 3.12*). It is found to the left of the **X** and **Y** values on the **Properties** panel.

Figure 3.12: The completed FUN RUN text with the adjusted parameters highlighted

Our first text object is completed. As you probably have discerned, the **Properties** panel is a really handy resource for manipulating all types of objects. We'll continue our typographic journey by creating reversed-out text next.

Creating reverse type

Reverse type is where the type color is reversed against a background color or object to match a design context. A typical example is white text on a black background, often referred to as **white on black** (**WOB**). Reverse type is simple to create. It requires a graphic object that interacts with a text frame. This is one of many (and arguably the easiest) method to create reverse type.

1. Choose the **Rectangle** tool and draw a rectangle of any size on the page. Make the following changes on the **Properties** panel:

   A. Under **Appearance**, set the **Fill** color to **Paper**.

   B. Click the **Corner** drop-down list and choose **Rounded**.

   C. Set the **Roundness** value to 18 px.

   D. From the **Transform** subset, ensure that the middle transformation point is selected.

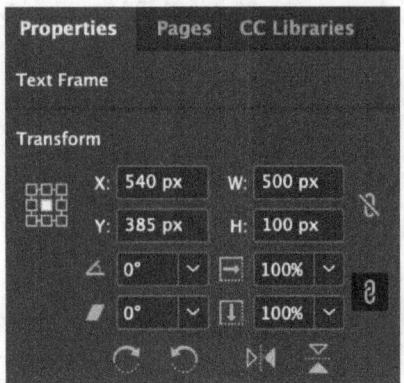

Figure 3.13: Close up of the Properties panel displaying the Transform controls

   E. Disable the constrain proportions chain-link icon and set the **W** value to 500 px and the **H** value to 100 px.

   F. You can choose to position the object by eye. Should you want the exact vertical value though, set the **Y** value to 385 px.

2. We need to align the rectangle to the text above. Click the rectangle with the **Selection** tool . Press *Shift* and click on the text to select it as well.

3. Release the *Shift* key and click the text for a second time to make it a key object. This allows for the rectangle to align with the text without the text being moved. The frame of the key object is highlighted in blue for easy identification. Next, click on the **Align horizontal centers** icon (third from left) from the **Properties** panel to center the two elements. If you refer to *Figure 3.14*, you can see that the **FUN RUN** text and, the rectangle are now perfectly aligned.

Figure 3.14: The completed rectangle that will form part of the reverse text

4. Let's add text in the rectangle. Choose the **Type** tool and click in the rectangle. This will convert the rectangle to a text frame. Type IN THE. Select the text with the **Type** tool and make the following changes on the **Properties** panel:

   A. Under **Character**, set the font to **Bebas Neue, Regular**.

   B. Set the size to **120 pt**.

   C. Under **Paragraph**, choose **Align center** (second icon).

5. We'll apply a color from the image to the type. To do this, we'll need to temporarily unlock the background image. On the **Layers** panel, click the padlock icon alongside **<03 Park Image.jpg>** to unlock it. With the text still highlighted, choose the **Eyedropper** tool from the toolbox. Click on the green foliage above the **FUN RUN** text. If you are unhappy with the color, simply click on a different part of the image to sample a new color. Click away from the text to see the result. Remember to lock the background image by enabling the padlock on the **Layers** panel.

Figure 3.15: The completed reverse text object

6. We'll now add the word PARK. We'll use a different technique to achieve this. Click the **FUN RUN** text with the **Selection** tool. Press and hold the *Alt* (Windows)/*Option* (macOS) and *Shift* keys. Drag the object below the reverse text rectangle we just completed with the words **IN THE**. By holding in *Alt/Option* as we drag, we are able to create a copy of the object we are dragging. The *Shift* key keeps the copied text perfectly aligned with the original.

7. Release the mouse then the *Shift* and *Alt/Option* keys. Select the **FUN RUN** text in the copied frame and type PARK to replace it. Then, change the text size on the **Properties** panel to **315 pt**.

> **Note**
> If the text frame is too small and the text is overset, choose the **Selection** tool. Double-click the bottom-right control of the text frame to resize it.

Figure 3.16: The copied text frame in place

8. We'll use the same technique for the last bit of text, the date of the event. This time, we'll make a copy of the reverse text and amend it. Click the **IN THE** reverse text frame with the **Selection** tool . Hold *Alt* (Windows)/*Option* (macOS) and *Shift*, and drag down to below the **PARK** text.

9. Highlight the text in the copied frame with the **Type** tool and make the following changes on the **Properties** panel:

    A. Change the font to **Bebas Neue Book**.

    B. The text size should be **50 pt**.

    C. Highlight the text with the **Type** tool and type SATURDAY, 20 JUNE

10. The final task at hand is to resize the rectangle frame and remove the rounded corners for the top part of the frame. Click the date frame with the **Selection** tool . Make the following updates on the **Properties** panel:

    A. Click the top-middle reference point under **Transform**. This will anchor the object to that point.

    B. Change the **H** value from 100 px to 45 px. I'm sure you see the value of changing the object reference point.

    C. Click the word **Corner** under **Appearance** to access the **Corner Options** dialog.

    D. Ensure the chainlink icon is inactive. Click on the drop-down lists for the top-left and top-right corners and set these values to **None**. The corners will return to a 90-degree angle. Click **OK** to dismiss the dialog.

11. If you need to move the object up or down, ensure it is still selected with the **Selection** tool . Then tap the up or down arrow keys till the object is where you want it to be.

12. To close out this part of the project, we'll group all the text objects. Choose the **Selection** tool and click each of the text objects while holding the *Shift* key. Once you've selected all the objects, right-click any one of them and choose the **Group** command from the context-sensitive menu.

Figure 3.17: The completed text objects aligned and grouped as a single unit

Well done! As you can see, working with and formatting type is relatively easy in InDesign. Combining text and graphic objects, gives us the ability to easily create reverse type. We'll explore importing graphic elements into our design in the next section.

Importing vector graphics

In this section, we will place a series of vector elements into our design. This includes a logo and three social media icons. Follow the steps below to get started:

1. Choose the **Selection** tool. Select **File | Place**. Navigate to the Chapter 3 - Designing Social Media Posts Example Files folder for *Chapter 3*. Select the file named 03 RTC Logo.ai. InDesign will load the file into its place gun. Click and drag in the space below the text group we created.
2. Let's sort out the alignment and size for the logo object.
3. Enable the **Constrain** proportions for the width and height chain-link switch under **Transform** on the **Properties** panel. Set the height to 200 px.
4. Click the first icon under **Frame Fitting** (**Fill Frame Proportionally**). This will ensure a perfect fit for the logo within its frame.
5. From the **Align** controls, ensure that **Align to Page** is enabled by clicking on the very first icon and choosing that option. Then, click **Align horizontal centers** (third icon) to center the artwork on the page.

Figure 3.18: The logo object placed on the page at the correct size and location

Placing vector objects, I'm sure you'll agree, is easy. In the next section, we will place of multiple objects, align them, and adjust the space between them so they are equidistant from one another.

Placing multiple objects

InDesign offers powerful controls to place and space multiple objects at once. We'll explore these options when placing the social media icons in our design. Follow these steps:

1. With the **Selection** tool active, click off the page to deselect all objects. Choose **File** menu | **Place**. Navigate to the Chapter 3 - Designing Social Media Posts Example Files folder. Select the following files using *Ctrl* (Windows) or *Cmd* (macOS) to make a non-contiguous multi-file selection:

    A. 03 Facebook icon.ai

    B. 03 LinkedIn icon.ai

    C. 03 Twitter icon.ai

2. InDesign will load all three files into its place gun. Use the arrow keys on your keyboard to move between the place gun image previews.

> **Important note**
> Do not release your mouse till all steps are complete. If you do inadvertently release your mouse, choose **Edit** | **Undo** and your place gun will be reloaded.

3. Click and drag toward the bottom right of the design, as shown in *Figure 3.19*. Tap the right arrow key twice. This will add two additional frames to accommodate all the social icons. You will get a live readout. Move your mouse till the **X** value is approximately 230 px and the **Y** value reads 50 px. Then, release the mouse, and voila! All three social icons are placed on the page. Use the arrow keys to nudge the objects in any desired direction.

Figure 3.19: Social media icons placed onto the artwork

The place gun offers us numerous flexible ways of importing content into InDesign. Everything from alignment, spacing, and content previews are catered for. In the next section, we'll generate a QR code directly in InDesign.

Generating QR codes

We'll close out this chapter by creating a QR code for our design. InDesign offers numerous options for QR codes, ranging from web links to digital business cards. Follow these steps:

1. Choose the **Selection** tool. Click off the page to deselect all objects on the page.
2. Choose **Object** menu | **Generate QR Code**. Choose **Web Hyperlink** from the **Type** dropdown. Type in a URL. We've typed www.packt.com.
3. Click the **Color** tab and select **Paper**. This will render our QR code in white. Click **OK**. The cursor will change to a place gun.
4. Click and drag in the space to the left of the logo to place the QR code in that location. Drag out till the **X** and **Y** values read around **125%**. Then, release the mouse. Voila! The QR code is placed into our design.
5. To ensure that the QR code and the social icons are aligned with the logo, we'll select all the elements with the **Selection** tool by clicking on them with the *Shift* key held in.
6. Release the *Shift* key and click on the logo again. The selection border around it will become more pronounced, indicating it is a key object. Then, choose **Align vertical centers** from the **Align** subset of the **Properties** panel.

That's us done. Please save your project. Should you wish to export your artwork for social media, choose **File** menu | **Export** and select **PNG** for the export format.

Figure 3.20: The completed social media post ready for export

QR code creation, as we've just seen, is native to InDesign. It has options for hyperlinks, electronic business cards, and everything in-between. Be sure to explore the many options available.

Summary

In this chapter, we designed a social media post from scratch. We started the project by setting up the document using the Web preset. This simplified our task by defaulting to pixels, and RGB as the document color space. We adjusted the page size to cater to social media. We used guides to define a grid system. We then placed images and cropped them. We adjusted the fill, stroke, and rounded corner values of objects. We worked with various text objects. This was achieved by creating new type elements and duplicating existing type objects. Reverse text was created by using objects as placeholders. Various vector graphics were imported and placed in the design including the logo and social media icons. We aligned and distributed elements in relation to one another and the page. We generated a QR code and tweaked its properties. These skills lay the groundwork for our creative journey in InDesign.

In the next chapter, we will explore the many typographic options available in InDesign to deliver high-impact communication pieces that exude finesse and flair.

Level: Intermediate

Designing with Text and Tables

InDesign is a powerhouse when it comes to designing communication pieces that are text and table-rich. It has industry-leading typographic functionality, ranging from time-saving styles to powerful formatting controls. You can easily incorporate source text from applications such as Microsoft Word, Excel, and many other applications. This chapter focuses on the text and table formatting fundamentals available in the software. Mastering this typographic functionality will put you in a strong position to maximize efficiency in your InDesign workflow.

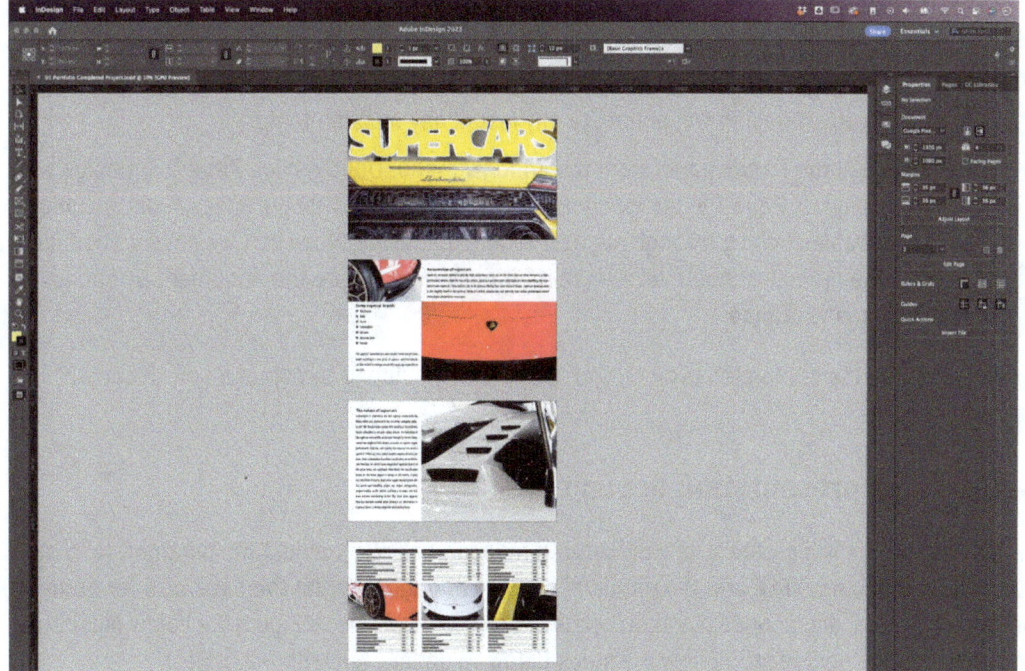

Figure 4.1: The completed four-page presentation project showing multiple slides (The image is intended as a visual reference; the textual information is not essential.)

Figure 4.1 above shows what we will design in in this chapter. We will focus primarily on importing and styling text and graphics to complete this project.

The main topics we will cover in this chapter are as follows:

- Setting up a presentation document
- Creating placeholder frames
- Importing multiple images at once
- Importing and formatting text from Microsoft Word
- Importing and formatting tables from Microsoft Excel

Since we are creating a presentation that will be projected on-screen, so we will set the project up using **pixels**.

This book is written in a practical, hands-on way. You can try concepts you've read about yourself by downloading the files referred to in this project. These example files can be downloaded from the following link: https://packt.link/a19oQ.

We'll start by exploring the completed project. Follow these steps to open the completed project:

1. Choose **File** menu | **Open**. Navigate to the Chapter 4 - Designing with Text and Tables Example Files folder. Open the file named Try it yourself 4 – Presentation Complete.indd. If you are presented with a missing fonts warning, please click **Activate**. InDesign will automatically install any missing fonts.

2. Access the **Pages** panel from the **Window** menu. Double-click **Page 1**. InDesign will present just **Page 1** in the viewport. Let's explore the rest of the pages in the document by double-clicking through pages 2 to 4 respectively. Now, that we have a good idea of the project at hand, let's recreate it ourselves. Close the document by choosing **File** menu | **Close**.

Having explored the completed project, you should feel equipped to set up a new document for our project.

Setting up a presentation document

In this section, we will create a new presentation document. We'll adjust the parameters to suit our desired outcome. We'll add the requisite number of pages, adjust the page size for optimal viewing on screen, and choose the appropriate units of measurement. *Figure 4.2* below illustrates how to set up the document. Follow the steps below to get started with the project:

Setting up a presentation document   87

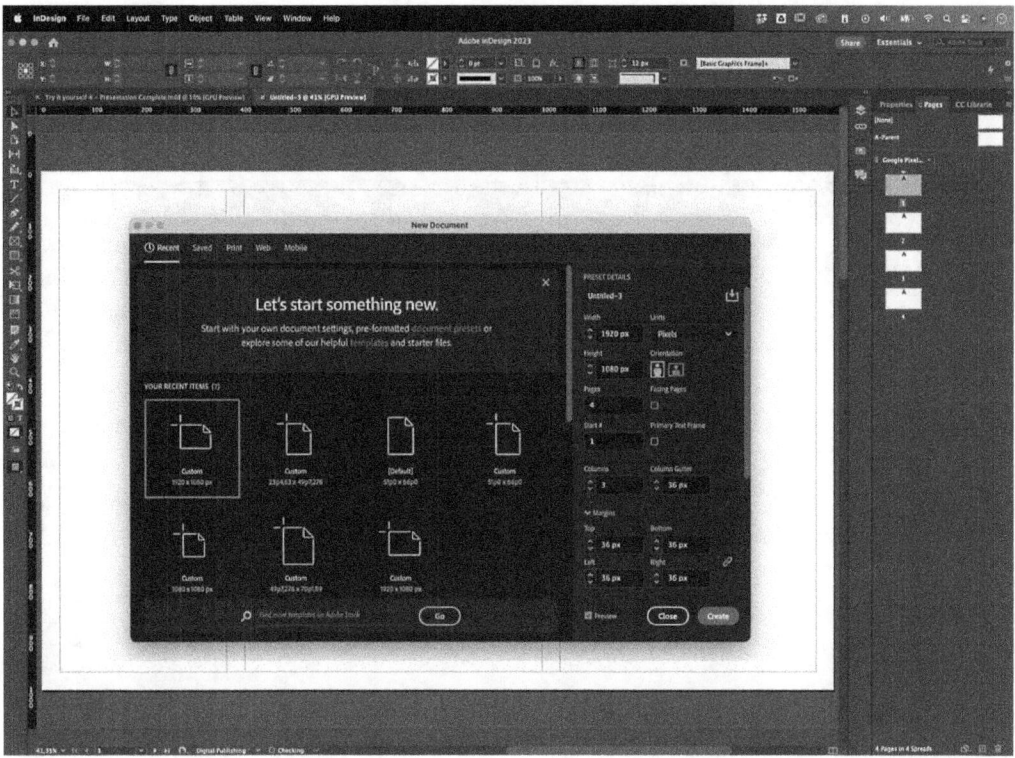

Figure 4.2: The four-page presentation setup
(The image is intended as a visual reference; the textual information is not essential.)

1. Click the **New File** button on the InDesign home screen. From the **New Document** dialog, choose **Web** subset. Then, make the following changes to the document settings:
2. Ensure the units are set to **Pixels**.

    A. Type 1920 for the width and 1080 for the height.

    B. Type 4 in the **Pages** field.

    C. Disable **Facing Pages**, as this only applies to multi-page documents.

    D. Disable the **Primary Text Frame** switch too, as this is used for large multi-page documents.

    E. Type 3 in the **Columns** field. Change the **Column Gutter** value to 36 pixels. *Gutter* in this context refers to the spacing between columns.

    F. Under the Margins sub-category, ensure that the chain-link icon is enabled. Set this value to 36 pixels as well.

    G. **Bleed** and **slug** can be ignored, as these are settings for printed documents.

3. Enable the **Preview** checkbox. InDesign will present the document to you behind the **New Document** dialog so that you can visually confirm that your settings are correct.

4. Click the **Create** button. You will be presented with the working document shown in the following screenshot:

Figure 4.3: The document showing Page 1 of 4, with the columns and margins visible

The document is now correctly set up for our presentation. It has the appropriate margins, units of measurement, and page columns. We'll add guidelines next, to create a rule-of-thirds grid that will assist us in the placement of elements onto the pages.

Adding guides to a document

As we did in the previous chapter, we'll add guides to our document to help position and align content in our design. Using a rule-of-thirds grid is a tried and tested tradition that can be traced back to the 18th century and prior. It helps you to organize content and create harmony between elements in a design. Let's get started:

1. Choose the page labeled **A-Parent**. It can be found at the very top of the **Pages** panel. Be sure to double-click it to make it active. Any elements added to the parent page will appear on pages associated with it. We will therefore place guides on the parent page. Note the capital letter **A** found on the top of each page in the **Pages** panel. This shows that **A-Parent** is the parent to all pages in the document. The **A** suffix helps us identify the parent. A document can have multiple parent pages for different subsections in a document.

Setting up a presentation document | 89

2. Choose **Layout** menu | **Create Guides**. In the **Create Guides** dialog, check the **Preview** checkbox for real-time visual updates as you make changes to settings.

3. Type a value of 0 for Columns (columns were created when we set up the document). Enter a value of 3 for the Rows field. Change the **Rows Gutter** value to 36 px. Set the **Columns Gutter** value to 0 px. Gutter refers to the spacing between columns and rows. Since we only require rows, the **Gutter** value for **Columns** has no material impact on our document setup.

4. Under **Options**, enable the **Margins** radio button. The guides and gutter values are positioned between document margins, as opposed to the page edge, which is what we want in this design.

> **Quick tip**
> Enable the **Remove Existing Ruler Guides** checkbox to eliminate any existing guides in the document. It ensures a clean and manageable guides workflow.

5. Click **OK** to accept the changes we've made in the **Create Guides** dialog.

6. Double-click on **Page 1** on the **Pages** panel to ensure that you are working on the document pages once more:

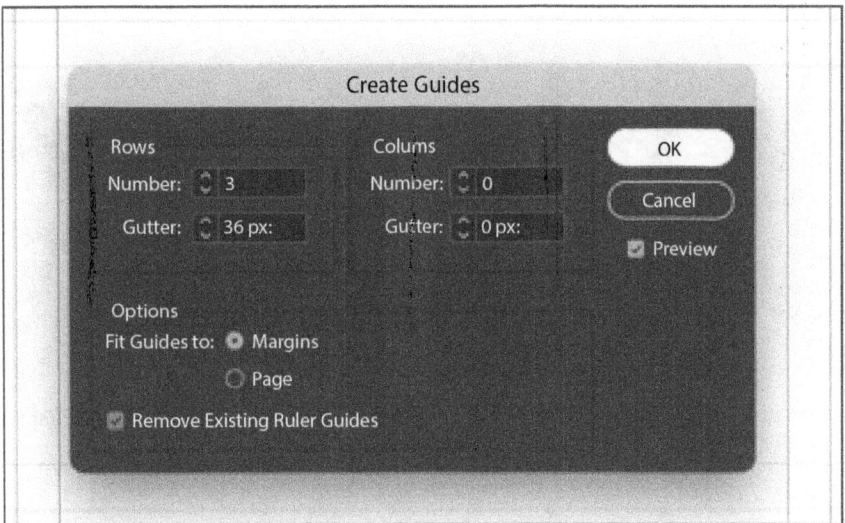

Figure 4.4: The Create Guides dialog displaying the required settings for the project

With the guidelines in place, we're ready to place content into our document. We'll start by creating placeholder frames. InDesign offers powerful controls for us to work with multiple assets quickly and efficiently. We'll use the guides we created to help our design decisions, including placeholder frames, which are discussed in the next section.

Creating placeholder frames

Placeholder frames allow us to plan and structure a document with ease. This is especially helpful if some content is still outstanding from contributors. Placeholder frames can contain text , graphics or photos. We'll explore all options available to us. In this section, we will first look a the completed design for each page. we'll then create the placeholder frames which will house the content for the various pages.

Figure 4.5: The completed design for Page 1

In this section, we will first look a the completed design for each page. we'll then create the placeholder frames which will house the content for the various pages. Let's get started:

1. Choose the **Rectangle Frame** tool ⊠ (F) from the **Tools** panel. Navigate to **Page 1**. Click and drag from the top-left corner to the bottom-right corner of the page. This frame will host our background image.

2. With the **Rectangle Frame** tool ⊠ still active, draw a second frame from the top-left edge to the top-right edge of the page. Note that the frame depth will only be as deep as the first-row guideline. Refer to *Figure 4.6* below for guidance.

Figure 4.6: The text and graphic placeholder frames for Page 1

3. Go to **Page 2**. We'll create two placeholder frames here.One for the small image at the top-left of the page, and a second, larger frame that will take up most of the space toward the bottom-right of the page. We'll place the text directly onto the page without creating frames. You can then decide whether you prefer using frames or using the column guides when placing text.

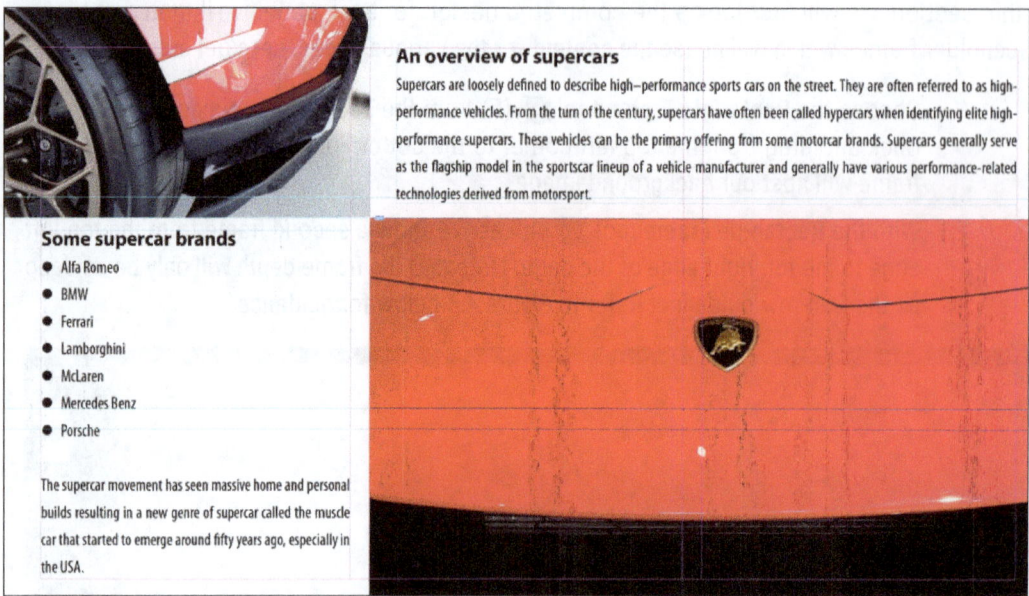

Figure 4.7: The design elements for Page 2

4. Draw a placeholder frame at the top-left of **Page 2**. As you can see, it spans one design unit on our design grid. Then, draw a second frame over the bottom four design units. Remember to draw your frame to the page edge in each case. The following screenshot shows the drawn frames on **Page 2**.

Figure 4.8: The graphic placeholder frames for Page 2

5. Pretty straightforward, right? Let's go to **Page 3**. This page super easy. We'll create a graphic frame for the image on the right of the page.

Figure 4.9: The completed version of Page 3

6. With the **Rectangular Frame** tool ⊠, selected, draw a frame from the top-right corner to the bottom of the page, taking care to leave the leftmost column open for our text.

Figure 4.10: The single frame required for Page 3

7. Now that we're on a roll, let's jump to **Page 4**. This time, as you can see in *Figure 4.11*, we have three images placed across the vertical center of the page. Read through the next step carefully before embarking on the task. We'll draw all three frames at once. Then, we'll apply tweaks to the left and right frames so that they touch the page edge.

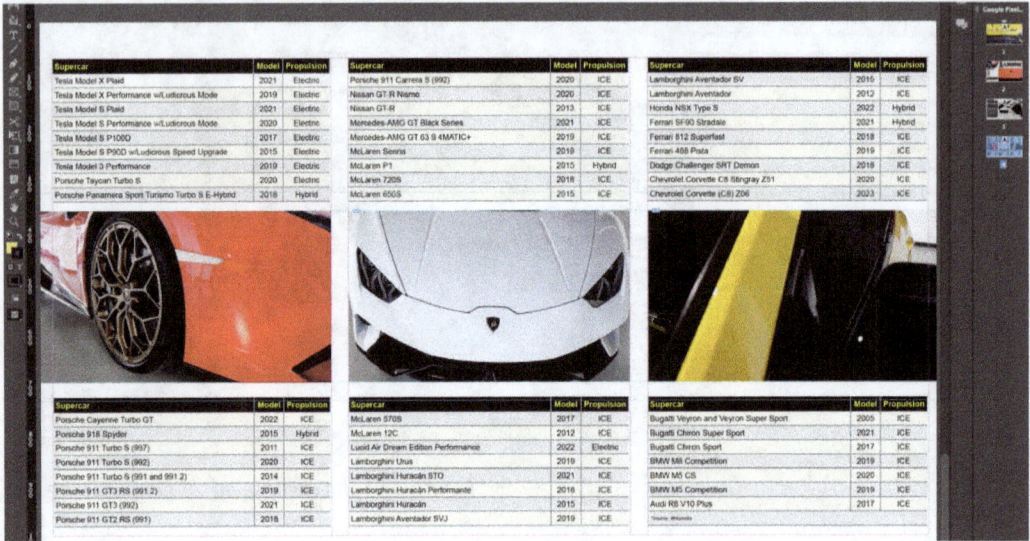

Figure 4.11: The completed design on Page 4 sporting three images and a table (The image is intended as a visual reference; the textual information is not essential.)

8. We'll create frames for the three images. We need the images to be placed in the middle third of the page. Start by drawing out the frames with the **Rectangular Frame tool** ⊠. Do NOT release your mouse button. Begin in the left margin, and drag to the right margin.

9. With the mouse held in, tap the right arrow key on your keyboard. This will result in two additional frames being drawn. Release your mouse once the three frames have been drawn and you are happy with the outcome. Pretty neat, huh?

Figure 4.12: The final image frames arrangement

10. Now, choose the **Selection** tool from the **Tools** panel. Click away from the frames to deselect them. Then, click on the left frame to select it. The frame will display nine little squares along its edge, called **control handles**. Click and drag out the left-middle control handle till it touches the left edge of the page.

11. Repeat the process for the right edge of the right frame on the page. Select the right frame. Choose the right-middle control handle, and drag it till it touches the right edge of the page.

12. Voila! Job done. Let's save our document at this point. Choose **File** menu | **Save**. Give your file a name such as Presentation.

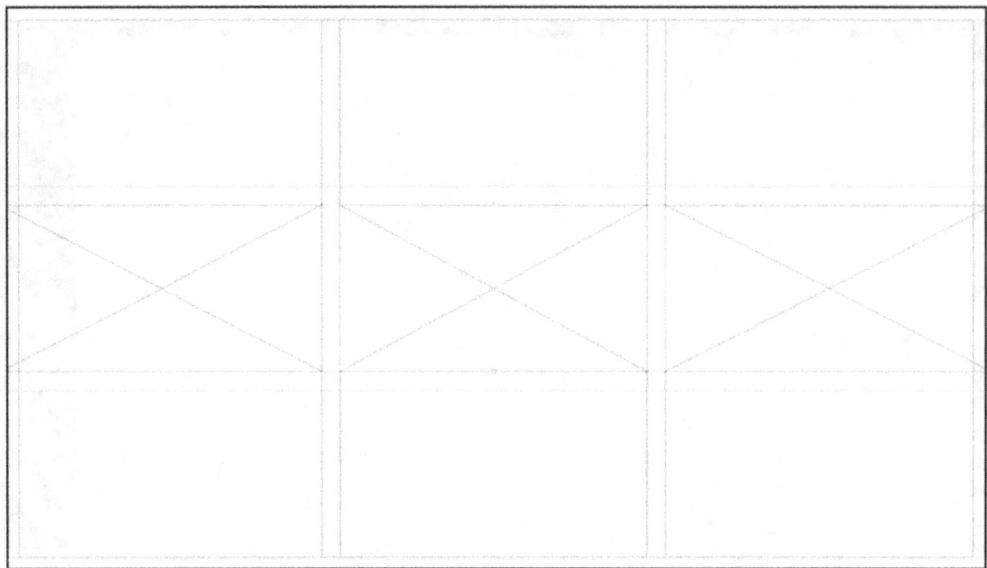

Figure 4.13: The left and right frames tweaked to meet the page edges

OK, let's recap real quick. To draw multiple frames at once, two critical criteria need to be met. You must keep your left mouse button pressed when starting to draw your first frame. Then, you tap the arrow keys to add or remove frames. We've now prepared our document for placing content from multiple sources into the frame placeholders we just created.

Importing multiple images into InDesign

This book progressively builds on the skills learned. We placed images on a single page in the previous chapter. We'll now place multiple images on multiple pages at once. As always, the source files can be found in Chapter 4 - Designing with Text and Tables Example Files folder. Let's get started:

1. Choose the **Selection** tool (*V* or *Esc*). Ensure that you have **Page 1** selected by double-clicking it on the **Pages** panel. Then, ensure you have nothing selected by clicking off the page.

2. Choose **File** menu | **Place**. Navigate to the **Example Files** folder. Choose the image file named 01 Cover Image.jpg. Then, while holding the *Shift* key, click on the 04c Yellow Side.jpg image. This will select all images in between for placement into the document. A total of seven images have been selected. Click **Open**.

3. The arrow icon ▶ will change to a **place gun** icon 🖼, with a thumbnail showing the first image that is to be placed. Observe the number (**7**) overlay on the image. This indicates that InDesign has loaded seven images for placement into the document.

4. Click in the larger frame on **Page 1**. Be careful not to click in the text frame at the top of the page. A safe place to click would be toward the middle of the larger frame. This will place the image into that frame.

> **Note**
> Note that the next image has been loaded in the place gun.

You may have also observed that the image does not span the full breadth of the page. We'll deal with that once we've placed all the images into their respective frames.

Figure 4.14: The first image placed on Page 1

5. Double-click **Page 2** on the **Pages** panel. Click in the top-left frame to place the side view of the vehicle, and then do the same for the larger front-view image. Again, the images don't fit in the frames perfectly. We'll resolve this soon enough.

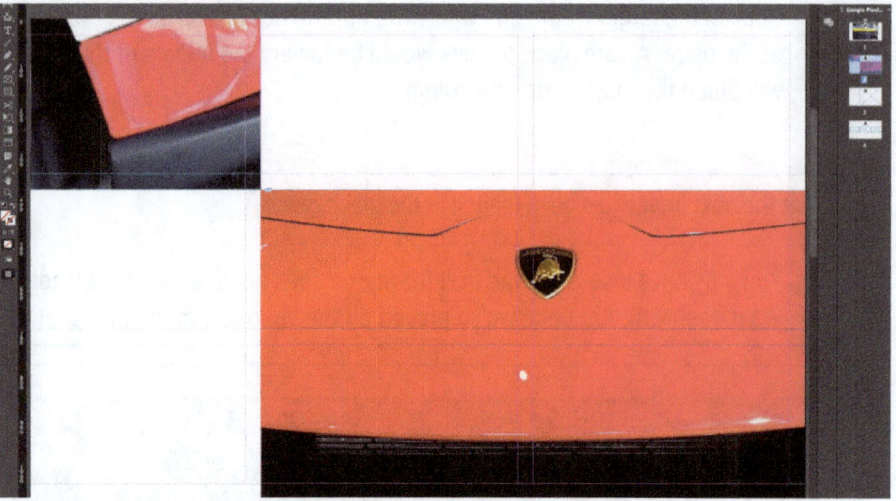

Figure 4.15: Multiple images placed into frames on Page 2

6. Double-click **Page 3** on the **Pages** panel. We need to place just a single image here. Click in the frame to place the image in it. The image may not fit the frame perfectly. Remember that we'll tweak the image placement in a moment, but since we have all the document images loaded into our place gun, we'll place them into the respective frames first and then adjust how they fit into the frames.

Figure 4.16: The image placed into the Page 3 placeholder frame

7. Double-click **Page 4** on the **Pages** panel to activate it. Starting from the leftmost frame, click once to place the first image. Click in the middle frame and the right frame to place the remaining images.

Figure 4.17: Page 4 with all the imported images placed

8. While we're on **Page 4**, let's resize and center the images perfectly within frames. Click the first frame with the **Selection** tool . Shift-click the remaining two image frames. Then then click on the first icon labeled **Fill Frame Proportionally** from the **Frame Fitting** subset on the **Properties** panel.

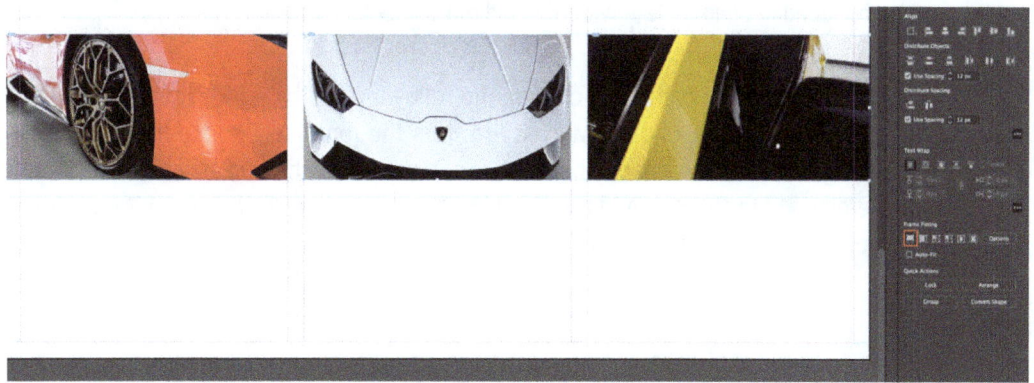

Figure 4.18: The images with Fill Frame Proportionally applied
(The image is intended as a visual reference; the textual information is not essential.)

9. Repeat *Step 8* on pages 1 through 3 in the document. Click an image frame/s with the **Selection** tool, and then click on the first icon labeled **Fill Frame Proportionally** from the **Frame Fitting** subset on the **Properties** panel.

You should now have a good understanding of how to work with individual and multiple images in your InDesign projects. We'll now turn our attention to working with and formatting text in the next section.

Typing and formatting text in InDesign

We can now turn our attention to the typographic elements of our design. Type can be dealt with in two ways in InDesign. The first option is where you draw a text frame and type directly into it. The second option is where text is imported into InDesign from a secondary source. We'll explore both in the following steps:

1. Navigate to **Page 1** by double-clicking the page on the **Pages** panel. Choose the **Type** tool (*T*). Click in the frame at the top of the page. You'll recall that we created this earlier in the chapter. The frame is automatically transformed into a text frame. You'll know you've done this correctly when the blue **X** icon running across the frame disappears.

2. Enable the *Caps Lock* key on your keyboard, and type SUPERCARS. The text by default is black and **12 pt** – virtually impossible to read. With the **Type** tool still active in the frame, choose **Select All** from the **Edit** menu. The text we just typed is highlighted as expected.

> **Note**
> You are most welcome to use keyboard shortcuts if you prefer. A list of curated keyboard shortcuts can be found in *Chapter 12* toward the end of this book.

3. Open the **Properties** panel and change the following attributes for the type. Under the **Character** subset, choose **Myriad Pro** from the font list. Choose **Black** for the type weight. It is found directly below the font name. Set the text size to **450 pt**, the kerning to **Optical**, and the **Tracking** value to **-100**. Under the **Paragraph** controls, choose **Justify** (the fourth icon from the left):

Figure 4.19: The main headline with formatting highlighted on the Properties panel

4. Let's change the color characteristics of the type. With the type still selected, make the following adjustments. Under **Appearance** on the **Properties** panel, change the stroke weight to **12 pt**. The default stroke color is black, but we'd like it to be white. Click the color chip to the left of the **Stroke**, and select **[Paper]** from the list.

Figure 4.20: The headline text with a 12 pt stroke applied

> **Note**
> It's pretty difficult to see text color attributes when it is selected. Inverts the colors to show that it is selected. InDesign does have a nifty way of making text color changes and showing you the changes in realtime without having to deselect the text first.

5. Start by choosing the **Selection** tool. The text frame is still selected. Our text has a black fill with a strong white stroke.

6. This step is quite important. Locate the **Formatting affects** text icon on the **Tools** panel. It can be found close to the bottom of the **Tools** panel and is presented as a capital T. When selected, the frame properties change to the text properties on the **Properties** panel. It is found just above this is the **Fill** and **Stroke** properties. Note that it will now display **T** as as opposed to a rectangle as it typically does.

7. The fill (the black **T**) should be in front of the white one. Click it once to bring it to the front. This action tells InDesign is that you want to change the fill properties of the type.
8. We'd like to pick up a warm yellow color from the car image. Choose the **Eyedropper** tool (*I*) . Then, click on the yellow color alongside the Lamborghini badge. The color is transferred to the fill of the text.

> **Tip**
> Should you want to sample another color with the **Eyedropper** tool, press the *Option* (macOS) or *Alt* (Windows) key, which will allow you to click a new sample color. We encourage you to experiment. If you need to go back to a previous color, you can always use the **Undo** command.

Figure 4.21: The text after having sampled the yellow color using the Eyedropper tool

The design is starting to take shape don't you think? We've explored some of the typographic controls, including character and paragraph controls, fills and outlines, and color sampling. This sets us up perfectly for the following section, in which we will import a Word document into InDesign and apply text formatting to imported text.

Importing text from Microsoft Word documents

We'll now turn our attention to importing type from third-party applications. After placing the type onto the relevant pages in our document, we'll style the type so that it fits our design objectives. This will include choosing typefaces, adjusting size, tweaking leading, and selecting the weight of the font for emphasis and legibility.

1. Navigate to **Page 2** by double-clicking its thumbnail on the **Pages** panel. Ensure that no objects are selected by choosing the **Selection** tool (*V* or *Esc*) and clicking away from the page.

2. Choose **File** menu | **Place**. Navigate to the Example Files folder. Choose the Word file named 05 Text.docx. Should you get a missing fonts warning message, click the **Replace Fonts** option at the bottom-left of the dialog.

3. The missing fonts are shown with an exclamation point in the top half of the dialog. In my case, **Segoe UI Regular** is missing. Under **Replace With:**, choose **Myriad Pro** from the **Font Family** drop-down list and **Regular** from the **Font Style** option. Check the **Redefine Style When Changing All** checkbox. Then, choose the **Change All** option to the center-right of the dialog. You will receive a message indicating that the updates have been made. Click **OK** to accept the changes. Then, click **Done** to close the **Find/Replace Font** dialog.

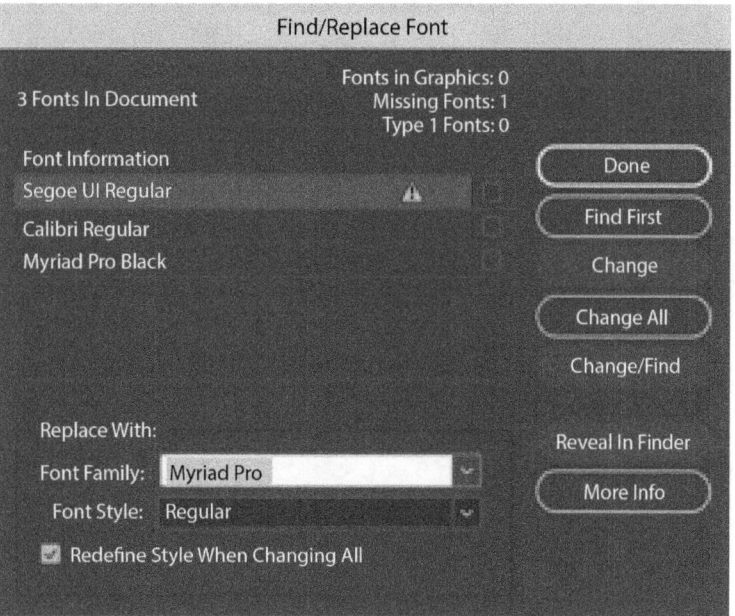

Figure 4.22: The Find/Replace dialog showing the missing font replacement options

4. We are now presented with the place gun icon once more. However, note that this time, it shows that it is ready to place text. Click and drag from the right edge of the top image to the light blue guideline above the larger image. Aim for the space between the right edge of the image and the left edge of the text frame to be equal to the gutter space. Have a look at *Figure 4.23* for reference.

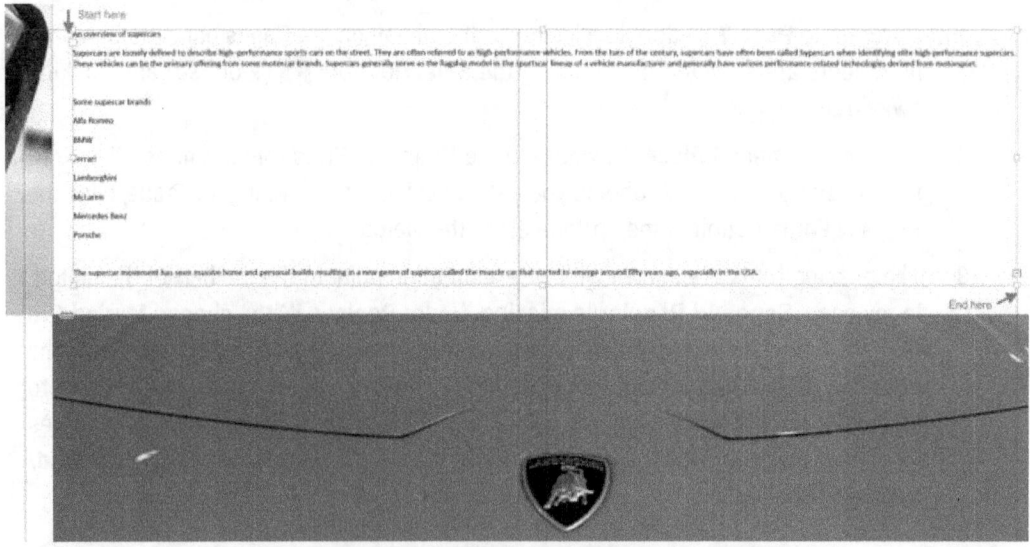

Figure 4.23: The Word file placed into a text frame at the top of Page 2 (The image is intended as a visual reference; the textual information is not essential.)

5. Toward the bottom-right of the placed text frame, there is a red square with a plus sign. This is the text overset icon. This means that the frame is too small to accommodate all of the text. We will have the overflow text flow from this frame to the another that we will create now. Click the **Selection** tool on the **Tools** panel. Then, click the red overflow icon. The place gun icon will appear once more. This indicates that we're now able to create a new text frame to allow the text to flow from one frame to the next. This is called *threading text* in InDesign terminology.

6. Click and drag below the top image, starting in the left margin and dragging across to the guide to the left of the larger image. Be sure to accommodate for space below the top image. *Figure 4.24* can be used for reference.

Figure 4.24: *The second text frame thread at the bottom-left of the page*

7. The red overflow icon does not appear on the second text frame indicating all text fits in the two frames. Click on the Out port, the blue box where the overflow icon appeared previously ⊕ with the **Selection** tool ▶, and then choose **Page 3** on the **Pages** panel. Nest your icon into the guides to the top left of the page (the pink and purple guides). See *Figure 4.25*. Simply click this time. InDesign will create a text frame that spans the column width and height automatically.

> **Note**
> Type frames, by default, respect margin and column guides, making text placement in large documents a whole lot easier.

Text will flow into this third text frame automatically as we adjust type size and add headings to the imported Word text.

Figure 4.25: The third text frame on Page 3

As you can see, placing text from Microsoft Word is a cinch. In this section, we explored how to import a Word file and thread text across multiple frames and pages. With this task completed, we'll format the imported text to improve its legibility and flow in the next section.

Formatting text attributes

Changing the appearance of text is something that you will do often in InDesign. When text is selected, the **Properties** panel displays an extensive list of options to change the font, size, color, leading, paragraph alignment, and much more.

1. We'll improve legibility and text fitting across the pages we placed (threaded) the text. Return to **Page 1**. Click anywhere in the first text frame at the top of **Page 1** with the **Text** tool (*T*) . Then, choose **Select All** from the **Edit** menu. This selects all the text in the text thread across all pages.

2. Head over to the **Properties** panel. Let's make the following text attribute changes. Under **Character**, change the font to **Myriad Pro** and the weight to **Condensed**. Set the text size to **30 pt** and the leading to **48 pt**.

3. Under the **Paragraph** subset on the **Properties** panel, choose the fourth icon Justify with last line aligned left. Disable the **Hyphenation** checkbox to prevent unsightly line breaks.

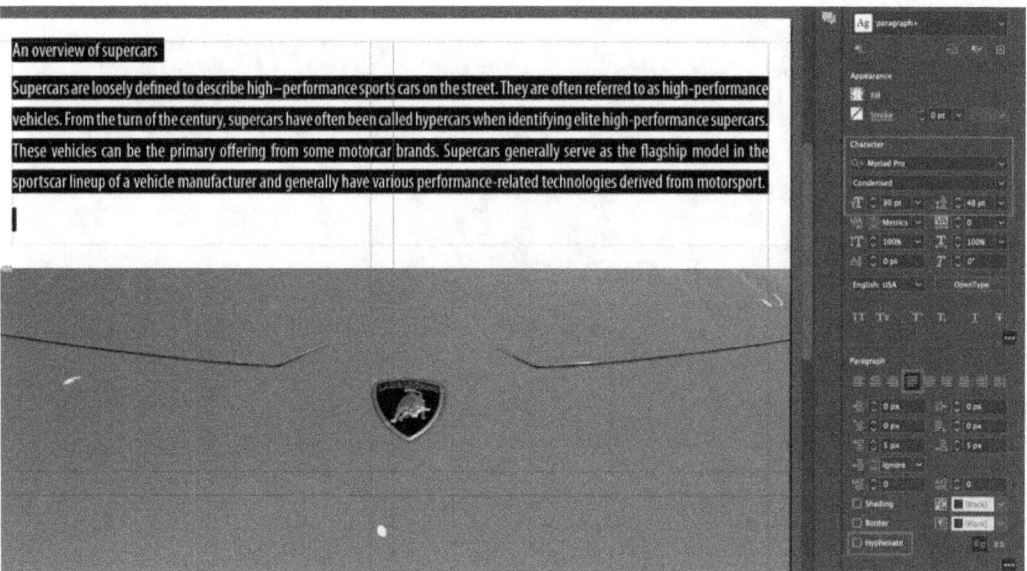

Figure 4.26: The body text styled across the entire story

As you've probably noticed, this book scaffolds on knowledge we've acquired to in an incremental manner. We've just looked at some of the text controls to style our copy. This can prove tedious when working with lots of text. With text formatting under our belts, we can now explore styles to help capture text attributes, for quick and easy application across a document. Styles help streamline monotonous formatting tasks.

Working with styles

When making intricate text formatting changes, you can enhance efficiency by capturing the text formatting settings within a style. This ensures consistency across your documents, lending a professional, polished look to your designs.

1. Choose **Window** menu | **Styles** | **Paragraph Styles** to open the panel. As you can see, there are many style options which we will discuss in more detail later. There is a style called *paragraph*, which was imported from the Word document. We'll first save our typographic parameters as a paragraph style. We'll then delete the Word style named paragraph. This will limit any unexpected formatting in your work.

2. With your text still selected, click the **Create new style** icon 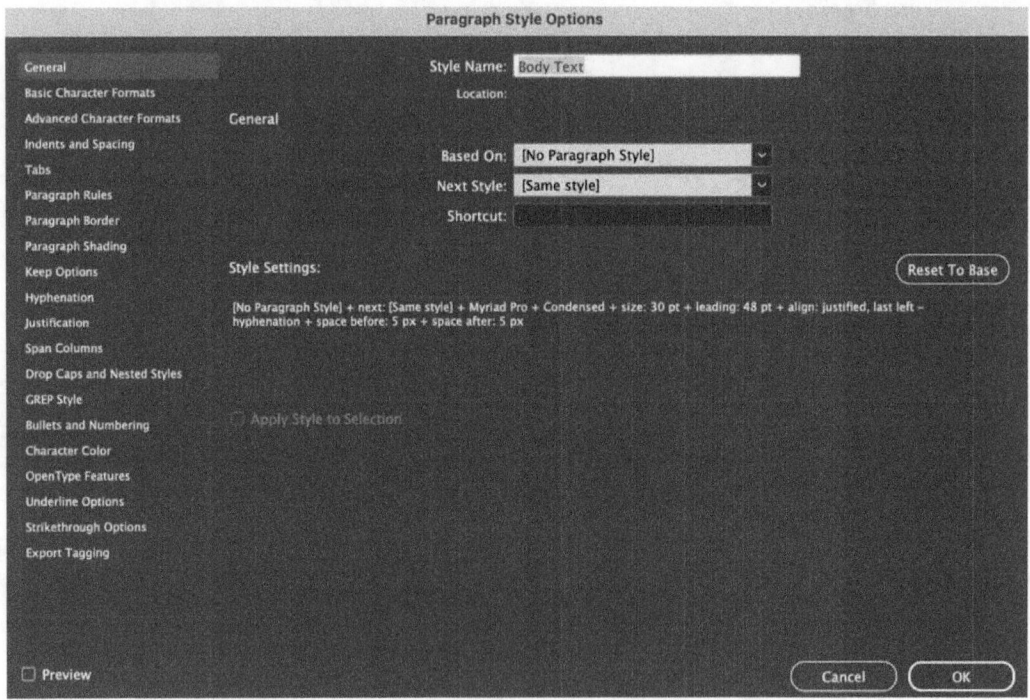 (second from right) at the bottom of the **Paragraph Styles** panel. This will create a new style called Paragraph Style 1. Let's rename the style and have a look at its properties. Double-click **Paragraph Style 1** on the **Paragraph Styles** panel. The **Paragraph Styles Options** dialog will open.

Figure 4.27: The Paragraph Styles dialog with the paragraph controls list on the left

3. Change the style name to Body Text. From the **Based On** drop-down list, choose **[No Paragraph Style]**. To the left of the dialog, every aspect of formatting can be accessed and personalized. It may seem a bit daunting at first, but it offers infinitesimal levels of control that are hard to match. Choose **OK** to accept your changes, and to close the dialog.

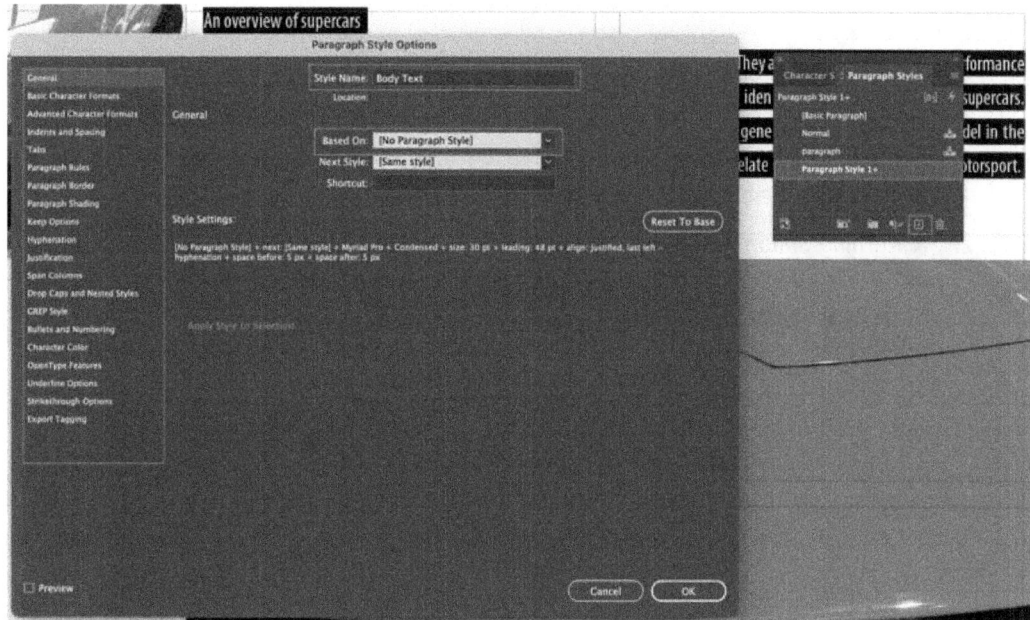

Figure 4.28: The newly created Body Text paragraph style highlighting the changes made

This section should have given you a good first glance into working with paragraph styles. We covered how to create, edit, and update styles. Remember that InDesign by default automatically imports styles from Word to maintain the look and feel of the document which can lead to clutter and unwanted styles. We'll do some style spring cleaning by removing unwanted imported Word styles in the following section.

Removing imported Word styles

When importing some file types, InDesign imports the styles too to ensure document integrity. This is the case with two styles from the Word file we imported, namely **Normal** and **Paragraph**. Note the disk icon to the right of these style names. This is an indicator that the styles are from an external source. The **Body Text** style we just created doesn't have that icon, as it is native to InDesign.

1. Choose the **Selection** tool from the **Tools** panel. Click away from all objects to ensure nothing is selected. This is important before embarking on the next step. Head to the **Paragraph Styles** panel, and delete **Normal** and **Paragraph** by selecting them and clicking the bin at the bottom of the panel.
2. A warning dialog will appear. Choose **Body Text** from the **Replace with** drop-down list. Please do this step for both Word styles. We'll be left with **[Basic Paragraph]** and **Body Text** styles.

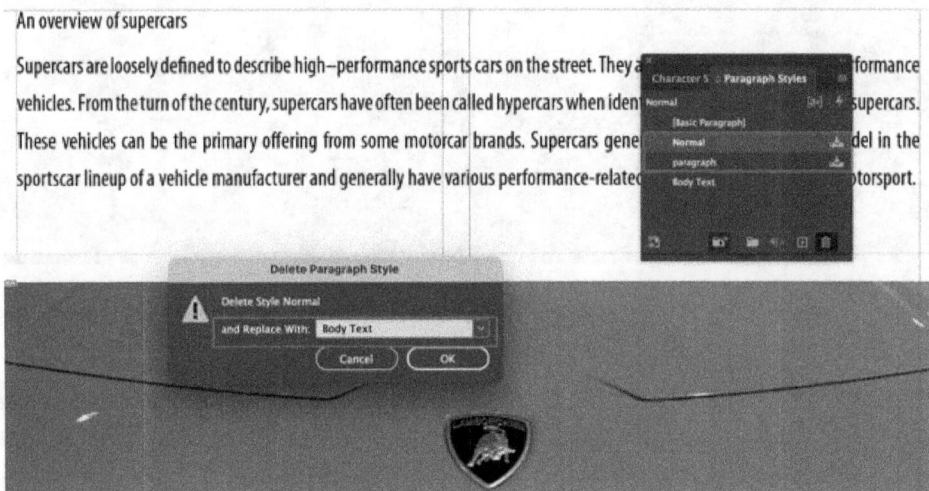

Figure 4.29: The two Word styles (note the disk icon alongside) being deleted updated to Body Text style

Remember that the **Paragraph Styles** panel is the repository for this type of style. There are many other types of styles which we will look at later. In this section, we looked at how to use this panel to remove unwanted Word styles that were imported when the text was imported. Remember that you control which part of the text is affected by a style. We'll look at how this is done in the next section.

Applying a style selectively

To close out the styles conversation, we'll create and apply a subheading style that we can apply to specific paragraphs of text. This will create the differentiation needed and break the monotony of a single text style.

1. Select the first paragraph of the text, **An overview of supercars** text with the **Type** tool . A neat way to do this is to click thrice in rapid succession on the paragraph.

> **Super tip**
> A single click places the cursor at your chosen location in the text.
>
> A double click selects a word.
>
> A triple click selects a line of type.
>
> Four clicks selects a multi-line paragraph.
>
> Five clicks select all the text in that thread, even across multiple pages.

2. There are multiple ways to create styles in InDesign. We'll create a subheading style from the **Paragraph Styles** panel. Click the panel menu icon on the top right of the **Paragraph Styles** panel.

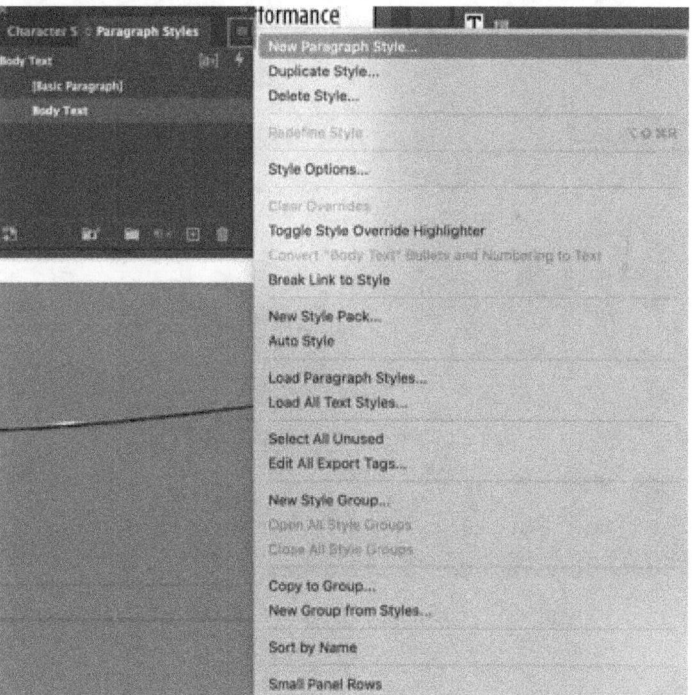

Figure 4.30: The Paragraph Styles panel menu is located at the top-right of the panel

Designing with Text and Tables

3. The **New Paragraph Style** dialog will open. Change the style name to Subheading. Then, choose **[No Paragraph Style]** from the **Based On:** drop-down list.

4. We'll now make some formatting changes. Check the **Preview** checkbox found at the bottom-left of the dialog. This will give us real-time visual feedback on any formatting decisions we make.

5. Click on the **Basic Character Formats** category from the list on the left. It is the second option from the top. Make the following changes:

   A. **Font Family**: Myriad Pro
   B. **Font Style**: Bold
   C. **Size**: 36 pt
   D. **Leading**: 48 pt

6. Then, click on the **Hyphenation** category. Ensure that the **Hyphenation** checkbox is unchecked. Click **OK** to confirm the updates and close the dialog.

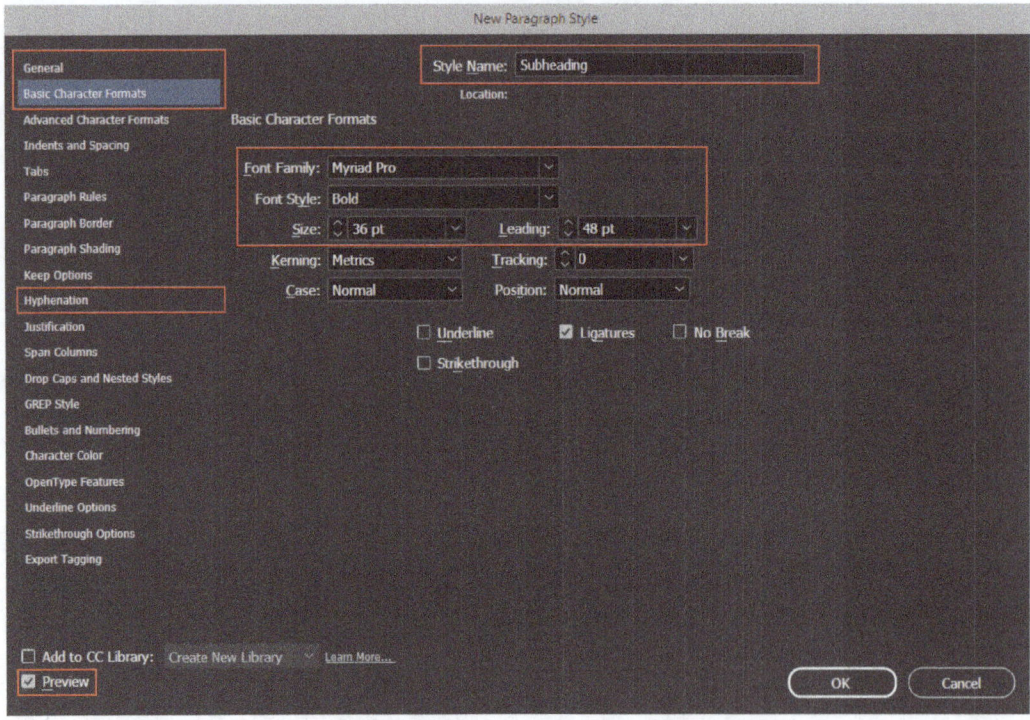

Figure 4.31: The Subheading style with the categories and formatting options highlighted

7. Now comes the easy part. With the first sentence, **An overview of supercars**, selected, ensure that the **Subheading** style is chosen from the **Paragraph Styles** panel. Then, select **Some supercar brands**, and choose the same style. Apply the **Subheading** style to **The nature of supercars** too.

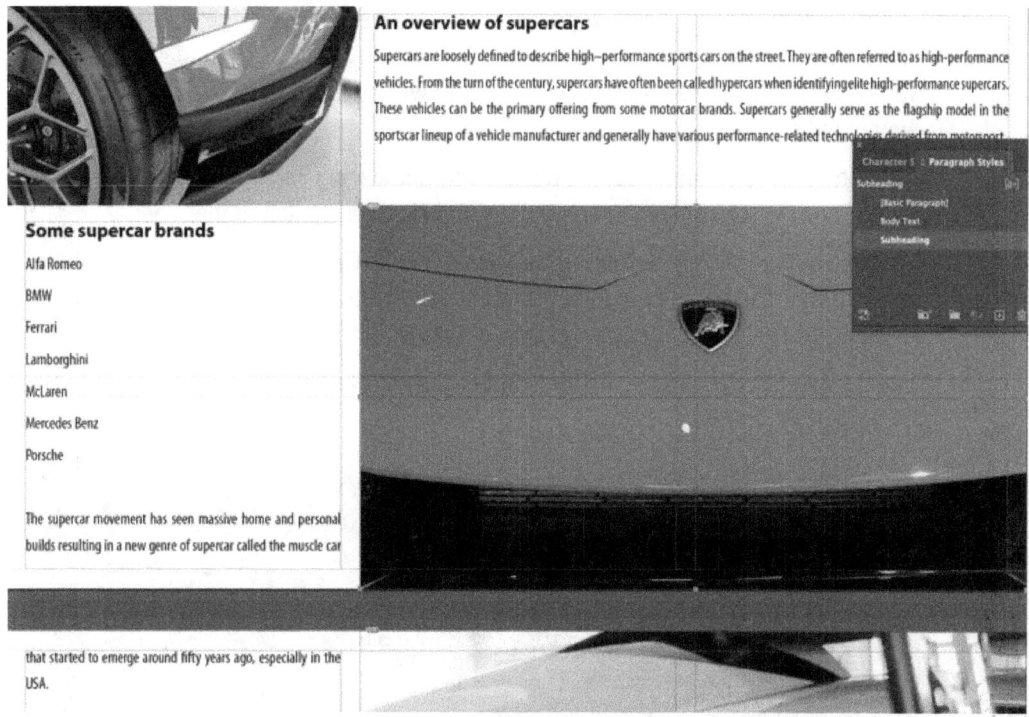

Figure 4.32: The Subheading style applied to the relevant text on pages 2 and 3

As you can see, applying styles to text selections is relatively easy. In this section, we created and applied a subheading style that we could apply to specific parts of our text. In the next section, we'll add some finishing touches to our imported Word file so that it fits better into the allocated frames in the design.

Formatting text for a perfect fit

We have a few tweaks to make to get our text in tip-top shape. We'll remove unnecessary carriage returns and add a bulleted list to a selection of text in this section.

1. Select the list under the **Some supercar brands** subheading on **Page 2**. The list starts with **Alfa Romeo** and ends with **Porsche**. Choose the first icon under **Bullets and Numbering** on the **Properties** panel. Bullets will be added. We want to choose a custom bullet.

2. Click the **Options** button under the **Bullets and Numbering** category on the **Properties** panel. Click the **Add** button on the **Bullets and Numbering** dialog that opens.

3. A sub-dialog named **Add Bullets** will appear. Choose **Wingdings** from the **Font Family**. Scroll through the list of characters, and choose the large round bullet icon. Click the **Add** button. Then, click **OK** to close the **Add Bullets** dialog.

4. Choose the newly added bullet from the **Bullets and Numbering** dialog, and click **OK** to apply it to the text.

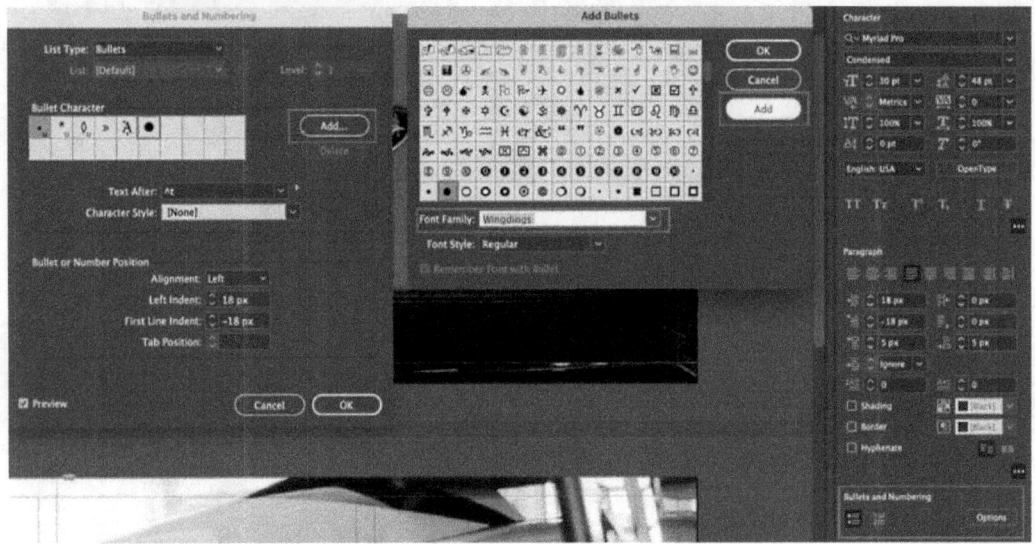

Figure 4.33: Applying a custom bullet to the selected text list

5. Let's have the text fit perfectly from top to bottom within the text frames. This is called vertical justification. Apply vertical justify to where it's warranted in your work. In this design, we'll apply it to the narrow vertical frame on **Page 2** and the frame on **Page 3**.

6. With the **Selection** tool active, click the bottom-left frame with the **Some supercar brands** subheading on **Page 2**.

7. Head to the **Object** menu and choose **Text Frame Options**. Check the **Preview** checkbox. From the **Vertical Justification** subset, choose **Justify** from the **Align** drop-down list.
8. Go to **Page 3**. select the text frame with the **Selection** tool and repeat the process.

This brings our Word import task to a close. Of course, there are many additional options that are available to you. You should be proud of yourself for getting the essential text functionality under your belt. We can now turn our attention to the import and formatting of tables in the next section.

Importing Microsoft Excel tables

Importing tables into InDesign is as easy as importing other assets. As is always the case, we'll use the **Place** command to import a table. We'll then look at some of the formatting capabilities in InDesign to create a pleasant, visually rich reading experience.

1. Choose the **Selection** tool (*V or Esc*). Double click the **Page 4** thumbnail on the **Pages** panel. Click off the page to purge any active selections. Choose **File** menu | **Place**. Navigate to the Chapter 4 - Designing with Text and Tables Example Files folder. Choose the Excel file named 06 Table.xlsx.

2. Should you get a missing fonts warning message, click the **Replace Fonts** option at the bottom-left of the dialog. If like us, you have **Times New Roman Condensed** missing, do the following. A missing font has an exclamation point alongside it. Select it by clicking on it. Under **Replace With:**, choose **Myriad Pro** from the **Font Family** drop-down list and **Regular** from the **Font Style** option. Check the **Redefine Style When Changing All** checkbox. Then, choose the **Change All** option to the center-right of the dialog. You will receive a message indicating that updates have been made. Click **OK** to dismiss the **Warning** dialog. Then, click **Done** to close the **Find/Replace Font** dialog.

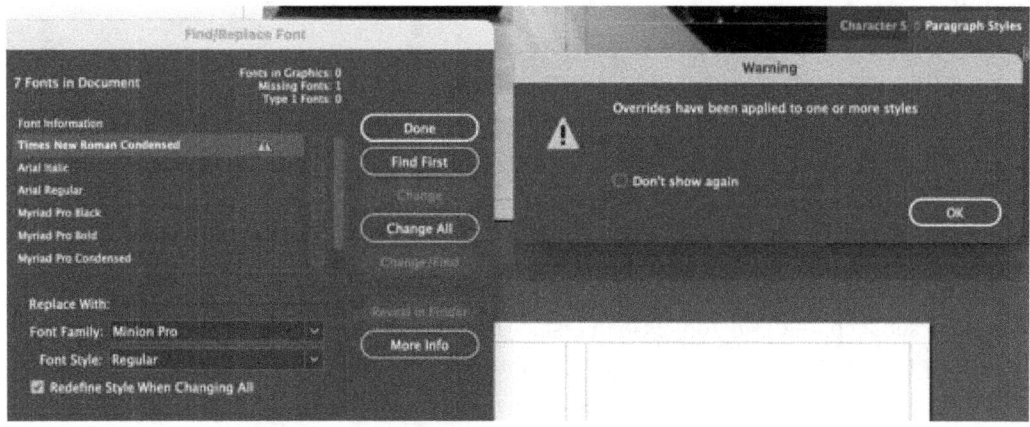

Figure 4.34: Missing fonts being replaced as the table is being imported

3. We are presented with a place gun once more. Note that the cursor looks exactly like the text placement we worked with earlier when placing the Word file. This is because tables are a subset of text in InDesign.

> **Note**
> Should you want to manipulate and format tables, you can deal with it by and large as you type.

4. Nest your cursor in the top-left corner of the page guides. Press and hold the *Shift* key and click your mouse. This will automatically flow the type to the next column.

> **Note**
> The *Shift* key invokes auto-threading, which is especially handy when working with large documents.

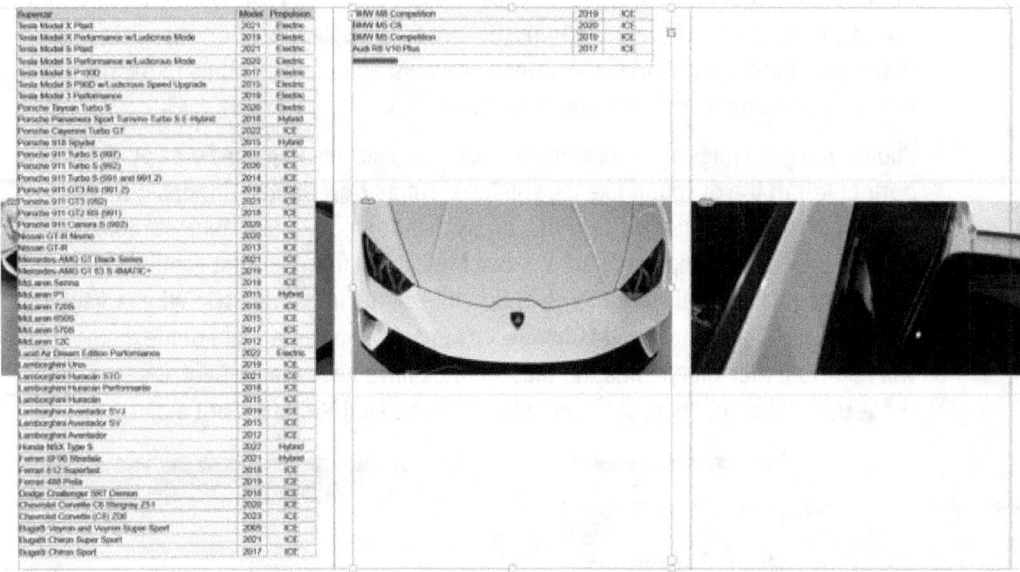

*Figure 4.35: The unformatted table placed on Page 4
(The image is intended as a visual reference; the textual information is not essential.)*

Having placed the Excel table in its designated space in our design on **Page 4**, you can see that tables are a subset of the **Type** tool in InDesign. The table we placed obscures the images we placed earlier. To fix this problem, we'll apply a text wrap to the images, which will effectively push the text away from the images, in the next section.

Wrapping text around objects

Where text runs over other elements, a boundary around the object needs to be created to push the text away from the object text. This is called a **text wrap**. The object that has the text wrap is called a wrap object.

1. You've no doubt spotted the table running over the images we placed earlier. We will apply a text wrap to the image objects to have the text flow around and not over them. Click on the second column of out table text using the **Selection** tool. The text frame will be highlighted.

> **Note**
> Remember that the object hierarchy is determined as you place content into the document. Objects created or placed first appear below objects that are created later.

2. Since the images were placed first in the design, they are below the table in the object hierarchy. Press and hold the *Command* (macOS) or *Control* (Windows) key, and click the image of the white vehicle in the center of the page. This instructs InDesign to choose the object directly below the currently selected table in the object hierarchy.

3. Then, press the *Shift* key, and click on the left edge of the image with the red car. Be careful not to click the table frame, as this will select it instead. If that does happen, click a second time on the table frame to deselect it.

4. Now, click on the yellow car image on the far right. Remember that the *Shift* key is still being pressed. All the car images should now be selected. If you mis clicked or would like to try again, simply click away from all objects on the page and work through the steps again.

5. From the **Properties** panel, head to the **Text Wrap** subset. Choose **Wrap around bounding box** (the second icon from the left). Ensure that the chainlink icon is enabled, type 16 px for the first offset value, and then strike the *Return* key. All offset values will be updated to **16 px** thanks to the chainlink icon. The table has now been successfully pushed away from the images.

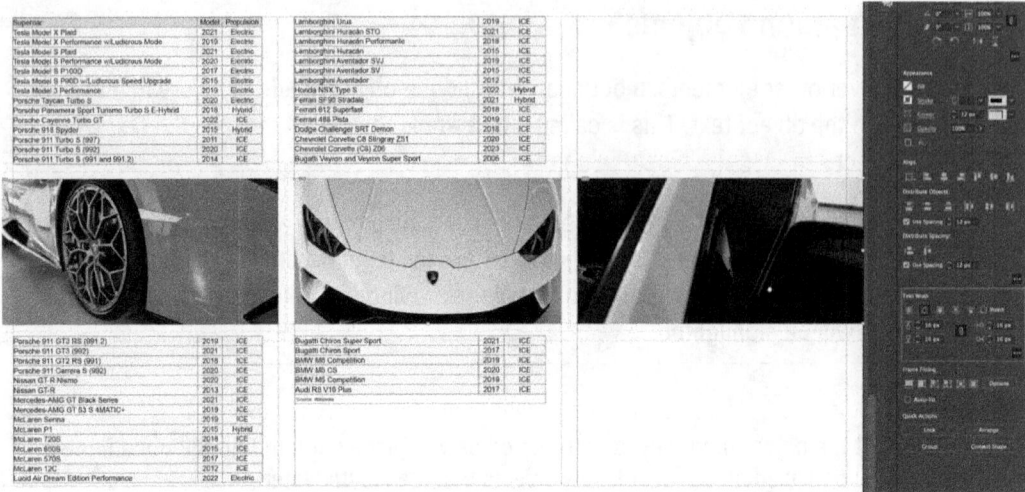

Figure 4.36: The text wrap successfully applied to all images on Page 4

Wrapping text around objects creates a more harmonious relationship between graphic and text objects. With the table flowing correctly, we can turn our attention to formatting the table to improve its appearance on the page.

Formatting tables

Whether you have worked with tables in other tools or are new to them, the formatting options in InDesign are relatively easy to work with. As stated before, tables are a subset of the **Type** tool. Any formatting is done using the **Type** tool.

1. Let's familiarize ourselves with selecting table components first. Select the **Type** tool (*T*). Hover over the edges of the table. If you move your cursor over a column, you will be presented with a downward-facing arrow. Should you click, InDesign will select that column. Similarly, if you hover to the left of a row, you will be presented with an arrow pointing to the right. Should you click inDesign will select the row you clicked. To select the entire table, move your cursor to the top-left corner of the first text frame containing the table. A diagonal arrow pointing down and to the right will appear. This will select the table in its entirety. Please explore.

2. Let's define the width of the columns. With the **Type** tool active, move your cursor over the Supercars column. Remember, you want to place your cursor just above the column. When you see the downward pointing arrow, please click to select it. Head over to the **Properties** panel. From the **Table Dimensions** category, locate the drop-down list that reads **At Least**, and choose **Exactly**. Choose the input field for the column width, and set the value to **416 px**.

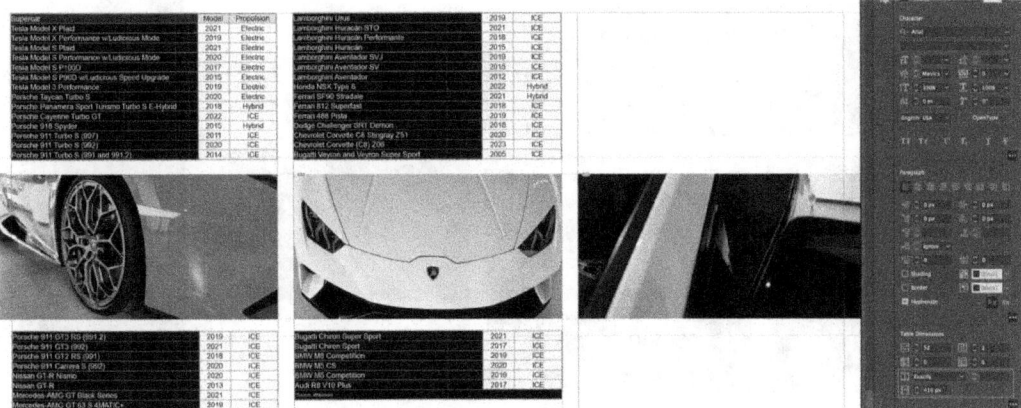

Figure 4.37: The Supercars column width being adjusted on the Properties panel

3. We'll need to define the widths of the remaining two columns. With the **Type** tool active, move your cursor over the **Model** column, and click to select it when presented with the downward pointing arrow. Head over to the **Properties** panel once more. Change the column width dimensions to exactly **70 px**.

4. We'll do this one more time for the **Propulsion** column. Its value should be exactly **105 px**. That takes care of the column widths. The table now fits perfectly in the columns.

5. We'll now adjust the rows for a better fit. Click in the top-left corner of the table using the **Type** tool . Remember to look out for the diagonal arrow to select the entire table. With the table selected, click in the input field alongside the **Row Height** drop-down list that reads **Exactly**, under the **Table Dimensions** category on the **Properties** panel. This is the input field for the row height. Set it to **33 px**.

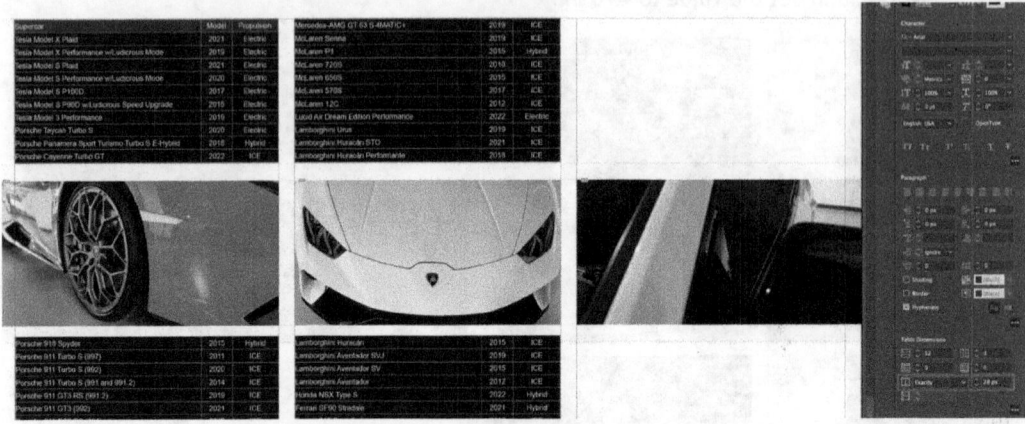

Figure 4.38: The row heights of the table being adjusted

6. The table is now overset. It needs to be flowed into the empty third column. To resolve this, choose the **Selection** tool . Click on the red overset icon found at the bottom-right of the second column. This action will change the cursor to a place gun . Click in the top-left corner of the third column. The table will flow into that column.

The column widths and row heights have been adjusted to our liking. However, with the table flowing across multiple columns, making sense of the data becomes a bit challenging. We'll convert the first row to a header row to resolve this problem. By doing so, the header information will be repeated at the top of each frame in the table thread.

Header and footer rows

Header and footer rows automatically repeat at the top and bottom of a table to make it easier to read the information being presented. In our design, creating a repeating header row makes sense, so let's do so.

Select the **Type** tool . Hover to the left of the header row in (the first row of the table). Click to select it. Choose **Table** menu | **Convert Rows** | **To Header**. This action will automatically place the header row above each instance of the table across columns, making it much easier to navigate.

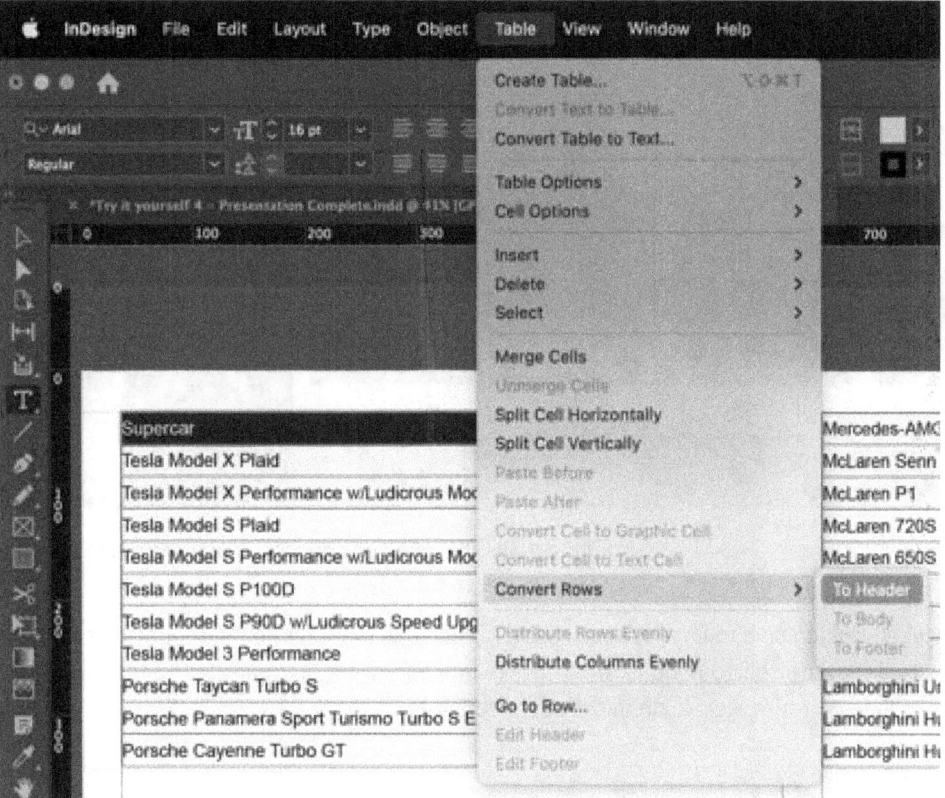

Figure 4.39: Converting the first row to a header row for enhanced legibility

Converting a row to a header row automatically places it at the top of each new instance, as the text flows through the design. Making a change to the first instance of the header row updates all instances. In the next section, we'll turn our attention to adjusting cell spacing to improve the relationship between the text and borders the individual cells.

Adjusting spacing in table cells

The space between a cell boundary and the contents of a cell can be easily changed to accommodate any design need. This is called a **cell inset**. We'll change the cell inset to help create a more easy-to-read table. The text inside the cells appear too close to the cell edge. This is particularly obvious in the first column.

To do that, select the entire table by clicking with the **Type** tool the top-left corner of the first table instance in the left column on the page. Then, change all the **Cell Inset** values on the **Properties** panel to **4 px**.

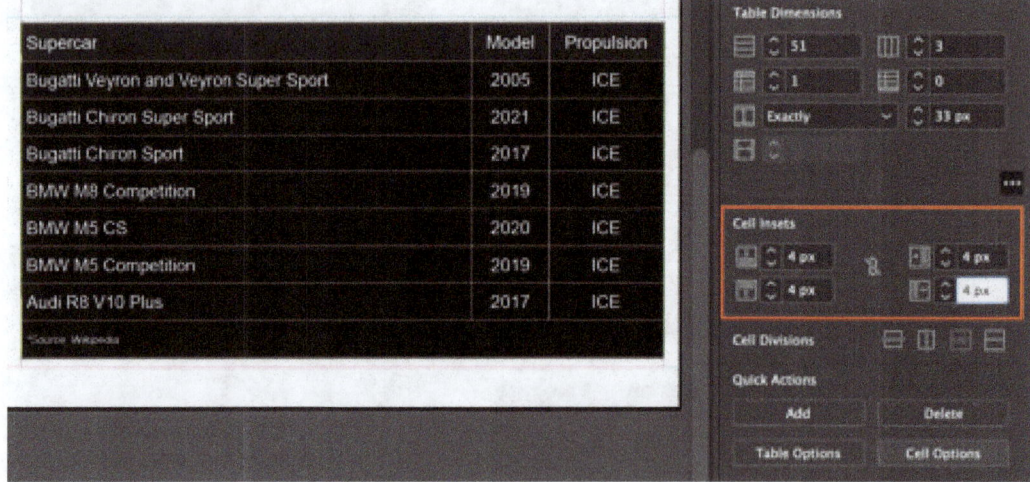

Figure 4.40: The adjusted cell inset and and its effect on the table

We used cell spacing to increase the space in each cell to better accommodate the text. We also ensured that the cell spacing is uniform. We can now work on coloring the table for maximum visual impact, which we will do in the next section.

Changing cell and text color

InDesign offers powerful controls to easily change the fill, stroke, and text colors of a cell or table. We'll now turn our attention to the color properties of the table in this section.

1. Let's tackle the table header first. Select the table header row of the first text frame. All the table header rows are selected, since they are clones of the first instance. Therefore, changing the properties of the first instance will ripple throughout the document. From the **Properties** panel, click the **Fill** swatch and select **Black** from the list of colors. The text will not be visible because we have black text in cells that we filled with black. The text will not be visible because we have black text in cells that we filled with black.

2. Click the **Formatting affects text icon** on the toolbox. This is the little **T** found toward the bottom of the panel. It will allow us to change the color of the text, which is currently also black, hence not visible. Click the **Fill** swatch, which has changed to a letter **T** (to indicate we are changing the text attributes) on the **Properties** panel, and choose **RGB Yellow**. The text should be visible now. Choose the **Selection** tool and click away from all objects to see how the changes we made affect the table design.

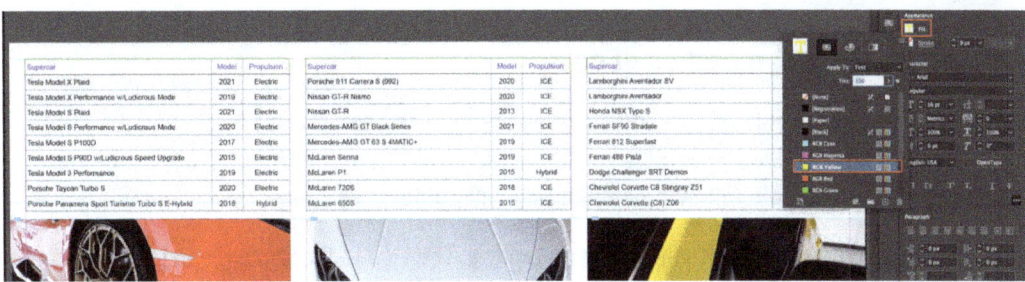

Figure 4.41: The text formatting and color controls on the Properties panel

As you have seen, moving between the type and cell color controls in InDesign is relatively easy if you know which controls to choose. With our color choices bedded down, we'll revisit the font properties and make some adjustments to further enahnce our design.

Adjusting the font and weight properties

Changing the text properties, such as font, weight, and color, is no different to manipulating regular text properties. You should be relatively comfortable with this. We'll adjust the font and weight properties of the text in the table, to differentiate between header rows and regular table cells.

1. Select the table in its entirety using the **Type** tool (T) . Change the font to **Myriad Pro Regular** on the **Properties** panel.
2. Then, choose the header row, and make its weight **Bold**. Click away from the table to see the results.

As we near the conclusion of this chapter, you should be very comfortable with making changes to text properties. Note that we used the **Properties** panel, as we did previously, to change the font and weight properties of our text. In the following section, we'll address the stroke or outline properties of our table.

Changing the stroke properties of cells

Cell strokes can be manipulated individually or all at once. You can choose to change the stroke properties of a cell, a collection of cells, or the entire table. In the following steps, we'll remove the vertical lines in the table whilst maintaining the horizontal lines.

1. Select the entire table with the **Type** tool . Then, go to the **Table** menu | **Cell Options** | **Strokes and Fills**. Enable the **Preview** checkbox to see the changes in real time.
2. In the **Cell Options** dialog, choose the **Strokes** and **Fills** tab at the top of the dialog. You will be presented with a proxy. See *Figure 4.42*. Any strokes that will be affected appear light blue on the proxy. Any strokes not selected, and therefore not affected by changes, are gray. You can activate and deactivate strokes by clicking on them. For our project, we will deselect all the horizontal strokes and ensure that only the vertical ones are blue.

Formatting tables   125

3. Choose the **Weight** option, and set the value to **0 pt** (zero). This will remove the vertical strokes. Click away from the table to view the results.

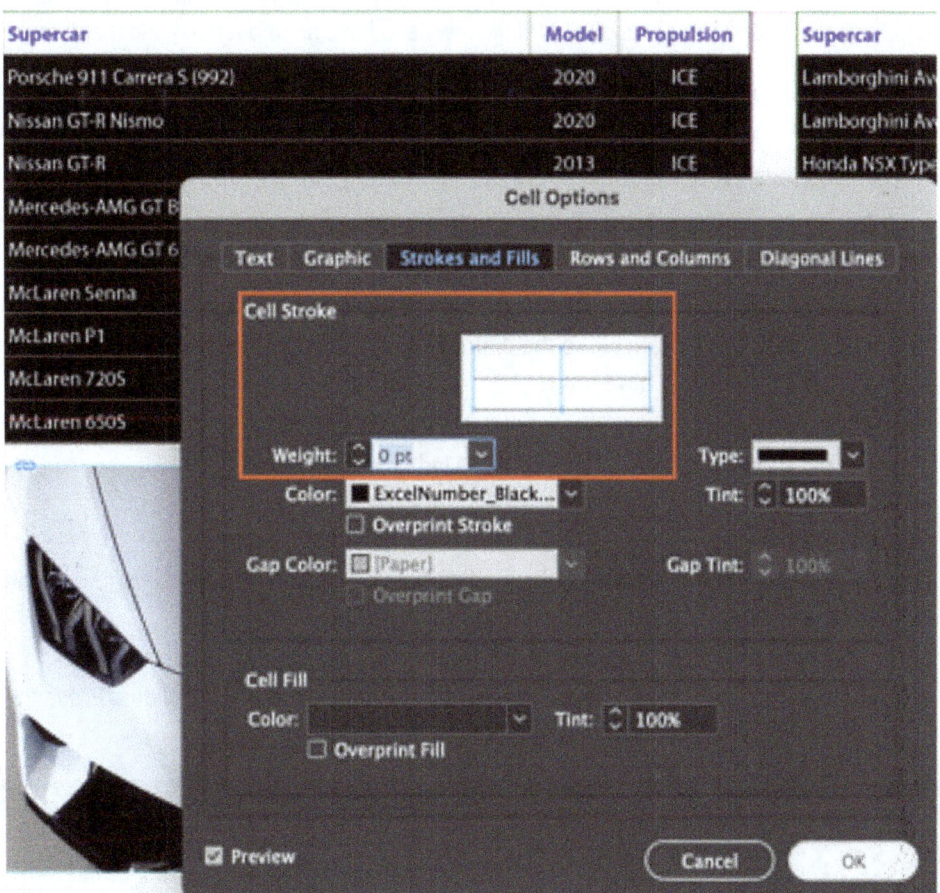

Figure 4.42: The Cell Options dialog with the changes highlighted and a sample of the table behind displaying its effect.

You may have noticed that even though we made stylistic changes to the strokes of table cells, we continue to work with the **Type** tool . We'll now explore the exciting options available to us for changing the fill colors of our table cells.

Applying alternating fills to the table

By using alternate strokes and fills, you can drastically improve the visual impact of a table. Typically, alternating strokes and fills are applied to table rows and have no impact on header and footer rows.

1. We'll select the entire table once again by using the **Type** tool . Then, choose **Table Options | Alternating Fills** from the **Table** menu. Enable the **Preview** switch in the dialog.
2. Choose **Every Other Row** from the **Alternating Pattern** drop-down list.
3. There are two color dropdowns in the middle of the dialog. Click the one to the left, and choose **RGB Yellow** from the color options. Set the **Tint** value to **20%**.
4. Now, click the **Color** dropdown to the right and choose **Black**. Then, set the tint value to **10%**. Click **OK** to close the dialog. Then, click away to deselect the table and see the changes you have made.
5. Let's view the completed project unhindered by guides and construction lines. Choose the **View** menu, and select **Screen Mode | Presentation**.

> **Note**
> You can use InDesign as a presentation tool without any export or converting to compatible file formats.

6. Use the arrow keys on your keyboard to navigate through the slides. Press the *Esc* key to exit **Presentation** mode.

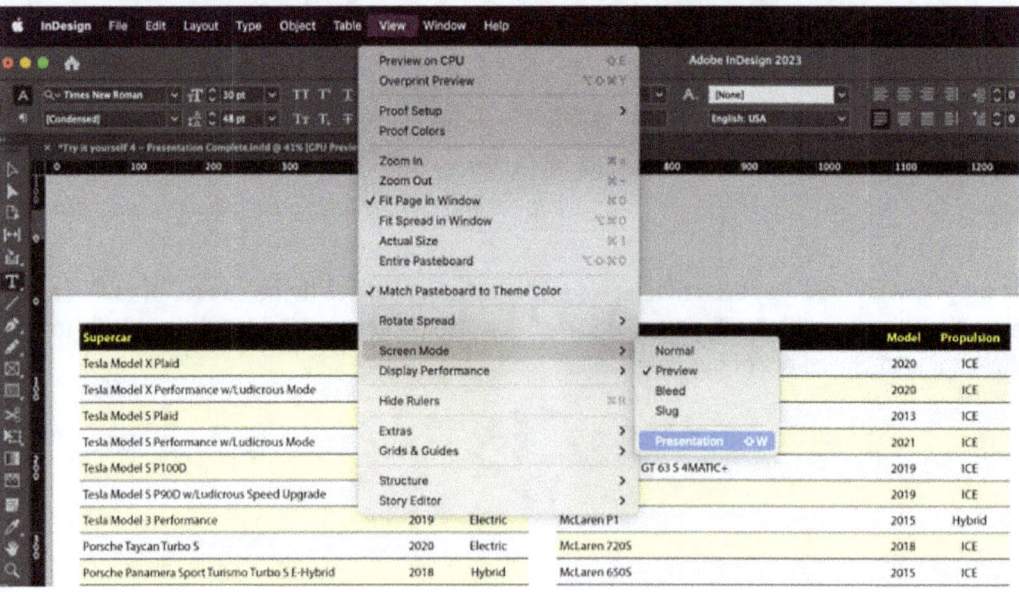

Figure 4.43: The Presentation screen mode is a great way to assess your design

Well done! This brings us to the end of this chapter on working with type and tables. As you no doubt have observed, InDesign has a rich palette of possibilities to help you realize pretty much any typographic goal.

Summary

In this chapter, we created a presentation by setting up a document using the web preset. This preset uses pixels for measurement units and RGB as the document color space. The document dimensions were set to 1920 px by 1080 px. We explored the completed design. A nine-unit rule-of-thirds grid system was put in place. We imported multiple images into the presentation and fit them to their frames. We then typed headline copy directly into a frame and changed its fill and stroke properties. Type was imported from Microsoft Word and formatted using paragraph styles. A bullet list was included. An Excel table was imported and placed into the presentation. The table was formatted to cater for header rows, cell inset spacing, stroke properties, and alternating fills. A text wrap was applied to ensure the table flowed correctly around graphic elements in its proximity.

In the following chapter, we will explore color theory in preparation for the chapter that comes after it. We'll look at the formats and color spaces appropriate for different types of output, be it for print or on-screen viewing.

Level: Intermediate

An Overview of Color Models

Understanding color is imperative in pretty much all design and publishing projects. Choosing the wrong color model can result in expensive cost overruns, and lead to disappointing output outcomes. This chapter aims to avoid that. It explores the CMYK (process), RGB, and spot color models. It is a precursor to working with color in *Chapter 6*. This chapter gives an overview of color models and how you can use them in professional design and communication practice. We will look at color for different contexts. Whether you are creating content for screens or print, or want a specific bespoke spot color, this chapter should help as a primer to the world of color.

Here are the main topics we will cover in this chapter:

- Understanding Color Models
- CMYK color
- RGB color
- Spot color

After having read this chapter, you should have a reasonably good grasp of when to use which color model and in what context. It has been written in a way that demystifies the world of color by focusing on the design outcomes while building on the important scientific foundation on which the design experience rests.

You can find the relevant projects/examples for this chapter here: https://packt.link/a19oQ

Exploring the chapter resources

This book is written in a practical, hands-on way. You can try concepts you read about yourself by downloading the files referred to in this project. These example files can be downloaded from the following URL: https://packt.link/a19oQ

Understanding Color Models

This is a color theory discussion in preparation for the next chapter. Our hope is that it helps your understanding of color models and their use in different contexts. Please note that this topic is broad as well as deep and could easily fill a book by itself. We will, however, demystify some of the core principles that you will encounter on a daily basis. We'll look at **Red, Green, Blue (RGB)**, **Cyan, Magenta, Yellow, Black (CMYK)**, and **Spot** colors. It is essential at this stage to discuss the fundamental tenets of color theory before we continue our design exploration.

Color models help designers express colors across different mediums. Color models use numeric values to describe colors. Specific color models help to define colors for certain types of output. Understanding color models and the space they occupy in the electromagnetic spectrum will assist you in making informed color choices when designing. The following figure shows a comparison of the CMYK color model (top), which is used when printing, and the RGB color model (bottom), which is used primarily for digital devices such as monitors and mobile phones.

Figure 5.1: The CMYK and RGB color models

We'll explore these color models by opening a print-ready document, a digital RGB document, and a document with spot colors. These documents have been prepared for you.

CMYK color

CMYK color is used when content is printed on paper or other substrates. CMYK color consists of three primary colors – cyan, magenta, yellow, and a key color, typically black. It is a subtractive color model. This means that as the primary colors are mixed or overlaid, the result is a darker color. When light strikes the surface on which the inks reside (typically paper), different ink combinations absorb different wavelengths of light, while reflecting other wavelengths. The vast majority of office printers and high-end commercial printing presses print with CMYK inks or toners. By creating mixes of cyan, magenta, yellow, and black inks, many secondary and tertiary colors can be achieved.

Now that we have a fundamental understanding of color theory, let us explore these color models tangibly by opening and analyzing pre created InDesign files for the relevant models. This is done to fast-track your journey through the book and avoid repetition.

1. Choose the **Open** button on the InDesign home screen. From the Chapter 5 - An Overview of Color Models Example Files **folder you've downloaded, open the file named** Try it yourself 5 – 02 CMYK Color.indd.
2. With the document open, let's explore the CMYK color model.
3. The three large circles are filled with primary colors cyan, magenta, and yellow.
4. Where two colors overlap, for example, cyan and yellow, a secondary color, red, is produced.
5. Where three colors overlap, we see a tertiary color, which should, in theory, be black. We get a dark, muddy gray-black color instead. This is due to the limitations of printing inks.

6. A fourth key color, black, is added to compensate for this shortfall. The small circle in the center of the following screen capture (*Figure 5.2*) illustrates the difference between a CMY mix and K. You can see that black has more visual weghting than just a CMY mix. Choose the **File** menu | **Close**.

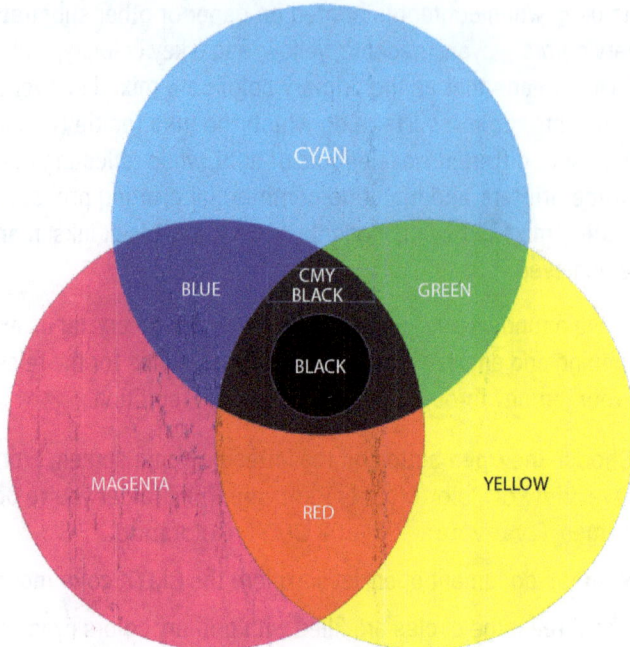

Figure 5.2: The subtractive CMYK color model

Now that we understand the colors used in print documents, let's turn our attention to documents created for digital devices that use the RGB color model.

RGB color

RGB color is primarily used for content on screens. Monitors, mobile phones, and televisions are examples of devices that use the RGB color space. RGB color consists of three primary colors – red, green, and blue. It is an additive color model, resulting in white as the primary colors are mixed or overlaid. Colors are created when the three primaries projected as light combine. Let's look at a real-world example file to make it easier for us to digest. The following steps walk you through a pre-created document:

1. Choose the **Open** button on the InDesign home screen. From the Chapter 5 - An Overview of Color Models Example Files **folder you've downloaded. Open the file named** Try it yourself 5 - 03 RGB Color.indd.

2. With the document open, let's explore the RGB color model.
3. The three large circles are filled with the red, green, and blue primary colors.
4. Where two colors overlap, a red and blue mix, for example, results in a secondary color, magenta.
5. Where three colors overlap, we perceive a tertiary color, which is white.
6. The black background represents the absence of light.
7. Choose **File | Close** when you are done exploring.

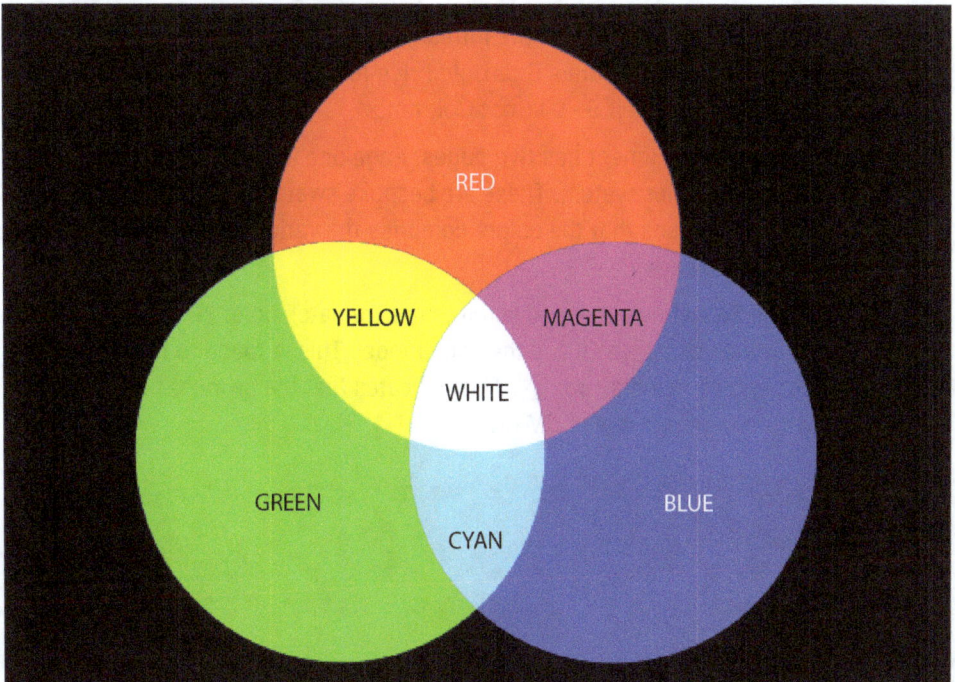

Figure 5.3: The additive RGB color model

Now that we understand the colors used in digital documents, we can turn our attention to bespoke spot colors. These are colors that are pre-mixed and printed as individual colors. They can add value to your work when you wish to use a custom brand color or a metallic, neon, or pastel color.

Spot colors

Spot colors are premixed inks that assist in achieving a specific result. Florescent and metallic colors are examples of spot colors. Since these colors exist outside of the the color gamut or range of CMYK color, they require additional printing plates and thereby increase the cost of the print run. A print run refers to the technical aspects of a print job and how it will be printed. For example, you could request a print run of 1,000 copies to be printed digiitally on a certain type of paper. Let's explore spot colors by working in InDesign. We have prepared a file that we will be using to expedite the discussion.

1. Choose the **Open** button on the InDesign home screen. From the Chapter 5 - An Overview of Color Models Example Files **folder you've downloaded, open the file named** Try it yourself 5 - 04 Spot Color.indd.

2. Note that the document has two pages. Page one is a collection of swatches from the Trumatch color system. These are bespoke swatches that are made up of CMYK colors. This means that the colors comprise the various component primary colors we discussed earlier.

3. Open the **Swatches** panel and scroll to the Trumatch color swatches. Alongside any color swatch name, you'll find the color model. This is found to the far right . Next to this swatch is a gray box . This indicates that the swatches are process colors or in other words, a mix of CMYK.

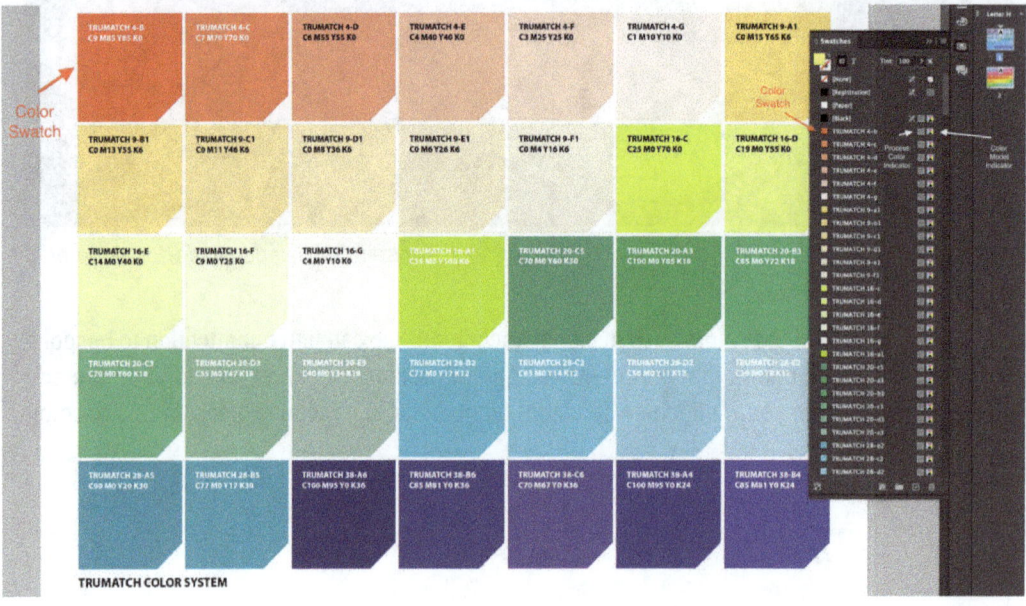

Figure 5.4: The Trumatch color system consists of CMYK inks (The image is intended as a visual reference; the textual information is not essential.)

4. Double-click **Page 2** on the **Pages** panel to go to it. Here, we have the **Dainippon Ink and Chemicals** (**DIC**) collection of color swatches. These are spot color swatches. While the colors are derived from a CMYK base, note that the gray box alongside color swatches has a circle inside of it to indicate it is a spot color.

Figure 5.5: The DIC color system consists of spot color inks
(The image is intended as a visual reference; the textual information is not essential.)

5. To make this easier to understand, choose **File** menu | **Open**. From the Chapter 5 - An Overview of Color Models Example Files **folder, open the file named** Try it yourself 5 – 06 Spot Color Separations.indd.

6. Choose **Window** menu | **Output** | **Separations Preview**.

> **Note**
> The reason we've opened a document with fewer swatches is that InDesign has a twenty-five-spot color swatch limit.

7. Change the **View** drop-down option to **Separations** from its default **Off** status.

8. Observe that the colors in the top row, using Trumatch, are not listed separately, as they are comprised of CMYK inks. The DIC colors, on the other hand, are spot colors and are listed separately.

An Overview of Color Models

9. Drag the bottom of the panel to reveal all the colors in the document.
10. Click on the eyeball alongside **Cyan**. Then do the same for **Magenta** and **Yellow**. As you do this, you'll get a good sense of the colors that make up a particular swatch.
11. Let's do the same for the DIC colors in the second row. When you click the eyeball visibility icon alongside a particular color, you can see it is not visible altogether, as it is an ink of that specific color and not a combination of primary colors.
12. Set the **View** switch back to **Off** to view all the colors once again. Close any open InDesign files in preparation for the steps that follow.

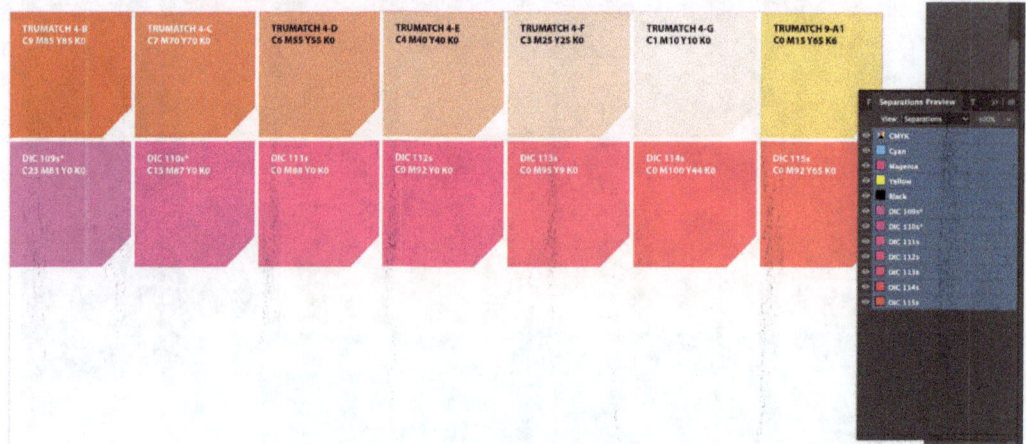

Figure 5.6: The Separations Preview panel showing CMYK and spot printing inks (The image is intended as a visual reference; the textual information is not essential.)

With this fundamental understanding of color, we are in a good position to embark on the execution of our project. Please be aware that this is not an exhaustive discussion of color models. We'll take what we learned here and apply it to a design in *Chapter 6*.

> **Note**
> Pantone colors are no longer in InDesign due to licensing changes, requiring users to purchase them separately or use alternative color systems.

Summary

In this chapter, we explored the CMYK, RGB, and spot color spaces. We now have an understanding of additive, subtractive, and spot colors. We looked at how primary colors mix and blend to produce secondary colors, and in turn how tertiary colors can be created by mixing secondary colors across these models. We also had a look at color separations for print and prepress. This helped us further discern the differences between spot and process colors. This knowledge assists in predicting with confidence the way printed material will be produced on a printing press.

This chapter is a prelude to the one that follows. We'll use what we learned here to work with color and graphics in a print brochure design. We'll work with both color and graphics to create a vibrant design. We will explore various types of imported color models, vector graphics, raster images, and business graphics. We'll ensure that content is created in the correct color space for the specified print output.

Level: Intermediate

Working with Graphics and Color

This chapter dovetails neatly with the previous one. You'll recall we explored the process (CMYK), RGB, and premixed ink (Spot) color spaces, covering the full gamut of color models available in InDesign. Armed with an understanding of primary, secondary, and tertiary color mixes, as well as how color separations are determined for high-quality printing, we are able to deal with the content of this chapter with a greater level of confidence.

In this chapter, you will learn how to use color and graphics to create vibrant designs while managing these resources across your projects. You will place (import) content from multiple sources. This chapter explores various types of imported color models and graphics formats. We will import vector graphics such as logos from applications such as Illustrator. We'll also place images from applications such as Photoshop. Then, we'll import business graphics from Acrobat. We'll ensure they are in the correct format and color space for the required output. In this chapter, we'll create a print brochure that mimics the form factor of a mobile phone.

140   Working with Graphics and Color

Figure 6.1: A mockup of the project for this chapter

Figure 6.1 shows a mockup of the project for this chapter. We will work with color and graphics to add vibrancy to our design. We will produce a brochure in the form factor of a mobile phone. The areas we will focus on are listed as follows:

- Applying color to objects
- Fill and stroke colors
- Text colors

- Using colors from images and graphics
- Importing graphics
- Changing the view quality
- Amending the object layer options

You can find the relevant projects/example here: https://packt.link/a19oQ

> **Important note**
> When creating print projects, this book uses picas and points for measurement units. This caters to readers using either imperial or metric units. If you prefer to work in inches or millimeters, you can type the pica value into the entry fields and InDesign will convert it into your preferred unit of measure. For example, 21p0, which is 21 picas and 0 points, will be translated to 3.5" or 89 mm. A reminder that this holds true for print documents only.

Exploring the completed project and resources

This book is written in a practical, hands-on way. You can try the concepts you read about yourself by downloading the files referred to in this project. These example files can be downloaded from the following link: https://packt.link/a19oQ

1. Open the completed project by choosing **File** menu | **Open**. Navigate to the Chapter 5 Example Files folder. Open the file named Try it yourself 5 - 01 Mobile Mockup Complete Id.indd. If you are presented with a missing fonts warning, please click **Activate**. InDesign will automatically install any missing fonts.

2. Let's familiarize ourselves with the project. Access the **Pages** panel from the **Window** menu. Double-click **Page 1**. Then, navigate to the remaining three pages to get a sense of what we will be building in this chapter. Try to identify the different elements that make up the design by using the **Links** and **Properties** panels. When done, please close the document by choosing **File** menu | **Close**.

The following section explores the completed InDesign project. We'll build the design from the ground up using the color models we discussed in the previous chapter.

Getting started

In this section of the chapter, we'll work with the completed project as a visual reference and a pre-populated design simultaneously. We'll create graphics and apply color to various components in the partially completed design. Note that the final result is meant to be a brochure that takes the form factor of a mobile phone. We won't get into imposition or die traces in this chapter since it falls into the domain of print finishing. Follow these steps:

1. From the InDesign **Home** screen, choose **Open**. Navigate to the Chapter 6 - Working with Graphics and Color Example Files folder you downloaded from Packt.com. Open the file named Try it yourself 6 - 01 Mobile Brochure Complete.indd.

2. Access the **Pages** panel. Walk through the document by double-clicking each of the four individual page thumbnails if you need a refresher. Then go back to **Page 1**. Keep this document open. We'll refer to it as we build out the design.

3. Now choose **File | Open**. Navigate to the Chapter 6 - Working with Graphics and Color Example Files. Open the file named Try it yourself 6 - 07 Mobile Brochure Start.indd.

4. Select the completed document. Choose **Window | 2-up Vertical** to view both documents at the same time. The completed project should appear to the left of the screen. If it does not, select its name tab and drag it to the left. Choose the **2-up Vertical** command again. Then drag the divider between the two documents to reduce the completed document screen space as shown in *Figure 6.2*.

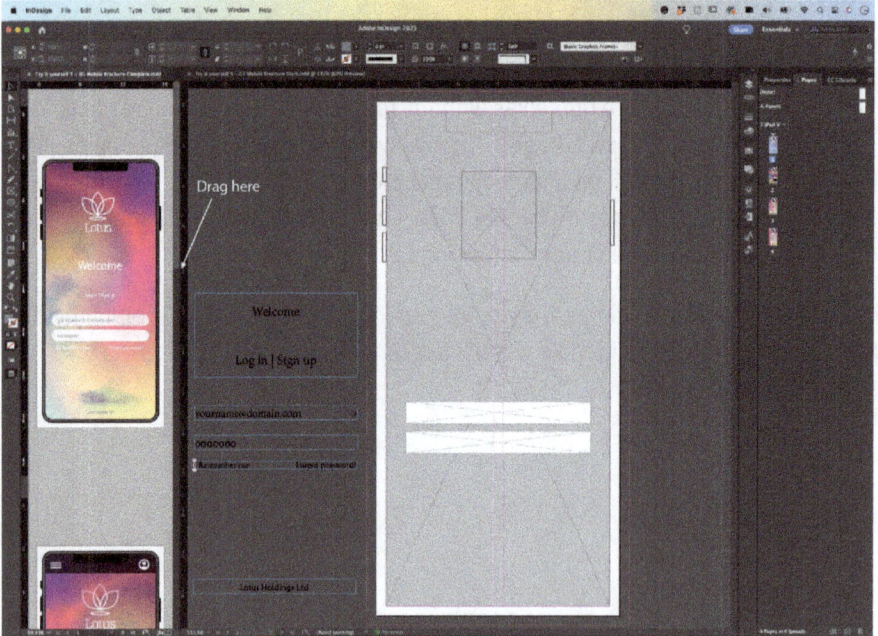

Figure 6.2: The documents arranged for optimal workflow

Getting started   143

The document we'll be working with has been populated with a wireframe of the design for you. We'll start by building out the mobile phone body and then populate the user interface elements.

5. Let's draw the phone body. Choose the **Rectangle Frame** tool ⊠ (*F*). Click into the top-left corner of the page where the guides and wireframe are and drag to the bottom right.

6. With the phone body drawn from margin to margin and the object still selected, make the following changes on the **Properties** panel:

7. Under the **Appearance** section, set **Fill** to **None**.

    A. Set **Stroke** to **6pt**. Ensure that the **Stroke** color is **[Black]**.
    B. Choose **Thin Thick Thin** for the stroke style.
    C. Set the **Corner** value to **1p6**.
    D. Choose **Rounded** for the corner style.
    E. Set the **Align stroke** ▣ value to inside.
    F. Click on the word **Stroke**, choose the **Gap Color** dropdown and select **[Paper]**.

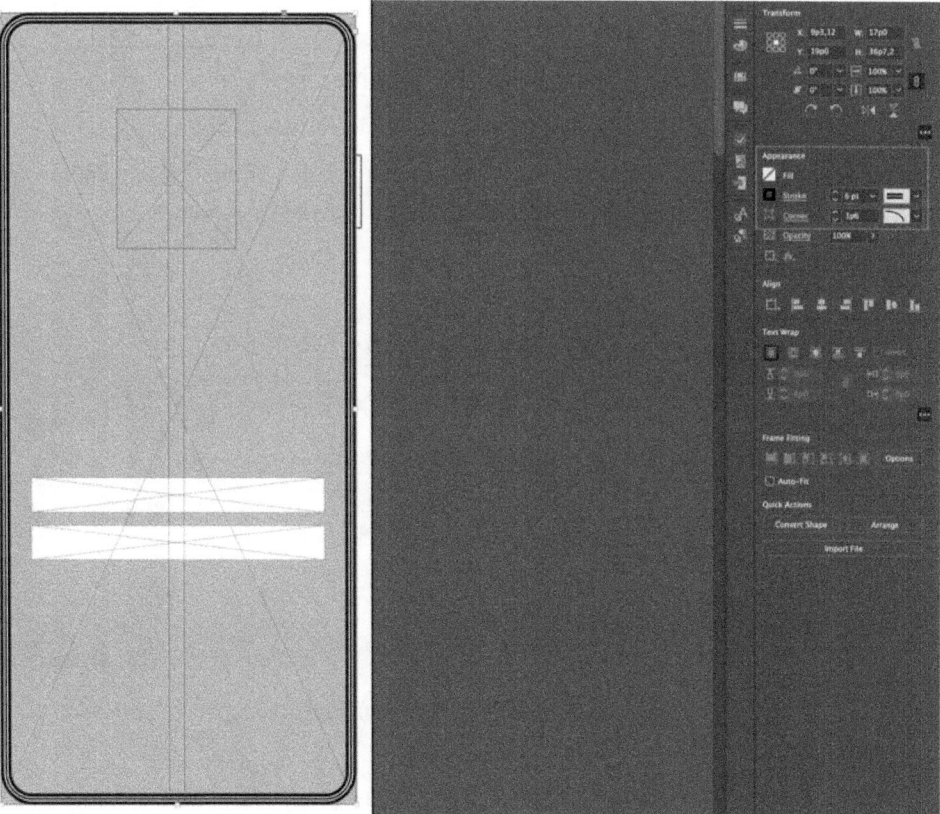

Figure 6.3: The body of the phone with updated appearance values on the Properties panel

Having drawn the frame for the phone body, we can turn our attention to the buttons and notches which we will cover in the next section.

Drawing the buttons and notch

In this section, we'll design to the buttons and the notch at the top of the screen, adjust their properties, and place them in the correct location in the design:

1. Choose the **Zoom** tool (Z) and zoom into the button found toward the top right of our phone object.
2. Choose the **Rectangle** tool (M) from the Toolbox. Draw a rectangle using the wireframe as a reference, then make the following adjustments on the **Properties** panel:
3. Set the **Fill** color to **[Black]**.
4. Set the **Stroke** value to **0pt**.
5. Now, for this object, we need to round out only two of the four corners. With the drawn rectangle still selected, choose **Object** menu | **Corner Options**. Make the following updates in the resultant **Corner Options** dialog box:

    A. Enable the **Preview** switch.

    B. Ensure that the chainlink icon is not active.

    C. Set the top-left and bottom-left corners to **None** and **0p0**.

    D. Set the top-right and bottom-right corner values to **Rounded** and **0p2.16**. We now have rounded corners on just the right corners of our shape.

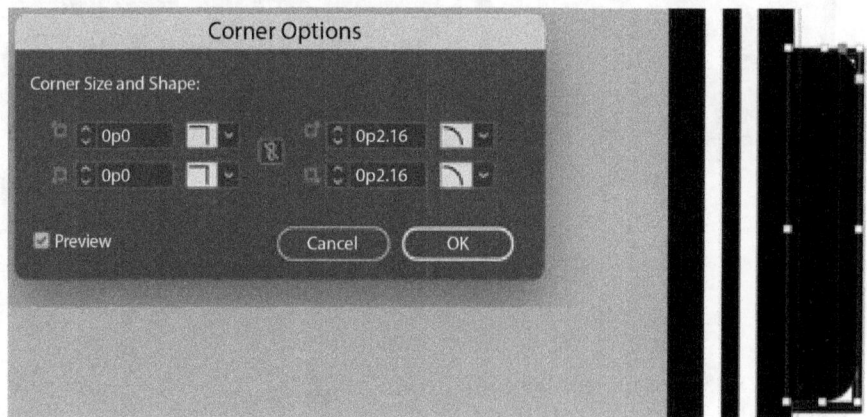

Figure 6.4: Adjusting corner roundness for specific corners of the button

6. We'll now do the same for the buttons to the right of the screen.

7. Choose the **Hand** tool (*H*) ![hand icon] from the Toolbox and drag the page left so the three buttons to the left of the screen come into view on the wireframe layer.

8. Draw out the top rectangle using the **Rectangle** tool ![rectangle icon]. Use the wireframe as a guide. Make the following adjustments on the **Properties** panel:

   A. Set the **Fill** color to **[Black]**.

> **Note**
> Colors such as black that appear in square brackets are default colors and cannot be deleted, moved, or renamed.

   B. Set the **Stroke** value to **0pt**.

9. Next, we'll make a copy of the drawn rectangle. Click inside the rectangle you just drew with the **Selection** tool ![selection icon] and drag down to the second button position. Focus on aligning the top of the copy to the top of the second button on the wireframe. Press and hold the *Shift + Alt/Option* keys as you do this to make a copy. Release the left mouse button, then the *Shift + Alt/Option* modifier keys.

> **Note**
> The *Shift* key locks the vertical direction, while the *Alt/Option* key makes a copy as you drag.

10. With the copied rectangle still active, click the middle control point off the bottom and drag it down to make the rectangle taller using the **Selection** tool ![selection icon]. Once again, use the wireframe as a reference.

11. The third and final button happens to be the same size as the second button. To make a copy, click and hold inside the second rectangle with the **Selection** tool ![selection icon], and drag the copy to its position over the third button on the wireframe grid. Release the left mouse button and *Alt/Option* and *Shift* modifier keys. See *Figure 6.5*.

12. Let's round out the leftmost two corners of the three rectangles all at once. With the **Selection** tool ![selection icon], click inside the top rectangle to select it. Then press and hold the *Shift* key and click once each on the second and third rectangles. Release the *Shift* key. All three rectangles should now be selected.

13. Choose **Object** menu | **Corner Options**. Make the following updates in the resultant **Corner Options** dialog box:

   A. Click the **Preview** checkbox.

   B. Ensure that the chainlink icon ![chainlink icon] is inactive.

   C. Set the top-left and bottom-left corners to **Rounded** and **0p2,16**. There you have it.

14. We now have rounded corners on just the left corners of our three rectangle shapes. Choose **View** | **Fit Page** under **Window** to see the entire page.

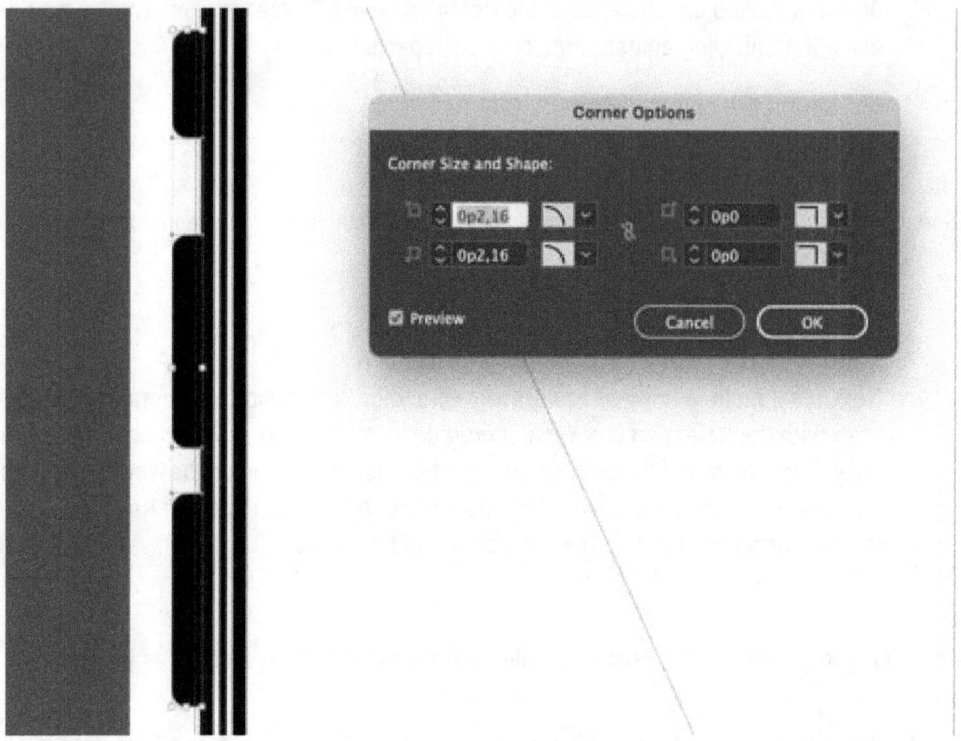

Figure 6.5: Button rounded corner values applied

To complete this part of the project, let's introduce the notch at the top of the screen. You have probably worked out that this is yet another rectangle with the bottom corners rounded. Follow these steps:

1. Zoom into the top of the page with the **Zoom** tool.
2. Using the wireframe as a guide, draw out a rectangle for the notch.
3. Make the following adjustments on the **Properties** panel:

    A. Set the **Fill** color to **[Black]**.

    B. Set the **Stroke** value to **0pt**.

    C. Adjust the size of the rectangle if required by clicking and dragging any of the control points.

4. Choose **Object** menu | **Corner Options**. Make the following updates in the resultant **Corner Options** dialog box:

   A. Click the **Preview** checkbox.

   B. Ensure that the chainlink icon is inactive.

   C. Set the bottom corners to **Rounded**. Change the rounded corner value to **1p0**.

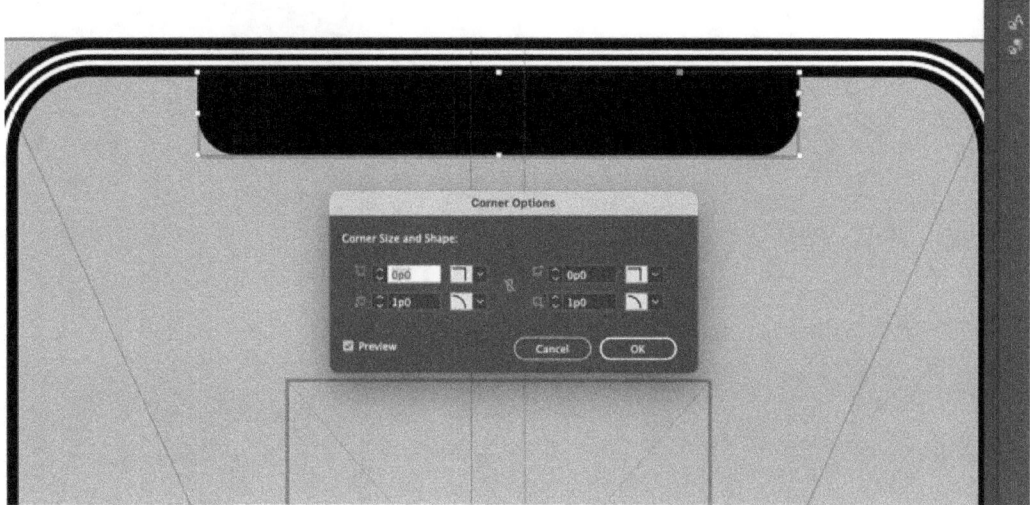

Figure 6.6: The notch with its rounded corner settings

This concludes the shape-drawing component of the project. We can now turn our attention to the user interface elements. To recap, we covered how to draw objects, change the fill and stroke properties, apply default colors, interactively copy objects, and apply rounded corners to objects.

Importing graphics into InDesign

The elements required for **Page 1** of our design include a background image that was prepared in Photoshop, a logo that was crafted in Illustrator, and text and graphic elements that we'll create and color directly in InDesign. The following screenshot shows the completed design for **Page 1**. We'll build each of the elements in the design in the steps that follow.

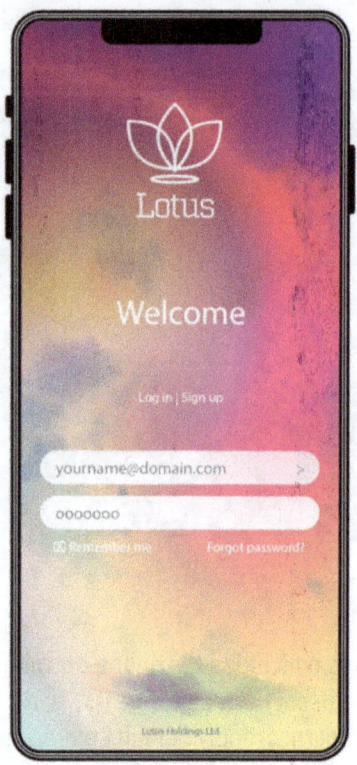

Figure 6.7: The completed page layout design for Page 1

The steps we'll undertake next are for the creation of a frame to house the Lotus logo, as can be seen in *Figure 6.7*. We'll adjust its size and alignment properties for a perfect fit.

1. Choose the **Rectangle Frame** tool (F) ⊠ from the **Tools** panel. Navigate to **Page 1**. Click and drag over the wireframe rectangle at the top of the screen. This frame will host the Lotus logo.

2. With the drawn frame active, choose **File** menu | **Place**. This allows us to place the logo into our freshly drawn frame.

3. **Navigate to the** Chapter 6 - Working with Graphics and Color Example Files folder. Select the file named **03 Illustrator Logo.ai**.

4. The file is placed into the frame, but it is too large. To correct this, head to the **Frame Fitting** subsection on the **Properties** panel. Click the second icon which is **Fit Content Proportionally**. Then, click the fifth icon which is labeled **Center content**. With the content resized and centered, we can move to the next task.

Figure 6.8: The logo placed into its frame on the page

5. We'll now draw out the two input boxes found toward the bottom of the interface. **Zoom** into that area of the page.

6. Choose the **Rectangle** tool . Draw the top box using the wireframe as a guide.

7. Make the following adjustments on the **Properties** panel:

   A. Under the **Appearance** subset, set the **Fill** color to **[Paper]**.

   B. Set the **Stroke** value to **0pt**.

   C. Change **Corner value** to **1p0** and choose **Rounded** from the corner drop-down list to round all corners of the input box.

Figure 6.9: The first input box with rounded corners applied

8. We'll now make a copy of the input box as we did with the buttons earlier. Choose the **Selection** tool . Click inside the rectangle we just drew. Press and hold the *Shift + Alt/Option* keys and drag down to place a copy just below. Use the wireframe as a guide.

We'll format the text next. We'll tweak the formatting properties of prepopulated text which you will find on the pasteboard alongside the page. Since you know how to create type, we've created this element for you so that we don't waste time and we can focus on its formatting properties.

Formatting type

We can now format the type on the page. The type has been prepopulated for you and placed on the pasteboard to the left of the page.

1. Choose the **Selection** tool . Click and drag over all of the text boxes to select them at once. We'll align them to the phone object we drew earlier.

2. Press and hold the *Shift* key and click on the phone frame on the page. Release the *Shift* key and click on the phone a second time. You will notice a thicker selection border around it. This makes it a **key** object. This means that when the objects are aligned with one another, the phone outline will remain in place.

3. Head over to the **Properties** panel and choose **Align horizontal** centers from the **Align subset** (third icon). The text now appears centered on the phone body.

4. We need to move the text to the front. Press and hold *Shift* and click on the phone stroke object to deselect it. You should now have just the text elements selected. Click **Arrange** under the **Quick Actions** category of the **Properties** panel and choose **Bring to Front** from the drop-down list. This ensures that the text appears in front of all elements.

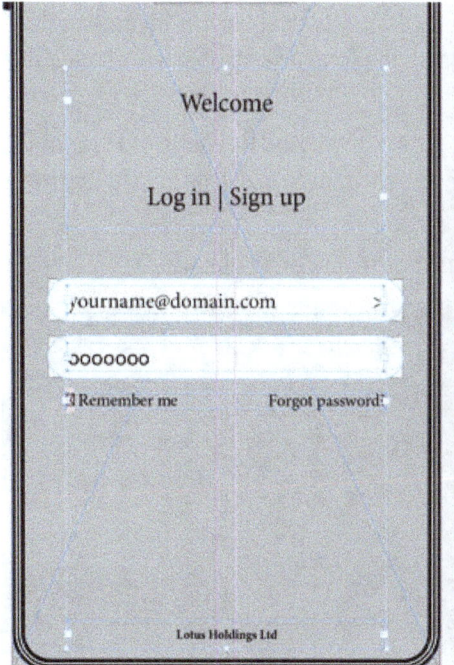 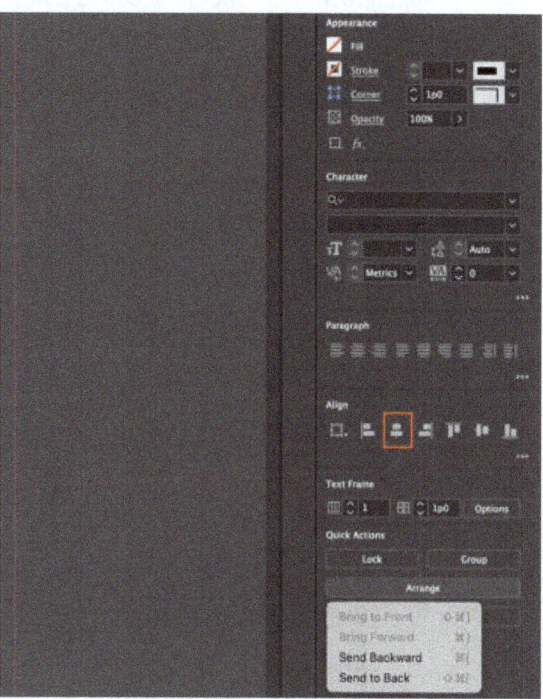

Figure 6.10: The text elements aligned to the center and moved to the front of the object stack

5. We'll now change the type characteristics by applying pre-created paragraph styles. We will create our own paragraph, character, and object styles in a later lesson. Choose the **Type** tool and double-click the word **Welcome** to highlight it. On the **Properties** panel, under the **Text Style** subset, click the drop-down list alongside **[Basic Paragraph]+** and choose **Heading Main** from the dropdown.

6. Click three times on **Log in | Sign up** to select all the words in that line of text. Choose the paragraph styles dropdown on the **Properties** panel once again, and choose **Sub Heading**.

7. Triple-click on **yourname@domain.com** > and choose **Type Entry Fields** from the styles dropdown. Do the same for the password symbols, **ooooooo**. Then, click **Align left** (first icon) under **Paragraph** on the **Properties** panel.

8. Select the **Remember me Forgot password?** text and choose the **Sub Heading** text style from the **Properties** panel. Then, choose **Align Right** (third icon) under the **Paragraph** options, a little lower down on the **Properties** panel.

9. You may have noticed that the symbol in front of the words **Remember me** does not appear correctly. That is because its font needs to be changed. Click and drag over it with the **Type** tool. Then, from the **Fonts** drop-down list under **Character subset** of the **Properties** panel, choose **Wingdings** as the font. The symbol will change to a checkbox ☒.

10. We have one more text element to format. That's the **Lotus Holdings Ltd** text at the bottom. Select the text with the **Type** tool and choose the text style named **Copyright** from the Properties panel.

11. Well done, we've now dealt with all of the text elements on the page.

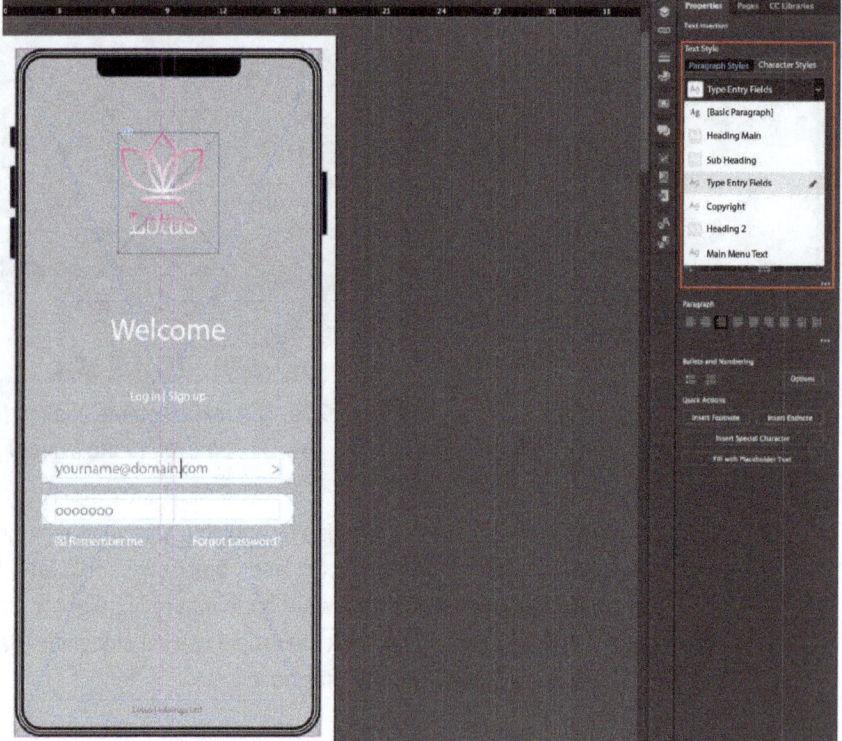

Figure 6.11: The text elements formatted with stylesheets from the Properties panel

Importing graphics into InDesign

By now, you should be very comfortable with importing vector objects such as Illustrator files. We'll work on importing another popular file type, Photoshop files, next. You can import native Photoshop files without the need for any conversion to other file formats into InDesign.

Importing a Photoshop image

The background image is the next task at hand. We will place a layered Photoshop file into the phone frame we created earlier and tweak it to best fit our design.

1. Choose the **Selection** tool . Click away from the page to ensure nothing is selected.
2. From the **File** menu, select **Place**. From the Chapter 6 - Working with Graphics and Color Example Files **folder, select the file named** 02 Photoshop Background .psd.
3. Your mouse pointer will be replaced by a thumbnail icon of the image. Click in the frame of the phone object.

   Caution: Don't click in a text or graphic frame, as InDesign will place the background object into that shape instead. If that were to happen, choose **Edit | Undo** and try again.

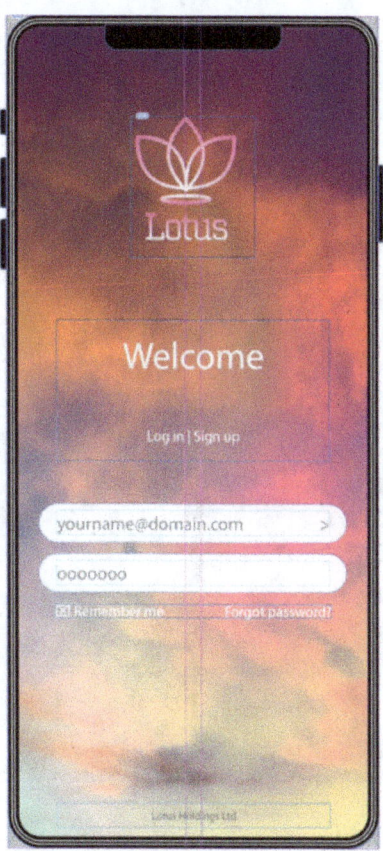

Figure 6.12: The Photoshop background image placed into the phone frame

Having placed the background into the document, we can turn our attention to the logo. Per the completed design, a white, non-gradient version of the logo will work better. InDesign is capable of accessing layers directly in Illustrator and Photoshop files. We'll look at how this is done in the next section.

Adjusting object layer options

Working within an Adobe Creative Cloud workflow allows for certain attributes of native file formats to be manipulated directly in InDesign. This is no different from the tight integration of Word and Excel, for example. Since the logo we placed in InDesign was designed as a multi-layer document in Illustrator, we can target and enable the layer that works best for our design.

1. Choose the **Selection** tool . Click on the **Lotus** logo to select it.
2. Right-click the logo to open the **Contextual** menu and choose **Object Layer Options**. As with pretty much everything in InDesign, there are many ways to achieve the same result. You can also choose **Object** menu | **Object Layer Options** if you prefer.
3. In the **Object Layer Options** dialog, check the **Preview** icon.
4. Under the **Show Layers** section, click the eyeball visibility icon alongside **Pink White Gradient** and **Pink**. This will hide those layers and allow the white version of the logo to be visible. Click **OK** to close the dialog.

Figure 6.13: The Lotus logo with the correct layer enabled

As you can see, making layer adjustments to imported assets is fairly easy to achieve. This is true for pretty much all of the Adobe file formats.

Object transparency and blending modes

InDesign offers powerful transparency and blending mode options for objects, fills, and strokes. Using these controls assists in unifying designs and creating rich interactions between page elements.

1. Choose the **Selection** tool . Click on the white rounded corner text entry frame under the **yourname@domain.com** text. Be sure to click on the white frame behind the text and not the text frame above it.

2. Press and hold the *Shift* key and click on the frame behind the password **ooooooo** placeholder text.

3. With both white frames selected, head over to the **Properties** panel. Under the **Appearance** subset, click on the word **Opacity** to access the options available.

4. Click on the drop-down arrow alongside the word **Normal**. These are referred to as blending modes.

5. Select **Overlay** from the list. We now have the background coming through ever so subtly.

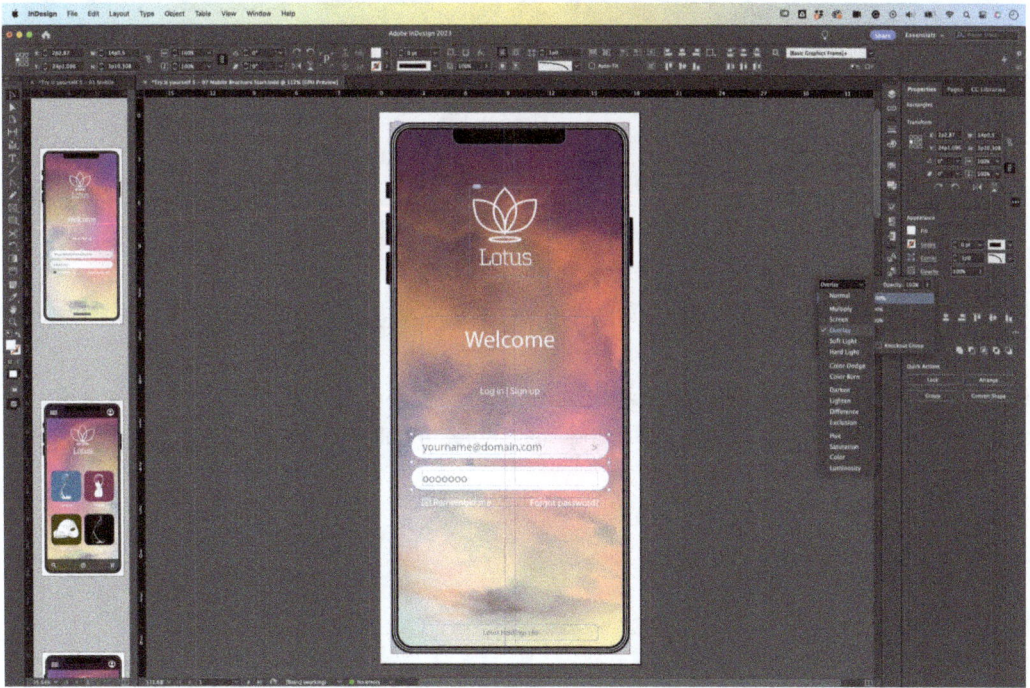

Figure 6.14: The text entry fields with the Overlay blend mode applied

6. Let's preview the final result. Choose the **Layers** panel and click the eye visibility icon alongside the Wireframe layer to hide it from view.

7. Then choose **View** menu | **Screen Mode** | **Preview**. This hides all construction lines and object frames.

8. When you are done, turn on the visibility of the **Wireframe** layer and choose **View** menu | **Screen Mode** | **Normal**.

9. Let's save a copy of this file. Choose **File** menu | **Save as**, and save it to a preferred location on your computer and give it a name. This will keep the original example file intact should you want to refer back to it.

Figure 6.15: The Wireframe layer is hidden and the Preview screen mode selected

Well done. This concludes all the required tasks for **Page 1**. In the next section of the chapter, we'll copy the required elements from **Page 1** and make adjustments to them on **Page 2** to complete its design.

Duplicating page elements

The following screenshot illustrates what the final design of **Page 2** ought to look like. In preparation for copying over the page elements, ensure that the **Artwork** layer is selected and the **Wireframe** layer is visible and locked on the **Layers** panel. Confirm that you are on **Page 1** on the **Pages** panel.

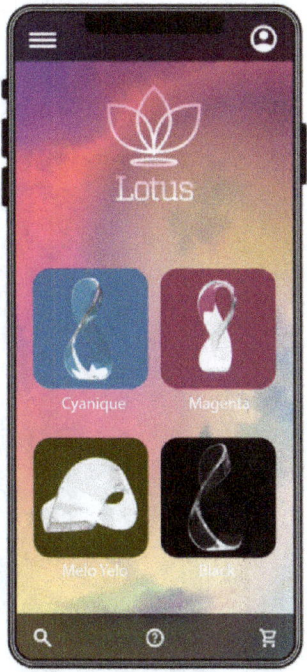

Figure 6.16: The completed design for Page 2

InDesign offers numerous options to copy and place objects between pages. We'll copy elements from our completed design on **Page 1** and place them perfectly in place on **Page 2**. We'll then delete elements we do not need.

1. Ensure that you are on **Page 1**. Choose the **Selection** tool . Head to the **Edit** menu and choose **Select All**.
2. Choose **Copy** from the **Edit** menu.
3. Double-click **Page 2** on the **Pages** panel. Note that the wireframe design is slightly different compared to **Page 1**. This is also evident in the completed example file.
4. We'd like to paste the copied content in the exact same location as it is on **Page 1**. The **Paste** command won't suffice as it has an offset. Choose **Edit** menu | **Paste in Place** instead.

5. With the pasted elements still selected, choose **Object** menu | **Arrange** | **Send** to back. This will push the elements to the back of the layer.

6. The text fields for **Page 2** become visible. With the **Selection** tool , click away from all elements to deselect them.

7. Let's delete the elements we do not require. Use the completed project as a guide. Starting at the top, the notch is not required. Click on it and press the *Delete* key.

8. Do the same for the **Welcome** text, the text entry fields, and the **Lotus Holdings** text at the bottom of the page. *Figure 6.17* shows what should be left on the page.

Figure 6.17: The remaining design elements on Page 2 ready for editing

The **Direct Selection** tool , allows for selecting parts of groups or individual objects without the need to ungroup elements or objects first. This offers powerful possibilities when editing and manipulating artwork. We'll use the **Direct Selection** tool to select a background image in a frame and eliminate it.

Working with the Direct Selection tool

You may have noticed that the wireframe is being obscured by the image background. We will remove it from the frame for now. A quick explanation first, though. Remember that all objects in InDesign reside in a frame, irrespective of whether you create it consciously or not. In the case of our background element, the frame is the object with a thick stroke. The image resides inside it. When you select an object with the **Selection** tool ▶, you select the object and all its component parts. When you click an object with the **Direct Selection** tool ▶, you select its subcomponents.

1. Choose the **Direct Selection** tool ▶. Click on the background image. Note that the selection is much bigger than the page because this is the extent of the image is a lot larger than the frame.
2. Press the *Delete/Backspace* key. If selected correctly, the background should be deleted. The phone frame should still be visible on the page. Refer to *Figure 6.18*.

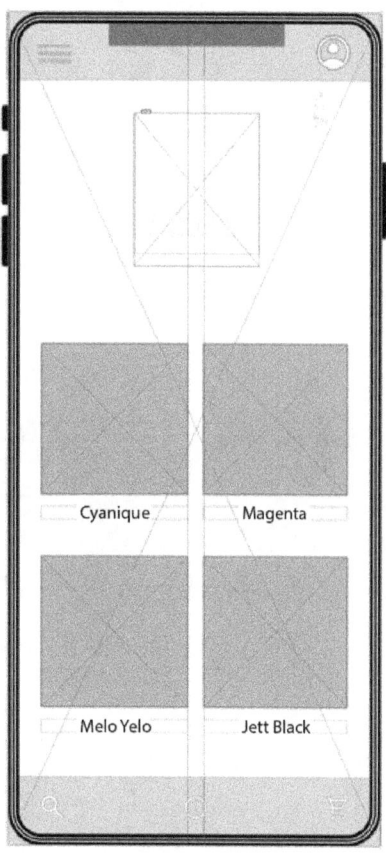

Figure 6.18: The image background removed with the Direct Selection tool

Adjusting object layer options

We worked with object layer options previously. As you can see, the white logo is hard to discern on the current background. Let's rectify this:

1. Choose the **Selection** tool . Click on the **Lotus** logo to select it.
2. Right-click the logo to open the contextual menu and choose **Object Layer Options**.
3. In the **Object Layer Options** dialog, check the **Preview** icon.
4. Under the **Show Layers** section, click on the visibility box alongside **Pink White Gradient** and **Pink** to make them visible. The eyeball will return to indicate it is indeed visible. Since this is the topmost layer, it does not matter whether the other layers are visible or not. Click **OK** to close the dialog.

Figure 6.19: The Pink White Gradient layer made visible in the Object Layer Options dialog

Assigning frame content

You may have noticed a faint **X** running across the phone frame. This indicates that the frame is optimized to contain graphic content. We'd like to change this:

1. Choose the **Selection** tool and click the phone object.
2. With the object selected, choose **Object** menu | **Content**. The frame is currently set to **Graphic**. Select **Unassigned** from the list of options. The blue **X** in the frame disappears on choosing this command.

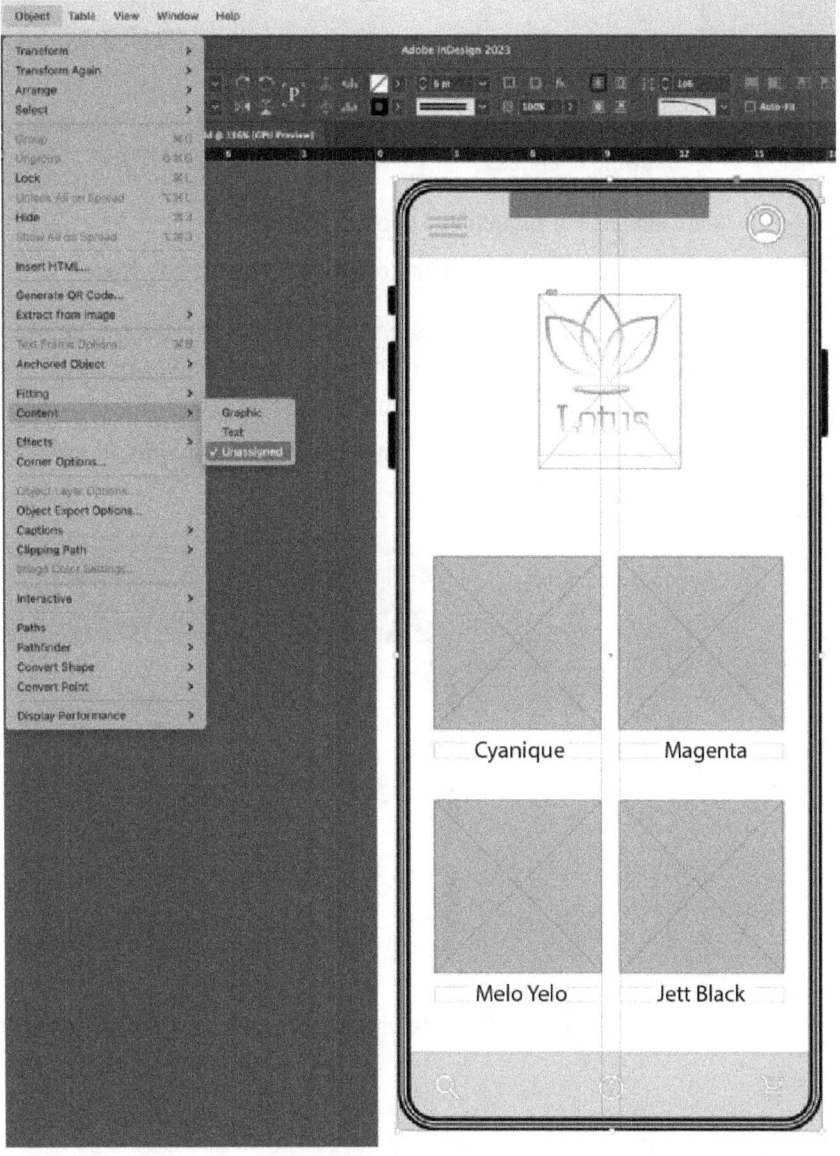

Figure 6.20: The phone object with its content set to Unassigned

Creating the status bar

The status bar is found at the top of a mobile phone interface. We'll create this element next. If we analyze the shape, it is the same as the phone shape with sharp corners for the bottom corners. Since phones have notches or slots at the top, we'll use the same color for a seamless transition.

1. We'll make a copy of the phone body shape and tweak it to meet the new shape requirements. Choose the **Selection** tool from the Toolbox.

2. Click the phone body frame and choose **Edit** menu | **Copy**. Then, select **Paste in Place** from the **Edit** menu to place it directly on top of the original.

3. Pick up the middle control handle off the bottom of the copied frame and drag it up to the desired size. Use the wireframe as a guide.

4. We'll now make changes to the properties of the shape. In the **Properties** panel, make the following changes:

   A. Click the **Fill swatch** and choose **[Black]** from the color swatch list.

   B. Set the **Stroke** width value to **0pt**. This will set it to **None**.

5. To resolve the rounded corners, choose **Object** menu | **Corner Options**. From the **Corner Options** dialog, change the corner type from rounded to square for the bottom corners only. Click **OK** to close the dialog.

6. The newly drawn rectangle obscures the phone frame. Right-click the object and choose **Arrange** | **Send to Back**.

Figure 6.21: The status bar with color, corner options, and hierarchy updated

Creating the navigation bar

The navigation bar is is found toward the bottom of the user interface. The process is a repeat of the previous step, with a few minor differences. We'll duplicate the phone shape again and introduce sharp corners for the top corners instead of the bottom ones. We'll also introduce transparency to create a translucent look:

1. Make another copy of the phone body shape by choosing the phone frame with the **Selection** tool .

2. Choose **Edit** menu | **Copy**. Then, choose **Edit** menu | **Paste in Place** to place it directly over the original.

3. Pick up the top-middle control handle at the top of the copied frame. Drag it downward to the desired size. Once again, use the wireframe as a guide.

4. You should be fairly comfortable with the changes that need to be made in the **Properties** panel. They are as follows:

   A. The **Fill swatch** should be set to **[Black]** from the color swatch list.

   B. Set the **Stroke** width value to **0pt** to disable it.

   C. Set **Opacity** to **60%**.

5. Choose **Object** menu | **Corner Options**. From the **Corner Options** dialog, change the corner type from rounded to square for the top corners this time, and click **OK**.

6. The newly drawn rectangle obscures the phone frame and needs to be sent back in the object hierarchy. Select **Object** menu | **Arrange** | **Send to Back**.

Figure 6.22: The navigation bar placed in its respective locations

Having completed the status and navigation bars, we can populate them with the relevant icons.

Working with libraries

The icons for the status and navigation bars have been derived from the Google Material Symbols library and saved in an InDesign library for easy access. Visit https://fonts.google.com/icons to view the full library. InDesign libraries (not to be confused with Creative Cloud libraries) are compact asset files that are saved to your local drive or server and are opened and accessed like any other InDesign file. One key difference is it opens as a panel.

1. Choose **File** menu | **Open**. Navigate to the Chapter 6 - Working with Graphics and Color Example Files **folder. Select the file named** 07 Icon Library.indl.
2. The library will open as a panel. If it obscures your page, drag it to a better location in the interface.
3. We'll start by placing the status bar icons at the top of the page. The black bar we drew earlier makes it difficult to see the icons below. We'll cut the opacity of this element temporarily, so we can use the wireframe below to help us place the elements correctly. Click the status bar object at the top of the page with the **Selection** tool . Change its opacity to **50%** on the **Properties** panel.
4. Click and drag the icon named **02 Menu** and place it on the top left of the status bar at the top of the page using the wireframe as a guide See *Figure 6.23*.
5. Follow the same steps for the icon named **02a Profile**. Click and drag it from the library and place it on the top right of the status bar at the top of the page.
6. **02b Search** should be placed on the left-bottom. Place **02c Help** in the bottom-center and **02d Basket** on the bottom-right of the navigation bar.
7. Let's return the status bar to its full opacity. Select it and take the **Opacity** value back to **100%**.
8. We'll use the library again on **Page 4**. For now, we can close it by clicking the **x** icon at the top left of the **07 Icon Library** panel.

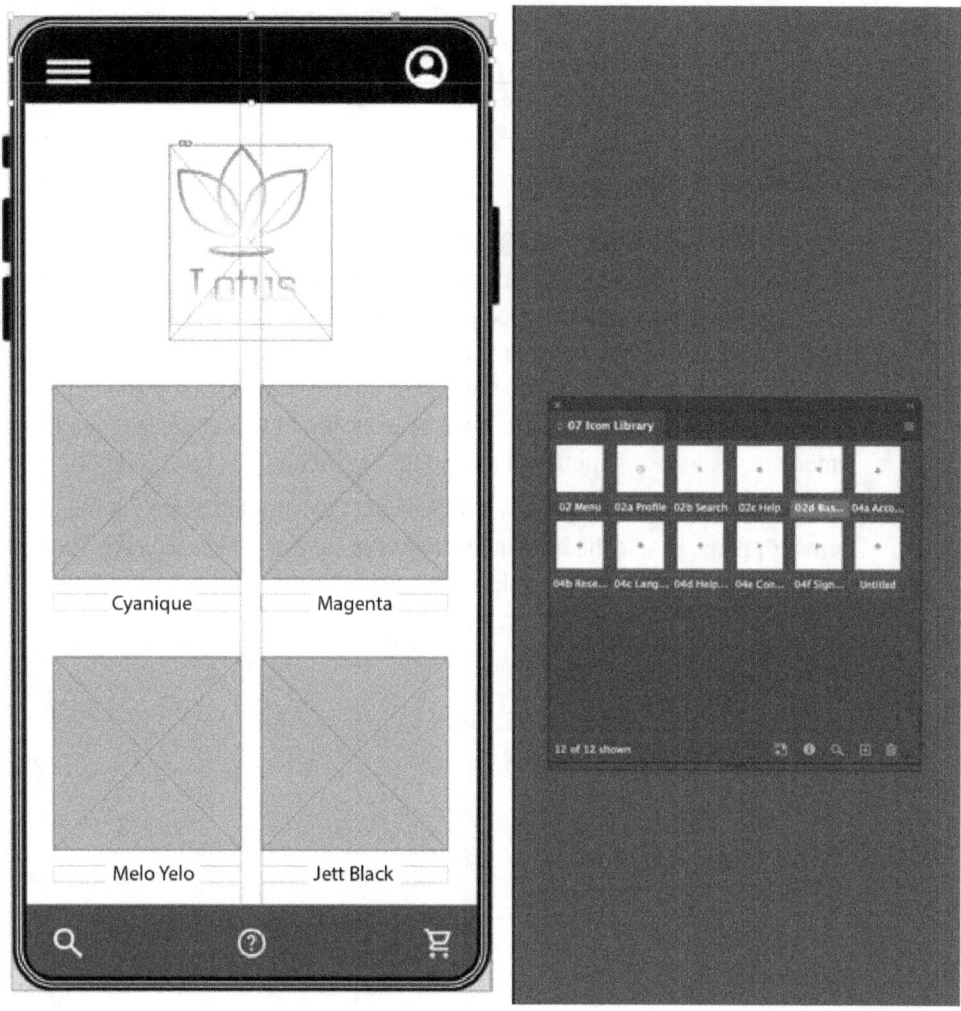

Figure 6.23: The relevant icons placed onto the design from the library

Having completed the status and navigation bars, we can turn our attention to the four image and their descriptions in the center of the design.

Drawing a multi-frame grid

InDesign allows for the placement of multiple elements into a user-defined grid on the fly. It makes working with multiple objects that much easier. We'll explore this functionality for the images in our design on **Page 2**.

> **Important note**
> For the following steps, do not release the mouse until the entire process is complete. We'll indicate when it is appropriate to do so.

To get started, follow these steps:

1. Select the **Rectangle Frame** tool ⊠. Using the wireframe as a guide, drag out a rectangle from the top left frame to the bottom right of the four image frames in the middle of the design. Keep your mouse button pressed in. Tap the up arrow key on your keyboard once. This will create two rows. Now tap the right arrow key once. You can see we have four rectangle frames drawn. Size the frames so they match the top and bottom edges in the wireframe guide below. They will be taller for now. We'll resize their heights in a moment. Release the mouse at this point. See *Figure 6.24* for reference.

2. With the four frames highlighted, we'll round out the corners. Select the **Object** menu | **Corner Options**. Enable the **Make all** settings the same chainlink icon 🔗. Then choose rounded for the corner style and key in a value of 1p0.

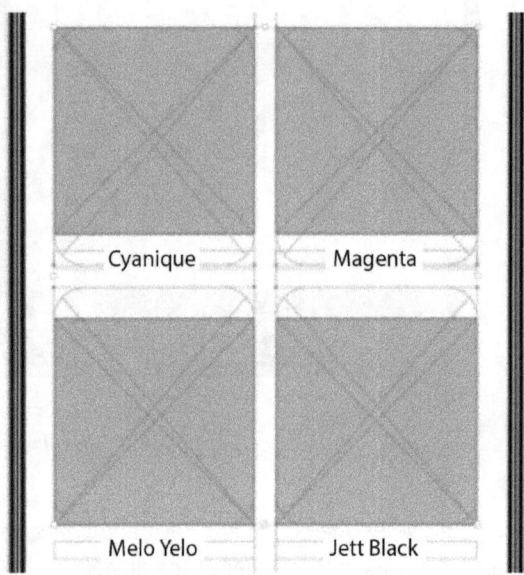

Figure 6.24: The four image placeholder frames with corner roundness applied

3. We'll now tweak the heights of the rectangles so they are the correct height. As you can see, they are too tall. Choose the **Selection** tool ▷. Click off the page to deselect all the elements. Then, click the top left frame, hold *Shift*, and click the top right frame. With the two frames selected, you will see a bounding box that envelops both. Click the middle bottom control point of the bounding box and drag it up until it locks into the wireframe.

4. We'll now do the same for the frames at the bottom. Click on the pasteboard away from any elements to deselect the two selected frames. Then, click the bottom left frame, press *Shift*, and click the bottom right frame. Release the mouse and *Shift* key. Select the top-middle control point this time and drag downward using the wireframe as a guide. See *Figure 6.25*.

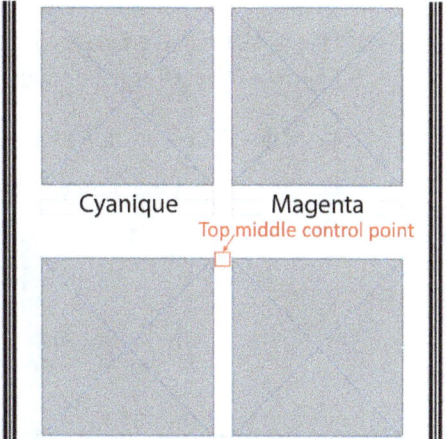

Figure 6.25: A zoomed-in view showing the control point used to manipulate the height of the frames

Well done. With the frames in place, we can turn to coloring them. We'll be using swatches to achieve this task.

Applying color to objects

We're now ready to color the frames. We'll be working with the **Properties** panel to complete this task:

1. Choose the **Selection** tool . Click inside the top left frame we just drew. In the **Properties** panel, under the **Appearance** subset, make the following changes:

    A. Click the **Fill swatch** and select **Cyan Process**.

    B. Ensure that the **Stroke swatch** is set to none.

2. With the **Selection** tool , click inside the top right frame we just drew. In the **Properties** panel, under the **Appearance** subset, make the following changes:

    A. Click the **Fill swatch** and select **Magenta Process**.

    B. Ensure that the **Stroke swatch** is set to **none**.

3. With the **Selection** tool, click inside the bottom left frame we just drew. In the **Properties** panel, under the **Appearance** subset, make the following changes:

    A. Click the Fill swatch and select **Yellow Process**.

    B. Ensure that the Stroke swatch is set to none.

4. Finally, still with the **Selection** tool, click inside the bottom right frame we just drew. From the **Properties** panel, under the **Appearance** subset, make the following changes:

    A. Click the Fill swatch and select **[Black]**.

    B. Ensure that the Stroke swatch is set to none.

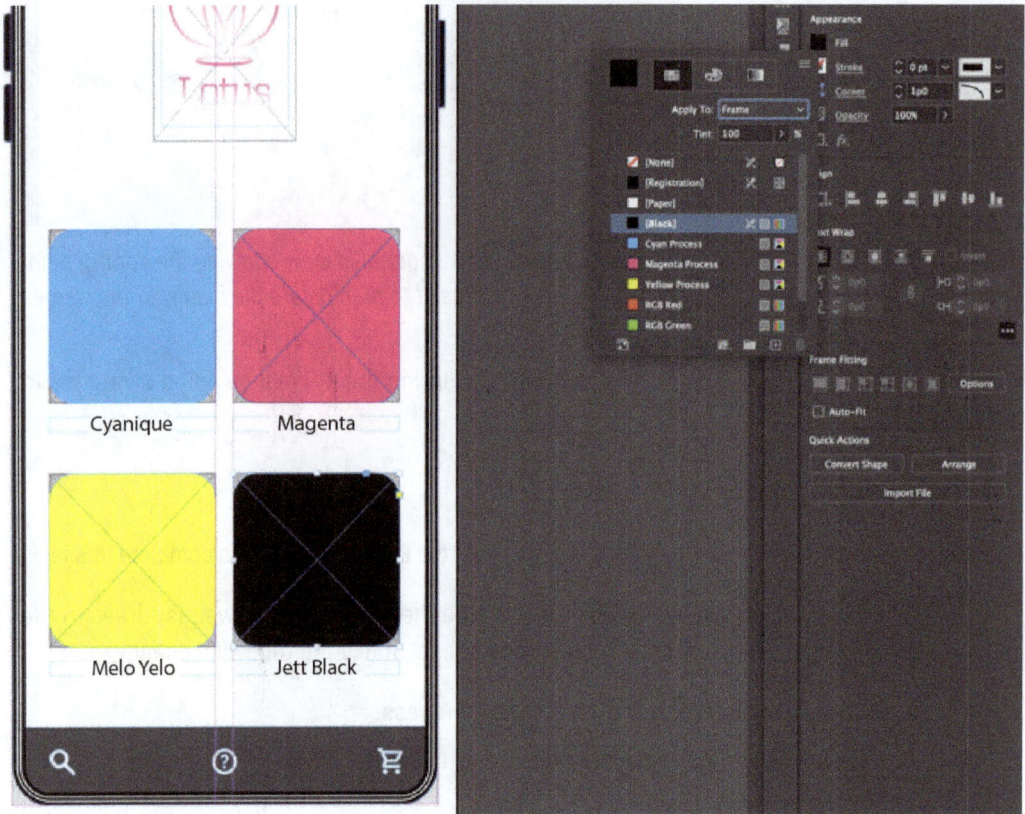

Figure 6.26: The four image placeholder frames with fill colors applied

Having applied the fill colors to the frames, we can now bring the image elements into the frames. This task will not affect the color as long as the image in question has transparency and is in a format that InDesign can understand.

Importing multiple files

We'll be importing several Mobius loop images into our design. These were designed in Adobe Dimension, rendered and finessed in Photoshop.

1. Choose the **Selection** tool . Ensure that no objects are selected by clicking away from everything.
2. We will be importing the following files:

   - 06a Mobius Loop Dn-Cyan.psd
   - 06b Mobius Loop Dn-Magenta.psd
   - 06c Mobius Loop Dn-Yellow.psd
   - 06d Mobius Loop Dn-Black.psd

3. Choose **File** menu | **Place**. Navigate to the Chapter 6 - Working with Graphics and Color Example Files **folder. Click on the** 06a Mobius Loop Dn-Cyan.psd **file once.** Then, press *Shift* and click 06d Mobius Loop Dn-Black.psd to select it and the files in between. With the four files highlighted, click **Open**.
4. Your mouse cursor will change to a place gun with a preview of the first image. Click inside the cyan frame to place it inside.
5. Then, head over to the magenta frame and click once to place its image.
6. Do the same for the yellow and black frames.

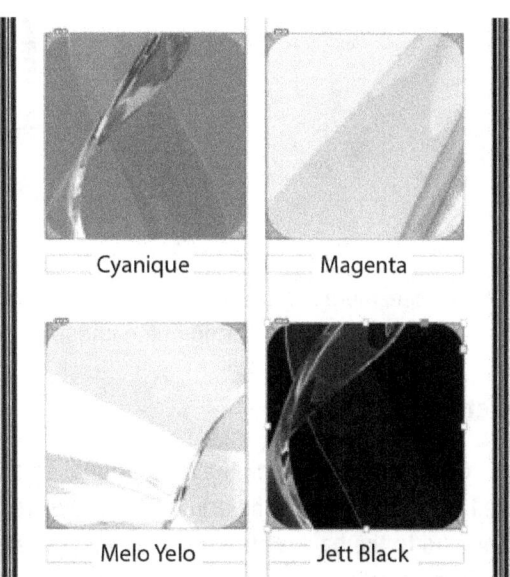

Figure 6.27: The images placed into their respective frames

You have no doubt observed that the images are too large for the frames they reside in. Let's correct this now.

1. With the **Selection** tool , click the first frame. Press and hold the *Shift* key and click once in the three remaining frames.
2. With all four image frames selected, head over to the **Properties** panel. Under the **Frame Fitting** subset, do the following:

    A. Click the second icon , which is **Fill content proportionally**.
    B. Enable the **Auto-Fit** switch. This ensures that the content will adjust to the frame size automatically.

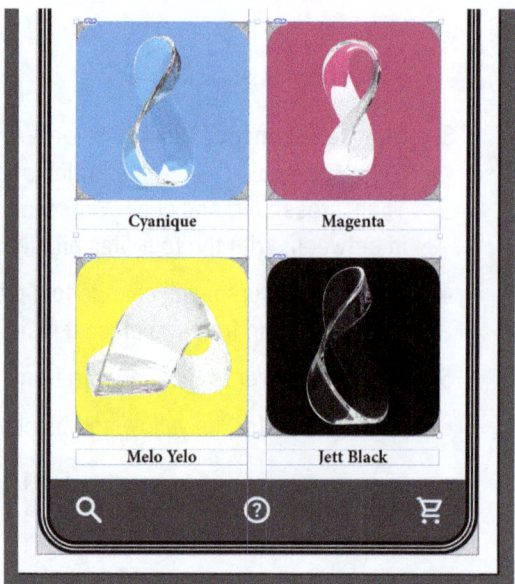

Figure 6.28: The images with the Fill content proportionally command applied

As you can see, there is relative flexibility in how content can be brought into and manipulated in InDesign. Our next task is to bring in the image background for **Page 2**.

Object hierarchy

We're now able to bring back the background. To do this effectively, we will create a copy of the phone form exactly above the original. The main reason for this is that if we move the frame and background to the back of the object stack, the status and navigation bars would obscure the phone frame stroke. See *Figure 6.29* for a visual reference:

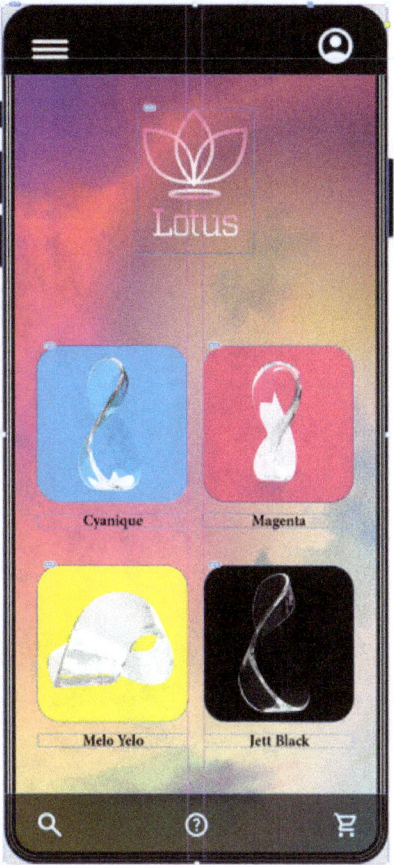

Figure 6.29: The phone frame with the background obscured by the status and navigation bars when sent to the back of the object stack

The next series of steps take us through how to enable the background, resolve the phone stroke/border, and work with the object hierarchy so that content appears correctly to the viewer.

1. Choose the **Selection** tool . Select the phone frame by clicking its edge once.
2. Select **Edit** menu | **Copy**. Then choose **Edit** menu | **Paste in place**.
3. Head to **Page 1** on the **Pages** panel.
4. Choose the **Direct Selection** tool (*A*) and click on the background image. Since the background is already on **Page 1**, we can simply copy and paste it into our frame on **Page 2**. Click on the background. Be sure not to click on other elements such as text frames or the logo. Then, choose **Edit** menu | **Copy**.

5. Head back to **Page 2**. Choose the **Selection** tool (*V*). Click the frame edge, right-click, and choose **Paste Into**. This will obscure all the other elements as it is above all these objects.

6. This is an easy fix. Right-click the object with the background fill and choose **Arrange | Send to Back** from the contextual menu.

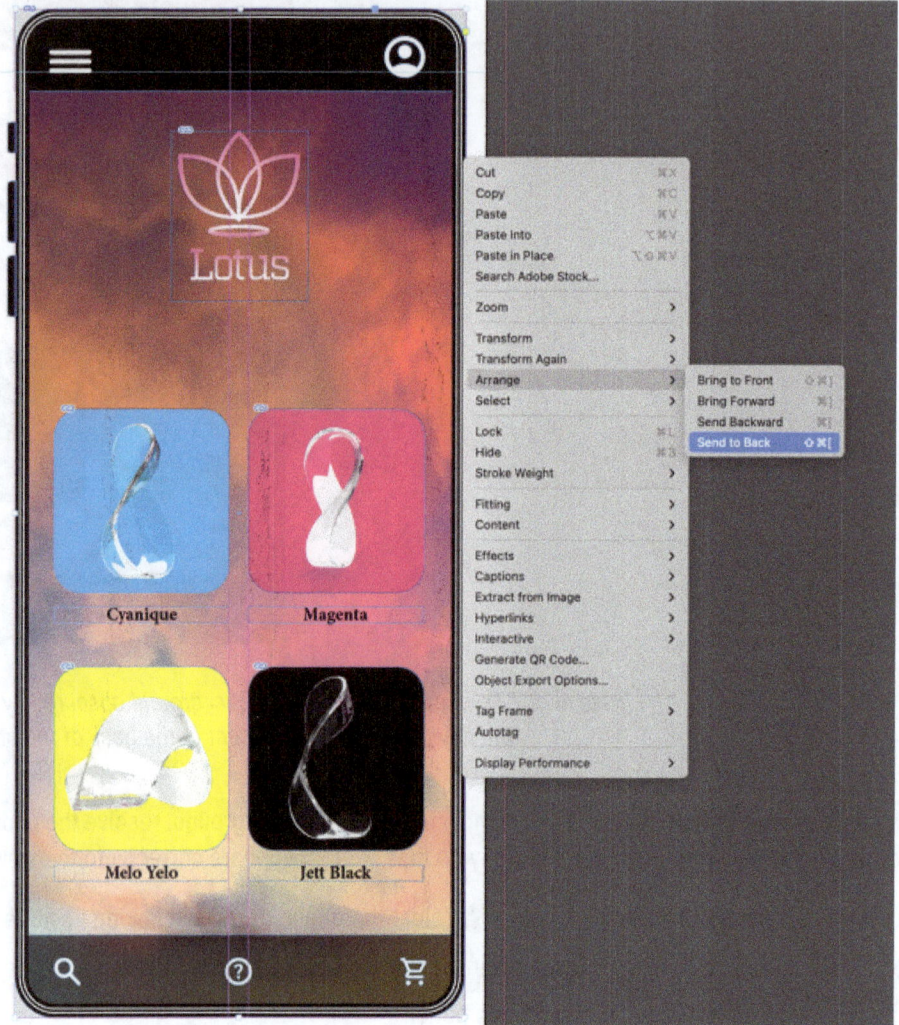

Figure 6.30: The background image frame sent to the back of the object stack

We have one final task for this page, which is to style the text below each image. We've done this before, so this should be good practice for you.

7. Choose the **Selection** tool . Click the first text object once. Then, press and hold *Shift* and click the remaining three text objects. Remember, it's one click each time. When you have them all selected, release the *Shift* key. Choose the **Sub Heading** paragraph style from the **Text Style** section on the **Properties** panel.

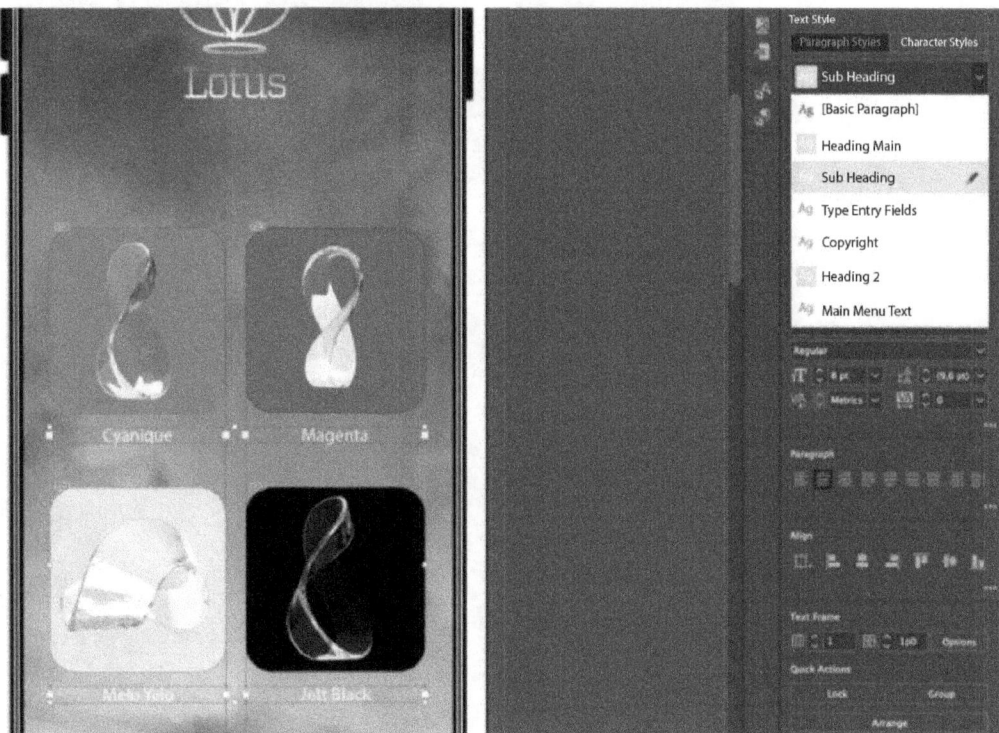

Figure 6.31: The text frames with the Sub Heading paragraph style applied

This concludes the design for **Page 2**. Let's recap what we covered real quick. We looked at duplicating objects to speed up our designs. We also worked with object layer options, libraries of icons, a multi-frame grid, and populating that grid with a multi-file import.

Placing chart objects in InDesign

For this segment of the chapter, we will look at how to import chart objects that originate from Excel. They have been saved as a PDF to maintain their visual integrity and to ensure maximum compatibility with InDesign. This is different from what we explored in the type and tables chapter. We'll copy across the elements from **Page 2** and modify them to fit the page design on **Page 3**. *Figure 6.32* shows the completed design for **Page 3**. As you can see, once the framework is in place, it is easy for us to copy and amend existing elements between pages to fit our design requirements.

174   Working with Graphics and Color

Figure 6.32: The completed Page 3 design

As we did previously, we'll copy and place elements from **Page 2** a completed design from **Page 2** to **Page 4**. It makes the most sense for us to copy over the design from **Page 2** as it has the most common elements.

1. Ensure that you are on **Page 2**. Choose the **Selection** tool, and from the **Edit** menu, choose **Select All**.
2. Select **Edit** menu | **Copy**. Then, head to **Page 3** and choose the **Edit** menu | **Paste in Place**.
3. The background is obscuring the wireframe. We'll hide that object from view temporarily. Click on the background image with the **Selection** tool. Choose **Object** menu | **Hide**. The wireframe should now show through.

4. With the **Selection** tool , click on the four image and text objects whilst holding the Shift key on the screen and press *Delete/Backspace once you have them all selected*.

Figure 6.33: The background image frame hidden from view

5. Choose the **Rectangular Frame** tool (*F*) and draw out the three frames per the wireframe in *Figure 6.33*. When drawing the two smaller frames, you can draw them individually or with the grid functionality we looked at earlier. Since these are perfect squares, use the *Shift* key to maintain equal horizontal and vertical proportions.

6. Choose **File** menu | **Place** and select the following objects from the Chapter 6 - Working with Graphics and Color Example Files folder. Press and hold the *Ctrl* (Windows)/ *Command* (Mac) key to select multiple individual files:

   A. **06a Mobius Loop Dn-Cyan.psd**: This image will be placed in the large frame

   B. **04 Donut Chart Ac.pdf**: This is a donut chart that will be placed in the smaller frame on the left side of the design

C. **05 Bar Chart Ac.pdf**: This is a bar chart that will be placed in the smaller frame on the right side of the design

7. You will be presented with the place gun. Place the content as has been done in the completed project to the left of the screen. See *Figure 6.34* below.

8. Select all three objects with the **Selection** tool . Head over to the **Properties** panel. Under the **Frame Fitting** subset, do the following:

    A. Click the second icon , which is **Fill content proportionally**.

    B. Enable the **Auto-Fit** switch. This ensures that the content will adjust to the frame size automatically.

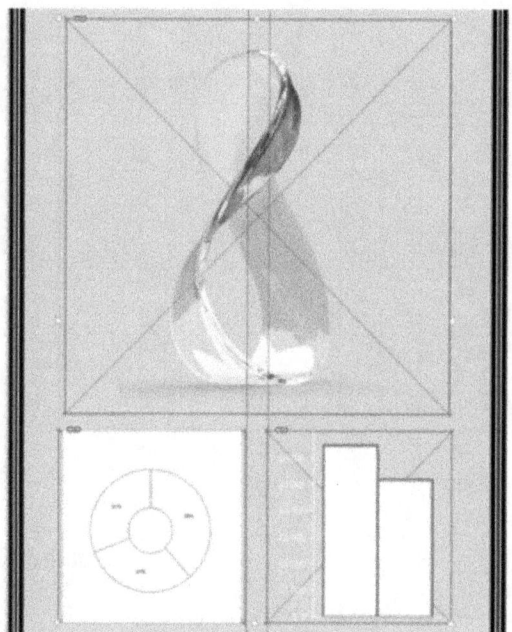

Figure 6.34: The image and charts placed into their respective frames

9. At this stage, we can unhide the background object. With any object selected, right-click and choose **Show All on Spread**.

10. The donut chart has a background layer that we do not want. We'll remove this. Right-click the donut chart object and choose **Object Layer Options**. Click the visibility (eye) icon to hide the background. Click **OK** when done.

11. Awesome. Our final task for this page is to change the blend mode of the two chart objects.

12. Select both objects with the **Selection** tool. Click **Opacity** on the **Properties** panel and change it to **Soft Light**.

Figure 6.35: The final design for Page 3 with the blend modes applied to the chart objects

With the design on **Page 3** complete, you should be well into the swing of things. At this stage, you should be relatively comfortable with copying, placing, manipulating, and creating objects from scratch.

In the next section, we'll explore inline graphics. These are graphic elements that are embedded in text objects and move with the paragraph text in which they are embedded. This ensures that the inline graphic element is always associated with the relevant text.

Inline graphics

There are occasions where the design requires type and graphics to work as a single unit. Of course, there is the option of grouping objects, and that works for certain scenarios. However, if you want graphics to flow with text, inline graphics deliver the most consistent results.

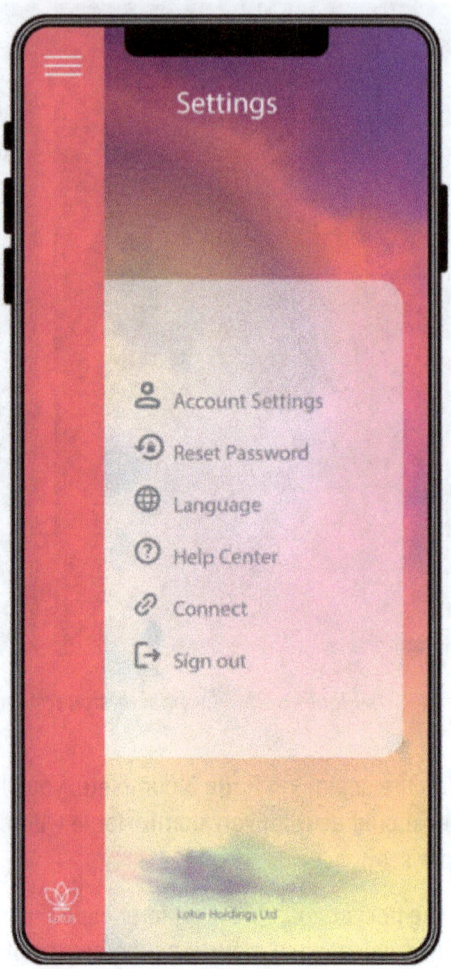

Figure 6.36: The completed design on Page 4 showing inline graphics

1. Go to **Page 1** from the **Pages** panel. Choose the **Selection** tool ▶, and from the **Edit** menu, choose **Select All**.

2. We'll mix things up once again. Go to **Page 1**. We do not need the text elements and entry fields except for the Lotus Holdings imprint at the bottom of the design for **Page 4**. Let's deselect those elements before we initiate a copy. Press and hold the *Shift* key and click on the following elements to deselect them:

   A. The **Welcome** text

   B. The text entry fields and their white rounded rectangle input fields

   C. The **Remember Me** text

3. Select **Edit** menu | **Copy**. Then, head to **Page 4** and choose **Edit** menu | **Paste in Place**.

4. The background is obscuring the wireframe once again. We'll hide that object from view temporarily, like we did previously. Click on the background image with the **Direct Selection** tool . Choose the **Object** menu | **Hide**. The wireframe should now show through.

5. Let's draw out the pink navigation bar to the left of the design. Select the outer phone frame. Right-click and choose **Copy**. Right-click again and choose **Paste in Place**.

6. You'll recall we hid the image in the original object. It is visible in the copy, though not required. Select the **Direct Selection** tool. Click on the image and hit *Delete/Backspace*.

Caution
Ensure you delete the frame contents and not the frame.

---

7. Let's resize the copied frame. Choose the **Selection** tool and click the outer frame copy. Then pick up the midpoint control handle on the right edge of the frame and drag it to the left to create a tall, thin rectangle. Use the wireframe as a guide.

8. We need to resolve the corners. The rightmost ones need to be square. With the object selected, go to the **Choose Object** menu | **Corner Options**. Ensure the chainlink icon is disabled. Then, set the top and bottom-right corners to **None**. Enable **Preview** to see the updates in real-time.

9. The object needs some color adjustments. With the object selected, head over to the **Properties** panel and make the following changes:

   A. Choose the **Fill Swatch** and then **Magenta Process**.

   B. Choose the **Stroke swatch** and set it to **None**.

Working with Graphics and Color

Figure 6.37: The vertical navigation bar correctly sized and colored

10. We need two elements from **Page 3**. The menu hamburger icon on the top left and the empty outer phone frame object to cover the pink navigation tab on **Page 4**. Head to **Page 3**. Click the Menu icon with the **Selection** tool . Press and hold *Shift* and click the frame of the phone object.

11. Choose the **Edit** menu | **Copy**. Head to **Page 4** and choose the **Edit** menu | **Paste in Place**. Excellent! See *Figure 6.38* for a visual reference.

12. We need to place and resize the logo at the bottom of the page. The vertical menu bar is obscuring the wireframe. We'll temporarily change its opacity. Select the menu bar with the **Selection** tool . Change the **Opacity** to **50%** in the **Properties** panel.

13. Align the bottom-right edge of the logo to the bottom-right edge of the frame placeholder on the wireframe at the bottom right of the page. See *Figure 6.38*.. Ensure that **Auto-Fit** is enabled in the **Properties** panel. Pick up the bottom-right corner of the logo frame and drag it toward the wireframe guide while holding the *Shift* key. Release the mouse and then the *Shift* key once you have the correct size and alignment.

14. With the logo still selected choose **Object | Arrange | Bring to Front** to bring it in front of the vertical magenta menu bar.

15. With this task done, we can return the vertical menu bar to full opacity. Click it with the **Selection** tool . Then change its **Opacity** value to 100%.

16. We can quickly resize and reposition the Lotus Holdings text while we're working in that zone. Choose the **Selection** tool icon . Then, click the text object and drag the corners so they align to the wireframe. Click the top-middle control point and drag it up until it locks into the wireframe. Then, select the bottom-left control point and drag it until it locks into the bottom-left corner of the wireframe. Done! See *Figure 6.38* below.

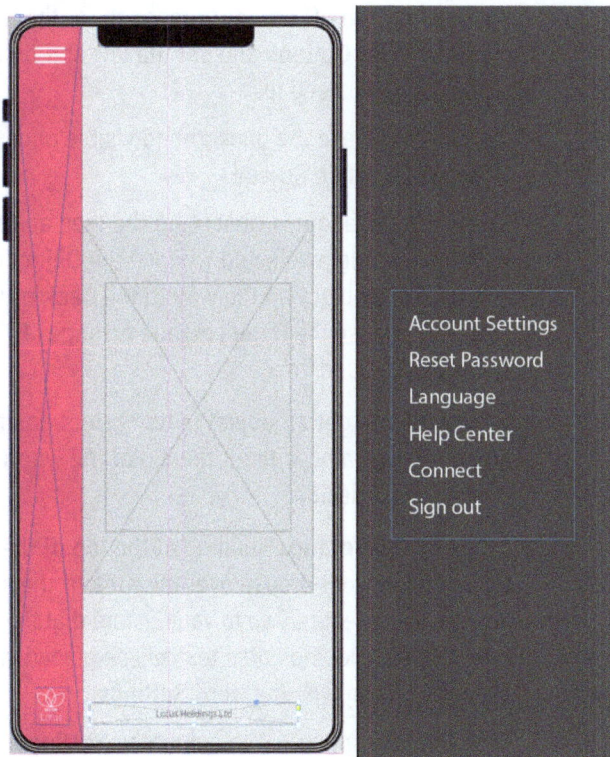

Figure 6.38: The navigation bar logo and copyright info box resolved correctly per the wireframe

17. We can now move the text frame from the pasteboard onto the page. Click and drag it with the **Selection** tool ▶ onto the page using the wireframe as a guide.

18. With the text frame highlighted, choose the **Main Menu Text** style from the **Properties** panel. This will apply the relevant font and styling characteristics to the text.

19. We're ready to draw in the white background object behind the text. Select the **Rectangle** tool ▭. Using the wireframe as a guide, draw a rectangle from the top-right edge until it meets the right edge of the vertical menu bar.

20. Make the following changes in the **Properties** panel:

    A. Set **Fill** to **[Paper]**.

    B. Set **Stroke** to **None**.

    C. Set **Opacity** to **50%**.

    D. Set **Corners** to Rounded with a value of **1p0**.

21. We need to turn off corner roundness for the leftmost corners. Head to the **Object** menu | **Corner Options** and set the left and right corner values to **None**. Resize the rectangle if you need to.

22. We can now make the background visible once more. Choose the **Object** menu and select **Show All on Spread**.

23. The white rectangle is obscuring the type and needs to be pushed back one level. With the rectangle selected, choose the **Object** menu | **Arrange** | **Send to Back**. This will send the object all the way to the back of the layer stack. With the object still selected, choose the **Object** menu | **Arrange** | **Bring Forward**. This will bring it in front of the background image.

    A nifty trick to get an object in its correct position. To close out this chapter, we'll create a text frame without the aid of the wireframe. This is for the **Settings** text at the top of the design.

24. Let's add the **Settings** heading at the top of the page design. Choose the **Type** tool T and move your mouse over the area of the screen you would like the text box to appear. This is entirely up to you. Ensure that the text cursor icon has a square border. A rounded border indicates text will be placed into an existing object. Click and drag the frame. Then type the word **Settings**.

25. Type *Ctrl/Command + A* to select the **Settings** text and choose the **Heading 2** style from the **Properties** panel.

26. Resize the frame by clicking it with the **Selection** tool ▶. Then drag the left and right edges so they are same with of the semi-transparent rectangle below it.

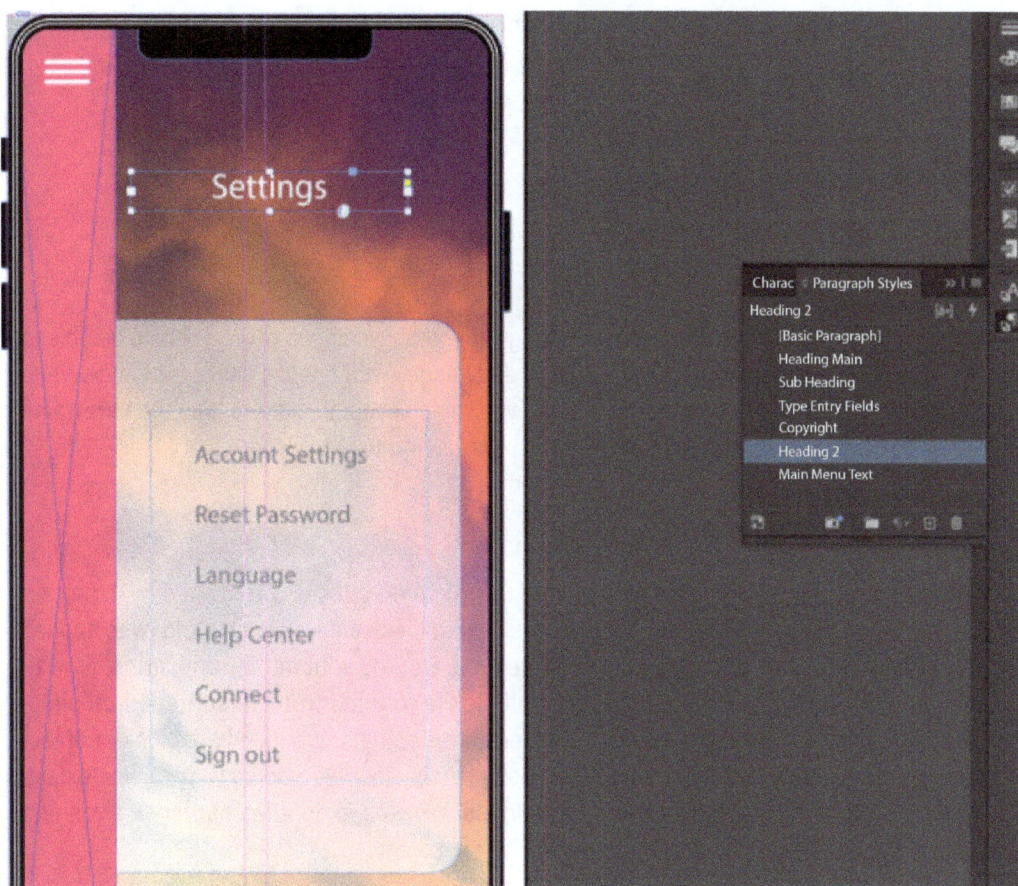

Figure 6.39: The artwork with styles applied

We can now close out this chapter by placing the inline graphics alongside each of the setting text entries. We'll use the icon library once more to achieve this.

1. Choose **File** menu | **Open**. Navigate to the Chapter 6 - Working with Graphics and Color Example Files **folder. Select the file named** 07 Icon Library.indl.

2. Drag the icon named **04a Account Settings** on the artboard alongside the page. This is a free-floating icon.

3. Choose **Edit** menu | **Cut**. Then, choose the **Type** tool and click in front of the **Account Settings** text and choose **Edit** menu | **Paste**. Ensure the text cursor is after the icon and press the *Tab* key to push the icon away from the text.

4. Repeat steps 2 and 3 to place the following icons:

   A. **04b** alongside **Reset Password**
   B. **04c** alongside **Language**
   C. **04d** alongside **Help Center**
   D. **04e** alongside **Connect**
   E. **04f** alongside **Sign out**

This brings us to the end of this chapter on working with graphics and color. You should be able to use InDesign's powerful tools to work with vectors and images with relative confidence. Be sure to walk through the completed project to see all that you've achieved. Be sure to hide the **Wireframe** layer on the **Layers** panel and choose **View** menu | **Screen Mode** | **Preview**.

Summary

In this chapter, we created a four-page brochure using a print subset. We started by exploring the completed design. We used a wireframe to assist with the design process. Color was applied to objects using the CMYK and spot color palettes. We worked with multi-frame grids, as well as color and graphics in detail. We imported multiple file formats from Illustrator, Photoshop, Dimension, and Acrobat. We explored how to access layer options. We then had a look at object transparency and blend modes. From a page geometry perspective, we worked with duplicate page elements, working with libraries and multi-frame grids. We closed out the chapter by arranging object hierarchies and embedding inline graphics in text objects.

In the next chapter, we will apply transparency and effects to content to create that winning design. The chapter's focus is on taking advantage of these powerful tools in InDesign to help create compelling content for a UI experience.

Level: Intermediate

Transparency and Effects: Part 1

In *Chapter 6*, we created a four-page brochure for print. Let's quickly recap what we covered there. We applied color to page elements, utilizing process and spot palettes. We set up multi-frame grid systems. This is a common thread throughout this book as it helps facilitate accurate placement of content, be it for print or digital delivery. We learned how to place multiple file formats. We touched on object transparency and blend modes. We'll discuss these in more detail in this chapter. Finally, we looked at arranging object hierarchies and embedding inline graphics in text frames.

In the next two chapters, we'll explore transparency, blend modes, and effects in detail. Now that we have a good grasp of working with text, graphic objects, and imported assets, we have the opportunity to explore how we can use InDesign effects to achieve professional design outcomes. We'll do so by designing a user interface (UI) for a heads-up display. While this is not typically created in InDesign. Let's see how far we can push the creative envelope with InDesign.

In this UI design, we'll create multi-layered backgrounds. We'll then work with parts of drawn objects, and apply 3D effects such as bevels, embossing, inner/outer shadows, and glows. We'll then seamlessly blend the design elements on page by exploring basic, directional, and radial feather effects. We'll also look at the satin effect to create additional visual interest. To truly have the design come together, we'll incorporate blending modes and transparency.

*Figure 7.1: The completed UI design project
(The image is intended as a visual reference; the textual information is not essential.)*

Figure 7.1 shows the completed futuristic UI design. As you can see, there is a high level of complexity and design options one can achieve with InDesign. We will recreate this artwork from the ground up. Since we've covered a number of the concepts in the design, such as drawing basic shapes, we've pre-created those elements in an InDesign library to to speed up our workflow.

These are the main topics we will cover in this chapter:

- Adjusting the opacity of design elements
- Working with object blend modes

- Using InDesign effects
- Applying multiple effects to different object properties
- Effects and output

You can find the relevant projects/examples for this chapter here: https://packt.link/a19oQ

Exploring the completed project and resources

By now, you should be quite comfortable with how this book is layed out. It is practical and hands-on. Explore the concepts you read about by downloading the files referred to in this project and following along. These example files can be downloaded from https://packt.link/a19oQ.

1. Open the completed project by choosing **File** menu | **Open**. Navigate to the Chapter 7&8 Transparency and Effects Example Files folder. Open the file named Try it yourself 7 - 01 Try it yourself 7 - 01 UI Design Complete.indd. If you are presented with a missing fonts warning, please click **Activate**. InDesign will automatically install any missing fonts.

2. Let's explore the project and become familiar with the various elements. This is a single-page digital project that uses a common screen form factor of 1920 px by 1080 px.

3. We'll reset the workspace so that it mimics the screenshots shown in the chapter as closely as possible. Choose the **Window** menu | **Workspace** | **[Essentials]**. Confirm that **[Essentials]** has a checkmark to its left. Then choose the **Window** menu once more and select **Reset Essentials**.

4. Access the **Layers** panel from the **Window** menu. As you can see, the various elements in the design have been named. The layer we will be working on is called **Artwork**. Click on the selection widget alongside any object name. That object will be highlighted on the page.

5. You can also click the **Visibility** icon 👁 (*eye icon*) to the right of the chosen object name to hide it. Click in the same location a second time to bring the eyeball back and make the object visible once more.

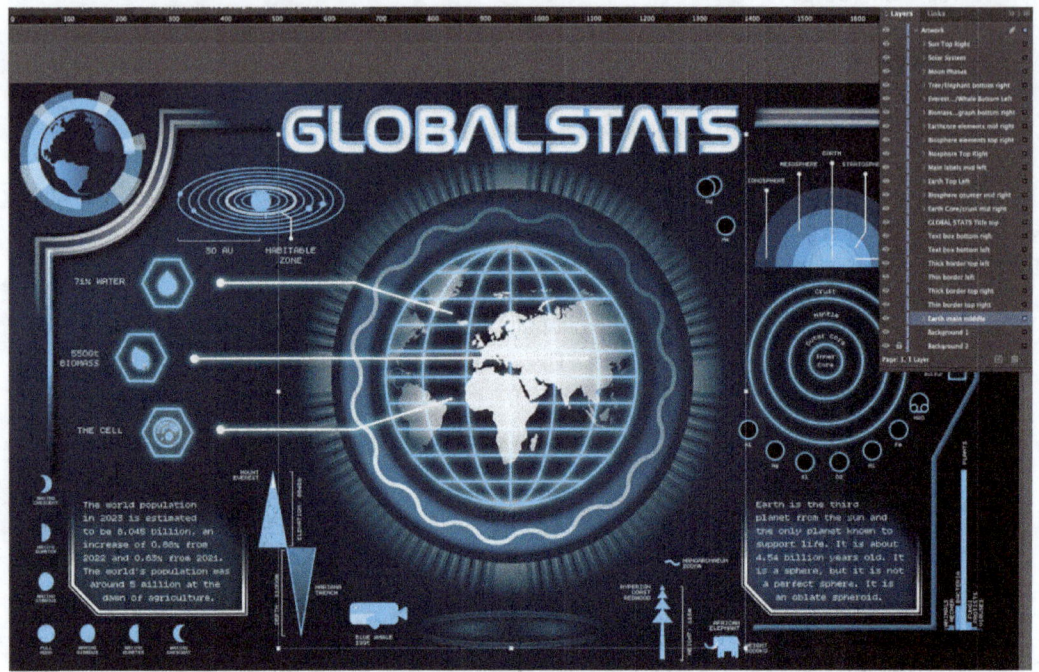

Figure 7.2: The Layers panel with the main Earth element selected (The image is intended as a visual reference; the textual information is not essential.)

6. Take some time to familiarize yourself with the design by clicking through the various design elements.
7. When done, please close the document by choosing **File Menu | Close**. If you are prompted to save the file, choose **Don't Save**.

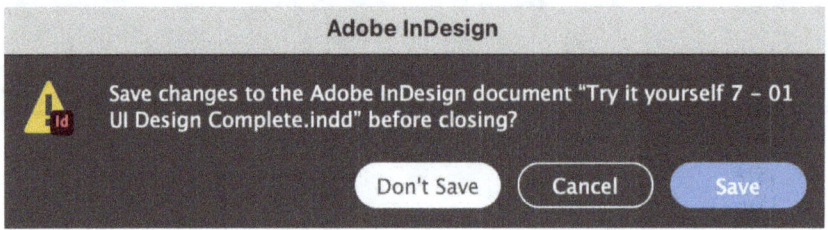

Figure 7.3: Choose Don't Save from the Save dialog box

In the next section, we'll set up our InDesign project. We'll build the design framework by setting up the page, choosing the page units, and setting up the grid system for our design.

Getting started

Let's get going by setting up our document. We'll set up a single-page document with the type area, columns, and a grid system that will help guide our design placement and composition. Follow these steps:

1. Launch InDesign. From the top left of the InDesign home screen, choose **New File**. In the resultant **New Document** dialog, choose the **Mobile** category of presets.

2. Click the **View All Presets +** button. Then select **Google Pixel/Pixel 2**. This preset gives us a good basis to work from. Be sure not to type Return or Enter, as this will accept the current changes and close the **New Document** dialog. Please make the following changes:

    A. Check the **Preview** checkbox found at the bottom left of the dialog. By doing so, we'll get real-time visual feedback as we tweak the document parameters.

    B. Let's name our document. We'll call it UI Design. Type the name in the text input area at the top right of the dialog box. This is just below **PRESET DETAILS**.

    C. Under **Orientation**, choose **Landscape**.

    D. Ensure that **Width** is **1920 px** and **Height** is **1080 px**.

    E. Uncheck the **Primary Text Frame** checkbox.

    F. We will work with one column for this project.

    G. Under **Margins**, ensure the chain-link icon is engaged. This allows us to make changes to one value, and all values update accordingly.

    H. Set the **Top** value to **72 px**, then press the *Tab* key to see the changes ripple through.

3. Click the **Create** button.

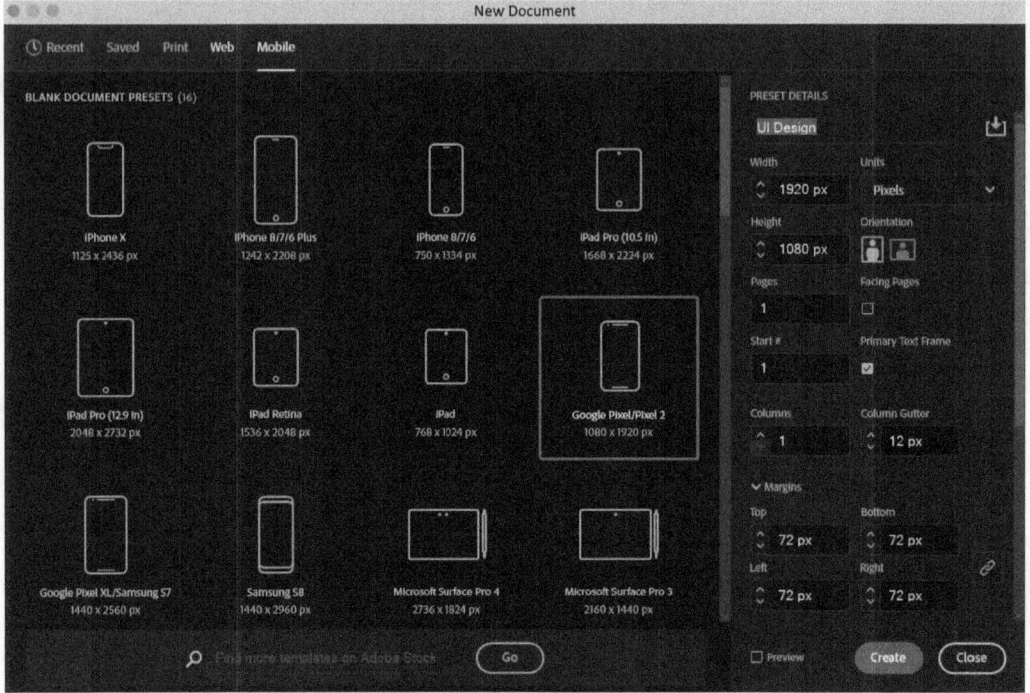

Figure 7.4: The document parameters for our project
(The image is intended as a visual reference; the textual information is not essential.)

With our document set up and ready to go, we'll move on to adding grids and guidelines to assist with the alignment and placement of design elements next.

Setting up guides and grids

A grid system, I'm sure you'll agree, is super valuable in keeping a professional-level alignment protocol for any design project. We'll set up a rule-of-thirds grid system to help us along with this process. This will be done by using the **Create Guides** command. It's worth remembering that grid systems are meant to guide the design. This means that you have creative license to step outside its bounds where you deem appropriate. Follow these steps:

1. Head to the **Layout** menu and choose **Create Guides**.
2. Ensure that the **Preview** checkbox is checked so we can see changes as we make them.

3. Set the number of **Rows** and **Columns** to 3 and double the **Gutter** value from 12 px to 24 px.
4. Under **Options** and **Fit Guides to**, choose the **Margins** radio button.
5. Leave the **Remove Existing Ruler Guides** checkbox unchecked. You can verify your settings by referring to *Figure 7.5*:

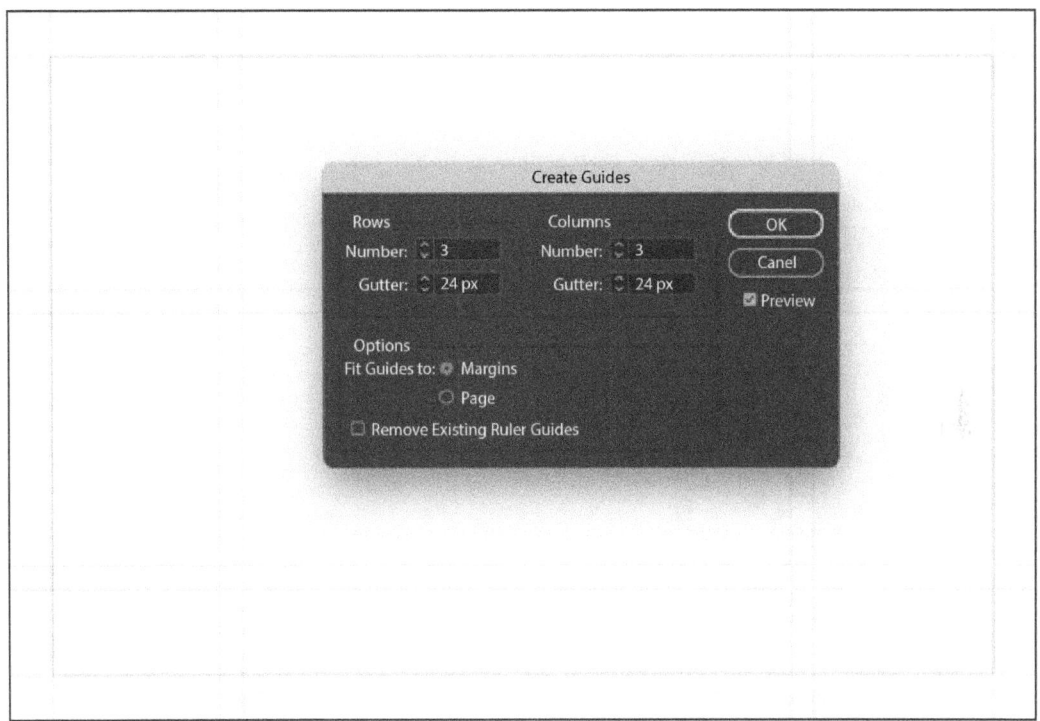

Figure 7.5: The rule-of-thirds grid setup

Setting up midpoint guides

To complete our grid setup, we'll add two guidelines in the center of the page. You can do this manually, but it is way more efficient and accurate using the **Create Guides** command.

1. Choose the **Layout** menu | **Create Guides**.
2. Confirm that **Preview** is checked.
3. Set the number of **Rows** and **Columns** to 2 and set the **Gutter** value to 0 px.
4. Under **Options**, and **Fit Guides to**, click the **Margins** radio button once more.

5. **Remove Existing Ruler Guides** should remain unchecked. You should see two additional guides denoting the horizontal and vertical midpoint. See *Figure 7.6*.

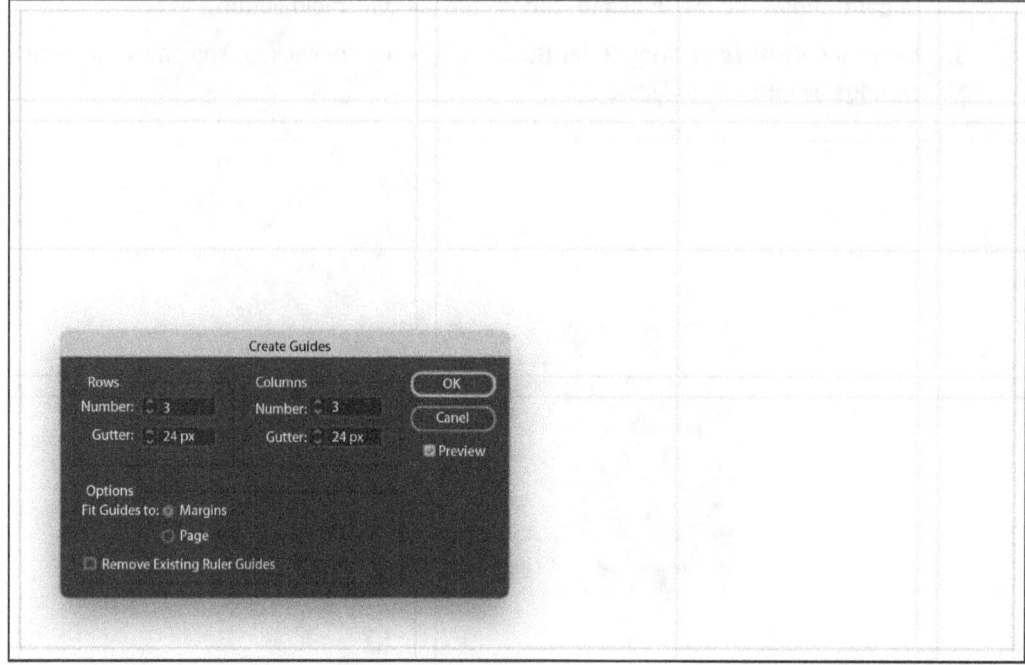

Figure 7.6: Additional ruler guides delineating the center of the page

With our grid system in place, we're ready to start building out our design. The first task will be to set up our background objects to help ground our design. Before we do that, let's save our document. Choose **File | Save**. Save the file to a location of your choice. Click **Save**.

To recap, we looked at the completed design and set up a new document with the appropriate dimensions, type area, and core grid system. We're now ready to start designing. We'll start with the background elements.

Creating the background

OK, we're good to begin our design journey. We'll create a background with a twist. Since we're exploring opacity and effects, we'll overlay two rectangles that will make up our background.

Drawing and coloring the background

The following steps demonstrate the drawing and accurate placement of a rectangle object that will form the basis of our background:

1. Choose the **Rectangle Tool** (*M*).
2. Draw a rectangle from the top-left corner of the page to the bottom right. You can tweak the values of the rectangle on the **Properties** panel, under the **Transform** subsection.

    A. Select the top-left reference point from the proxy.

    B. The values for **X** and **Y** should be 0 px. This means the object's top-left point will begin where the page begins.

    C. The value for **W** (width) is 1920 px and **H** (height) is 1080 px.

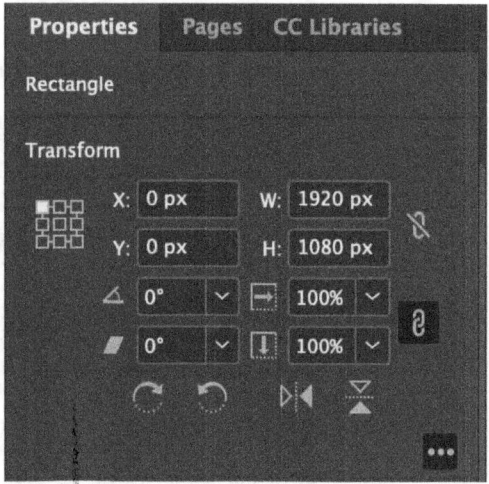

Figure 7.7: The values for the background rectangle

Applying a custom gradient

With the geometry sorted, we'll make changes to the rectangle fill and stroke properties. We'll create a dark blue to black radial gradient with no stroke properties.

1. Do the following under the **Appearance** sub section of the **Properties** panel:

    A. Click the **Fill** color chip. From the flyout, choose the **Gradient** option.

    B. Choose **Apply to Frame**. This means the gradient applies to the object in its entirety.

    C. Choose **Radial** from the **Type** dropdown.

    D. Click on the white **gradient stop**.

    E. Choose the flyout menu and ensure you are working in **RGB**.

    F. Set the stop values to **R = 0, G = 20, B = 25**.

    G. Select the black **gradient stop** on the far right.

    H. Set its values to **R = 0, G = 0, B = 0**.

    I. Now click around just below the gradient ribbon, about a quarter of the distance away from the left gradient stop. A new stop will be placed at the point you clicked.

    J. Set the location to **25%**.

    K. Click this newly added stop and change its values to **R = 0, G = 50, B = 70**.

Figure 7.8: A snapshot of the gradient settings

Duplicating the background

The gradient we created is perfect for highlighting our focal point object. We'll now duplicate the gradient object and apply additional changes such as adjusting the gradient position and applying a satin effect to further enhance our background. Follow these steps:

1. Select the **gradient** object using the **Selection** tool (*V + Esc*) from the Toolbox.
2. Choose **Edit | Copy**, then select **Edit | Paste in Place**.
3. To make adjustments to the gradient we copied, follow these steps:

   A. Select the **Gradient Swatch** tool (**G**) from the Toolbox.

   B. Drag a gradient path that starts at the top left and ends toward the bottom right of the middle design unit.

   C. Feel free to experiment and settle on a different gradient arrangement if you wish.

4. Now for the easy bit. Ensure that the object has no stroke by choosing the **Stroke** color chip on the **Properties** panel. Then choose **None** from the flyout menu.

> **Quick tip**
> It's worth remembering that if you draw long gradient directional lines, it results in smooth color gradations, whereas shorter ones result in more immediate color gradations.

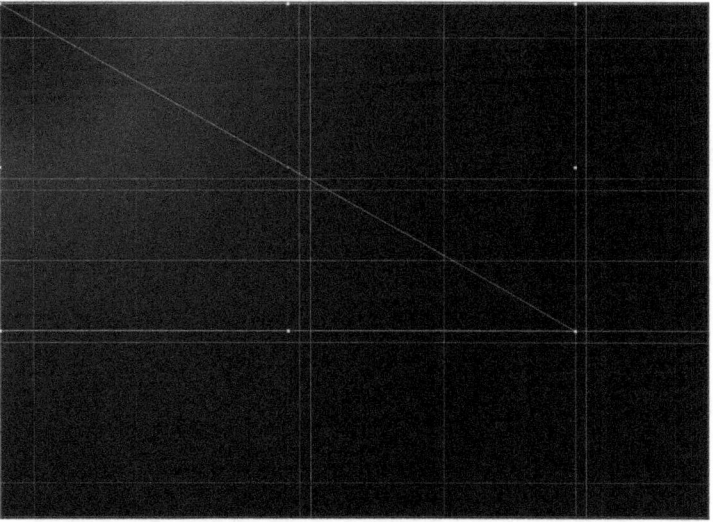

Figure 7.9: The indicative line direction and length for the second gradient

At this point, the duplicate background rectangle obscures the first rectangle we drew. We'll resolve this in the steps that follow.

Applying a satin effect

The gradient highlight color for our duplicate copy has moved toward the top left of the object. To add dynamism to our gradient, we'll apply a satin effect and blending mode to the object.

1. Let's organize and label our artwork before we continue.
2. Access the **Layers** panel.
3. Click-pause-click the layer named **Layer 1** and change the layer name to Artwork.
4. Click the arrow to the left of the **Artwork** layer. Click the **Select Item** icon ▫ for the top background rectangle. It is found to the right of the object name on the **Layers** panel.
5. Click-pause-click the top rectangle named **<rectangle>**. Rename it to Background 2.
6. Repeat the process for the bottom rectangle. Change its name to Background 1.
7. Select the duplicate (top) background rectangle (**Background 2**).
8. Choose **Edit** menu | **Effects**.
9. Identify and click the *fx* icon ▫ toward the bottom right of the panel. Choose **Satin**.
10. Observe that there is a checkmark alongside the **Satin** effect on the left of the resultant **Effects** dialog box.
11. Click on the name **Satin** to access the satin effect's parameters.

> **Caution**
> Do not click the checkbox as this will disable the effect. If you do this in error, simply enable the checkbox again by clicking it a second time.

12. Ensure that the **Preview** checkbox is checked, then make the following changes for the **Satin** effect:

    A. Under **Structure**, change **Mode** to **Lighten**.
    B. Click the color swatch alongside the mode drop-down list, choose **[Paper]** from the **Effect** color dialog that appears, and click **OK**.
    C. Set **Opacity** to 100%.
    D. **Angle** should be 120°.
    E. Change the **Distance** value to 5 px.

F. The **Size** value should be 100 px.

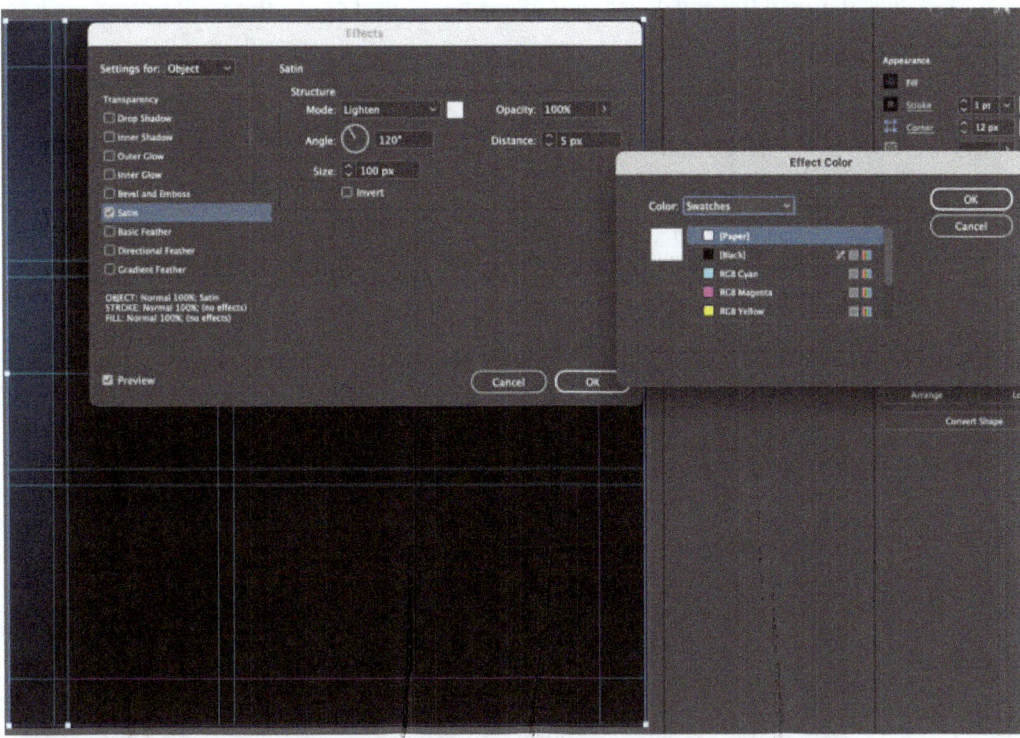

Figure 7.10: The Satin effect applied to Background 2. Also visible are the Effects and Effect Color dialog boxes

You should be relatively comfortable with changing the labels of objects, layers, as well as applying and tweaking effects now. Our next task is to rearrange the object hierarchy.

Rearranging objects and applying blend modes

You'll recall that we created the original background object with the specific intent of having the gradient in the center of the object. It is currently being obscured by the copy we made. We'll swap the order of these objects and change the blend modes so the colors between the two background objects interact to give a rich fusion of color.

1. Head to the **Layers** panel.
2. Select **Background 1** and drag it above **Background 2**. The objects have now been swapped in the hierarchy. You will notice that the original center gradient is visible once more.

3. Select **Background 1** with the **Selection** tool (*V + Esc*).
4. Click the word **Opacity** under the **Appearance** subset on the **Properties** panel.
5. Choose **Lighten** from the flyout. The colors between the two objects can now merge due to the blend mode change.
6. Select both background objects and choose the **Object** menu | **Group**. Then rename the newly created **<group>** object to Background on the **Layers** panel.
7. We'll lock the **background** group, so we don't inadvertently move or edit it. Click between the visibility eyeball and the layer color strip on the **Layers** panel. A lock icon appears.

Feel free to experiment with different blend modes and effects. When you are done, choose **File | Save**.

Figure 7.11: The completed background object group

Let's have a look back at our journey thus far. We created and duplicated objects, applied gradients, made adjustments to those gradients, applied a **Satin** effect, changed blend modes, and arranged, labeled, and locked objects. We will now create the main graphic element in our design.

Creating the primary user interface graphic

With the background object completed, we can turn our attention to the individual design elements. Many of the elements use the fundamental building blocks and basic shapes we've already covered in earlier chapters.

Creating the primary user interface graphic 199

Figure 7.12: A snapshot of the main UI element against the background

We've created a library of elements to speed things up and avoid repetition. In this next section, we will be working with strokes and stroke properties, transparency, the gradient feather, and outer glow effects.

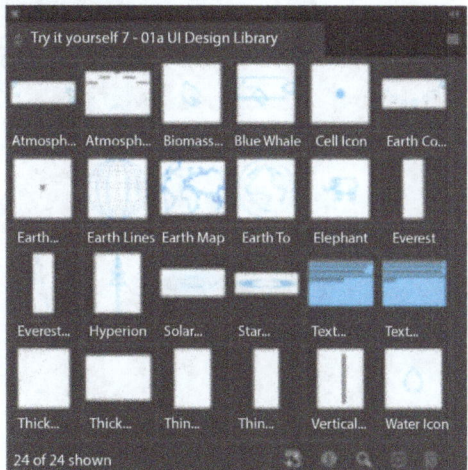

Figure 7.13: A view of the library we will use for this project

This section explores the creation of the primary graphic elements, creating borders, applying text, and other elements. As we tackle each topic, you'll have an opportunity to fully explore transparency, blend modes, and effects that InDesign has to offer.

Working with InDesign libraries

Libraries are a great way to organize and reuse the graphics, text, and other design elements that are most often used in InDesign. A library opens as a panel but is saved like any regular InDesign file with one exception. Its file extension differs, which helps distinguish it as a library. The InDesign library file extension is .indl, as opposed to the regular .indd InDesign document file extension.

Follow these steps to open the InDesign library:

1. Open the library project by choosing **File | Open**. Navigate to the Chapter 7&8 Transparency and Effects Example Files folder. Open the library file named Try it yourself 7 - 01a UI Design Library.indl. The library will open in InDesign as a floating panel.
2. Choose **Large Thumbnail View** from the panel library panel menu.

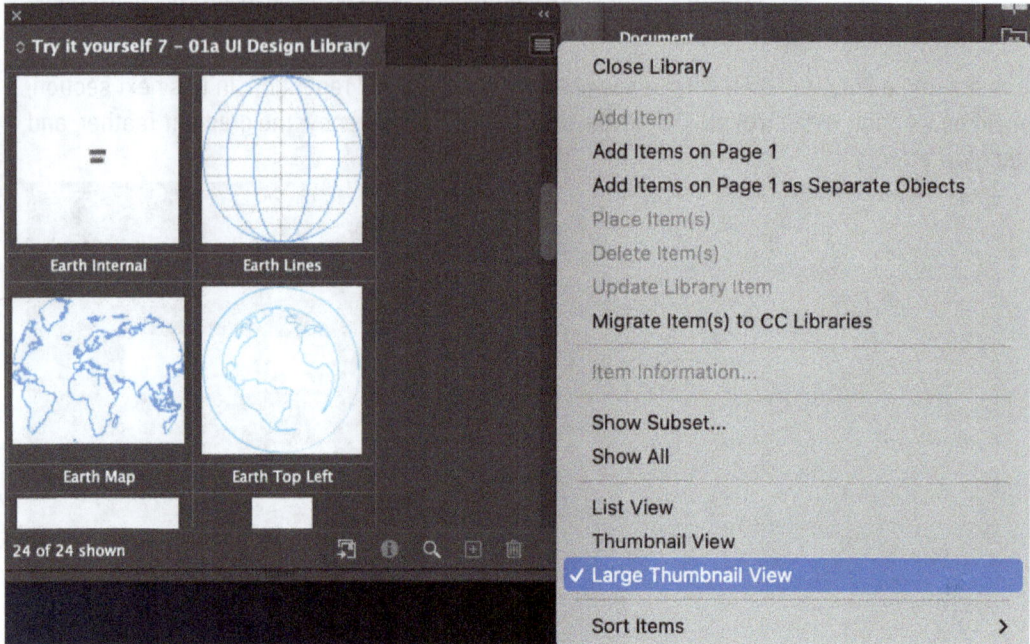

Figure 7.14: The panel menu with viewing options

3. Select the **Earth Lines** element and drag it from the library onto the page.
4. Align the **Earth Lines** object with the center of the page with **Align to page** from the **Properties** panel. Then click the **Align horizontal** and **Align vertical** center icons.

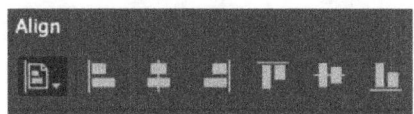

Figure 7.15: The Align controls with Align to page enabled

5. This is a series of ovals and lines. Make the following adjustments to the object under the **Appearance** subset on the **Properties** panel:

   A. Set the stroke width to 4 pt.
   B. Click the **Stroke color** swatch.
   C. Choose the **Swatches** icon from the flyout.
   D. Let's delete unwanted swatches. Click the flyout panel menu and choose **Select All Unused**.
   E. Click the **Bin** icon to delete the unwanted swatches.
   F. We'll now import color swatches from the completed project. Click the **Swatches** panel menu and choose **Load Swatches**.
   G. Locate the Chapter 7&8 Transparency and Effects Example Files folder and choose Try it yourself 7 - 01 UI Design Complete.indd.
   H. The swatches will now appear in the panel. Click the swatch labeled **Blue**. The lines will turn a bright blue color.

Having changed the color properties of the artwork, we'll apply an **Outer Glow** effect next to differentiate it from the background.

Adding an Outer Glow effect

The **Outer Glow** effect extends off the outer edges of artwork to create a soft halo along an object's geometry. It works best on dark backgrounds.

1. With the **Earth Lines** element selected, choose the *fx* icon and choose **Outer Glow** from the list.

2. Choose the following settings in the **Effects** panel:

    A. **Mode**: **Screen**

    B. **Colour**: **White**

    C. **Opacity**: **100%**

    D. **Size**: **15 px**

    E. **Spread**: **5 px**

3. Click **OK** to accept the changes. Remember to periodically save your work by choosing **File | Save**.

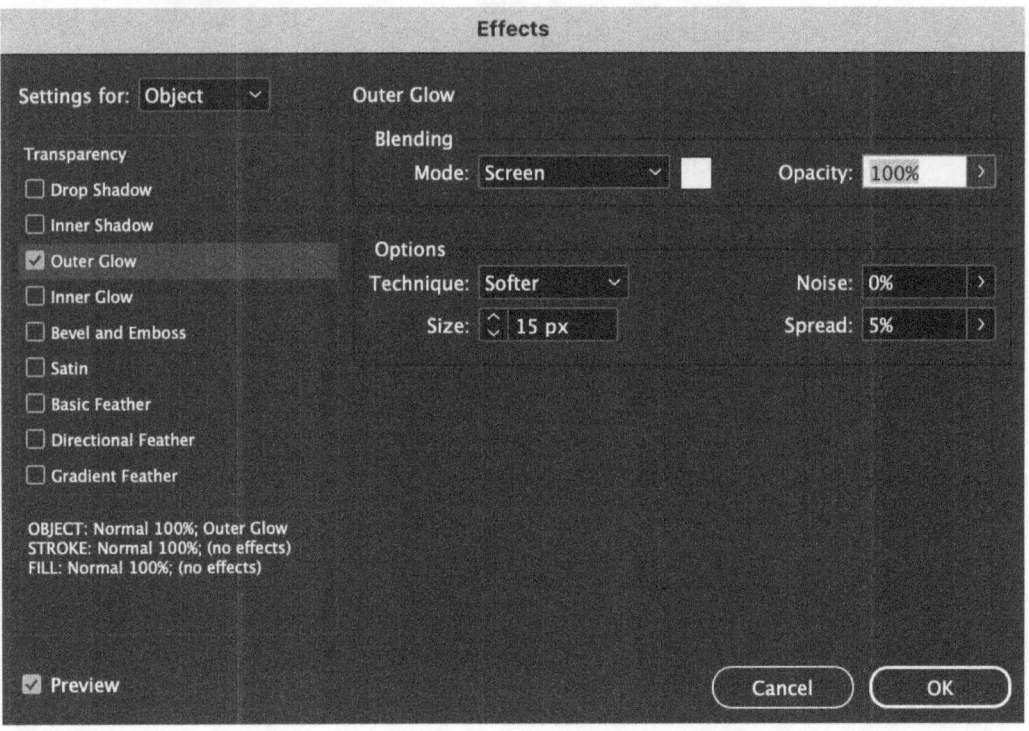

Figure 7.16: The Outer Glow effect settings

Working with object styles

To save time, you can save complex object properties like what we just worked on as an object style. Object styles can be used to quickly format objects with a variety of properties. We'll be using this feature multiple times in this design instead of retracing steps multiple times. All of the object properties have been captured in an object style named **4pt Blue Outer Glow**. This is brought in with the library we opened earlier. When we next need to apply these properties, we'll be able to do so in a single-click operation.

1. Access the **Object Styles** panel by choosing **Window | Object Styles**.
2. You'll see that we have several styles that have been created for different elements of the artwork. Since we've already worked with and mastered styles, there's no need to create a new one at this point.
3. Close the **Object Styles** panel for now. We'll work with it later.

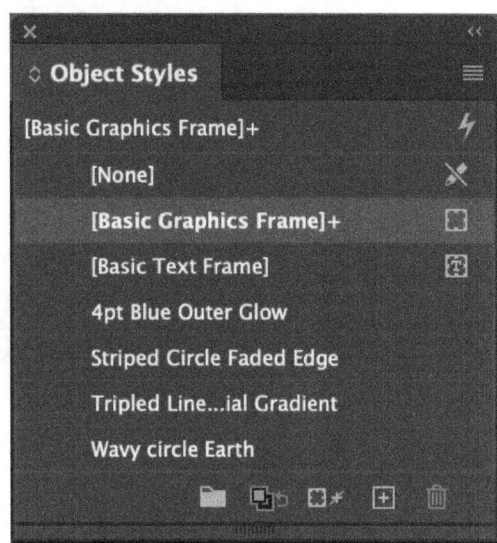

Figure 7.17: The Object Styles panel

Placing and formatting the world map

We'll bring in the world map next. To make it fit with the latitude and longitude lines, we'll adjust its fill color and opacity and finish off with a gradient feather effect.

1. Access the object named **Earth Map** in the library and drag it onto the page.

Figure 7.18: The document library with the Earth Map object selected

2. Swap the fill and stroke properties by clicking the **Swap fill** icon and **Stroke** icon in the Toolbox. It is found just above the **Fill** and **Stroke** swatches. The object should now have a white fill with no outline.

3. *Shift*-select the **Earth Lines** object. Release the *Shift* key and click it a second time to make it a key object.

4. Then click the **Align horizontal centers** and **Align vertical centers** icons on the **Properties** panel.

5. Select just the **Earth Map** object and nudge it into place using the up arrow key on the keyboard.

Creating the primary user interface graphic   205

6. Under the **Appearance** subset on the **Properties** panel, click the *fx* icon and select **Gradient Feather**.

7. Choose the following settings in the **Effects** dialog box that comes up:

   A. Ensure that **Preview** is enabled.

   B. Click the gradient midpoint found above the horizontal gradient ramp and set its location value to 85%. This will result in a more acute drop-off in the object opacity.

   C. Under **Options**, change the gradient type to **Radial**.

   D. Click **Transparency** on the list to the right of the dialog.

   E. Set **Mode** to **Screen** and **Opacity** to **70%**.

   F. Click **OK** to accept the changes and close the dialog.

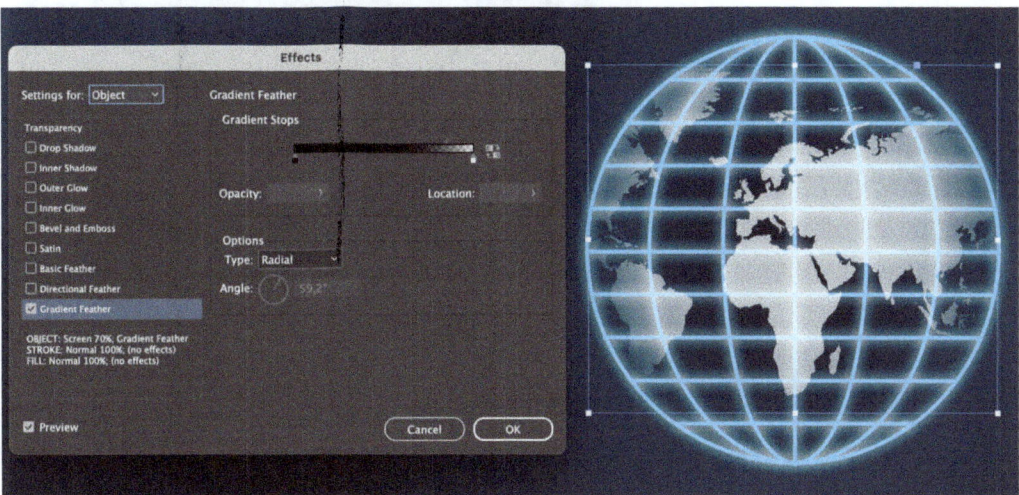

Figure 7.19: The Earth design element with the Gradient Feather settings visible

Let's rename group these elements. To do that, follow these steps:

1. Rename the map object from its current name of **<compound path>** to Map Main. Do this by click-pause-clicking the object on the **Layers** panel.

2. To keep things manageable, it makes sense to group the lines with the map. Select both the **Map Main** object and the **Earth Lat/Long Lines** group. Choose **Object | Group**.

3. The grouped object will have a default name of <group>. Let's rename it to Map Main Middle.

Creating the border elements

The border elements that surround the earth object are a series of concentric circles with various weights, effects, transparencies, and styles applied. We'll create these one at a time, so you have an idea of how they build up to the final design.

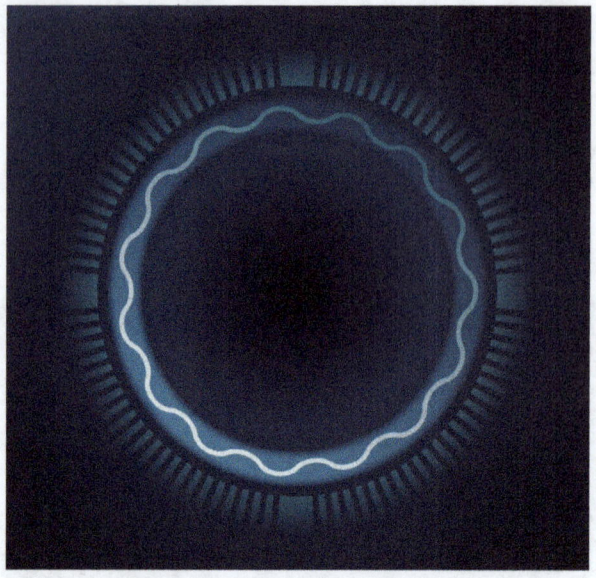

Figure 7.20: A preview of the series of outlines in this task

1. Select the **Ellipse** tool (**L**) from the Toolbox.
2. Draw a circle of any size by dragging anywhere on the page with the *Shift* key engaged.
3. Set the **W** and **H** values to **690 px** on the **Properties** panel.
4. Align the just-drawn circle to the center of the page using the **Align horizontal** and **Align vertical center** commands.
5. Make the following changes on the **Properties** panel:

   A. Ensure the stroke color is **[Paper]**.
   B. Set the stroke weight to **60 pt**.
   C. Click the word **Stroke** to open the **Stroke Properties** flyout. Click the word **Stroke** to open the **Stroke Properties** flyout. Click the stroke type dropdown and choose **Dashed** from the list.
   D. Click the word **Stroke** to open the **Stroke Properties** flyout and choose **Align Stroke to Outside** ( ) to push the stroke away from the earth object.

E. Click **Opacity** and set **Mode** to **Screen** and **Opacity** to **50%**.

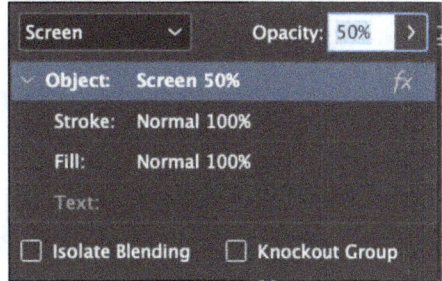

Figure 7.21: The object transparency and blend mode updated

F. Click the *fx* icon ![fx] and set a Gradient Feather effect up as follows:
G. Under **Type**, choose **Radial**.
H. Then move the gradient midpoint ◇ found above the horizontal gradient ramp and set its location value to **75%**.
I. Set the location of the white gradient stop on the right to **87%**.

Figure 7.22: The artwork with the outline

6. Rename the border circle object. Click-pause-click the object named **<circle>** on the **Layers** panel. It will be the topmost element. Change its name to Outer Border 1.

We'll add extra depth to our artwork by working with a duplicate in the next series of steps.

Duplicating and adjusting element properties

The border element can now be duplicated and offset on its rotation axis to create additional depth in the artwork.

1. Select the **Outer Border 1** circle object.
2. Choose **Edit** | **Copy** and **Edit** | **Paste in Place**. This will position the copy directly on top of the original. You will notice that the copy interacts with the original, resulting in a brighter outcome.
3. Make the following changes on the **Properties** panel:

    A. Under the **Transform** subset, ensure that the middle reference point is selected.

    B. Change **Rotation Angle** to **6°**.

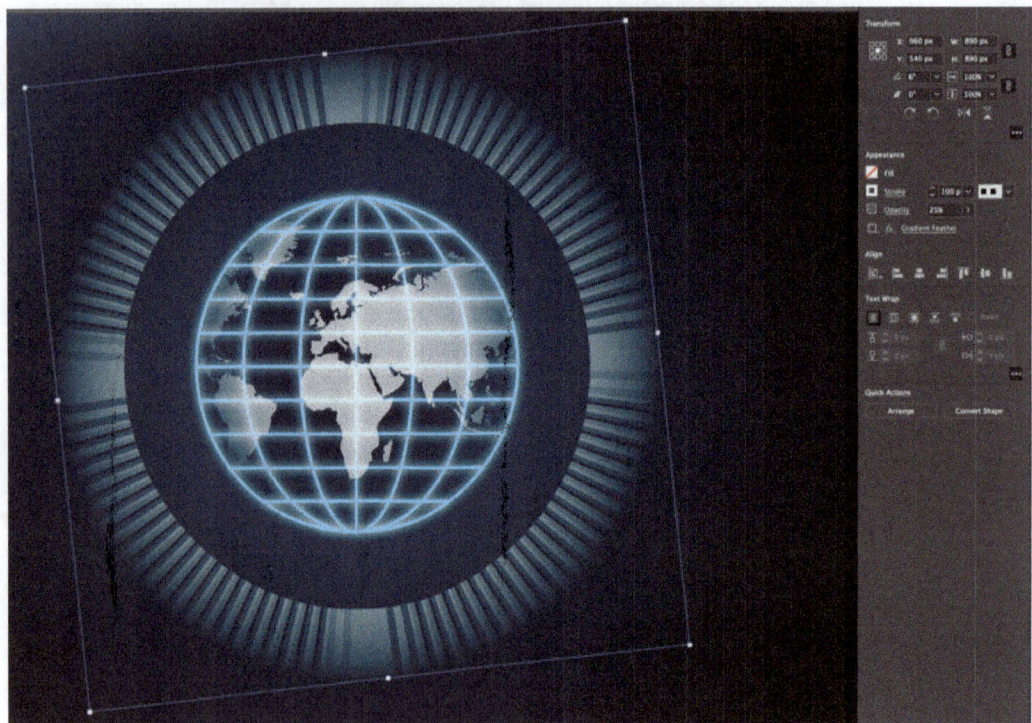

Figure 7.23: The artwork showing the completed outer borders and the Properties panel settings for the duplicate circle object

4. Rename the object to Outer Border 2 by click-pause-clicking the duplicate object on the **Layers** panel.
5. Select both border objects and group them by choosing **Object | Group**.
6. Rename the group object to Outer Border.
7. With the **Outer Border** object still selected, confirm the middle transform control is selected on the **Properties** panel and change the **W** and **H** values to **810 px**.

With the outer border complete, we can turn our attention to the two inner borders, which will complete the primary focal point design element.

Applying multiple feather effects to elements

The inner border is made up of a circle that has multiple gradient effects applied. A copy lies on top of it. They copy has a wavy line style applied to it.

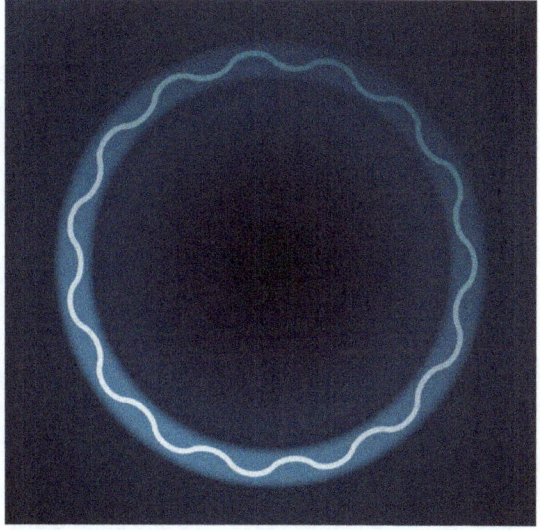

Figure 7.24: The two inner borders that we'll be creating next

Figure 7.24 illustrates how you can use multiple effects and overlapping elements to deliver compelling design results. Follow these steps:

1. Select the **Ellipse** tool (**L**) from the toolbox.
2. Draw a circle of any size by dragging anywhere on the page with the *Shift* key engaged.
3. Set the **W** and **H** values to **596 px** on the **Properties** panel.

4. Align it to the center of the page using the **Align horizontal** and **Align vertical center** commands on the **Properties** panel. Make sure that the **Align to page** option is chosen.

Figure 7.25: The Align to page option is the leftmost icon

5. Make the following changes on the **Properties** panel:

    A. Under the **Appearance** subset, set the fill to **[None]**.
    B. Change the stroke color to **Blue**.
    C. Set the stroke weight to **60 pt**.
    D. Click the stroke type dropdown and choose **Solid** from the list.
    E. Click **Opacity** and set **Mode** to **Screen** and **Opacity** to **50%**.

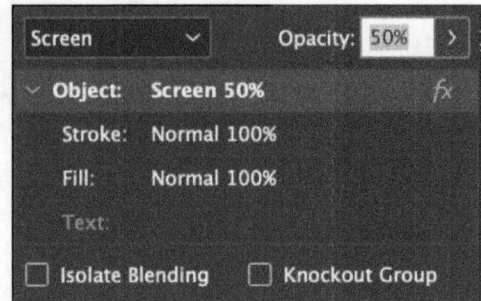

Figure 7.26: The object mode and Opacity settings

    F. Click the *fx* icon and set the effects up as follows:
    G. Choose **Basic Feather**.
    H. Set the **Feather** value to **15 px**.
    I. Leave the rest of the values as the default.
    J. Now apply **Gradient Feather** by enabling its checkbox.
    K. Set it to **Linear**.
    L. Change **Angle** to **60°**.
    M. Click **OK**.

6. Rename the object to Inner Border Feather on the **Layers** panel.

Figure 7.27: The artwork showing the inner border and the feather settings

With this element complete, we'll create a copy of it in the next step and change its style to a wavy line.

Varying stroke styles

The inner border has an additional copy lying on top of the **Feather** object. This copy has a wavy line style applied to it. Follow these steps to create it:

1. Select the inner **Border Feather** circle object.
2. Choose **Edit** | **Copy and Edit** | **Paste in Place**. This will position the copy directly on top of the original. You will notice that the copy interacts with the original, resulting in a brighter outcome.

3. Make the following changes on the **Properties** panel:

    A. Change the stroke color to **[Paper]**.
    B. Set the stroke weight to **30 pt**.
    C. Click the stroke type dropdown and choose **Wavy** from the list.
    D. The opacity should be 100%.
    E. Click **Multiple Effects Applied** to open the **Effects** dialog box.
    F. Uncheck the **Basic Feather** checkbox.
    G. Click **OK**.

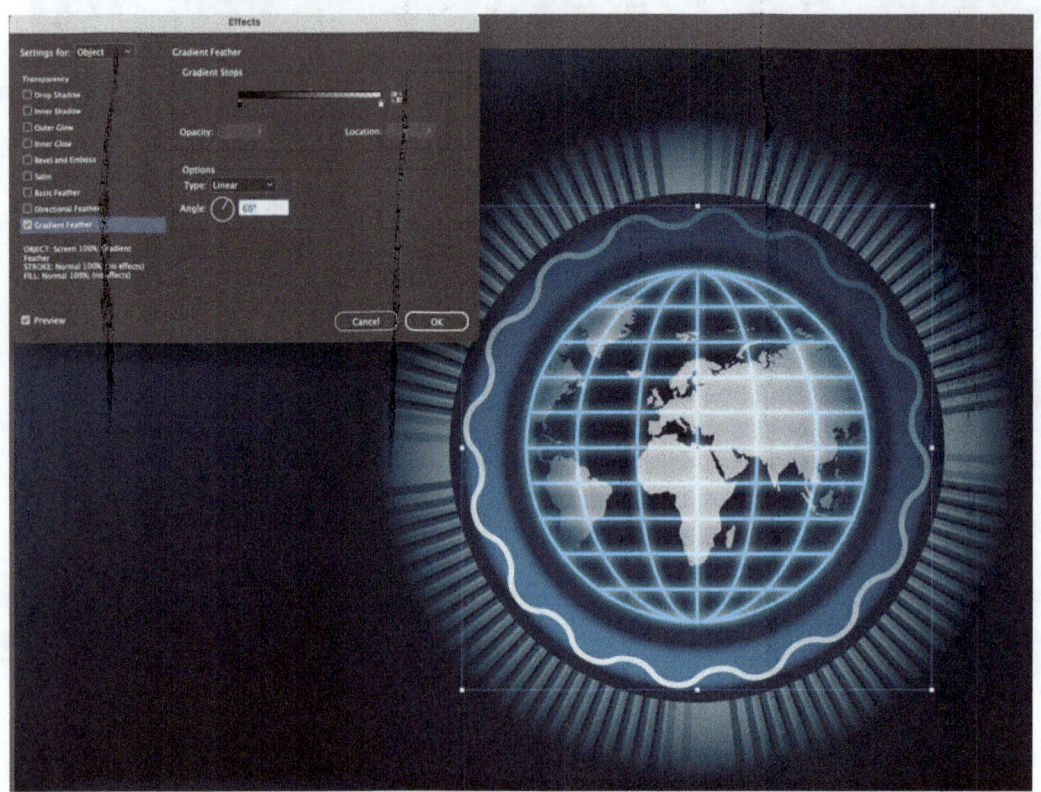

Figure 7.28: The artwork showing the wavy and Effects settings are visible for easy reference

4. Select both inner border objects and group them by choosing **Object | Group**.
5. Rename the group object to Inner Border.

The border elements are complete. We'll now move these border elements into the **Map Main Middle** group.

Moving elements between groups and subgroups

Generally, it's a good idea to name elements as you progress in your designs for easy identification or if they are handed over to another designer. We'll consolidate the borders into the **Map Main Middle** group.

1. Select the **Inner Border** group by clicking it with the **Selection** tool.
2. Twirl open the **Map Main Middle** element on the **Layers** panel.
3. Drag the **Inner Border** element into the **Map Main Middle** object and place it below the **Earth Lat/Long Lines** object.
4. Repeat the process for the **Outer Border** group by clicking it with the **Selection** tool.
5. Drag it into the **Map Main Middle** object and place it below the **Inner Border** object.
6. Lock the **Map Main Middle** object, so you don't inadvertently make changes to it.
7. Save your work at this point.

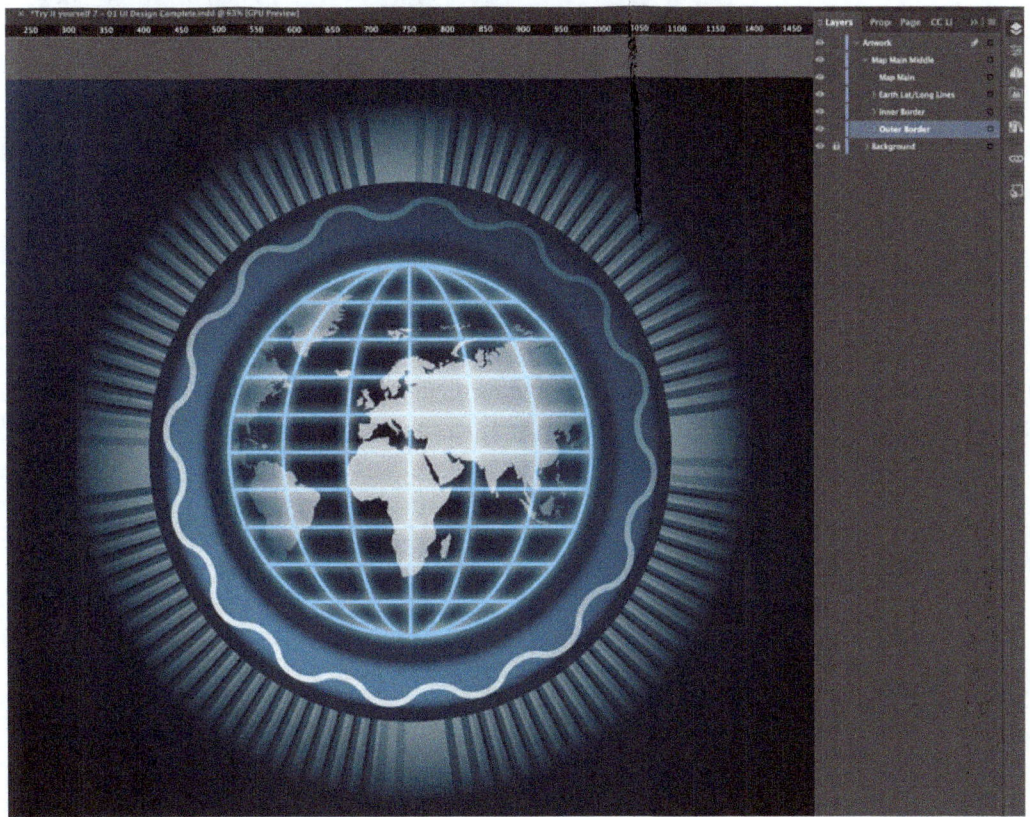

Figure 7.29: The completed Main Earth element with the Layers panel is visible, showing the hierarchy of objects

This completes the main **Earth** element design. We'll continue our exploration by creating the **Oval** halo object found below the **Earth** element next. We have explored transparency, blend modes, feathers, and stroke styles thus far. We'll use these skills to create the halo elements found below the **Earth** object.

Working with ovals and polygons

To visually nest the **Earth** object onto the canvas, we'll create a dual object halo beneath it. A star and oval will be used for this task. We'll then apply transparency, blend modes, and effects to finesse their look and have them gel with the rest of the design.

Figure 7.30: The design with the completed dual objects beneath

In this next section, we will design the halo shadow elements found beneath the main **Earth** design element.

1. Drag the object named **Starburst Bottom** onto the page from **01a UI Design Library**. If you have closed it, choose **File** menu | **Open** and reopen it from the Chapter 7_8 Apply Transparency and Effects files folder.

2. With the objects selected, make the following positional changes on the **Properties** panel:

    A. Under **Transform**, choose the middle reference point on the proxy. Set the **X** value to 960px and **Y** to 1010 px.

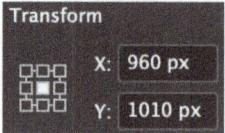

Figure 7.31: The reference point and x and y values

3. Deselect the objects by clicking on the **Pasteboard**.
4. Then select the **Oval**.
5. Make the following changes on the **Properties** panel:

   A. Change the stroke color to **[Paper]**.
   B. Set the stroke weight to **10 pt**.
   C. Click the stroke type dropdown and choose **Thick-Thin-Thick** from the list.
   D. The opacity should be **20%**.
   E. Change the blend mode to **Screen**.
   F. Click the *fx* icon and choose **Gradient Feather** from the drop-down list.
   G. Choose **Radial** under **Type**.
   H. Click **OK**.

6. Now select the Star object.
7. Make the following changes on the **Properties** panel:

   A. Set **Fill** to **[Paper]**.
   B. Choose **[None]** for the Stroke color.
   C. Make the object opacity **20%**.
   D. Choose **Screen** for the Blend mode.
   E. Click the *fx* icon and choose **Gradient Feather** from the drop-down list.

8. In the **Effects** dialog box that comes up, make the following changes:

   A. Under **Gradient Stops**, click the leftmost black stop and set **Opacity** to **0%**. The stop will turn white.
   B. Then click about halfway, just below the gradient bar. This action will add an additional stop at the location you clicked.
   C. Set the location to **50%**. Exactly halfway.
   D. Change its **Opacity** value to **100%**.
   E. Choose **Radial** under **Type**.
   F. Click **OK**.

9. Select the <oval> and <polygon> objects and choose **Object | Group**.
10. Then rename the <group> object to Earth Main Halo.
11. Drag this group into the **Map Main Middle** group on the **Layers** panel.

12. Lock the **Map Main Middle** group.
13. Save your work by choosing **File | Save**.

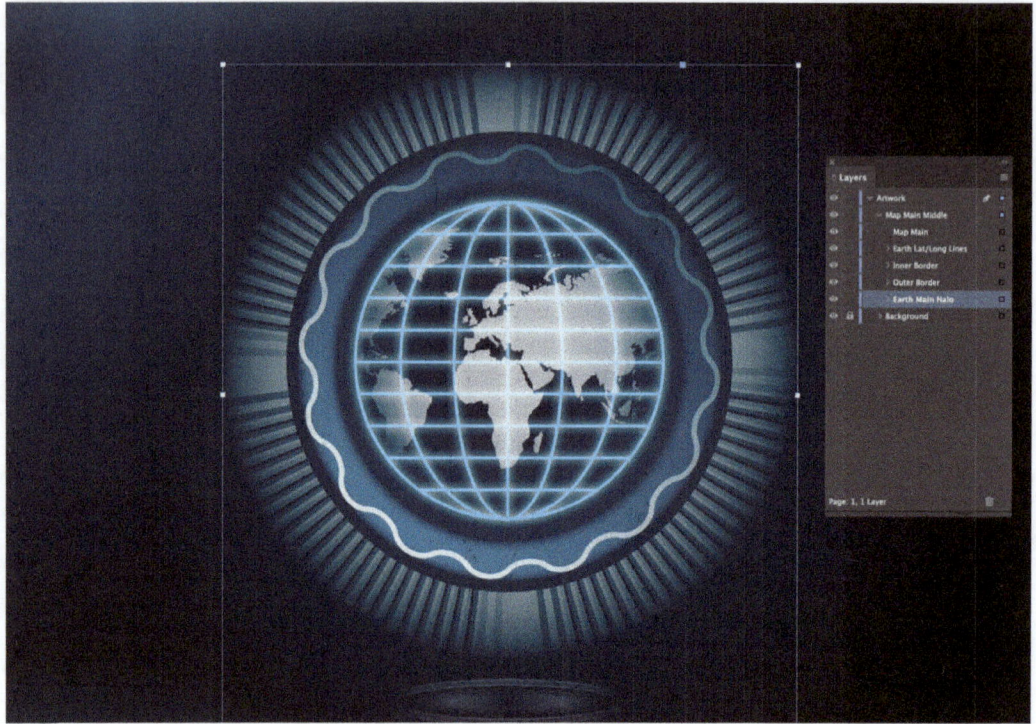

Figure 7.32: The completed halo and earth artwork with the layer hierarchy visible to the right

With that, we come to the end of the chapter. Remember, the fun continues in the next chapter, since this is a two chapter project.

Summary

In this chapter, we kickstarted the core elements of a UI design. We explored how to set up the document, by setting up guides and a grid system to help us design with ease and accuracy. We then created a multi-object background, to which we applied gradients, effects, and blend modes. Next, we created the primary user interface graphic. This gave us a great opportunity to work with InDesign libraries, explore additional effects, and create object styles. We closed out the chapter by creating and refining the properties of stroke objects.

The next chapter is a continuation of this one. We will create borders to frame our design, apply effects to typographic elements, make controlled changes to elements quickly and efficiently, and place elements with precision.

Level: Intermediate

Transparency and Effects: Part 2

In the previous chapter, we created the base elements of a user interface design. This chapter continues from where we left off. Let's recap what we covered in *Chapter 7*. After setting up the document and grid system, we created a multi-object background using gradients, effects, and blending modes. We also completed the primary user interface graphic. We worked with InDesign libraries, effects, object styles, and stroke properties.

This chapter follows on from the previous chapter. We will explore applying effects to specific attributes of a chosen design element – for example, a fill, a stroke, or text. Speaking of text, we'll apply effects to text elements whilst maintaining full editibility. We'll apply object styles to objects and duplicate elements precisely where we need them, using the step and repeat functionality found in InDesign. We'll also create custom shapes using the Pathfinder commands.

The main topics we will cover in this chapter are as follows:

- Creating borders
- Combining elements
- Applying effects to text

You can find the relevant projects/examples for this chapter here: https://packt.link/a19oQ

Creating borders

In this section, we'll create multi-object borders that frames the design. The basic building block for this step is a rectangle with bevels and inverse rounded corners. Since you know how to create such objects, to save time, you can access these elements in the 01a UI Design Library we've been using in *Chapter 7*.

Figure 8.1: The borders we'll be creating

We're familiar with creating shapes. To save time, we'll bring in elements from our library and change their properties to meet our design requirements.

1. Locate the size library item in the 01a UI Design Library. If you have closed it, choose **File** menu | **Open** and reopen it from the Chapter 7&8 Transparency and Effects Example Files files folder.
2. Ensure that the guides are visible.
3. Drag the thin border left element from the library and place it against the top and left margin guides on the page.
4. Now, drag the item labeled thin border right onto the page and drag it so that it locks into the top and right margins on the page.

Figure 8.2: The screenshot shows the objects placed using the guides. The Library and Layers panels are also visible on the right (The image is intended as a visual reference; the textual information is not essential.)

5. Select the left border object and make the following changes to the **Properties** panel:

    A. Set the **Fill** value to **[None]**
    B. Change the stroke color to **Blue**
    C. Set the stroke weight to **10 pt**
    D. Ensure the stroke type is **Solid**

6. Click the *fx* icon and choose **Bevel and Emboss** from the list.
7. Change **Size** to **16 px** in the Effects dialog.
8. Enable the **Directional Feather** effect from the list on the left of the **Effects** dialog and make the following changes:

    A. Set the left and right feather widths to **100 px**
    B. Change the **Angle** value to **90°**

9. Click **OK**

Using the Eyedropper tool

We'll copy the effects to the right thin border with the help of the **Eyedropper** tool. InDesign allows you to control which properties are sampled.

1. Double-click the **Eyedropper** tool.
2. Check all checkboxes except for **Transform Options** in the **Eyedropper Options** dialog box, and then click **OK**.

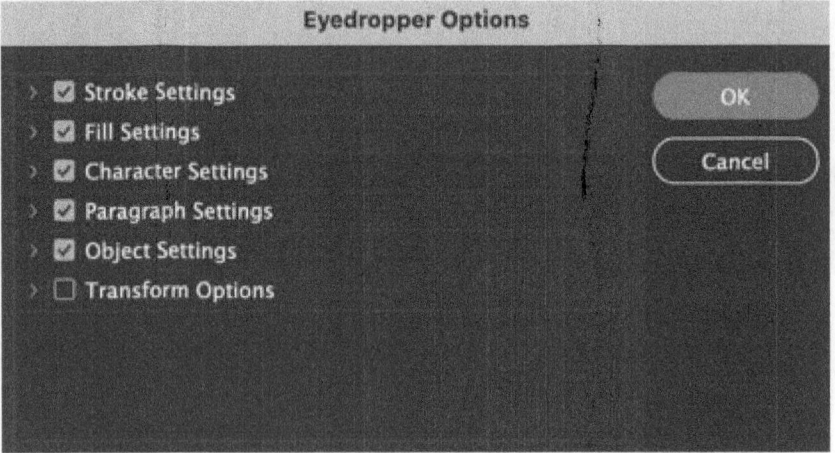

Figure 8.3: The Eyedropper Options dialog with possible attribute choices

You can be very specific about the properties you wish to capture with the **Eyedropper** tool.

3. Select the Thin border right element with the **Selection** tool.
4. Choose the **Eyedropper** tool. With the Thin border right object still selected, click on the thin border left object. The properties will be copied over to the thin border right object.
5. Select the Thin border right element with the **Selection** tool once more, and then click the **Multiple Effects Applied** label alongside the *fx* icon under the **Appearance** subset on the **Properties** panel.
6. Make the following changes in the resultant **Effect** dialog box:

    A. Choose **Transparency** at the top left of the list
    B. Set **Opacity** to **75%**
    C. Choose **Bevel and Emboss** from the list on the left
    D. Change the size to **10 px**
    E. Choose **Directional Feather** and set the left and right feather widths to **10 px**

7. Click **OK** when you're done.

Figure 8.4: The borders in place with multiple effects applied

The thin borders we placed on the page are complemented by thicker borders as shown in *Figure 8.4*, which we'll execute next.

Combining elements

In this section, we'll bring elements into the design from the library. We'll then apply multiline strokes, change the stroke and gap colors, and apply a gradient to the strokes. We'll then complete the object edits by adjusting its transparency and feather properties.

1. Locate the library item named Thick border top left **in the** 01a UI Design Library. If you have closed the library, reopen it from the Chapter 7&8 Transparency and Effects Example Files **files folder.**
2. Ensure that the guides are visible.
3. **Drag** Thick border top left **onto the page and place it against the top and left margin guides in the same location as our thin border.**
4. Now, drag the item labeled Thick border top right **onto the page and drag it so that it sticks to the top and right margins on the page.**
5. Ensure that both objects are selected with the **Selection** tool .

6. Head to the **Properties** panel and make the following changes:

   A. **Fill** should be set to **[None]**
   B. Set the **stroke width** to **40 pt**
   C. Click the stroke type drop-down list and choose **Thin-Thick-Thin**
   D. Click the word **Stroke** and choose **Gap Color**, found toward the bottom of the flyout. Set it to **[Paper]**

7. Click the **Stroke** color swatch once again and make the following changes in the flyout:

   A. Click the **Gradient** icon at the top of the flyout
   B. Change the type to **Radial**
   C. Click the leftmost gradient stop and set its RGB values to 255,255,255 (white)
   D. Now, click the right stop and set its RGB values to 0,50,70 (dark blue)
   E. Change the **Opacity** value to **80%**

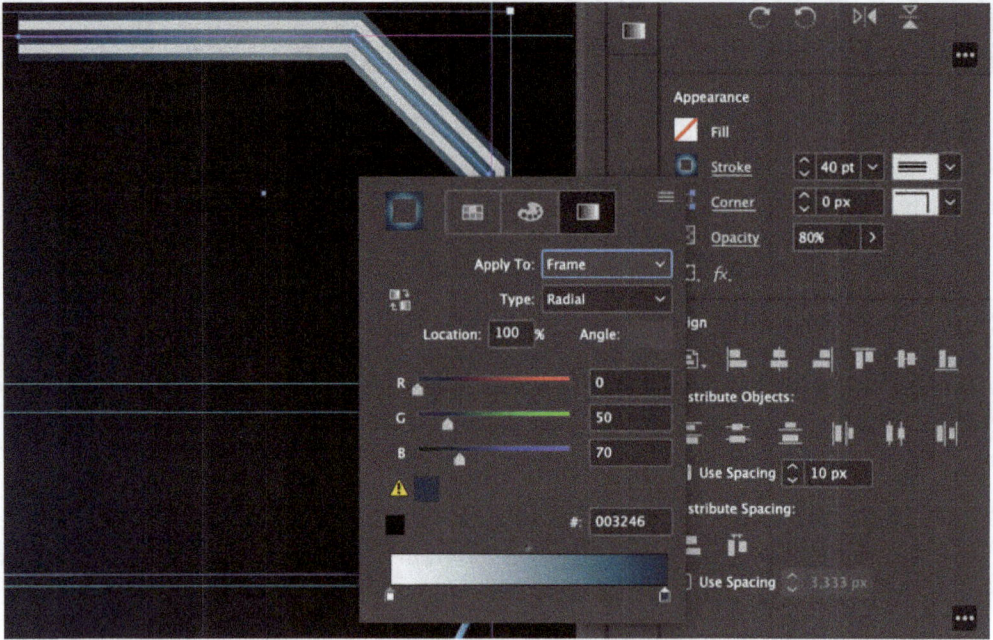

Figure 8.5: The Stroke flyout showing the stroke properties and the effect of the edits on the Thick border top right object in the background

8. Click the *fx* icon on the **Properties** panel, choose **Bevel and Emboss…**, and then make the following changes in the resultant **Effects** dialog box:

A. Change the size to **15 px**.
   i. Choose **Gradient Feather** and set the type to **Radial**.
   ii. Move the gradient midpoint by dragging the diamond icon found above the gradient as far right as possible. The maximum value is 87%. It can be typed into the **Location** input box too.
B. Click **OK** when you're done.

9. Let's group the border elements.
10. Select all four border elements, either by pressing *Shift* and clicking them on the page or from the **Layers** panel.
11. Choose the **Object** menu | **Group**.
12. To rename the newly created <group> object, click-pause-click <group> on the **Layers** panel. When highlighted, rename <group> to Borders.
13. Move the **Borders** object on the **Layers** panel so that it sits between **Map Main Middle** and **Background**.
14. Lock the object in the **Layers** panel or by choosing the **Object** menu | **Lock**.
15. We're done with this component, so save your work.

Figure 8.6: The completed borders with the Layer hierarchy visible in the Layers panel (The image is intended as a visual reference; the textual information is not essential.)

Let's recap real quick. We placed basic border shapes from our library. We then applied bevel and emboss, opacity, feather, and gap color properties to the elements. What's next? We'll work with text.

Applying effects to text

So far, we've applied effects to graphic objects. We'll now explore possibilities with text effects in this section. InDesign offers powerful text effect options for text and text frames.

Figure 8.7: The design with text elements we will edit in this section (The image is intended as a visual reference; the textual information is not essential.)

In this section, we'll create headline copy and apply effects to specific properties of that text. We'll add a bevel and inner shadow to give the headline three-dimensionality.

Headlines

Since text objects are fairly easy to create, we'll create a text frame and type out the headline. We'll apply bevel and emboss and inner shadow effects to the headline to make it pop.

1. Ensure that the guides are visible by choosing the **View** menu | **Grids & Guides** | **Show Guides**.

2. Select the **Type** tool and drag a text frame between the two border elements we just created. The size and location are unimportant for now. We'll resize and position the element in a moment.
3. Type GLOBAL STATS as the headline.
4. Select the headline text with the **Type** tool.
5. Click in the font name entry field on the **Properties** panel. The font we will use is a typeface from the Adobe Fonts library. Search for the Nasalization font name.
6. Click **Find More** at the top of the flyout, and then click the **Activate Now** icon to the right of the font name.

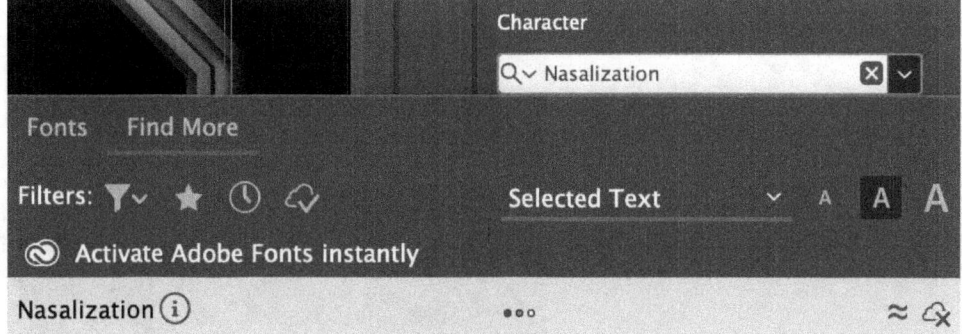

Figure 8.8: The font activated from the Adobe Fonts library

7. Select the text with the **Type** tool and make the following changes on the **Properties** panel:

    A. Ensure that the font is **Nasalization**
    B. Set **Weight** to **Regular**
    C. Set the **Fill** color to **[Paper]**
    D. Key in 118pt for the text size
    E. Set the stroke color to **Blue**
    F. Set the stroke weight to **6pt**
    G. Set the stroke type to **Solid**
    H. Click **Stroke** and from the flyout choose **Align stroke to outside** (the third icon)

Applying effects to type

You may have noticed the *fx* button is unavailable when text is highlighted with the **Type** tool. The reason for this is that effects are applied to objects and their properties. This means that we need to select the text object with the **Selection** tool and then apply any desired effects.

1. Select the type with the **Selection** tool.
2. We'd like to target specific properties for our effects. This is done through the **Effect** panel. Choose **Window** menu | **Effects** to access the panel.
3. You can see that stroke, fill, and/or text effects can be applied to the object in its entirety or individually choose the **Text** subset.

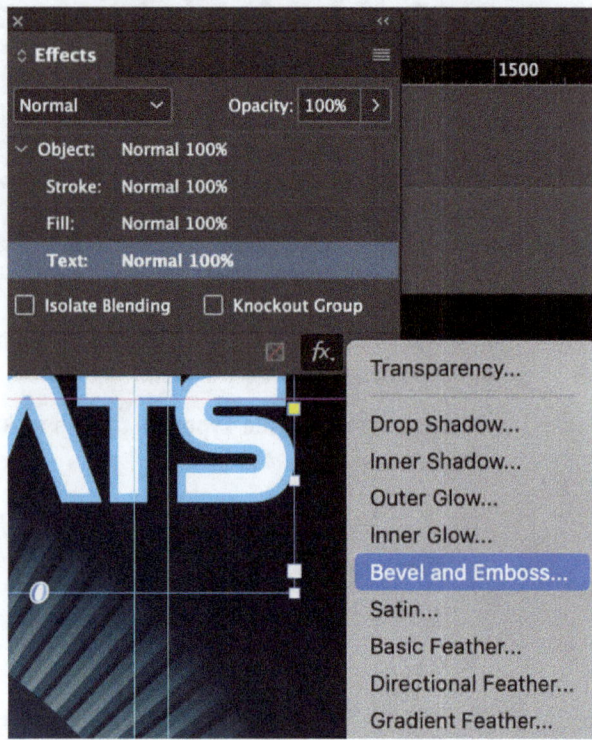

Figure 8.9: The Effects panel with the Text property selected and a Bevel and Emboss effect being applied. The text is partially visible in the background

4. Click the *fx* icon at the bottom of the panel and choose **Bevel and Emboss** from the list.

5. The default bevel and emboss settings are ideal and don't need to be changed. They are:

   A. **Style = Inner Bevel**
   B. **Size = 7 px**
   C. **Angle = 120°**
   D. **Altitude = 30°**

6. Check the **Inner Shadow** effect from the list to the left and update the settings as follows:

   A. Change the **X** and **Y** offset values to **7 px**.
   B. Under **Options**, change the **Size** value to **10 px**.
   C. The shadow is too dark and does not fit the overall design. We'll change its color to a dark blue.

Figure 8.10: Effects applied to the headline text

   D. Click the black color swatch alongside the **Multiply** blend mode at the top of the **Effects** dialog.
   E. An **Effect Color** dialog opens. Click the drop-down list alongside **Color** and choose **RGB**.
   F. Key in these values: R = 70, G = 120, and B = 150.

G. Click **OK** to close the **Effect Color** dialog, and click **OK** again in the **Effects** dialog to accept our changes.

Figure 8.11: The completed text with the Effects panel (top right), the Effects dialog (bottom left) showing the two chosen effects, and the Effect Color dialog (bottom right) showing the RGB color mix for the inner shadow color

We now need to optimize the text frame size and place it in the appropriate position on the page.

7. Ensure the text is selected with the **Selection** tool.
8. Double-click the bottom-right control handle to resize the text frame to fit the type perfectly.

Figure 8.12: Resizing the text frame using the bottom-right control handle

9. Choose **Align horizontal centers** from the **Properties** panel.
10. Under the **Transform** subset on the **Properties** panel, ensure the middle reference point is selected and change the **Y** value to **95 px**. This setting resolves the vertical position of the headline object on the page.
11. Lock the <GLOBAL STATS> object on the **Layers** panel.
12. Save the file.

Figure 8.13: The design thus far with the headline text in place

This step concludes our headline element. We'll continue working with type. We'll place the two text elements found on either side of the main earth element next and apply the necessary formatting changes.

Applying effects to text and text frames

This section is a continuation of our exploration of text effects, with a significant twist. We'll now apply effects to the fill and stroke of a text frame, leaving the text untouched.

*Figure 8.14: The two paragraph text elements we'll be editing
(The image is intended as a visual reference; the textual information is not essential.)*

The two text elements on either side of the bottom of this UI design have **fill** and **stroke** effects applied. We'll bring one instance into the design, apply the necessary styling, and then create a paragraph style nested inside of an object style so that the properties are applied to the second object with a single click. Follow these steps:

1. Ensure that the guides are visible by choosing the **View** menu | **Grids & Guides** | **Show Guides**.
2. Locate the library item named Text Bottom Left in the 01a UI Design Library. If you have closed the library, reopen it from the Chapter 7&8 Transparency and Effects Example Files files folder.
3. Drag it onto the page and place it in the bottom-left design unit.
4. Let's position the object in its final location. Under **Transform** on the **Properties** panel, ensure that the middle reference point is selected. Set the **X** value to 285 **px** and the **Y** value to 850 **px**.

5. Let's format the text and create a paragraph style. Select the text with the **Type** tool.
6. Click in the font name entry field on the **Properties** panel. The font we will use is a font from the Adobe Fonts library. Search for the Bitcount font name.
7. Click **Find More** at the top of the flyout, and then click the **Activate Now** icon to the right of the **Bitcount Mono Single** font name.

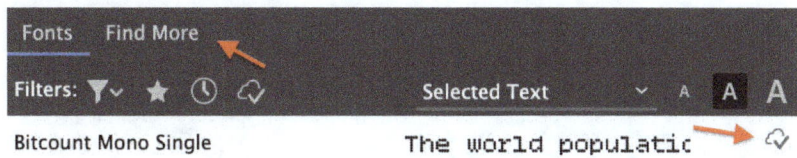

Figure 8.15: Activating the Bitcount font

8. The remaining text properties are as follows:

   A. **Size**: **18 pt**
   B. **Alignment**: **Left**

9. We'll format the text frame next. Choose the **Window** menu | **Effects**.
10. Select the **Stroke** property in the **Effects** panel and make the following changes on the **Properties** panel:

    A. Confirm that the fill color is **Blue** and the stroke color is **[Paper]**.
    B. Change the stroke width to **10 pt**.
    C. Confirm that **Thin-Thick** is the stroke style applied to the frame.

11. Click **Corner** and set the bottom-left and top-right values to **48 px**.

    A. The corner type should be **Bevel**.

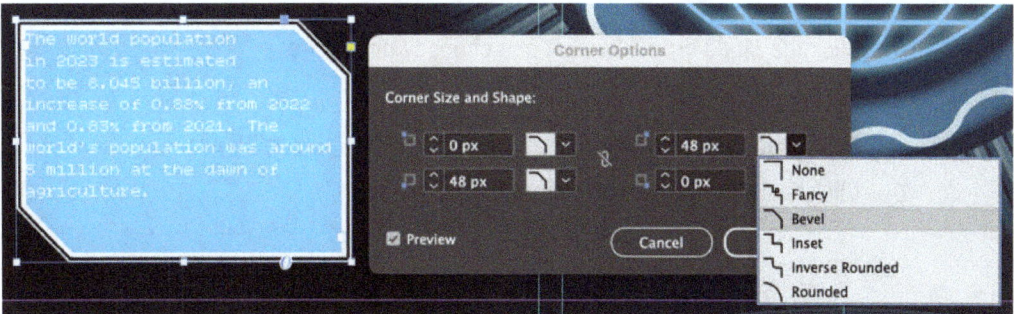

Figure 8.16: The text frame with the corner options set up

12. The text is too close to the frame. To offset it, select the object with the **Selection** tool.

    Choose **Object** menu | **Text Frame Options**. Check the **Preview** checkbox. Change the **Text Inset** to **18 px**. Click the **Align dropdown** and choose Justify. Click **OK**.

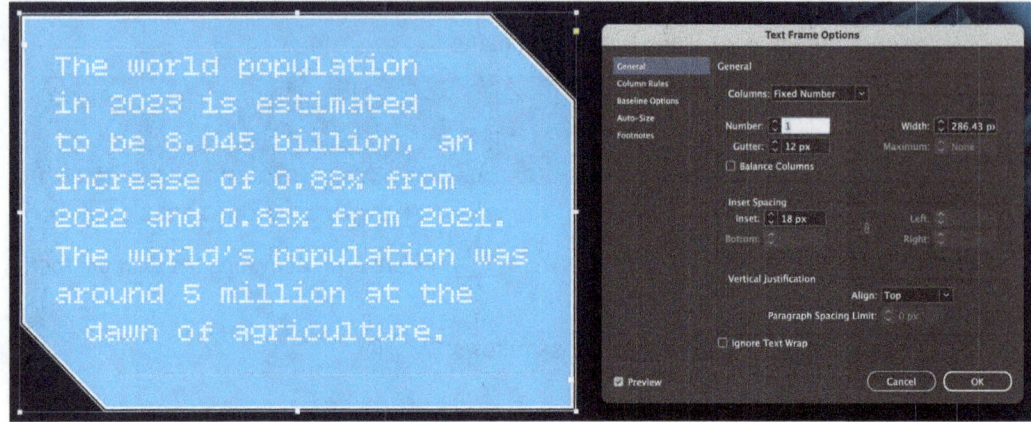

Figure 8.17: The text frame (left) with the text frame options dialog (right)

13. The design requires a directional feather on the stroke and fill. With the object selected, click **Stroke** on the **Effects** panel.

    A. Click the *fx* button at the bottom of the **Effects** panel and choose **Directional Feather**.

    B. Set the top value to **150 px**.

14. We'll use the same technique to apply a feather and transparency setting to the fill of the text frame. Click the **Fill** property on the **Effects** panel.

15. Choose the *fx* icon once more and click **Transparency**. Make the following updates in the **Effects** dialog that appears:

    A. Click the **Mode** drop-down list and choose **Luminosity**.

    B. Set **Opacity** to **20%**.

    C. Tick **Directional Feather** and set the top feather value to **75 px**.

    D. Click **OK**. We're done with formatting the element.

Saving and applying an object and paragraph style

We'll need to apply these changes to the text frame that will be positioned on the opposite side of the page. We'll save a paragraph style first. We'll then define an object style and embed the paragraph style inside it. By doing so, we'll take care of the styling for the frame and the text at once.

1. With the object still selected, head to the **Properties** panel and make the following changes:

    A. Under the **Text Style** subset, ensure **Paragraph Styles** is highlighted (in blue).

    B. Click the **New Paragraph Style** icon 🔳. Replace the default name of **Paragraph Style 1** with Body Copy and hit **Return** to accept the change.

2. To create an object style, we'll need to go to the **Object Styles** panel. Choose the **Window** menu | **Styles** | **Object Styles**.

3. Click the **Create new style** icon 🔳 at the bottom of the panel.

4. A new object style called **Object Style 1** is added to the object styles list. Double-click this style to open the **Object Style Options** dialog. We will make some minor tweaks as follows:

    A. Change the name to Text Frame

    B. Set **Based on** to **None**

    C. Click **Paragraph Styles** from the list to the left of the dialog

    D. Choose the **Body Copy** style we created earlier from the **Paragraph Style** drop-down list

    E. Click **OK** to close the dialog

This concludes the formatting of the text frame element and setting up of the associated paragraph and object stylesheets.

Applying an object stylesheet

We'll now bring in the right text frame onto the page and apply the properties we embedded into the object style we created previously.

1. Ensure that the guides are visible by choosing the **View** menu | **Grids & Guides** | **Show Guides**.

2. Locate the library item named Text Bottom Right **in the** 01a UI Design Library. **If you have closed the library, reopen it from the** Chapter 7&8 Transparency and Effects Example Files **files folder.**

3. Drag it onto the page and place it in the bottom-right design unit, using the guides as an aid.

4. Let's position this object in its final location too. Under **Transform** on the **Properties** panel, ensure that the middle reference point is selected. Set the **X** value to **1570 px** and the **Y** value to **850 px**.

5. With the text frame selected, click the **Body Copy** object style in the **Object Styles** panel. Voila! All properties have been copied over to the right text frame.

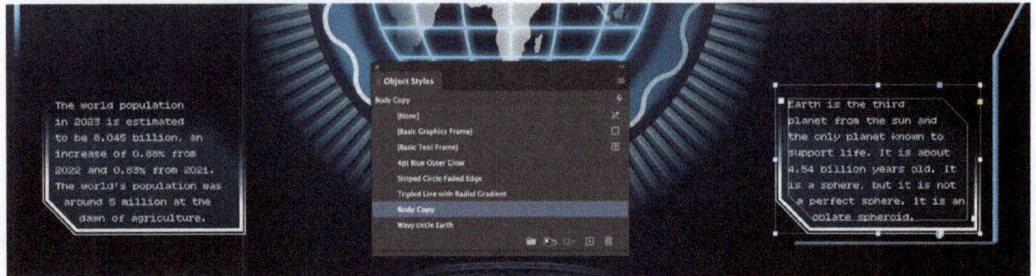

Figure 8.18: The Object Styles panel flanked by the two body copy text frames

As you can see, styles can help speed up your workflow tremendously. Especially if you are working with complex documents. We now know how to apply effects and transparency to different object properties, adjust text insets, activate fonts from the Adobe Fonts library, and create and apply object styles.

Creating outer glows

In this section, we'll work with a basic element group for the earth core elements shown in *Figure 8.19*.

Applying effects to text   235

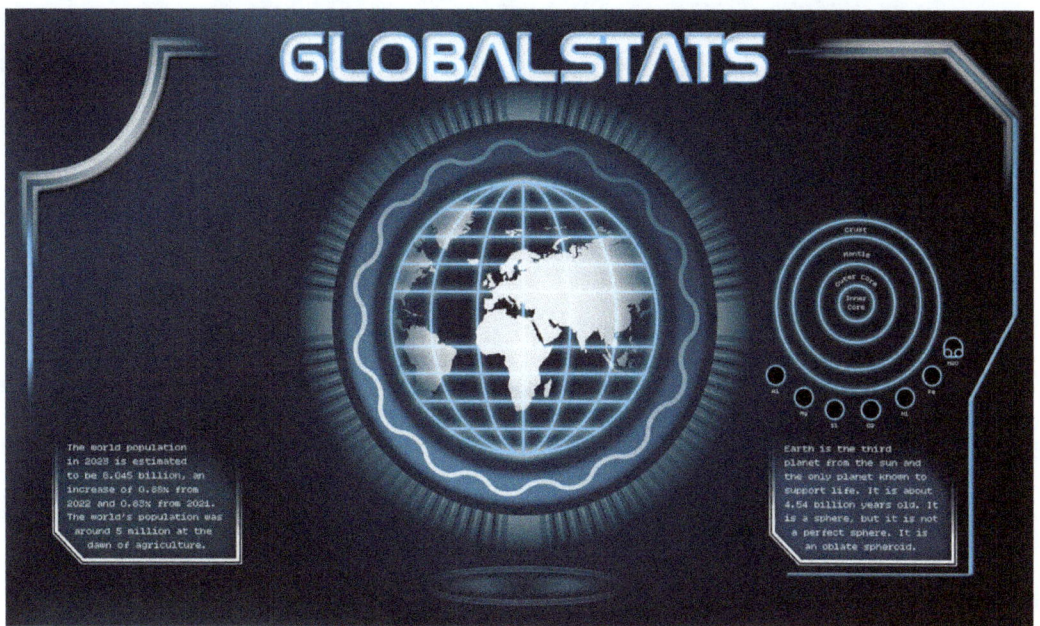

Figure 8.19: The design with the earth core elements we will edit on the right of the design

We'll apply an outer glow and use the **Eyedropper** tool to copy properties from one element to another next.

1. Drag the Earth Core object from the 01a UI Design Library onto the page.

2. Align the Earth Core object above and center of the Text Frame Right. With the Earth Core element still selected, *Shift* + click the Text Frame Right object. Release the *Shift* key. Click on the Text Frame Right element again to make it a key object. This will lock its location in place, and the Earth Core element will align with it.

3. Under the **Align** subset on the **Properties** panel, choose **Align horizontal centers** (the third icon from left).

4. We can now resolve the vertical position of the Earth Core object. *Shift* + click the Text Frame Right object to deselect it. This leaves only the Earth Core object selected.

5. Under the **Transform** subset on the **Properties** panel, make the following adjustments:

    A. Ensure that the middle reference point is selected
    B. Set the **Y** value to **515 px**

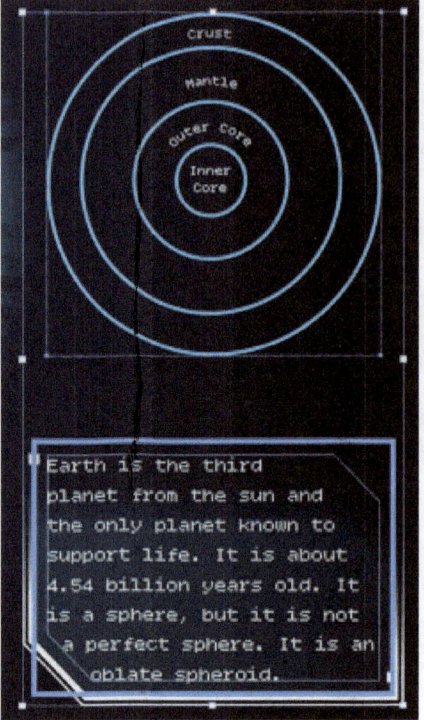

Figure 8.20: The two elements in perfect alignment

We'll look at how to select objects from the **Layers** panel next.

Selecting objects from the Layers panel

It's time to add an outer glow to each of the blue concentric circles representing the Earth's core, mantle, and crust. The entire element is a group. We'll work on sub-group objects by accessing the group and choosing only the components we require from the **Layers** panel for this purpose.

1. Click the twirl-down arrow alongside the object named Earth/core crust on the **Layers** panel. Select the four <circle> objects found below the object labeled <Inner Core>.

2. Right-click on any one of the highlighted objects and choose **Select Item(s)**. A highlight square will appear to the right of these object names, as shown in *Figure 8.21*.

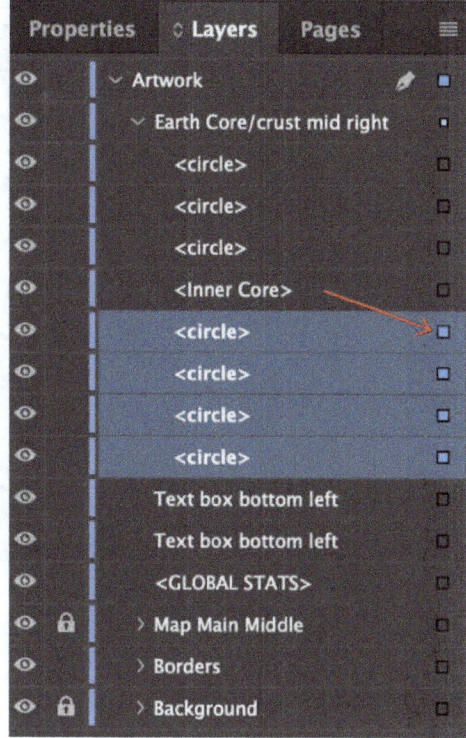

Figure 8.21: The four <circle> sub-elements selected on the Layers panel

3. We will add an **Outer Glow** effect to these elements. Make the following adjustments to the selected <circle> objects under the **Appearance** subset on the **Properties** panel:
4. Choose the *fx* icon and select **Outer Glow** from the list.
5. Choose the following settings in the resultant **Effects** panel:

   A. **Mode**: Screen
   B. **Color**: White
   C. **Opacity**: 100%
   D. **Size**: 10.5 px
   E. **Spread**: 5 px

6. Click **OK** to accept the changes. We'll save our work by choosing the **File** menu | **Save** before continuing.

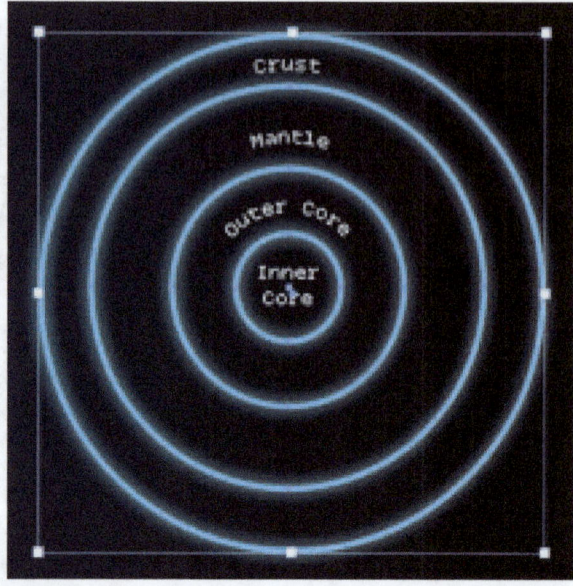

Figure 8.22: The design with the Earth core elements modifications completed

Adjusting object position

Next, we'll bring the object labeled Earth Core Elements onto the page. We'll reposition it to an exact location using the **Properties** panel. We cannot use the alignment controls in this instance, since the object is not symmetrical.

1. Under the **Transform** subset of the **Properties** panel, make the following adjustments:

   A. Ensure that the middle reference point is selected

   B. Set the **X** value to **1583 px**

C. Set the **Y** value to **655 px**

Figure 8.23: Positioning the Earth Core Elements object on the page

The object is pretty much finished, except for the two hydrogen atoms that make up the H20 molecule and the typeface for the labels under each element.

2. We'll start by resolving the fill on the hydrogen molecules. Double-click the object group with the **Selection** tool . This action allows you to drill down one level into a group of objects.

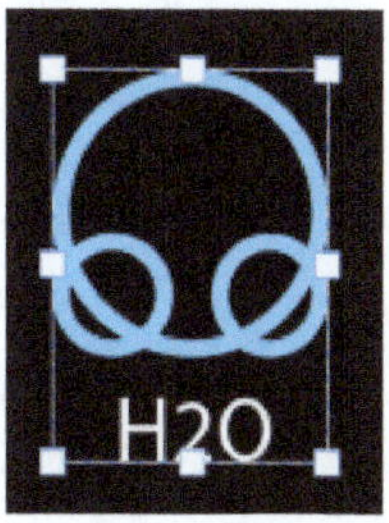

Figure 8.24: Sub-selecting the H20 element

3. Select the H2O elements, as shown in *Figure 8.24*.

4. Each subsequent double-click drops down one level further into the group. Double-click a second time on the right hydrogen molecule.

5. Click the **Fill** swatch and choose **[Black]**.

6. Repeat this process for the hydrogen molecule on the right.

Figure 8.25: Fill properties applied to the H2O group elements

Using Find/Change

The **Find/Change** command lets us make changes and updates to objects with specific characteristics really quickly and easily. We'll use this function to change the font for all of the text elements in the Earth Core Elements group. We'll change the font from Myriad Pro to Bitcount Mono Single.

1. To do that, ensure that the entire Earth Core Elements group is selected. Choose the **Edit** menu | **Find/Change** and make the following changes:

    A. Select the **Text** tab.

    B. Set the **Search** setting to **Document**.

    C. Under **Find Format**, click **Specify attributes to find** icon.

    D. Click **Basic Character Formats** from the list on the right.

E. Click the **Font** drop-down list in the middle of the dialog box and choose **Myriad Pro**. The other values do not need to be changed, as we are only changing the font. Click **OK**.

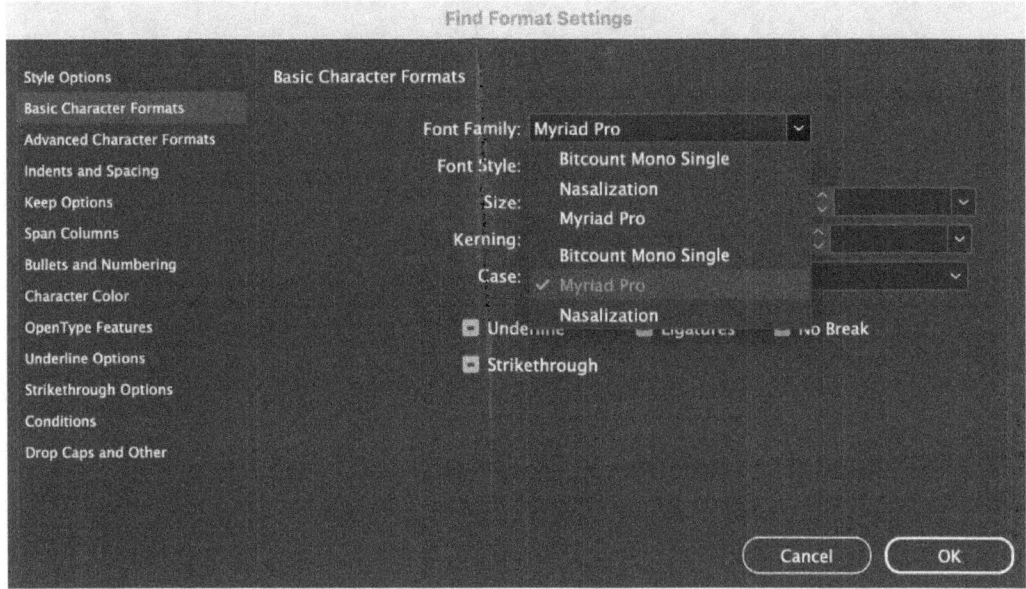

Figure 8.26: Finding objects based on specific formatting properties

2. We're now back in the **Find/Change** dialog. Make the following changes to the Change properties:

    A. Under the **Change Format** subset, click the **Specify attributes** to change the icon.

    B. Click **Basic Character Formats** from the list on the right.

    C. Click the **Font** drop-down list in the middle of the dialog box and choose **Bitcount Mono Single**. Once again, the other values do not need to be changed. Click **OK**.

3. Click the **Change All** button to affect the font change. You'll get an update dialog indicating how many elements were changed. Click **OK**.

4. Click the **Done** button to close the **Find/Change** dialog box.

Figure 8.27: Executing a font-based find and change

You may have noticed that the H2O text has disappeared on the far right of the graphic. This is because the text frame is too narrow to accommodate the **Bitcount** font. This is called overset text. We'll fix this in the next section.

Overset text

If the H2O label is overset, indicated by a red square with a plus sign inside it. This is because the Bitcount font is wider than Myriad Pro. To remedy this do the following:

1. With the **Selection** tool, double-click the text H2O element twice to select it.

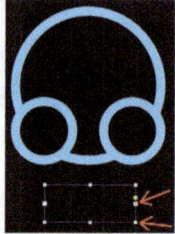

Figure 8.28: The H2O text frame with the red overset text indicator

2. Double-click the bottom-right control to auto-resize the text frame to accommodate the text. See *Figure 8.28*.

We're done with formatting this element. In this section, we looked at editing elements inside a group without having to ungroup first. We also worked with the **Find/Change** functionality and auto-resizing of text frames.

Step and repeat

In this section, we will work on the biosphere vertical counter element See *Figure 8.29*. This element is made up of text, a rectangle frame and a series of rectangles showing the concentration of elements in the Earth's biosphere.

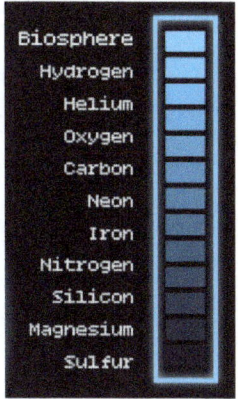

Figure 8.29: A view of the vertical counter element

Figure 8.30 illustrates the vertical counter element in its final position in the artwork.

Figure 8.30: The biosphere elements in the context of the overall design
(The image is intended as a visual reference; the textual information is not essential.)

To the biosphere counter object, we'll use the tranform controls and step and repeat command to achieve the desired outcome.

1. Drag the **Biosphere Counter** object from the 01a UI Design Library onto the page.
2. To position the **Biosphere** object in its correct location on the page, ensure that it is selected and make the following adjustments on the **Properties** panel:

    A. Under the **Transform** subset, select the middle reference point
    B. Set the **X** value to **1770 px**
    C. Set the **Y** value to **440 px**

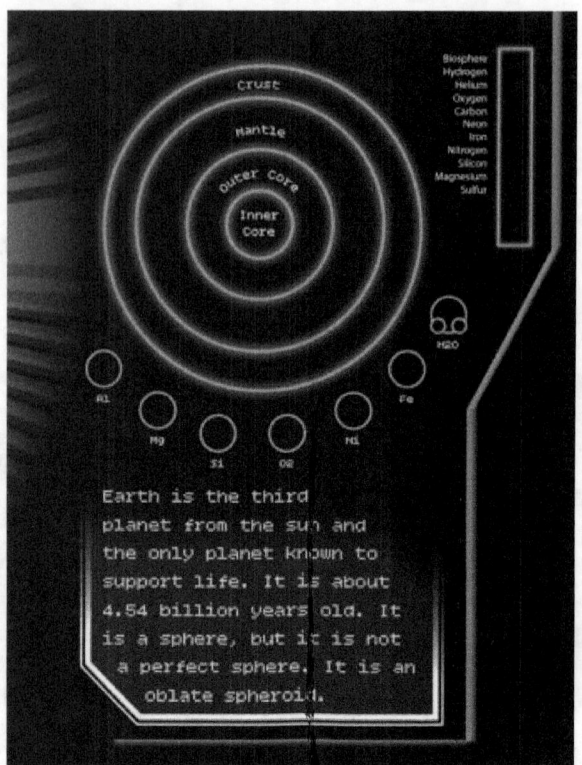

Figure 8.31: The Biosphere Counter object positioned correctly with the help of the Properties panel

3. We'll change the font and vertically align the text, so it fills the frame from top to bottom. Double-click the text element with the **Selection** tool and make the following changes:

   A. On the **Properties** panel, change the font to **Bitcount Mono Single**.

   B. Choose the **Object** menu | **Text Frame Options**. Ensure that the **Preview** tickbox is ticked.

   C. Under **Vertical Justification**, choose **Justify** from the **Align** drop-down list.

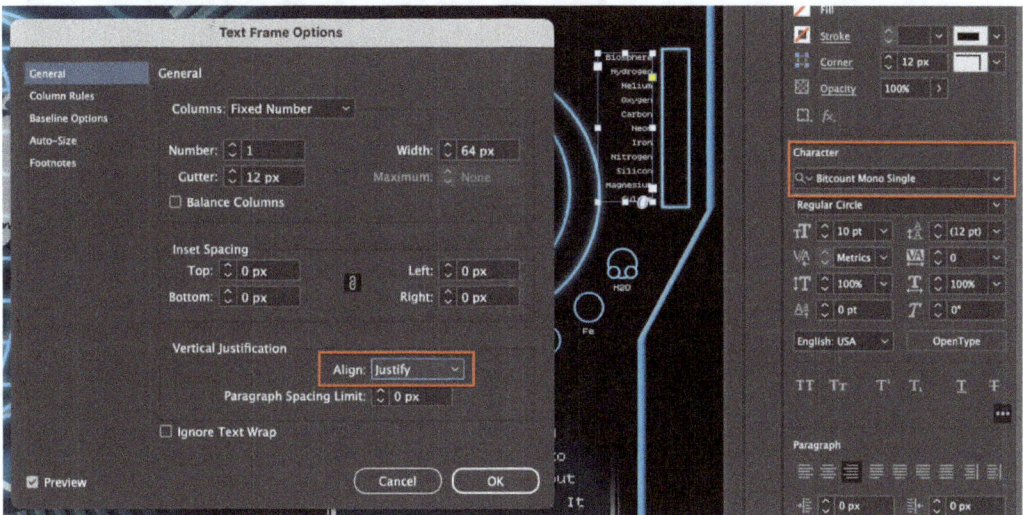

Figure 8.32: Vertical justification being applied to the text

Using the Step and Repeat command

The counter elements are a series of rectangles with varying degrees of opacity ranging from 9% to 100%. We'll draw the first rectangle and step and repeat copies to achieve the desired result.

Figure 8.33: The graduated result is achieved by progressively changing the opacity

1. Draw a rectangle of any size on the page.
2. With the rectangle object selected, make the following updates on the **Properties** panel:

    A. Under **Appearance**, set the **Fill** color to **Blue** and the **Stroke** color to **[None]**
    B. Under **Transform**, break the constrain proportions chainlink by clicking it
    C. Change the **W** value to **22 px** and the **H** value to **10 px**

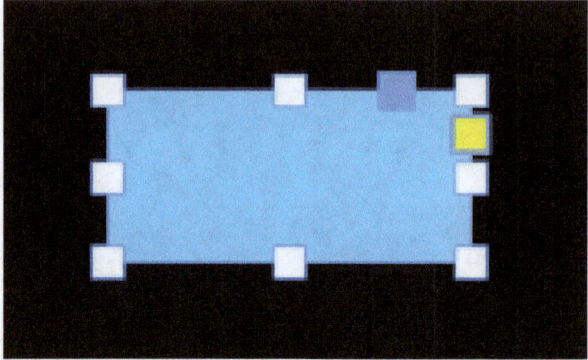

Figure 8.34: The drawn rectangle and its controls

3. We'll position this rectangle element by using the **Properties** panel. With the object selected, make the following changes under the **Transform** subset:

    A. Ensure that the middle reference point is selected.
    B. Set the **X** value to **1807 px** and the **Y** value to **359 px**. This will place the rectangle horizontally centered, and at the top of the border object.

4. With the rectangle in the correct location, we're able to place multiple copies using the **Step** and **Repeat** command. Ensure that the rectangle we drew is the only object selected.
5. Choose the **Edit** menu | **Step and Repeat**. Make the following changes in the **Step and Repeat** dialog:

    A. Enable the **Preview** switch
    B. Under **Repeat**, set the count to **10**
    C. Choose **16 px** for the **Vertical** offset and **0 px** for the **Horizontal** value

D. Confirm that the fit is perfect, as shown in the following screenshot, and then click **OK**

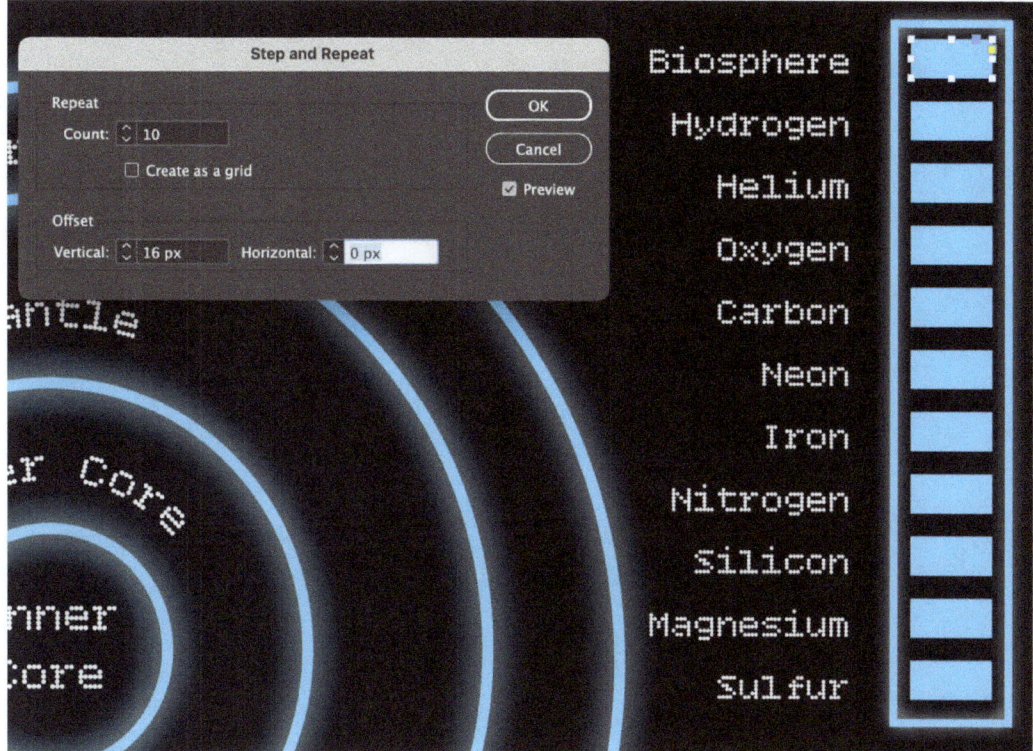

Figure 8.35: Step and Repeat offers controls for repeat count and offset

The next step is to adjust each of the rectangle opacities to create the graduated look. Since there are 11 rectangles in total, we'll adjust the opacity values from the bottom up in increments of 9%.

6. Choose the bottom-most rectangle with the **Selection** tool and set its opacity to **9%** on the **Properties** panel.
7. Select the second-from-bottom rectangle and set its opacity to **18%**.

8. The third rectangle should be 21%, and so on. The following list shows the opacity values from bottom to top:

    A. Rectangle 1: **9%**
    B. Rectangle 2: **18%**
    C. Rectangle 3: **27%**
    D. Rectangle 4: **36%**
    E. Rectangle 5: **45%**
    F. Rectangle 6: **54%**
    G. Rectangle 7: **63%**
    H. Rectangle 8: **72%**
    I. Rectangle 9: **81%**
    J. Rectangle 10: **90%**
    K. Rectangle 11: **100%**

Figure 8.36: The rectangle opacities from top to bottom

9. Let's group the text, outer border rectangle, and step and repeat rectangles so that they act as a single object. *Shift* + click each of the rectangles till they are all selected.

10. Choose the **Object** menu | **Group**. A dotted line will appear around our newly grouped object. This is a visual aid to help you identify grouped objects when they are selected. The word group also appears at the top left of the **Properties** panel.

11. Let's rename our newly created group. Select the <group> element from the **Layers** panel. Click-pause-click it to rename it, calling it Biosphere Counter. Then press **Enter/Return** to confirm the name change.

12. Save your work by choosing the **File** menu | **Save** before continuing.

Figure 8.37: The design with the counter in place to the right of the UI design

Let's recap briefly. We brought elements onto the page from the project library and changed the font and vertical justify attributes. We then drew a rectangle, colored it, and positioned it using its *X* and *Y* properties. With this done, we were able to apply the Step and Repeat command and adjust the opacity for each of the copies to achieve a graduated look from top to bottom. We then grouped and renamed the element. To avoid monotonous repetition, we'll point out the techniques we used for each object as we bring new objects into the design.

Applying arrowheads to strokes

We'll bring the biosphere design object onto the page next. We'll also explore how to apply arrowheads to the ends of strokes for the various labels. The concentric half circles use the same transparency technique we just looked at. The formatting of text elements were also covered in earlier steps. Try formatting these on your own. *Figure 8.38* shows the completed design element.

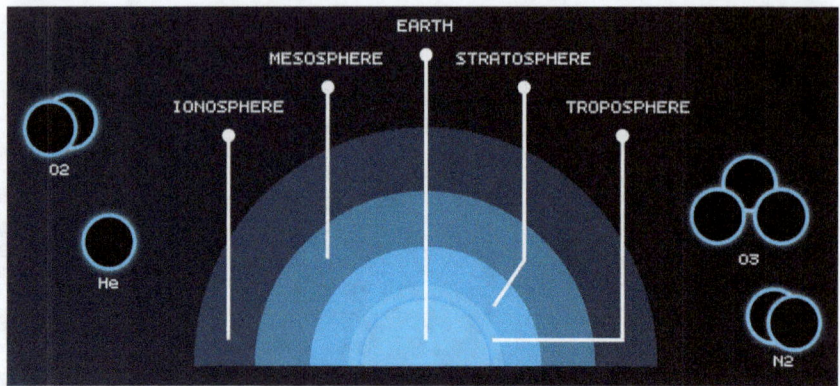

Figure 8.38: The biosphere element and its labels

We're ready to bring the Biosphere Top Right object onto the page. In the steps that follow, we'll position the element precisely. We'll also change the stroke properties of the leader lines to match the visual style of the overall design.

1. Drag the Biosphere Top Right object from the 01a UI Design Library onto the page.
2. To position the Biosphere Top Right object in its correct location on the page, ensure that it is selected and make the following adjustments on the **Properties** panel:

    A. Under the **Transform** subset, select the middle reference point

    B. Set the **X** value to **1565 px**

C. Set the **Y** value to **225 px**

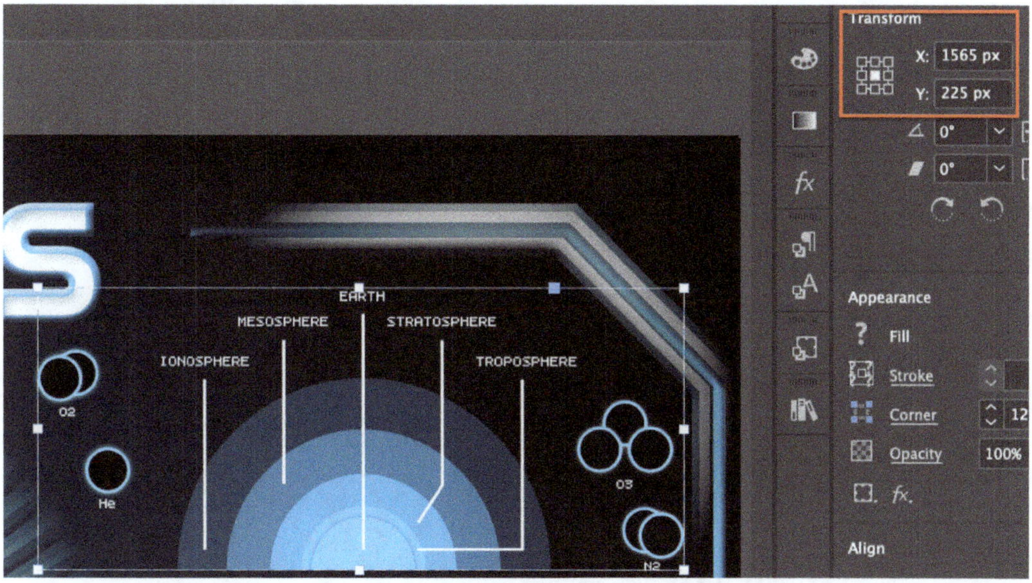

Figure 8.39: The positional values for the biosphere object group

3. We want to change the label leader lines to circular endpoints. Let's select the leader lines. Access the **Layers** panel and click the twirl-down arrow for the **Biosphere Top Right** group.

4. Select the **Leader lines** subgroup by clicking the **Select Items** box , found to the right of its name on the **Layers** panel.

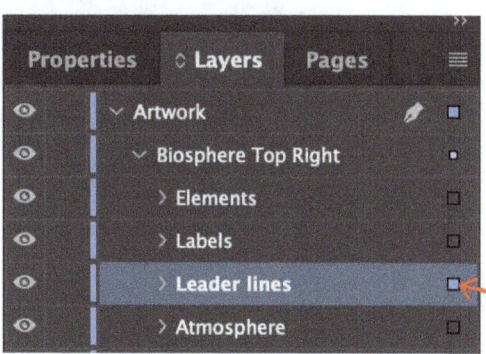

Figure 8.40: Making selections from the Layers panel can boost efficiency in complex designs

5. With the leader lines selected on the page, make the following changes on the **Properties** panel:

    A. Click the **Stroke** word under the **Appearance** subset to open the flyout menu.

    B. The **Start/End** dropdown controls the line arrowheads. These can be anything from arrows to geometric shapes. Choose the **Circle Solid** option from the **End** dropdown list (the fifth option from the top).

6. Deselect the object to see the result.

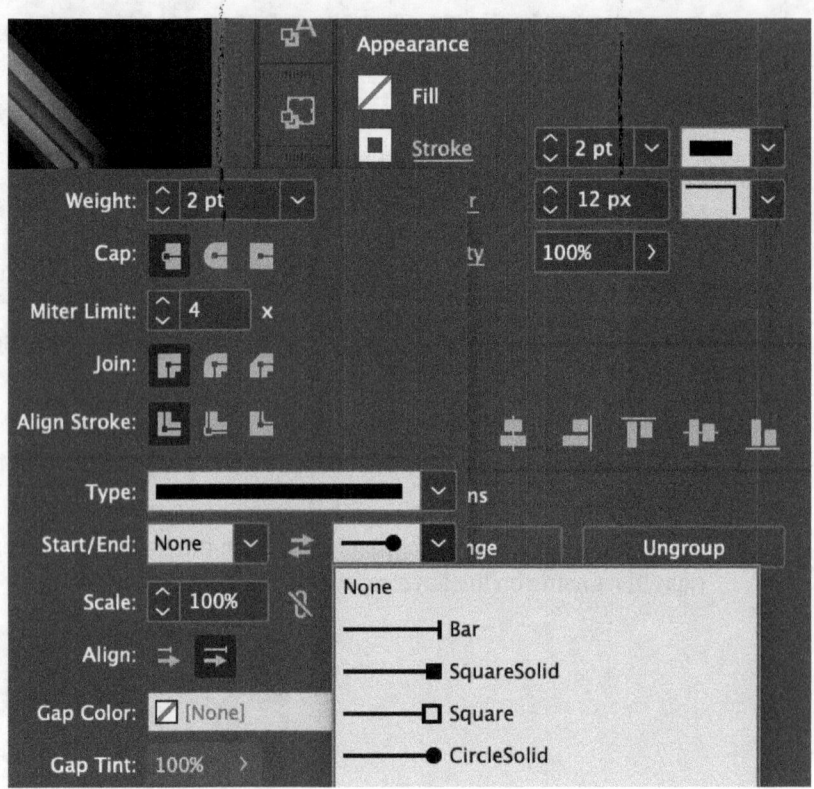

Figure 8.41: Settings for the leader line properties

That's us done with this element. *Figure 8.42* shows our progress thus far. As evidenced by the previous steps, changing line arrowheads to achieve the look you want is relatively easy. We encourage you to experiment by choosing different arrowhead styles and applying an arrowhead to the start of the lines too.

Figure 8.42: The updated design with the biosphere object styled correctly (The image is intended as a visual reference; the textual information is not essential.)

Placing the main sequence labels

The main sequence labels are made up of elements that have outer glows, custom fill and stroke properties, and type labels. All these options have been covered in this chapter, and you should be very comfortable with these concepts by now.

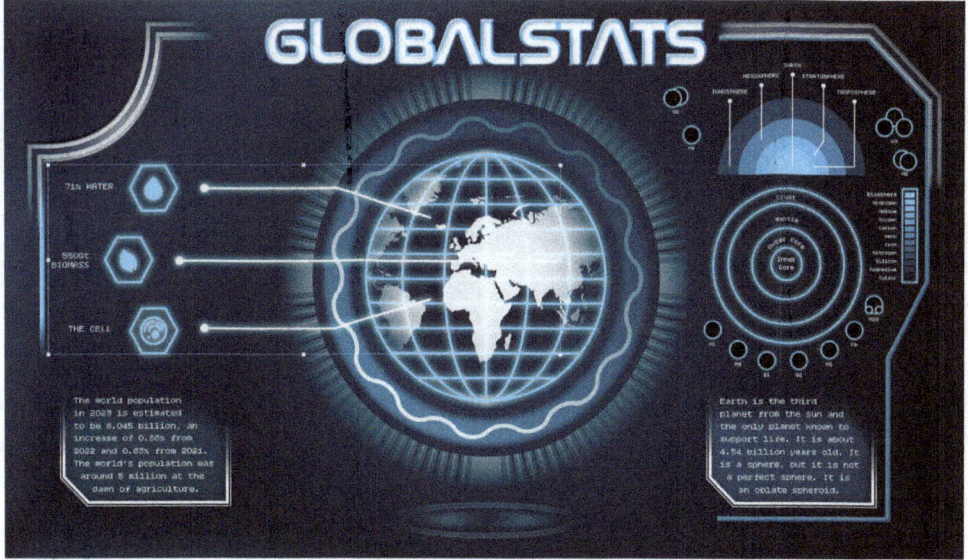

Figure 8.43: The completed design with the main sequence earth object labels highlighted (The image is intended as a visual reference; the textual information is not essential.)

To avoid rote repetition, we'll place the remaining objects for this design with the styling already applied. You can still explore the various properties of objects by working with individual unstyled assets from the library.

1. Drag the Earth Main Labels object from the 01a UI Design Library onto the page.
2. To position the Earth Main Labels object in the correct location on the page, ensure that it is selected and make the following changes on the **Properties** panel:

    A. Under the **Transform** subset, select the middle reference point.
    B. Set the **X** value to **620 px**
    C. Set the **Y** value to **505 px**

Placing the solar system graphic

The solar system graphic is made up of a series of concentric ellipses. The planets are circles with the basic blue fill color. We'll place the styled element on the page in its correct location. Should you wish to experiment, place the unstyled version of the solar system asset from the library instead.

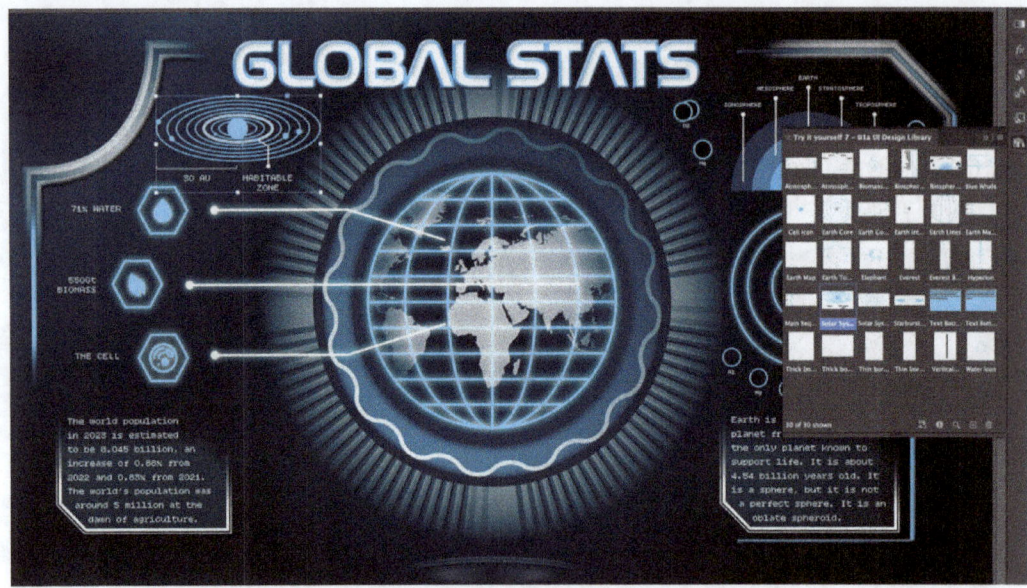

Figure 8.44: The solar system element placed on the page with the Library panel visible (The image is intended as a visual reference; the textual information is not essential.)

Let's place the Solar System object into the design. We'll then style it on the **Properties** panel.

1. Drag the Solar System object from the 01a UI Design Library onto the page. If you prefer, you can drag the Solar System Unstyled object onto the page and try your hand at styling it. This is optional.
2. To position the Solar System object in its correct location on the page, make the following changes on the **Properties** panel with it still selected:

    A. Under the **Transform** subset, select the middle reference point
    B. Set the **X** value to **470 px**
    C. Set the **Y** value to **245 px**

Placing the corner earth graphic

The Earth Top Left element is a different iteration of the map element found in the main graphic. It has a series of concentric circles with different stroke widths, colors, and transparencies applied. We'll place the styled version of the design element on the page in its correct location. As usual, the unstyled version of the asset is accessible from the library should you want to explore on your own.

Figure 8.45: A zoomed-in view of the design with the earth element selected

1. Click and drag the Earth Top Left object from the 01a UI Design Library onto the page.
2. Let's position the object appropriately on the page by making the following changes on the **Properties** panel while it is selected:
   A. Under the **Transform** subset, select the middle reference point
   B. Set the **X** value to **140 px**
   C. Set the **Y** value to **130 px**

Using Pathfinder commands

The Moon Phases object is made up of a series of circles that have either been left as is or trimmed using the Pathfinder. The Pathfinder commands allow you to trim or merge objects depending on your needs.

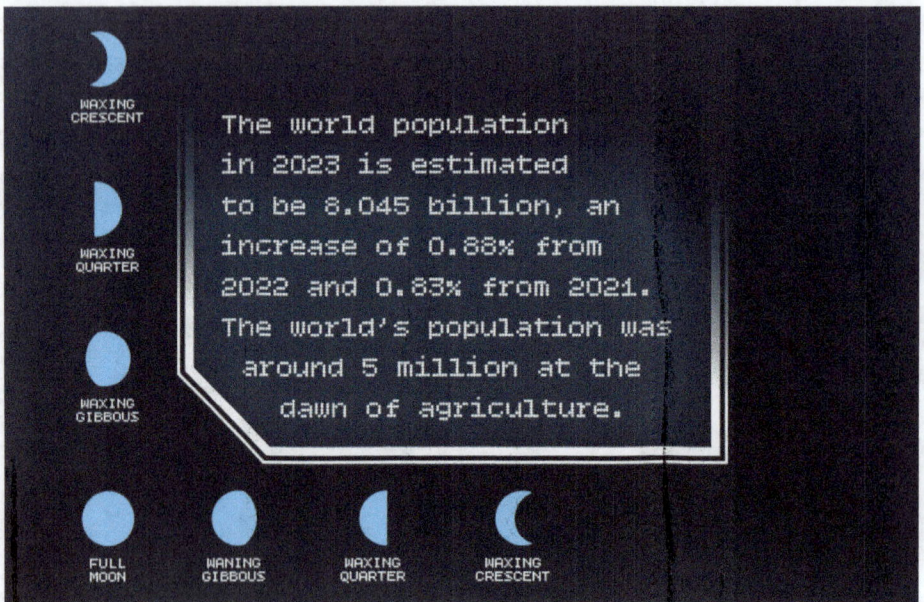

Figure 8.46: The completed Moon Phases object as it appears on the bottom-left of the page

In the steps that follow, we'll work with pre-created the elements for efficiency and speed. We'll use the Pathfinder commands to get the desired result, as shown in *Figure 8.46*.

1. Click and drag the Moon Phases object from the 01a UI Design Library onto the page. The icons on the horizontal axis are complete. The ones running vertically have been prepared for us so that we can explore how the Pathfinder commands work.

2. Let's position the object in its correct location on the page by making the following changes on the **Properties** panel while it is selected:

   A. Under the **Transform** subset, select the middle reference point
   B. Set the **X** value to **195 px**
   C. Set the **Y** value to **895 px**

3. Open the **Layers** panel and twirl open the **Moon Phases** group object. You can see that the group is made up of a series of sub-groups. We will work with the series of waxing groups.

4. Twirl open the groups labeled as follows:

   A. **Waxing Crescent**
   B. **Waxing Quarter**
   C. **Waxing Gibbous**

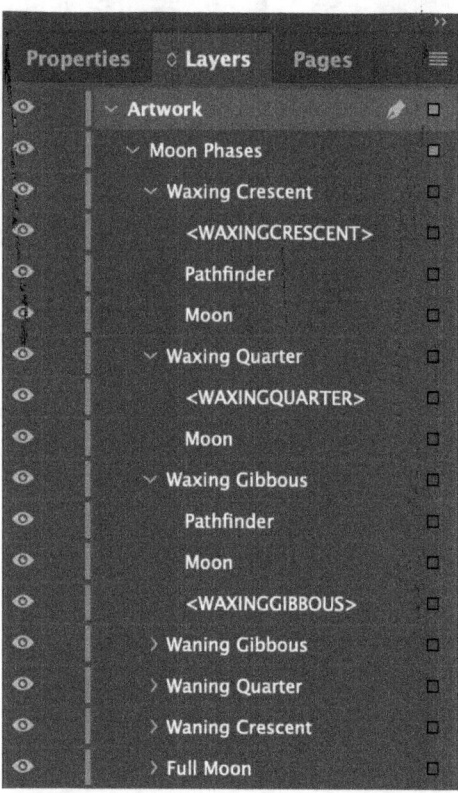

Figure 8.47: The Layers panel gives you powerful, complimentary object identification and selection options

5. Under the **Waxing Crescent** group on the **Layers** panel, click the selection box alongside **Pathfinder**, press the *Shift* key, and click the selection box for **Moon** as well.
6. The two objects will be highlighted on the page to confirm they are indeed selected. See *Figure 8.48*.

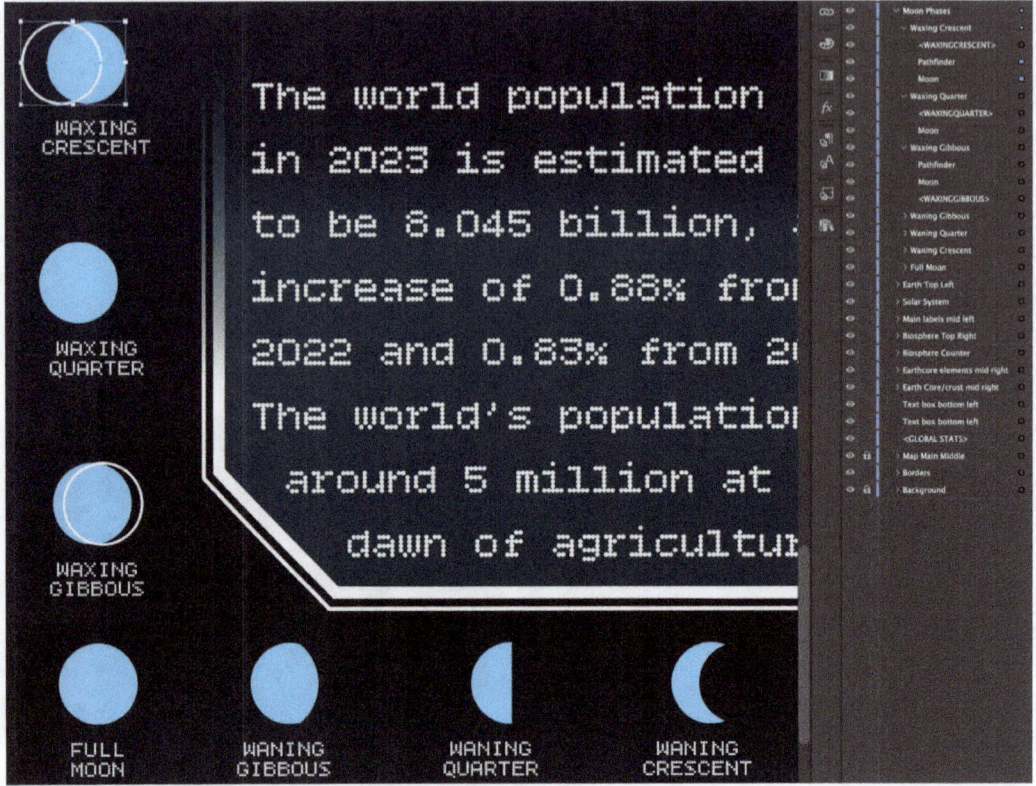

Figure 8.48: Ensure that you have both ellipses selected

7. Choose the **Object** menu | **Pathfinder** | **Subtract**. This command will use the **Pathfinder** object with the white outline and subtract the underlying blue circle to create the desired crescent shape.

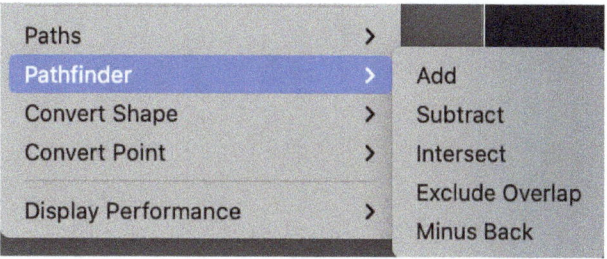

Figure 8.49: The Pathfinder controls in InDesign help to create complex shapes easily

8. Close the **Waxing Crescent** object by clicking its twirl arrow to reduce clutter in the **Layers** panel.
9. For the **Moon** object under **Waxing Quarter**, we need half a circle. We'll use the **Direct Selection** tool to eliminate the points we don't need.
10. Ensure that nothing is selected. Choose the **Direct Selection** tool (*A*).
11. Click the middle-left edge of the **Waxing Quarter** object to select just that control point Refer to *Figure 8.50*.

Figure 8.50: Selecting object sub-components with the Direct Selection tool

12. Tap the *Delete/Backspace* key to eliminate that point. Voila! We have a semi-circle.

Figure 8.51: Creating a semi circle by deleting a point

13. Let's clean up the view of the **Waxing Quarter** group by clicking on the downward pointing arrow to its left on the **Layers** panel. This should make it easier for us to navigate the assets.

14. Under the **Waxing Quarter** group on the **Layers** panel, click the selection box alongside **Pathfinder**, then press the *Shift* key, and click the selection box alongside the **Moon** object too. Both objects will show selection controls on the page.

15. Select the **Object** menu | **Pathfinder** | **Intersect** command. This **Pathfinder** will keep the common areas shared between the two shapes.

16. If the resultant shape adopts the **Pathfinder** color properties, head to the **Properties** panel and set the **Appearance** properties as follows:

    A. Click the **Fill** swatch and choose **Blue** from the color swatch list
    B. Click the **Stroke** swatch and set its value to **None**

As you can see, the **Pathfinder** commands give you powerful controls to create complex shapes with ease. We'll now bring in the three remaining elements to complete our design.

Placing the final design elements

We are now ready to wrap up our design. We'll bring in a supergroup of elements and position it in an appropriate location on the page. These elements employ the same techniques we covered earlier. The individual elements are included in the library should you wish to explore further.

Figure 8.52: The Final Elements supergroup placed in the design (The image is intended as a visual reference; the textual information is not essential.)

1. Click and drag the Final Elements object from the 01a UI Design Library onto the page.
2. We'll position the object in its allocated space on the page by making the following updates on the **Properties** panel whilst it is still selected:

    A. Under the **Transform** subset, select the middle reference point

    B. Set the **X** value to **1165 px**

    C. Set the **Y** value to **545 px**

That's us done, bringing to conclusion a juicy chapter. Choose the **View** menu | **Screen Mode** | **Presentation** to see the final result in its full glory without any user interface clutter. It's worth noting that while InDesign is not the first choice for this type of design. It is nonetheless very capable.

Summary

In this chapter, we created a UI design. Our starting point was to set up the document after exploring the completed design. We created unique backgrounds that integrated and meshed with each other. We explored the full palette of effects that InDesign has on offer. We also looked at object blending modes and opacity values, which allow objects to be semi-transparent and interact with other objects in unique and interesting ways. We looked at softening the edges of objects using **Feather** and varying their strokes too. We used the **Eyedropper** tool to quickly transfer properties from one object to the next. We used the **Layers** panel to arrange object hierarchies and select objects in complex multi-faceted groups. We used the **Step and Repeat** command to create copies of objects at specified intervals and steps. We concluded by creating unique shape combinations using the **Pathfinder** commands.

In the next chapter, we will explore the exciting world of advanced typography. We will look at a sample of Indesign's advanced typographic controls, and its value to you when creating sophisticated design projects.

Part 3: Advanced Techniques

This part includes in-depth explorations of typographic tools, styles, OpenType features, variable fonts, and QR codes. Learn how to prepare documents for high-quality output, by working with inks, separations, imposition, and ISO-aligned PDF exports. Create interactive digital content for devices using InDesign's multimedia capabilities. Learn how to take advantage of InDesign's evolving AI features such as layout suggestions, intelligent image fitting, and text to generative image features to streamline your design processes and boost creativity.

This part has the following chapters:

- *Chapter 9, Advanced Typography*
- *Chapter 10, Preparing Documents for Professional Print*
- *Chapter 11, Multimedia, Interactivity, and AI*
- *Chapter 12, Help and Troubleshooting*

Level: Advanced

Advanced Typography

Welcome to the advanced features section of this book. To avoid repeating steps that you are now very familiar with, we'll focus more on concepts and less on detailed explanations for steps we've already covered in previous chapters. We'll also work on pre-created files to allow us to fast-track the topics under discussion and to communicate an idea in the shortest possible timeframe. You're welcome to create the design elements presented from the ground up to truly hone your skills.

InDesign has one of the most comprehensive typographic toolsets available to professional designers and creative professionals. We could easily dedicate an entire book to this topic. In this chapter, we will cover the salient typographic tools and high-end text features that we feel would be of use to you in InDesign. These include **nested** styles, **nested line** styles, and **Generalised Regular Expression Print** (**GREP**) styles. This chapter also discusses how to use **OpenType** features, style mapping from **Microsoft Word**, and custom bullets. Our discussion on type would not be complete without exploring local overrides, type on a path, text variables spellcheck, and **QR** codes.

The main topics that we will cover in this chapter include the following:

- A deep dive into text styles
- Rapid-fire application of styles
- Exploring OpenType features
- Style mapping from Microsoft Word
- Nested styles
- Nested line styles
- GREP styles
- Customizing bullet lists
- Type on a path

- Variable fonts
- Local formatting overrides
- Generating QR codes

You can find the relevant projects/examples for this chapter here: https://packt.link/a19oQ

More on Styles

We looked at the fundamentals of formatting type and paragraph styles in *Chapters 2* and *4*, respectively. Now, we'll turn our attention to rapid formatting of text for quick and predictable results. This chapter scaffolds on concepts covered in previous chapters. We will be working with a menu design in this chapter. Let's open the completed menu as shown in *Figure 9.1* and have a look at the project outcomes.

Figure 9.1: The completed menu design showing the InDesign page layout (The image is intended as a visual reference; the textual information is not essential.)

Figure 9.1 shows a four-page tabloid-sized menu design graphic elements have been pre-populated. We will focus on the text elements.

Figure 9.2: The completed menu design in its print pagination order
(The image is intended as a visual reference; the textual information is not essential.)

Figure 9.2 shows this four-page menu as it will be printed. This is called **imposition**. The spread that appears at the top shows the menu cover to the right and the back of the menu on the left. The bottom spread shows the inside of the menu. This is how the document will be printed and folded.

Exploring the completed project and resources

By now, you should be quite comfortable with the approach in this book. It is practical and hands-on. You are encouraged to explore the concepts you read about by downloading the files referred to and following along. We'll explore the completed design first. We'll then open a partially constructed project file and explore the concepts covered in this chapter by working in that document. The example files can be downloaded from https://packt.link/a19oQ.

We'll do a cursory walk-through of the project and its various design components. This design is a four-page folded menu set to tabloid size.

1. Open the completed design file by choosing **File** menu | **Open**. Navigate to the Chapter 9 Advanced Typography Example Files folder. Open the file named Try it yourself - 01 Typography Complete.indd.

2. If you are presented with a missing fonts warning, please click **Activate**. InDesign will automatically install any missing fonts.

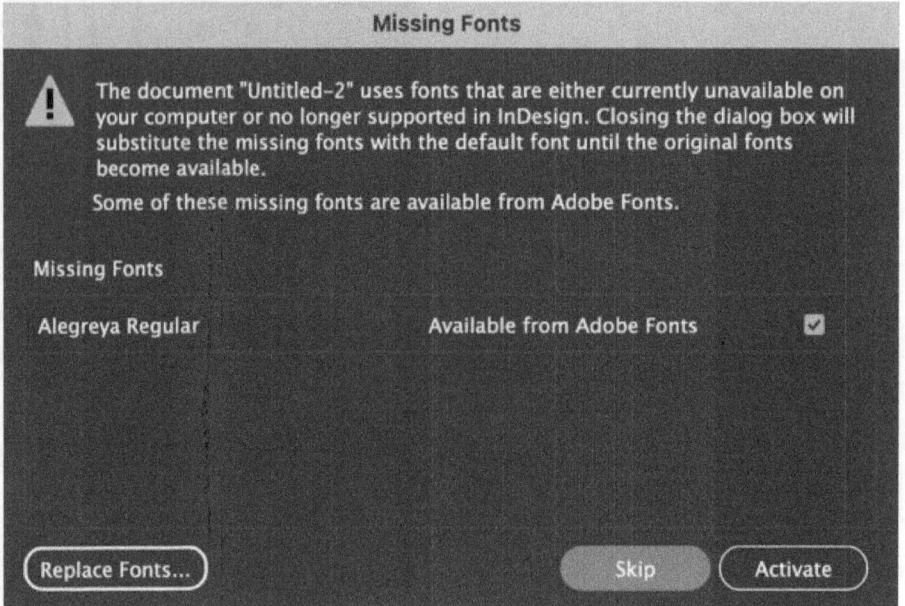

Figure 9.3: The Missing Fonts dialog box

3. Reset the workspace so that the view of the interface you have is as close to what is being shared in the book as possible. Do this by choosing the **Window** menu | **Workspace** | **[Essentials]** has a check in the box to its left. Choose the **Window** menu a second time and select **Reset Essentials**.

4. Access the **Pages** panel from the **Window** menu. Navigate through the document. **Page 1** is the front cover of the menu. Pages 2 and 3 are the inside pages, and **Page 4** is the back cover.

5. You can also click the visibility icon ▣ (the icon that looks like an eye) to the right of any chosen object name to hide it. Click in the same location a second time to bring the eye back and make the object visible once more.

6. Take some time to familiarize yourself with the design by clicking through the various design elements.

7. Once you are done, please close the document by choosing **File Menu | Close**. If you are prompted to save the file, choose **Don't Save**.

In the next section, we'll open the InDesign working document. We'll start by familiarizing ourselves with the various pages and applying formatting changes to the typographic elements.

Getting started with the menu design

After opening the project file, our first task is to acquaint ourselves with the core design elements and apply the appropriate formatting for each of the components. Remember, our intention is to work with speed and efficiency by leveraging the powerful type tools and automation options InDesign has to offer.

1. Choose **Open** from the top left of the InDesign home screen.
2. Navigate to where you saved the example files for this chapter.
3. **Select the file labeled** Try it yourself - 01 Typography Menu Design Start.indd **and click Open**. Activate any fonts if you are presented with the **Missing Fonts** dialog. InDesign will locate and install any fonts used in the document that may not be installed on your computer.

Figure 9.4: The working document with the Pages panel
(The image is intended as a visual reference; the textual information is not essential.)

Page 1 has a hero image of some plated food, unformatted **MENU** text, and a logo. We'll apply styles to the **MENU** element. We'll then move to all other headings through out the menu and apply appropriate styles through to **Page 4**.

Applying paragraph styles

Paragraph styles, as you know, host numerous properties that make for quick and easy formatting. Let's apply pre-created styles to the various heading elements. We've covered setting up paragraph styles previously, so we'll apply these quickly and move on to the next topic.

1. Navigate to **Page 1**. Select **Type tool (T)**. Click inside the **MENU** text frame. Choose **Edit** menu | **Select All** to highlight all the text. The keyboard shortcut is *Cmd + A* (macOS) or *Ctrl + A* (Windows).
2. Head to the **Properties** panel. Click the **Paragraph Styles** tab under **Text Style**.
3. From the drop-down list, choose the **01 OFC Menu Heading** paragraph style.

Figure 9.5: The 01 OFC Menu Heading style applied to the menu text

4. Navigate to pages 2-3. Select **Type tool (T)** . Click inside the **MAINS** text frame. Choose **Edit** menu | **Select All** to highlight all of the text.
5. Head to the **Properties** panel. Click the **Paragraph Styles** switch under **Text Style**.
6. Choose **02 Mains Heading**. Done!
7. We'll use a different technique to apply the **SWEETS** heading style on **Page 3**. Choose the **Selection** tool (*V/Esc*). Click the **SWEETS** text frame once to select it.
8. Choose the Style labeled **06 Sweets Heading** from the **Paragraph Styles** drop-down list on the **Properties** panel.
9. We have one more heading to apply. Navigate to **Page 4**. Select the **DRINKS** text frame with the **Selection** tool (*V/Esc*). Choose the style labeled **07 Drinks Heading** from the Properties panel.

Well done. All headings are now formatted correctly. We had a look at how to quickly format type by using styles to rapidly move through a document and style text as needed.

Exploring OpenType

OpenType in InDesign is essentially your key to unlocking a richer and more expressive typographic world, elevating your designs from basic to truly captivating. Overall, it empowers designers to push the boundaries of typography with OpenType. You can do this by using pre-defined collections of alternate characters and swashes (known as **stylistic sets**), using swashes and alternates to substitute characters for a specific look, or creating elegant letter combinations by using ligatures to enhance legibility. These are just some of the many benefits of OpenType. We'll explore some of the salient OpenType features offered by InDesign and apply them to the menu design. Let's begin:

1. Head to **Page 1**. Choose the **Zoom Tool** and zoom into the logo group at the bottom of the page.
2. The letter **e** in the word **Vibes** is clearly affecting on the letter **s**. We'll use OpenType to resolve this.

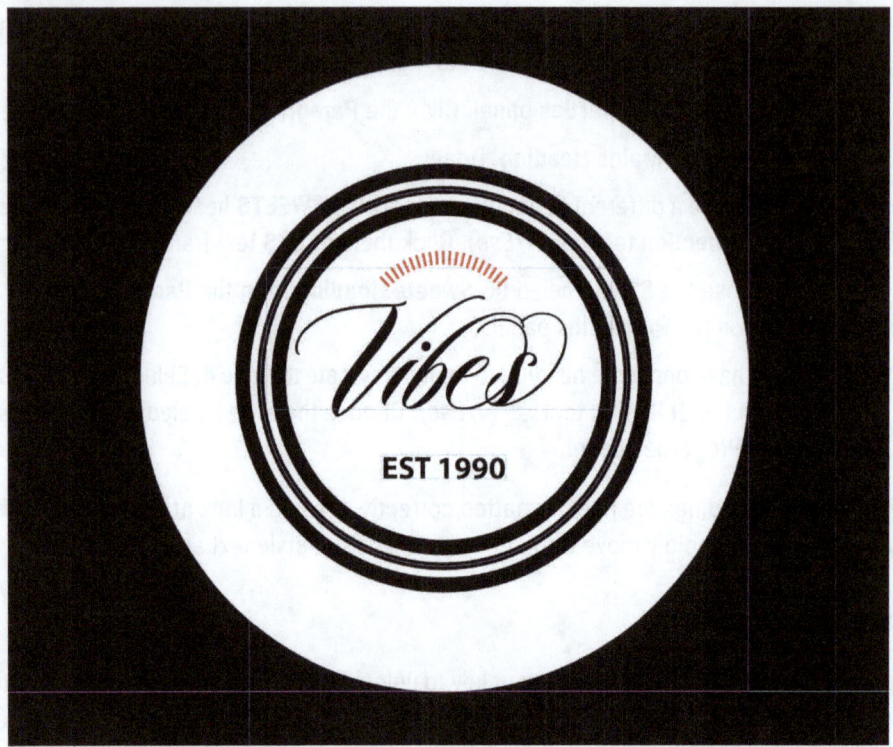

Figure 9.6: The finial or tail of the letter e impinges onto the spine of the letter s and runs just under the ascender of the letter b

3. Select the **Type** tool and highlight the letter **e**.

4. Hover over the character to activate an interactive pop-up list of alternates for the chosen letter. For the typeface we've chosen, there are a few variations available.

5. Choose a variation that does not have a swash.

> **Quick tip**
> You can use the **Glyphs** panel to get a comprehensive view of the entire font or alternate options for your selection. Choose **Type** menu | **Glyphs** to open the panel.

6. You are encouraged to experiment at this stage. Choose different letters and combinations of letters to explore the OpenType options available to you in that particular typeface.

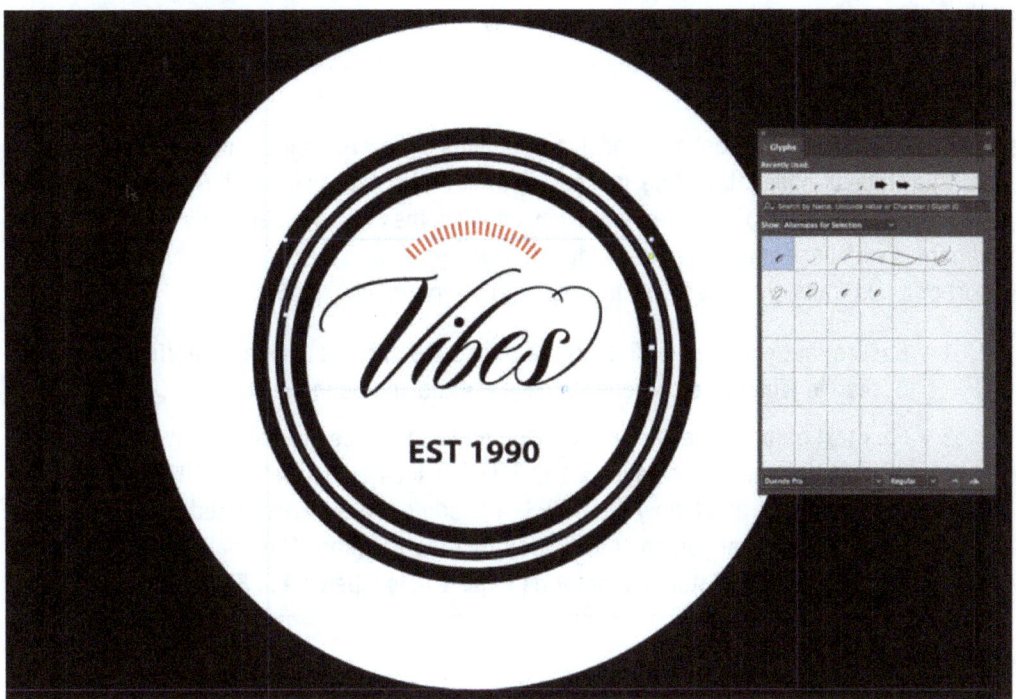

Figure 9.7: The Vibes logo with an alternate applied and the Glyphs panel visible (The image is intended as a visual reference; the textual information is not essential.)

That wraps up the design for **Page 1**. Type *Cmd + 0* (macOS) or *Ctrl + 0* (Windows) to center the entire page in the viewport. Toggle between the **Normal** 🖹 and **Preview** ▢ viewing (*W*) options off the bottom of the toolbox. Choose **File** menu | **Save** at this point. We'll move to the spread pages 2-3, where we'll bring in text from Microsoft Word and automatically format it on import.

Style mapping from Microsoft Word

Have you ever spent hours meticulously crafting styles in Microsoft Word, only to face the daunting task of recreating them in InDesign? With a bit of forward planning, style mapping between Word and InDesign can drastically speed up your workflow and streamline monotonous tasks.

Threading text frames

Text frames in InDesign can exist as standalone elements or flow through connected frames across pages. This process, called **threading**, makes use of in and out ports on each frame. Empty ports mark the beginning or end of a text thread. When enabled, the **Show Text Threads** option connects linked frames with lines and arrows denoting the flow direction of the text thread. A red plus in an out port of a text frame indicates overflow text. Let's explore how this works.

1. Ensure that you are working on the pages 2-3 spread. Choose the **View** menu | **Fit Spread in Window** to center both pages of the spread in the viewport.
2. Four text frames have been pre-created for you to place the text from Word into. Three of these frames are on pages 2 and 3. One is located below the **MAINS** heading, and two are above and below the **SWEETS** heading. These are marked as **1**, **2**, and **3** in *Figure 9.8* so that you can easily identify their location. The final text frame can be found in the left-bottom quadrant on **Page 4**. It is labeled **4** in *Figure 9.8*.

> **Note**
> The frames in *Figure 9.8* have a white border and numbers so that you can easily identify them. The design will have the frames in place without the white border or numbering.

Figure 9.8: The text frames that we will be threading and placing the Word text file into (The image is intended as a visual reference; the textual information is not essential.)

3. As a gentle reminder, threading text means connecting one text frame to another which allows text to flow between them. To get the process started, we'll enable the visibility of the thread sequence by choosing **View** menu | **Extras** | **Show Text Threads**.

4. Choose the **Selection** tool from the Toolbox. Click the first text frame below the **MAINS** heading on **Page 2** (See *Figure 9.9*).

5. Click the **Out** port as indicated in the screenshot that follows.

Figure 9.9: Text frame 1 with its Out port indicated

6. Move your cursor inside the second text frame. The icon will change to the thread icon, which is represented by two chain links and an arrow . Click to link the two frames. A text thread line will appear between the **out** port of text frame 1 and the **in** port of text frame 2, as shown in the screenshot that follows.

Figure 9.10: Text frames 1 and 2 successfully threaded with the text thread visible
(The image is intended as a visual reference; the textual information is not essential.)

7. We'll repeat the process for text frames 3 and 4. As you can see, text threads can span multiple pages and spreads.

Figure 9.11: The linked text threads across pages 2 to 4

With the text frames threaded and the direction of the flow of text correct, we can embark on placing the text from Microsoft Word and mapping the Word styles to their corresponding InDesign styles.

Mapping Word styles to InDesign styles

Style mapping helps bridge the gap between content created in Microsoft Word and ensuring that that content is professionally designed and laid out in InDesign. This function allows you to link your Word styles directly to InDesign styles, saving you hours of manual formatting.

Exploring the styles used in Word

This is an optional step. Let's have a quick look at the Word document to see how it has been created and how styles have been applied:

1. **Open the file named** 01 Word Import.docx **from the** Chapter 9 Advanced Typography Example Files | Links **folder.**

2. Make the **Styles Pane** visible from the **Home** ribbon bar. Choose **Styles in use** from the **List** dropdown toward the bottom of the pane and check the **Show styles guides** checkbox just below.

3. As can be observed in *Figure 9.2*, five styles have been used in the document. These styles have been renamed as follows:

    A. **Normal** has been changed to **Menu Item Description**, e.g., *Savory mix of tofu*

    B. **Heading 1** has been changed to **Category Heading**, e.g., *Appetizers*

    C. **Heading 3** has been changed to **Menu Item**, e.g., *Crispy Thai Springrolls 8.00*

    D. **Heading 4** has been changed to **Ingredient Notice**, e.g., *Made with...*

    E. **Heading 5** has been changed to **Ingredient Bullet Pts**, e.g., *Soy-free...*

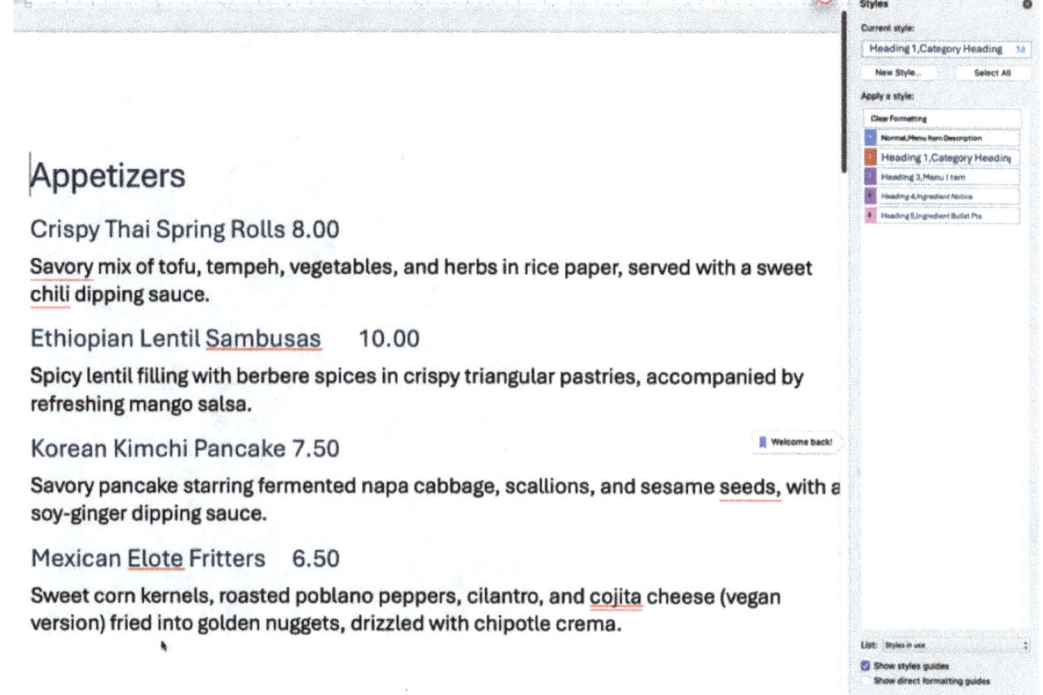

Figure 9.12: The Word document with the style pane visible

Having looked at the styles applied in Microsoft Word, we can turn our attention to styles and how to set them up in InDesign, next. Close the Word file and quit the application.

Exploring the styles setup in InDesign

Let's have a quick look at styles that have been set up for you in InDesign. With a little bit of forward planning, one can use style mapping to great advantage.

1. Open the **Paragraph Styles** and **Character Styles** panels in the menu document in InDesign.
2. Apart from having additional styles for formatting other design elements (as we have just done with the headings), you'll observe that we have styles that mimic the naming of the Word styles. We find that working this way helps streamline the style mapping workfow.

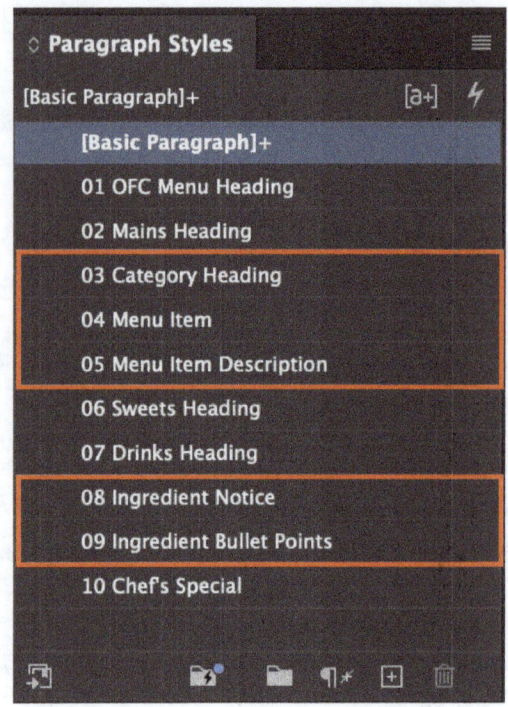

Figure 9.13: The InDesign Paragraph Styles panel with common styles highlighted

Now that we have an understanding of how the styles connect between InDesign and Word, we're ready to import the Word document. We'll do so in the next section. We'll also map the Word styles to the InDesign styles above for automatic flow and formatting.

Importing and mapping Word styles

InDesign can import Word files by either removing styles, preserving and importing them, importing them automatically, or customizing how the styles are imported. Which of these powerful choices you select will depend on the task at hand.

1. Choose the **Selection** tool and click off-page on the pasteboard to ensure nothing is selected. This is an important step as InDesign, by default, replaces any chosen element with objects or text being imported. If this happens by mistake, you can always undo the last set of actions and place your content again.
2. Choose **File menu** | **Place**. Navigate to **Example Files** | Chapter 9 Advanced Typography Example Files | Links folder and choose the file called 01 Word Import.docx. Do not click **Open** or **OK** just yet.
3. Toward the bottom of the **Place** dialog is the **Show Import Options** checkbox. Check it.

> **Note**
> Checking the **Show Import Options** checkbox results in the options dialog appearing for all subsequent elements you place in your design, which can be cumbersome. A handy tip is to press *Shift* as you click the **Open** button. This will trigger the **Show Import Options** dialog once-off for the element/s being placed.

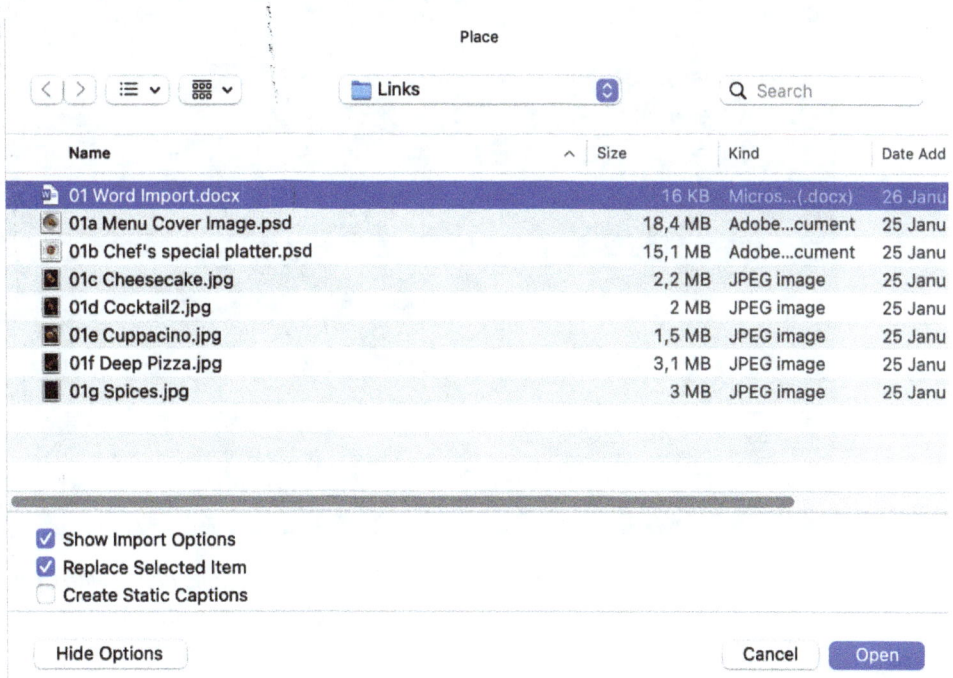

Figure 9.14: The Place dialog with Show Import Options checked

4. Set the following options in the **Microsoft Word Import Options** dialog:

   A. Uncheck all checkboxes except **Use Typographer's Quotes**.
   B. Click the **Customize Style Import** radio button near the bottom of the dialog.
   C. Then click the **Style Mapping…** button the right. See *Figure 9.15*.

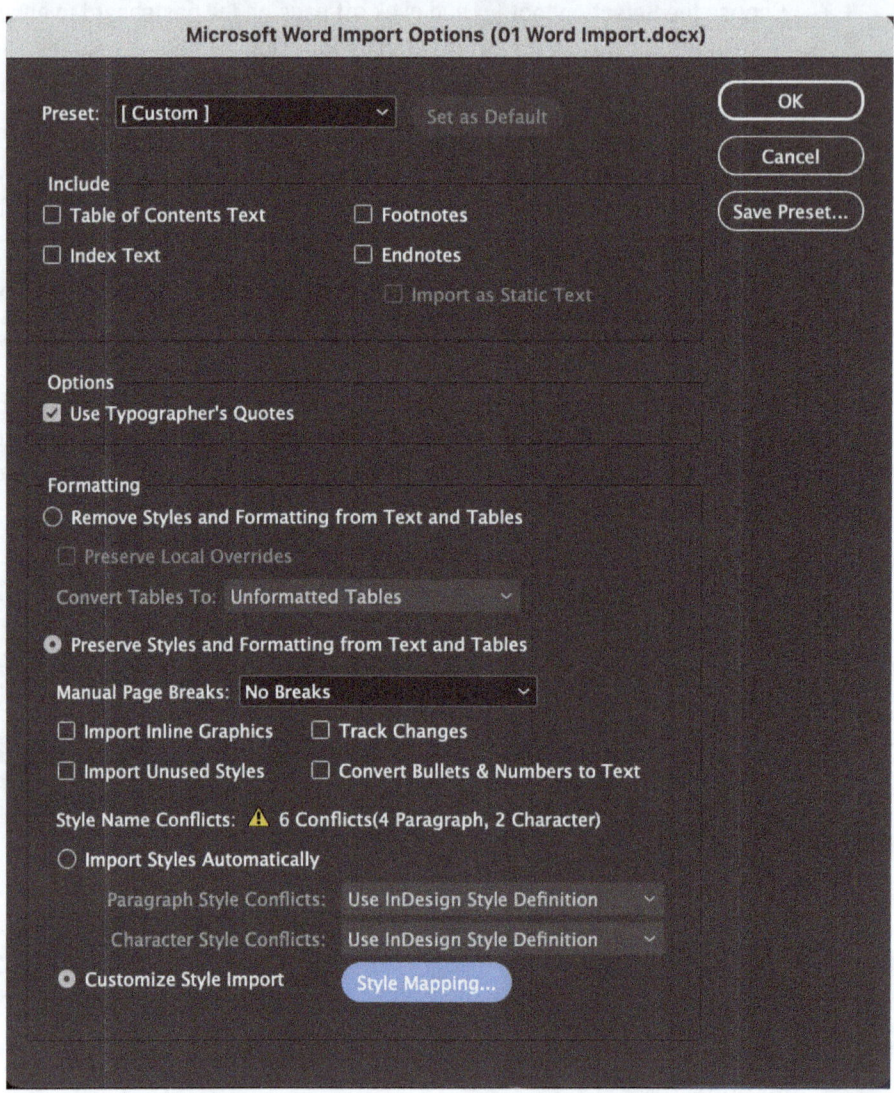

Figure 9.15: The Word Import Options dialog with Customize Style Import and Style Mapping selected

5. In the **Style Mapping** dialog that opens, you will be presented with a list of all the styles that are used in the Word document. You'll observe that since we used the same naming convention for styles used in the Word document and the InDesign document, InDesign maps them automatically. Unmapped styles can be mapped as desired. We'll map the styles that were used in Word as they appear in the Word style list found to the the left of the **Style Mapping** dialog with InDesign styles found on the right.

   A. **Map Normal** to **05 Menu Item Description**
   B. **Map Heading 1** to **03 Category Heading**
   C. Ignore **Heading 2** as it has not been used
   D. **Map Heading 3** to **04 Menu Item**
   E. **Map Heading 4** to **08 Ingredient Notice**
   F. **Heading 5** to 09 **Ingredient Bullet Points**
   G. The rest of the Word styles can be ignored, as they have not been used either

6. Click **OK** twice. Click in the first frame of our text thread on the left-bottom **Page 2**. The formatted text has been placed into all the text frames we threaded earlier. Notice that the text has been styled courtesy of **Style Mapping**.

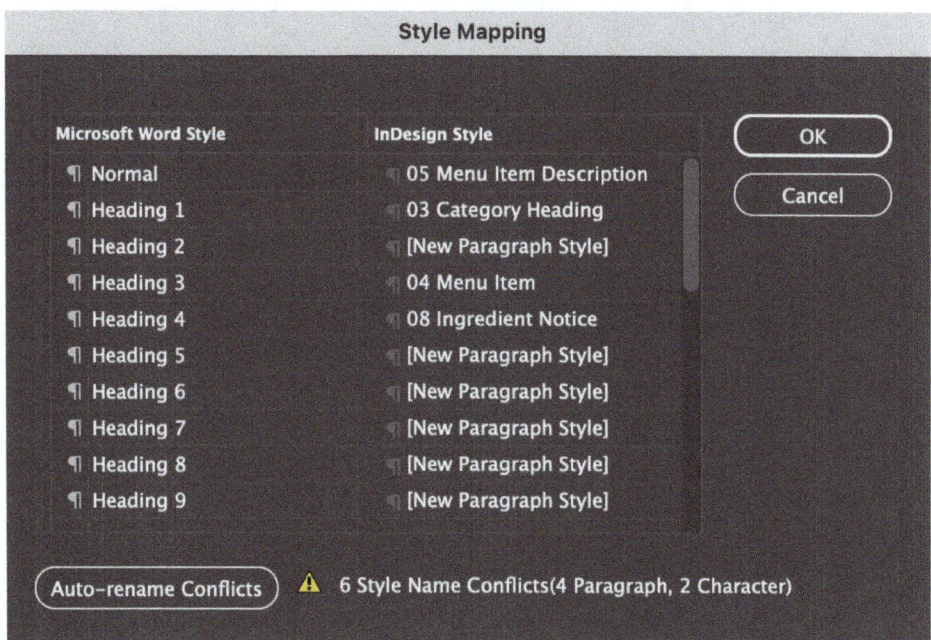

Figure 9.16: The Word styles mapped to relevant InDesign styles

As you can see, style mapping can save you many hours by having InDesign deal with the monotonous task of assigning styles based on the rules that you have defined for your project.

Customizing the properties of a defined style

For the next task, we'd like to increase the point size for the prices of each of the dishes on the menu. We'll do so by redefining the properties of the style and having it update the prices throughout the document.

1. Open the **Paragraph Styles** panel on the screen.
2. Ensure that no elements are selected. This is an important step.
3. Right-click the **04 Menu Item** style and choose **Edit** to open the **Paragraph Styles Options** dialog.
4. Enable the **Preview** checkbox on the bottom-left of the dialog to see any changes we make in real time.
5. The style constitutes nested styles that define the white color of the menu item and the gold color of the price. Remember that nested styles apply character formatting inside a paragraph style based on specific conditions such as word count or punctuation. In our example, that trigger condition is a *Tab* character between the menu item and the price.
6. GREP styles find and apply formatting that we specify to text based on custom search patterns. The style also has a GREP component, which looks like this: (?<=[\.])\d+.
7. This GREP style searches for one or more digits (\d+) that are preceded by a period using a positive lookbehind expression to identify and apply the superscript style to digits that follow the period in the text.

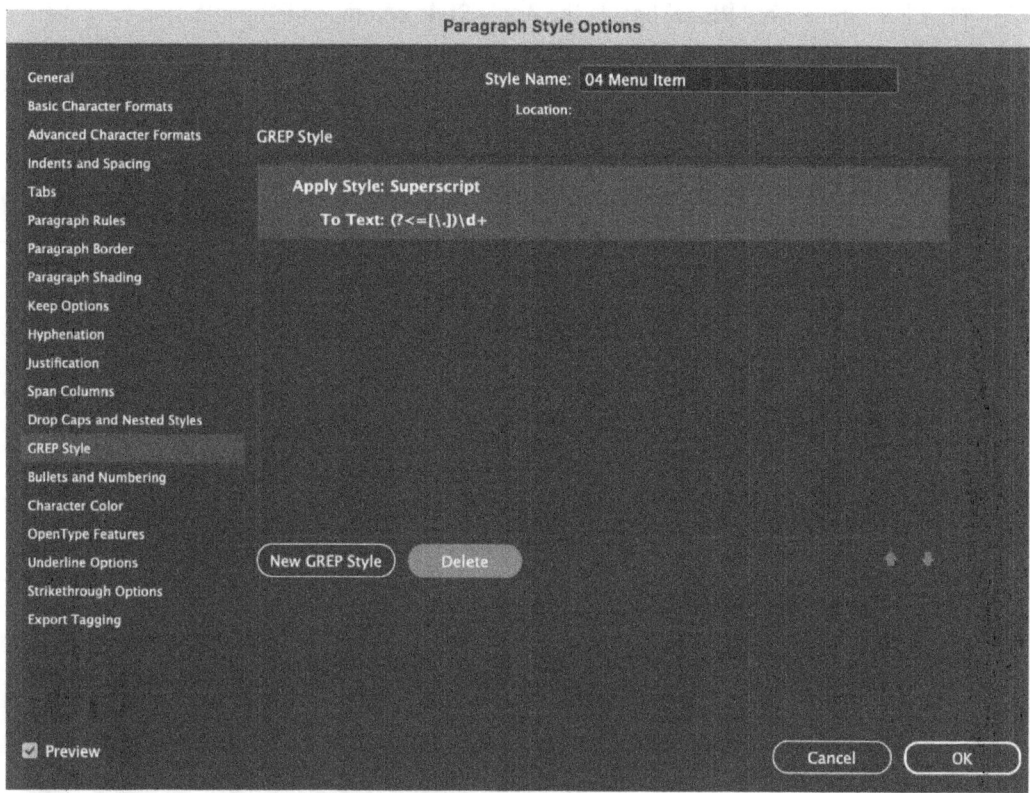

Figure 9.17: A GREP style that forms part of the 04 Menu Item paragraph style

8. We'd like to change the price point size of the price from 12 pt to 16 pt. To achieve this, we'll use a GREP style.

9. Click the **New GREP Style** button. We'll deal with the **Apply Style** command shortly. The default search string is \d+, which means find any string of digits. This matches our requirements perfectly.

10. We now need to define a **Character** style that we can apply to our query that will initiate the size change.

11. Click on the word **[None]** beside the **Apply Style** command to open a drop-down list. Choose **New Character Style...** from the bottom of the list so that we can define and apply our preferred text size.

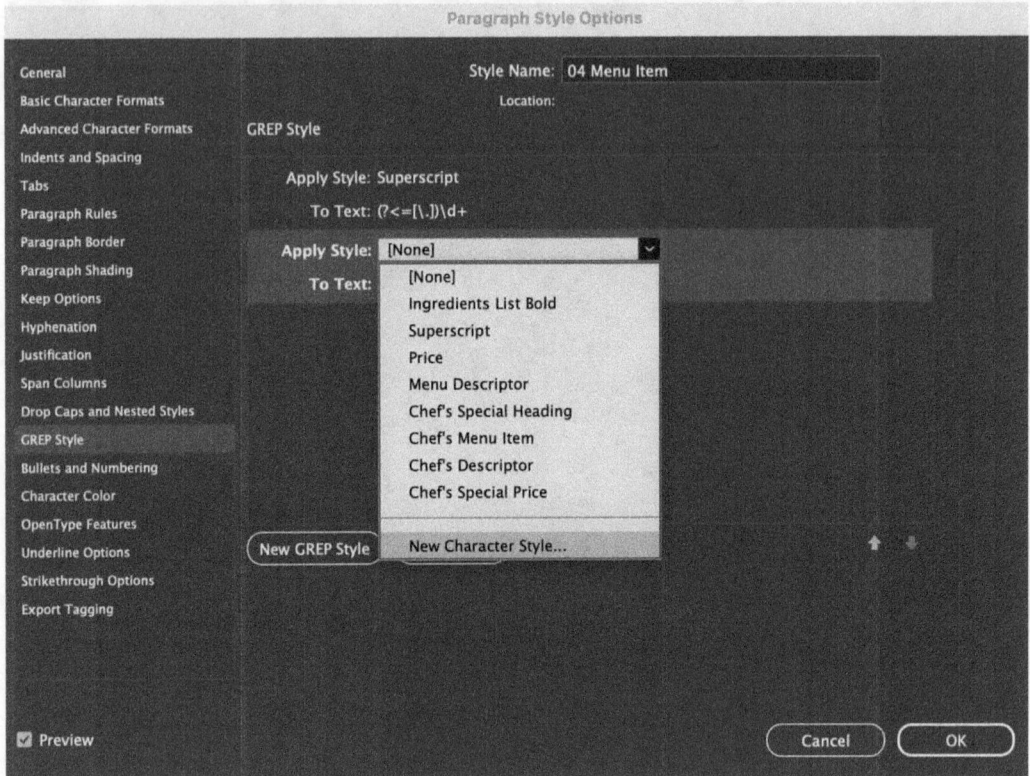

Figure 9.18: The newly created GREP style with the Apply Style dropdown

12. Rename the style. Call it **Price 16pt**.
13. Choose the **Basic Characters** subset from the left of the dialog and change the size value to 16 pt. With **Preview** enabled, you should see the change directly in the design. Click **OK** when you are done to close all open dialogs.

Figure 9.19: The design with the price size change highlighted and the newly created character style visible (The image is intended as a visual reference; the textual information is not essential.)

In the next section we will insert special characters called glyphs to help enhance our design further.

Using glyphs

Occasionally, we require a specific glyph, symbol, or icon in our designs. These are often referred to as **dingbats** in typography. We'll add a dingbat to a string of text to give it the look we want. We'll do this directly to the text, as there is only one instance where it is needed. A style here would be overkill.

1. Choose the **Selection** tool and click off-page on the pasteboard to ensure that nothing is selected.
2. Zoom into the frame found at the bottom left of **Page 4**. See *Figure 9.20*. Identify the text that reads **MADE WITH** [a]. We'd like to change the [a] placeholder to a golden heart symbol.
3. Select the [a] placeholder text with the **Type** tool.

4. Choose **Type menu | Glyphs**. Ensure that **Show: Entire Font** is selected.

5. Change the font from **Bebas Neue** to **Zapf Dingbats**. **Wingdings** can also be used if you do not have **Zapf Dingbats** installed on your computer.

6. Scroll through the font symbols until you locate the heart symbol and double-click it to replace the placeholder.

7. We'll make a quick color change to the heart from **Paper (White)** to **Gold**. You should be pretty okay with doing this. Select the heart symbol and choose **Gold** for its fill from the **Properties** panel.

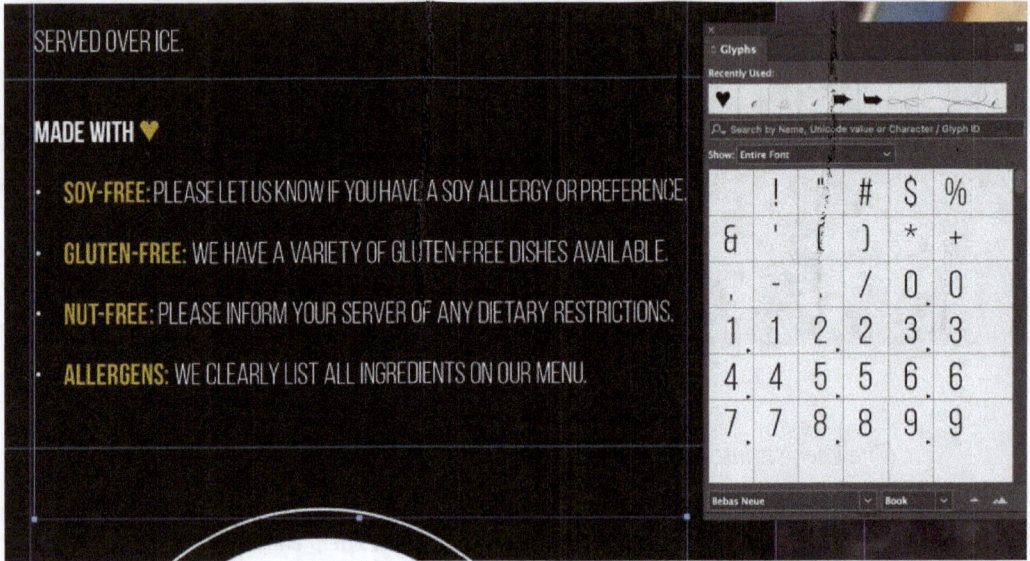

Figure 9.20: The design showing the heart dingbat and the Glyphs panel with the relevant elements

As you've just witnessed, accessing custom glyphs and dingbats is straightforward. Glyphs in InDesign offer a vast array of individual visual representations or characters within a font, encompassing letters, numbers, symbols, and special characters. They allow you to have precise control over typography and design elements in a document.

Adding custom bullets to a list

While we're on the topic of glyphs and special characters, you've probably noticed that the bullets in the list below the **MADE WITH** ♡ text are not as robust as we'd like them to be. We'll tweak the associated style to achieve the desired result.

1. Ensure that you have ingredients text selected with the **Type** tool 🅣. On the **Properties** panel, click the **Paragraph Styles** switch under **Text Style**.
2. From the drop-down list just below, click the **Edit** icon ✏ next to the **09 Ingredient Bullet Points** paragraph style name to make the necessary changes to the style.
3. Click **Bullets and Numbering** from the options list on the left. Then click the **Add** button.

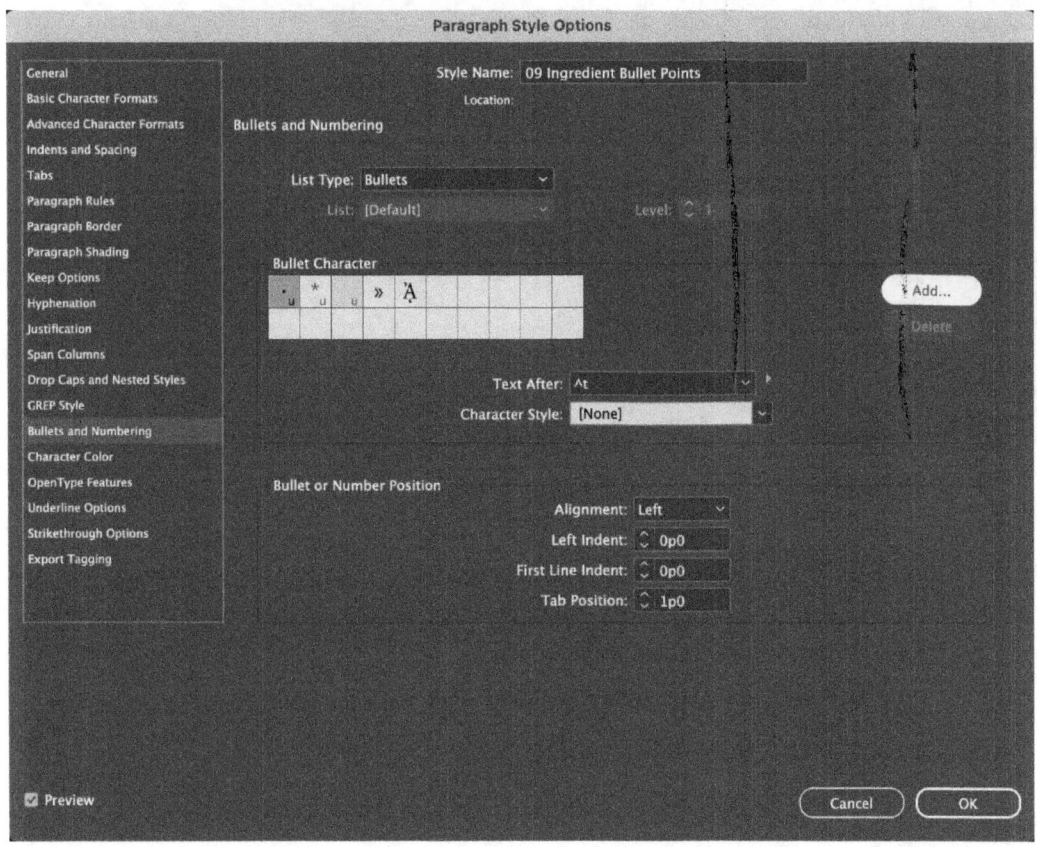

Figure 9.21: The Paragraph Style Options dialog showing options for Bullets and Numbering

4. In the resultant **Add Bullets** dialog, change the **Font Family** to **Zapf Dingbats**. You can use **Wingdings** if **Zapf Dingbats** is unavailable on your system.

5. We've settled on a large round bullet. You are welcome to experiment by choosing a dingbat of your choice.

6. Click **Add** and **OK**, in that order, to have the new bullet added to the **Bullet Character** list.

7. Ensure that the **Preview** checkbox is checked and choose the newly-added bullet. This will be displayed on the design in real time.

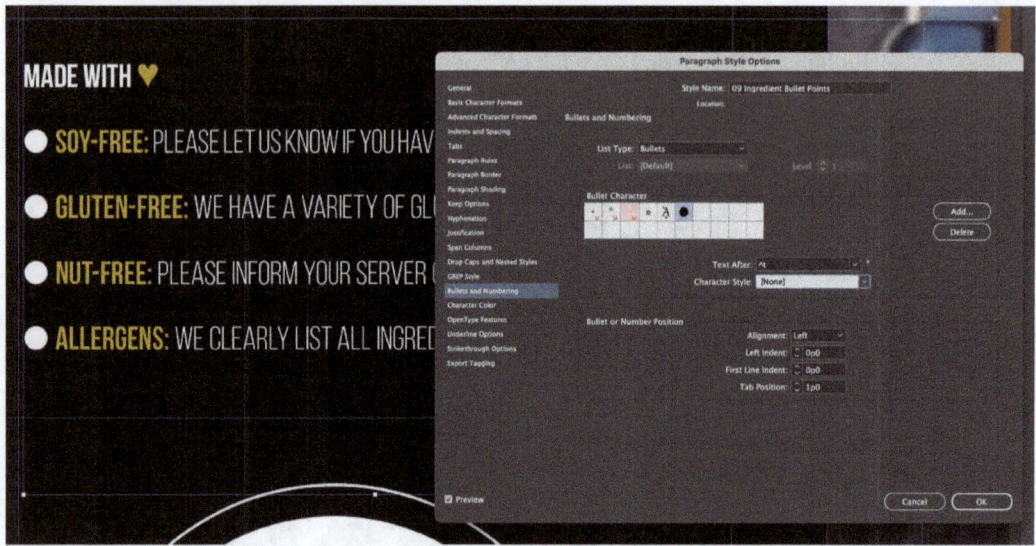

Figure 9.22: The bulleted list with the new bullet applied

8. We'd like the color of the bullet to be gold. We'd also like to adjust its size and apply a baseline shift to move its vertical position so it aligns better with the text. A character style will need to be created for this task.

9. Click the dropdown next to the **Character Style** command and choose **New Character Style**.

10. In the **Character Style Options** dialog, make the following changes:

    A. From the **General** category, set **Style Name** to **Ingredients Bullet**.

    B. From the **Basic Character Formats** category, change the size to **10pt**.

    C. Choose the **Advanced Character Formats** category and set **Baseline Shift** to 1pt. This will center the bullet better vertically against the height of the text.

D. Finally, select to the **Character Color** category and choose **Gold**.

Figure 9.23: The bulleted list with the new character style applied

InDesign offers you strong controls to customize bullets. These let you adjust the appearance, size, font, and styling of bullet characters used in lists, providing you with tremendous creative control. Be sure to experiment with other options such as OpenType features, as well as bullets.

Combining paragraph and character styles

Combining paragraph and character styles in InDesign streamlines design consistency and efficiency, enabling quick and unified formatting of both text blocks and individual text elements to create a cohesive and professional look throughout your documents. For the task that follows, we will format the chef's special element, taking it from its unformatted form on the left of *Figure 9.24* to its completed result on the right.

Figure 9.24: The bulleted list with the new character style applied
(The image is intended as a visual reference; the textual information is not essential.)

1. Navigate to **Page 2** and zoom into the **Chef's Special** element at the bottom of the page.
2. Let's look at the relationship between the type and the chef illustration. Select the chef illustration with the **Selection** tool . Then choose the **Window** menu | **Text Wrap**. You can see that a basic text wrap has been applied to the artwork to prevent the type from running into the graphic. You are welcome to close the **Text Wrap** panel.

Figure 9.25: A text wrap around the bounding box of the chef illustration has been applied

3. Select the text object with the **Selection** tool . Head to the **Text Style** segment of the **Properties** panel and ensure that the **Paragraph Styles** switch is active. Then choose **10 Chef's Special** from the drop-down list. This takes care of most of the formatting for us.

4. We now have an opportunity to harmonize between paragraph and character styles. Select the **CHEF'S SPECIAL** title with the **Type** tool. Switch to the **Character Styles** switch on the **Properties** panel. Choose the **Chef's Special Heading** character style and voilà, it is done.

5. Select the price with the **Type** tool. Choose the **Chef's Special Price** character style from the dropdown list..

> **Tip**
>
> You can triple-click the price with the **Type** tool too. Then choose the **Chef's Special Price** character style from the drop-down list on the **Properties** panel.

Making changes to vertical justification

We have to do one more task to complete the Chef's Special element. That is to resolve the vertical alignment of the type within the text frame. This is done by adjusting the controls in the **Text Frame Options** dialog.

1. With the text frame selected the **Selection** tool, choose **Object** menu | **Text Frame Options**. Under the **Vertical Justification** controls, change the **Align** value from **Center** to **Top**. Check the **Preview** checkbox for real-time feedback. Choose **OK** when you're done.

Figure 9.26: The design with the type vertically aligned

As you can see, working with advanced typographic controls in InDesign is straightforward. Typography in InDesign offer a vast array of individual visual controls for you to tweak. These settings give you precise control over typography and design elements in a document.

Placing type along a path

The InDesign **Type on a Path** feature wraps text along custom shapes or paths. Using the **Type on a Path** tool, you can have text follow custom curves or shapes, adapting to their contours. This versatility allows for the seamless integration of text into design elements such as circles, spirals, or other complex shapes.

Figure 9.27: Type applied to an ellipse with glyphs on either end

In this section, we'll place text on a designated path and style it so that it meets the design requirements for our menu.

1. Navigate to the bottom of **Page 4**. You'll observe that an additional circle has been drawn around the logo. This will host our text, which can be found just off-page.
2. Select all the **Yummy** text off-page with the **Type** tool . Then choose **Edit** menu | **Cut** to transfer it to the clipboard.
3. Click and hold on the **Type** tool and select the **Type on a Path** tool (*Shift + T*) from the resultant tool flyout.
4. Hover over the top of the circle and click to activate it as a type path. You'll observe a blinking cursor where you clicked.
5. Choose **Edit** menu | **Paste** to place the text on the path.
6. We now need to remove the stroke on the circle. It played the role of a visual aid and is not needed in the final design. Click the circle with the **Selection** tool . Then click the **Stroke** swatch on the **Properties** panel and select **None** from the flyout.

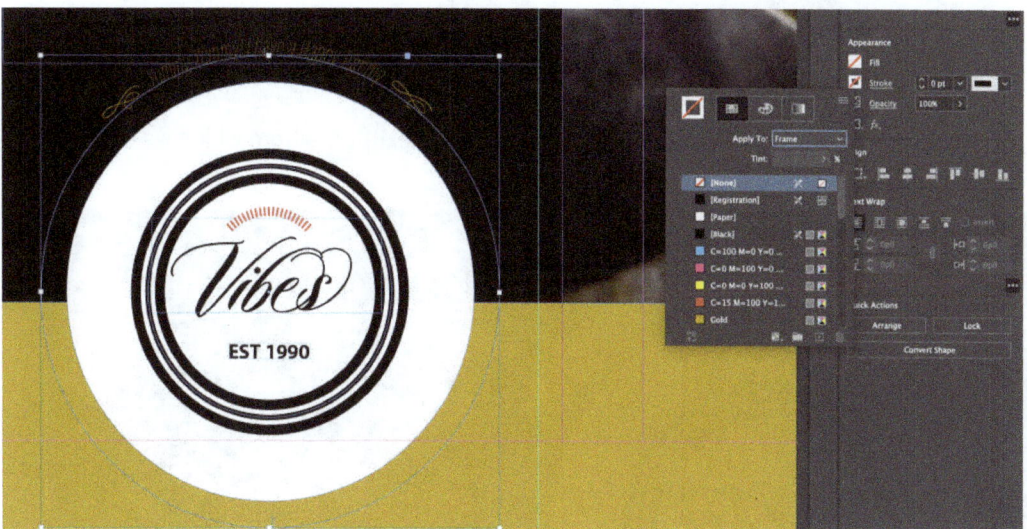

Figure 9.28: The type on a path execution with the circle stroke set to None on the Properties panel

InDesign supports a smorgasbord of different font formats. We'll look at the promising world of variable fonts in the next section.

Variable fonts

Variable fonts are a revolutionary type of technology. A single font file can contain a range of formatting options including weight, width, and slant. InDesign leverages variable fonts to provide designers with unprecedented flexibility in adjusting typograph attributes seamlessly. The biggest benefit is that you can achieve diverse typographic effects without the need for multiple font files. This enhances both design flexibility and workflow efficiency. In this section, we will apply a variable font to some copy and explore what we can do with this powerful font format.

1. The text that reads *Yummy, Yummy! I have a Happy Tummy* needs some work. Select this text only. Be sure not to select the decorative glyphs on either end of the text (See *Figure 9.29*).

2. Head to the **Properties** panel and click the **Variable Font** switch . It is found under the **Character** subset, nestled under the **Font** name. Refer to *Figure 9.29* if you need to.

3. In the **Variable Font** flyout, set the values as follows:

    A. Weight: 200

    B. Width: 115

    C. Slant: 0

4. Now for some housekeeping. Click the empty text frame from which we copied the copy with the **Selection** tool and delete it.

Figure 9.29: The type with the Variable Font controls visible

The **Variable Fonts** controls in InDesign offers great design flexibility by giving you access to fine controls over typographic properties in a single font file. We're sure that this will help streamline your workflow efficiency and enhance typographic expression.

Local overrides

Occasionally, you may want to quickly tweak type properties without creating a new style. Creating a style for one or two instances is unecessary. Local overrides in InDesign act like personalized branches for your text. While a paragraph or character style defines the overall format, local overrides allow you to tweak specific instances within that style for your desired needs.

Figure 9.30: The screenshots show the text before and after local overrides have been applied

For this section, we'll format text using a style as a base and tweak it to fit our design.

1. Click inside the **SCAN ME** text frame found at the bottom-right of **Page 4** with the **Type** tool (*T*). Then choose **Edit** menu | **Select All** to select all of the copy.

2. Head to the **Properties** panel and ensure that **Paragraph Styles** is selected. Click on the drop-down list and select the **05 Menu Item Description** style.

3. With the text still selected, make the following changes on the **Properties** panel. Refer to *Figure 9.31* for the parameters we need to change:

    A. From the **Appearance** subset, choose the **Fill** swatch and change the color from **[Paper]** to **[Black]**.

B. Go to the **Character** subset and change the leading to **Auto**.

C. Under **Paragraph**, click the **Align right** option.

D. Then change the **Space After** value from 1p0 to 0p0.

4. That's it. One final point worth noting is that InDesign shows you that local overrides have been applied by adding a **+** suffix to the style name. It now reads **05 Menu Item Description+**.

*Figure 9.31: The type with local overrides highlighted on the **Properties** panel*

Using local overrides for quick once-off edits can be done at your discretion in InDesign. It's worth noting that the type is connected to the style. Any changes made to the style that are not local overrides will update if changes are made to the style.

Generating QR codes

QR codes in InDesign open powerful doorways to connect your printed materials to augmented reality. Embedding a QR code in our menu design will augment the printed design by allowing diners to get instant information on menu ingredients, calories, and more. You can use QR codes to take users to a website, embed an email address, or trigger an augmented reality experience. We'll generate a custom QR code, style it, and place it in its final position in the layout.

Figure 9.32: The completed design with the QR code in place

1. With the **Selection** tool , click off-page to ensure that no elements are selected.
2. Choose **Object** menu | **Generate QR Code**. In the resultant dialog, make the following edits:

    A. For type, choose **Web Hyperlink**.

    B. In the URL entry field, type https://vibes.food/ingredients. This is a fictitious link for the sake of demonstrating the feature.

    C. Change the color to [**Black**]. You are welcome to experiment, as always. Click **OK** when you are done.

3. Click and release the loaded cursor off-page to prevent placing the element inside an existing element.
4. We now need to adjust the size and position of the element. With the QR code still active, make the following changes. See *Figure 9.33* for the properties that need to be updated. Make the folllowing changes on the **Properties** panel:

    A. Under the **Transform** subset, choose the middle proxy reference point.

    B. Set the **W** and **H** values to 7p0.

C. Set the **X** value to 58p0 and the **Y** value to 96p0.

Figure 9.33: The QR code placed onto the design

QR codes offer you the ability to extend the functionality of a printed or digital document you create in InDesign into a multi-dimensional user experience. When you use them judiciously, you can overcome the gimmicky trend that has been associated with QR codes.

Summary

In this chapter, we delved deep into the wonderful world of text styles in InDesign. From the rapid-fire application of styles to the nuanced control of OpenType features. We explored the seamless transfer of styles from Microsoft Word and unlocked the power of nested styles. We looked at how GREP styles can enable complex search strings. We also transformed bullet lists with unique design elements. Text was placed gracefully along paths and variable fonts were used for fine typographic control within the same font. By generating QR codes, we looked at how to bridge the gap between print and augmented reailty. In the next chapter, we will look at how to prepare this menu and other designs for high-end professional print.

Level: Advanced

10
Preparing Documents for Professional Print

InDesign is a print publishing powerhouse offering myriad print management features and customizable controls. This allows you to set up your print document with a high degree of quality assurance. You are warned of potential issues that could occur on output. InDesign also enables you to manage important factors such as inks and separations, imposition, step and repeat, ISO-aligned PDF/X exports, and soft proofing to get the quality print results your clients need and demand. It's worth noting that setting up documents for professional commercial print has to factor in a number of variables. These range from stock (paper/substrate) requirements, standards used in your country/region, press-specific requisites, ink considerations, and color settings for your specific printing environments, among a slew of other requirements.

In this chapter, the essential tenets of preparing documents for print will be discussed. We'll apply these concepts to InDesign documents to see how to get the best printed results. You should then be able to take these core concepts and tweak them to fit your print requirements with ease. Knowing how to prepare content correctly for print is the difference between a successful campaign and costly mistakes.

The main topics we will cover in this chapter include the following:

- Setting up Step and Repeat
- Data Merge
- Creating print-ready PDF files
- Color separations
- Preflighting

You can find the relevant projects/examples for this chapter here: https://packt.link/a19oQ

Setting up Step and Repeat

For this first segment of this chapter, we will use the business card design we worked with in *Chapter 1*. We'll use the **Step and Repeat** function to precisely duplicate and arrange artwork in rows and columns in preparation for printing. We'll look at the completed project in the steps that follow to help us understand our objectives. We'll then move on to preparing a project file for printing step-by-step. You can follow along by downloading the files referred to in this project. These files can be downloaded from https://packt.link/a19oQ.

1. In Adobe InDesign, open the completed project by choosing **File** | **Open**. Navigate to the Chapter 10 Professional Print Example Files folder. Open the file named Try it yourself 1 - Business Card Step and Repeat Complete.indd.

2. If you are presented with a missing fonts warning, please click **Activate**. InDesign will install any missing fonts from the Adobe type library.

3. Let's explore the project and become familiar with the various elements in the design. This is a single-page print setup of the business card project we worked on in *Chapter 1*. We'll work in picas and points to cater to folks who work in either imperial or metric units as best we can.

4. Reset the workspace so that it mirrors the screenshots shown in this book as closely as possible. Choose the **Window** menu and ensure **[Essentials]** is checked. Then, choose the **Window** menu again and select **Reset Essentials**. If you prefer to use your own custom workspace, you are more than welcome to do so.

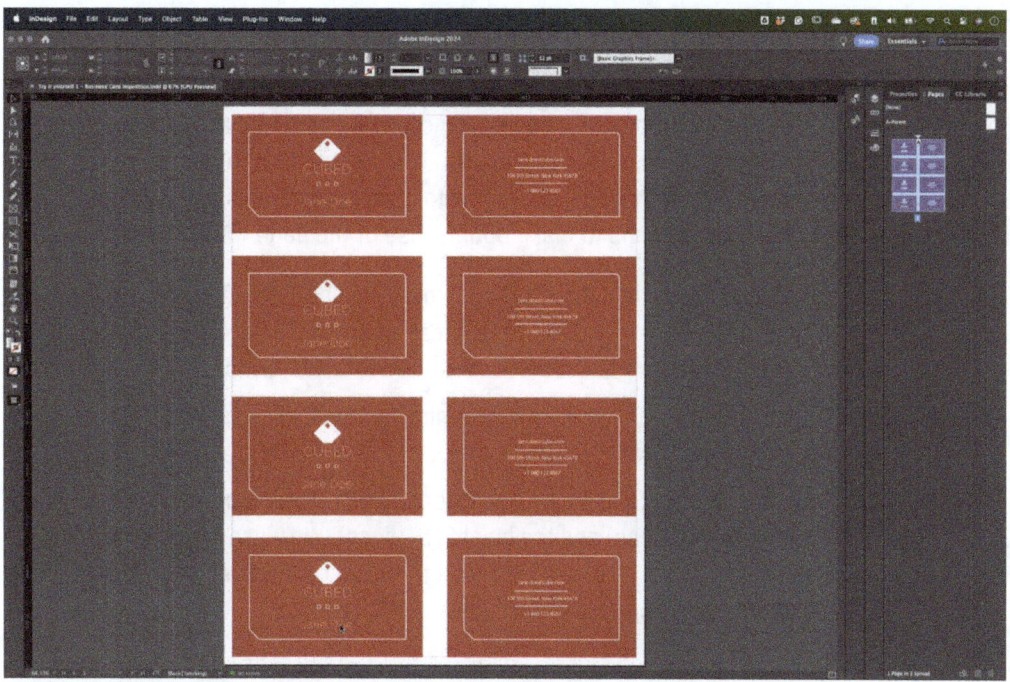

*Figure 10.1: The business card design ready for print
(The image is intended as a visual reference; the textual information is not essential.)*

Note that the business card has a front and back design. The designs have been repeated as many times as possible to accommodate a letter-sized sheet of paper.

5. Once you're done exploring the completed project file, please close the document by choosing **File | Close**. If you are prompted to save the file, choose **Don't Save**.

A few things we will work on for this project. Take note of the cut marks off the edges of each of the business cards. They were applied to the original artwork before the copy-and-paste operation. There is no bleed requirement for the overall page, as bleed has been incorporated into each individual copy of the business card design.

Preparing artwork for print

Preparing artwork for print is a career in itself. Professionals in this discipline study and work in print production for many years before mastering the nuances of prepress file preparation. Preparing files correctly for printing saves time, effort, and money. In the steps that follow, we will replicate the print outcome we just explored. We will look at how to create crop marks and duplicate copies of the design across rows and columns to make optimal use of the page when printing.

1. Open the project file we will be working on by choosing **File** | **Open**. Navigate to the Chapter 10 Preparing Documents for Professional Print folder. Open the file named Try it yourself 1 - Business Card Step and Repeat Start.indd.

2. If you are presented with a warning about missing fonts, click **Activate**, and InDesign will install any missing fonts.

3. Go to **Page 1** on the **Pages** panel. Then, choose **File** | **Document Setup**. Make a note of the page width (21 picas) and the height (12 picas). We'll use these values to run a script that will place cut marks for the final trim size of the business card. Click **OK** to close the dialog without making any changes for now:

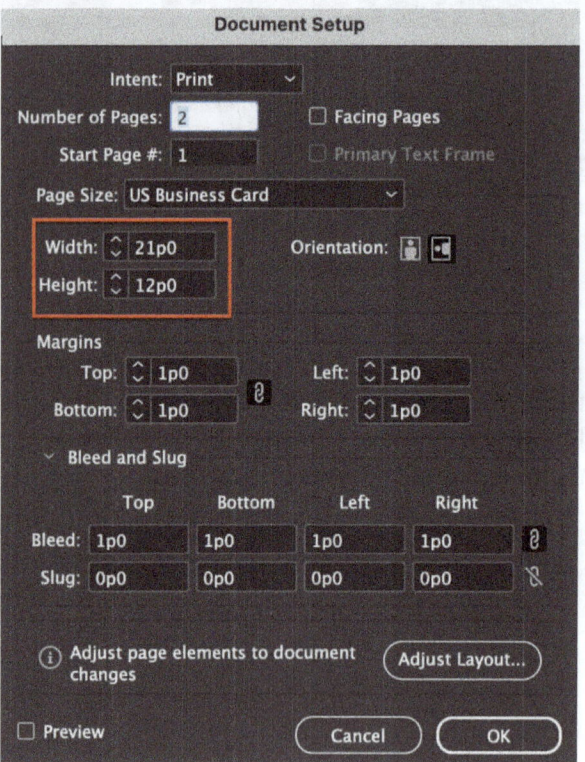

Figure 10.2: The document page size helps us determine the final cut size of the business card

4. Draw a rectangle of any size on the page using the **Rectangle** tool ▪ (*M*). With the rectangle selected, head to the **Properties** panel and make the following changes:

   A. Under the **Transform** category, ensure that the middle reference point is highlighted.

   B. Ensure that the **Constrain Proportions** switch is disabled.

   C. Set **W** to **21p0** and **H** to **12p0**.

   D. Then, set the position values for **X** to **10p6** and **Y** to **6p0**.

Good work. We'll use this object to create our cut marks for the front of the card by using a script that ships with InDesign.

Using scripts in InDesign

In the steps that follow, we'll run a script that will autogenerate cut marks along the outer edges of the business card design. These cut marks are used by the printer to cut and trim the printed cards to their final size.

1. Ensure that the rectangle we just drew is selected, then select **Window | Utilities | Scripts**.

2. In the **Scripts** panel, choose **Application | Samples | JavaScript**.

3. Locate the Cropmarks.jsx script and double-click it to run it.

4. In the **CropMarks** dialog box that appears, make the following changes:

   A. Ensure **Crop Marks** is checked.

   B. Under the **Crop Marks** options, set **Length** and **Offset** to **6pt**, and leave **Stroke Weight** at **0.25pt** (aka hairline).

   C. Uncheck **Registration Marks**.

D. Under the **Draw Marks Around** subset, choose **Entire Selection**:

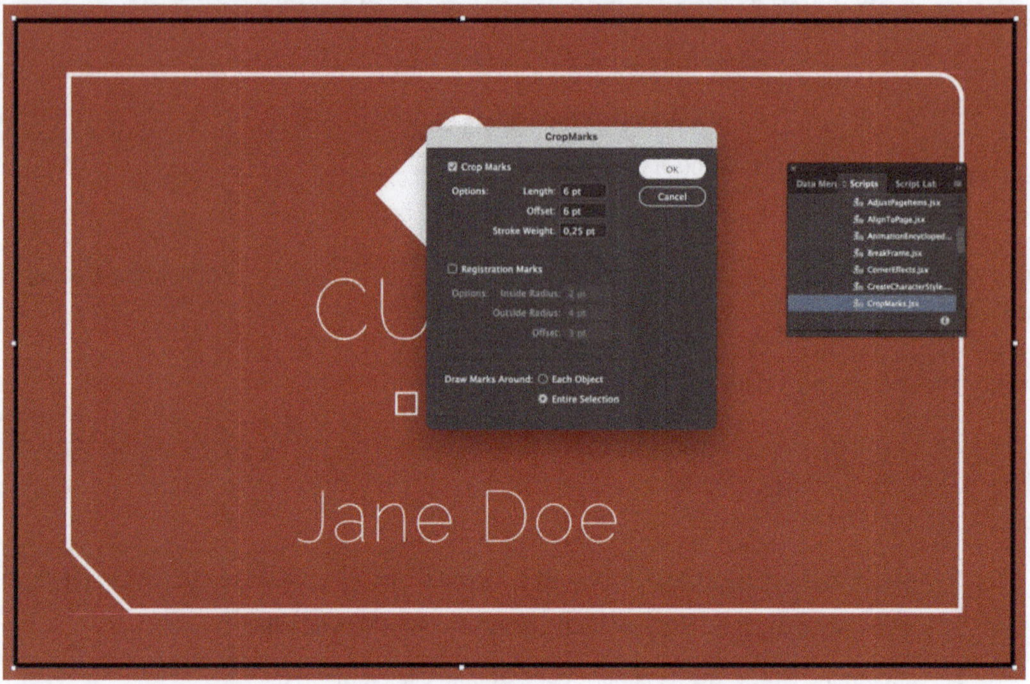

Figure 10.3: The design with crop marks, the Crop Marks dialog, and the Scripts panel

5. We'll repeat this process on **Page 2**. Select the rectangle object and cut it to the clipboard (**Edit | Cut**). Then, navigate to **Page 2** of the document, and choose **Edit | Paste in Place**.

6. With the pasted rectangle still highlighted, run the Cropmarks.jsx script again on **Page 2**. In the **CropMarks** dialog box, use the same parameters as were used in *step 4*

7. Now, delete the rectangle we used to define the crop mark parameters.

Figure 10.4: Page 2 with crop marks applied and the reference rectangle deleted

8. We'll now prepare the document elements for the **Step and Repeat** process. Since we're on **Page 2**, select all the elements on **Page 2** and group them.

9. Head to **Page 1** and group all the elements there as well. This will ensure that we keep the page elements intact relationally, and it makes it easier to work with.

With the elements grouped and crop marks in place, we can now change the document properties to accommodate multiple instances of the business card.

Adjusting the document setup

The document page size needs to be changed to match your print environment. We will be using **Letter** for our page size in this example. Should you work with metric measurements, it's worth noting that the concepts we cover can be customized to your unique design environment. Follow the next steps:

1. Choose **File | Document Setup** and make the following changes:

    A. Enable the **Preview** checkbox to see your changes in real time.

    B. Set **Page Size** to **Letter**.

    C. Change **Orientation** to **Portrait**.

D. Keep **Margins** at **1p0**.

E. Set **Bleed** to **0pt** all the way around. Once done, click **OK**.

2. On **Page 1**, select the group of the front of the business card and drag it till it locks into place in the top-left margin on the page.

3. We'll take the design of the rear of the card to **Page 1**. Go to **Page 2** and cut the group object that makes up the rear of the card to the clipboard (**Edit | Cut**).

4. Return to **Page 1**, paste the business card back and drag it so that it snaps to the top right of the page. See *Figure 10.5*:

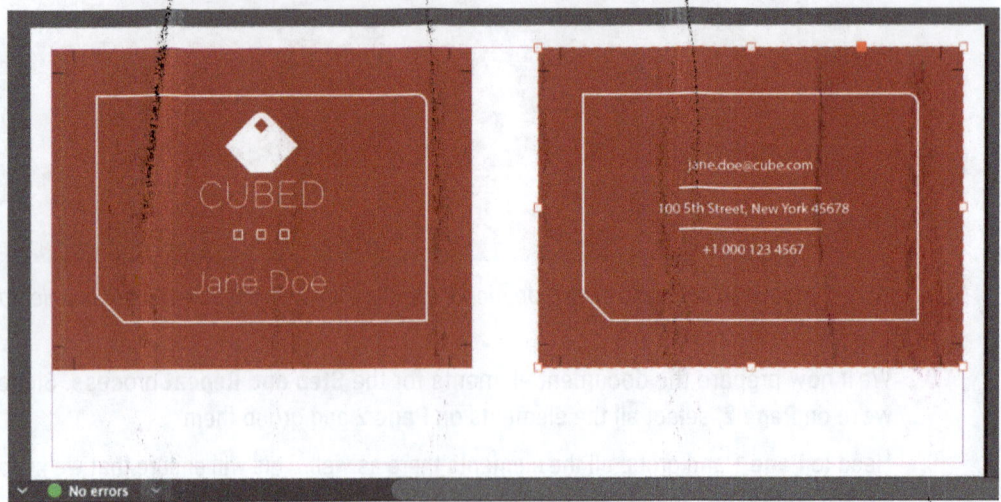

Figure 10.5: A zoomed in view of the front and rear of the business card placed side by side on Page 1

5. We can now delete **Page 2** as it is no longer needed. Select it on the **Pages** panel and click the bin icon to eliminate it.

With the front and rear of the business card in place on **Page 1**, we can execute a **Step and Repeat** command to create a multi-copy setup for printing.

Using the Step and Repeat command

InDesign's **Step and Repeat** command allows for designs to be duplicated at regular intervals horizontally, vertically, or in both directions as grid-aligned elements. The steps that follow explain how to use the **Step and Repeat** command to optimize paper usage on an appropriate paper size when the job is printed.

1. Select both the front and rear designs of the business card on **Page 1**. You can choose the **Select All** command from the **Edit** menu.

2. Choose **Edit | Step and Repeat** and make the following changes:

    A. Enable the **Preview** option.

    B. Under **Repeat**, set the **Count** value to 3.

    C. Disable **Create as a grid**.

    D. Under **Offset**, set **Vertical** to **16p8** and **Horizontal** to **0p0**.

    E. The three copies should be evenly spaced and start at the top margin and end at the bottom margin of the page, as illustrated in *Figure 10.6*.

3. Click **OK** to accept the changes made.

Figure 10.6: The Step and Repeat dialog with copies of the business card shown on the page

That's all there is to it. You can print this directly on a connected printer or save the file as a PDF/X file for high-end professional printing. We will explore how to prepare PDF/X files for print a bit later in this chapter.

In the next section, we'll look at how to set up the same design for different people using the **Data Merge** command.

Data Merge

Data Merge in is a powerful feature that enables the automated merging of variable data from a spreadsheet or database into a predesigned InDesign document template. This process streamlines the creation of personalized documents. We'll employ **Data Merge** to save time and ensure accuracy while maintaining consistency across multiple iterations of our business card design.

Figure 10.7: The completed variable data design with different names and contact information

We'll kick off this section by looking at how to set up data sources so that they are correctly interpreted by InDesign. We'll then import a data source, define variable placeholders, and merge the data into a multi-card design that is appropriate for printing.

Preparing the data source

The data input source is usually prepared in a spreadsheet application. This is typically how knowledge workers typically communicate with designers. InDesign can process a spreadsheet or database file saved as either a comma-delimited .csv file, a tab-delimited .txt file, or a semicolon-delimited .txt file.

To prepare the data source, follow the next steps:

1. Optional: If you wish to see how we prepared the data source file, open a spreadsheet application such as Microsoft Excel, Apple Numbers, or Google Sheets. Then, choose **File | Open**, navigate to the Chapter 10 Professional Print Example Files folder, and open the file named Try it yourself 2a - Business Card Data Merge.csv. The spreadsheet has four columns of information ranging from the person's name to their phone number.

	A	B	C	D	E
1	Name	Email	Location	Phone No	
2	Jane Doe	jane.doe@cube.com	100 5th Street, New York 45678	+1000123456	
3	Uncle Bob	uncle.bob@cube.com	202 Relative Road, London 6789(	+4400012345	
4	Joe Bloggs	joe.bloggs@cube.com	303 Sun Avenue, Mumbai 12345	+9100067890	
5	Mary Smith	mary.smith@cube.com	404 Main Road, Durban, 34567	+27100034567	
6					
7					

Figure 10.8: The data source which comprises four columns of information

2. Open the InDesign project file by choosing **File | Open**, navigate to the Chapter 10 Professional Print Example Files folder, and open the file named Try it yourself 2 - Business Card Data Merge Start.indd.

3. If you are presented with a missing fonts warning, click **Activate**, and InDesign will install any missing fonts.

4. The print setup departure point is the same as the **Step and Repeat** process previously. Notice that we've put in generic placeholders for the variable data inputs, such as the person's name and contact details, which will be populated in the print document.

5. Choose **Window | Utilities | Data Merge**.
6. Click the **Panel** menu of the **Data Merge** panel and choose **Select Data Source**.
7. Locate our data source file named Try it yourself 2a - Business Card Data Merge.csv in the Chapter 10 Professional Print Example Files folder and click **Open**.
8. The **Data Source** panel will be populated with the information from the source file depicting columns for **Name**, **Email**, **Location**, and **Phone No**.
9. We need to show InDesign where we'd like the data to go. With the **Type** tool ▮ (*T*), highlight the word **Name** on the front of the card. Then, drag the **Name** data point from the **Data Source** panel onto the highlighted text. Now, the word **<<Name>>** replaces the text placeholder. The angle brackets are visual cues indicating it is a variable data point.

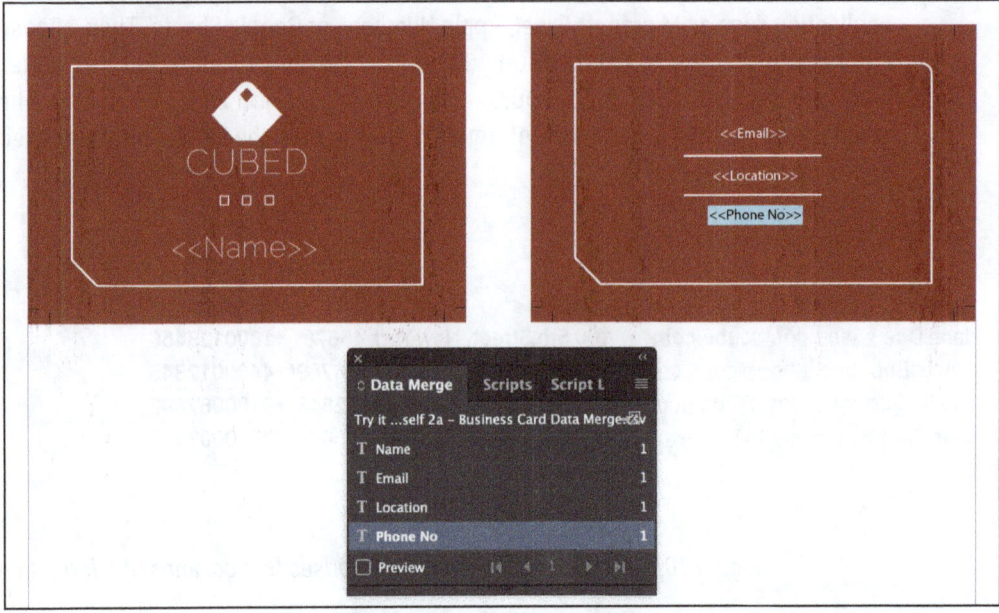

Figure 10.9: The artwork showing the <<Name>> data point in place

10. We'll repeat the process for the email address, location, and phone no. placeholders. Highlight each placeholder and double-click or drag the relevant data point over it to replace it with the variable. See *Figure 10.9*.

11. With that done, check the **Preview** checkbox off the bottom of the **Data Source** panel. The first row of information in the data source file is previewed.

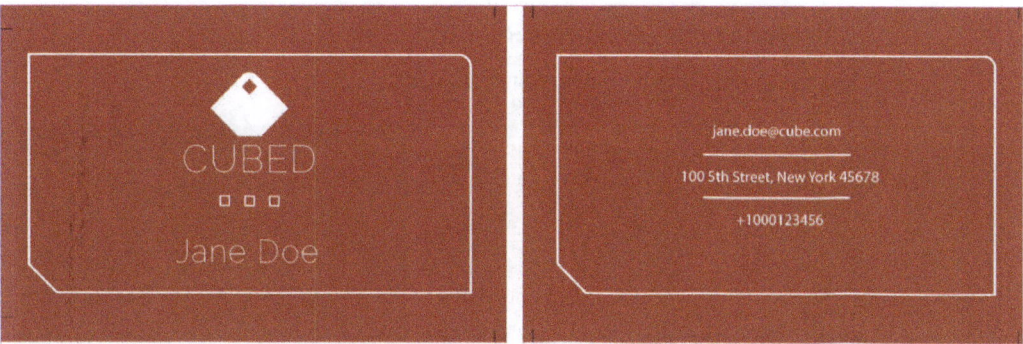

Figure 10.10: Previewing the artwork by checking the Preview checkbox

With our design showing the information correctly, the next task is to create a merged document that shows the relevant data for each of the four individuals whose business cards we are preparing for print.

Creating a merged document

Once the target InDesign document is formatted to your liking and data fields are correctly inserted from the data file, you can merge the document information in preparation for print. InDesign automatically generates a new document, keeping your original document safe from unwanted changes. In the steps that follow, we will prepare a print-ready merged document with unique data for each business card instance.

1. Click the **Data Source** panel menu ▤ | **Create Merged Document**.
2. In the **Create Merged Document** dialog, make the following changes:

    A. Under the **Records** tab, choose **All Records**.

    B. For **Records per Document Page**, choose **Multiple Records**.

    C. Keep **Generate Overset Text Report with Document Creation** checked. This will alert you to any text overflow in the merged file.

    D. Check **Preview Multiple Record Layout**.

    You should now see all records for the four business cards.

3. Click the **Multiple Record Layout** tab and make the following changes:

   A. Leave all values as is, except for **Spacing**.

   B. Under **Spacing**, change **Between Rows** to **31.5pt**.

   C. Click **OK** to generate your new print-ready InDesign file.

Figure 10.11: The layout with the Data Source panel and the Create Merged Document dialog visible

That's it. You have the option of printing directly to a connected printer or preparing a PDF file which you can send to a **print service provider** (**PSP**). We'll look at PDF file preparation for PSPs next.

Creating print-ready PDF files

Preparing PDF files in InDesign is a critical step in ensuring the integrity and compatibility of your documents for distribution and printing purposes. Utilizing the PDF/X standard, which was specifically designed for graphic arts, enhances this process by providing a reliable framework for creating files optimized for professional printing. Adhering to PDF/X standards ensures that your documents maintain consistent color management, font embedding, and other essential attributes. This guarantees reliable reproduction across different platforms and printing devices.

It is worth noting that you may need to tweak PDF settings to meet the requirements of your specific print requirements or those of your PSP.

That said, we will be using the most updated PDF/X standard currently available in InDesign in the steps that follow. We will be preparing an InDesign file for PDF/X-4 export and adjusting the parameters to include all necessary printer marks required in a typical professional print environment.

1. With the newly created merged file open, choose **File | Adobe PDF Presets | PDF/X-4:2008**.
2. Should you have the file open from the previous activity, please move on to *step 3*. If you have closed the file, choose **File | Open**, and choose the file named Try it yourself 2 - Business Card Data Merge Complete.indd from the Chapter 10 Preparing Documents for Professional Print folder.
3. Choose a location to save the PDF file on your computer and click **Save**.
4. In the resultant **Export Adobe PDF** dialog box, make the following changes:

    A. In the **General** section, check **View PDF after Exporting**.

    B. Choose **Marks and Bleeds** and **Check All Printer's Marks**. There is no bleed in this document, so we'll leave **Bleed and Slug** unchecked (See *Figure 10.12*).

> **Quick tip**
>
> If you are working on a document that has bleed, enable **Use Document Bleed Settings**. An example of this is the menu design we worked on in the previous chapter.
>
> You are welcome to look at the settings in the other subcategories, but the PDF/X setting we have chosen takes care of all of this for us.

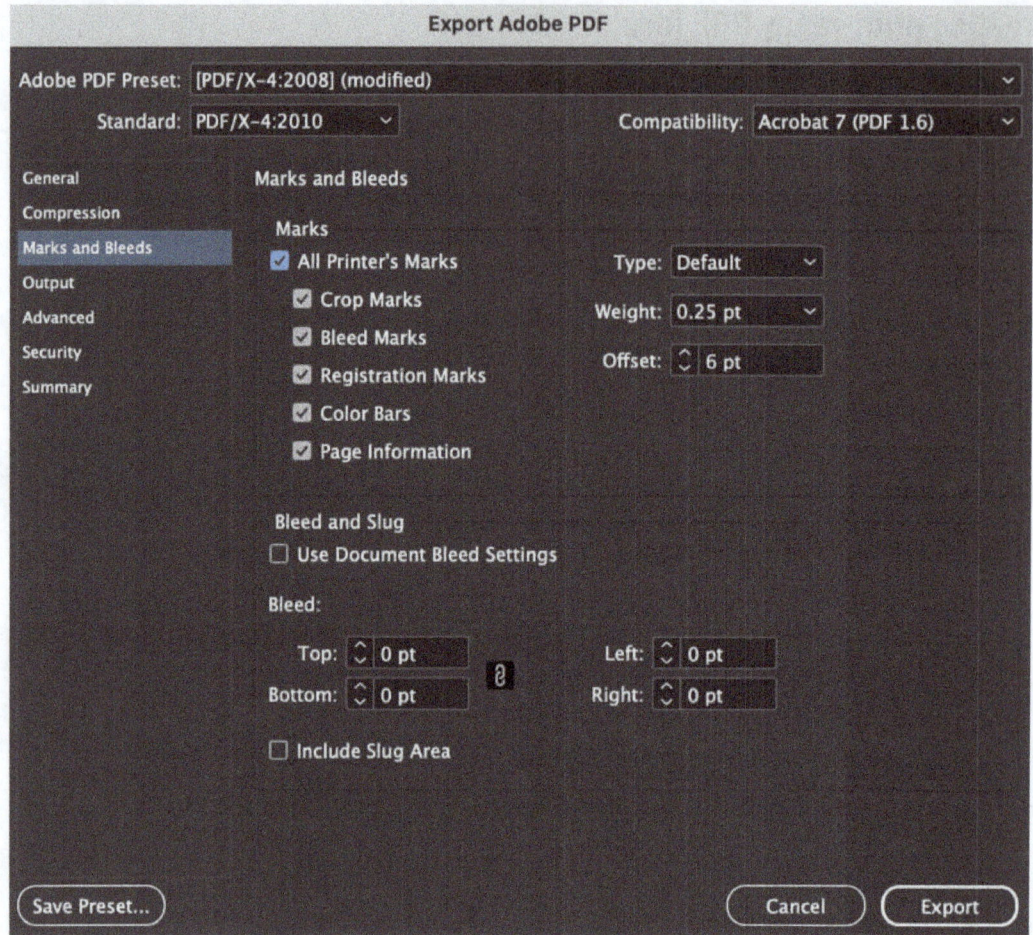

Figure 10.12: The Export Adobe PDF dialog showing the chosen PDF/X standard with marks and bleeds enabled

5. Choose **Export** to generate a PDF/X-4 file. InDesign will generate a PDF file and preview it for you in Adobe Acrobat if you have it installed on your computer.

A print-ready PDF called Try it yourself 2 - Business Card Data Merge Complete.pdf **can be found in the** Chapter 10 Professional Print Example Files **for reference.**

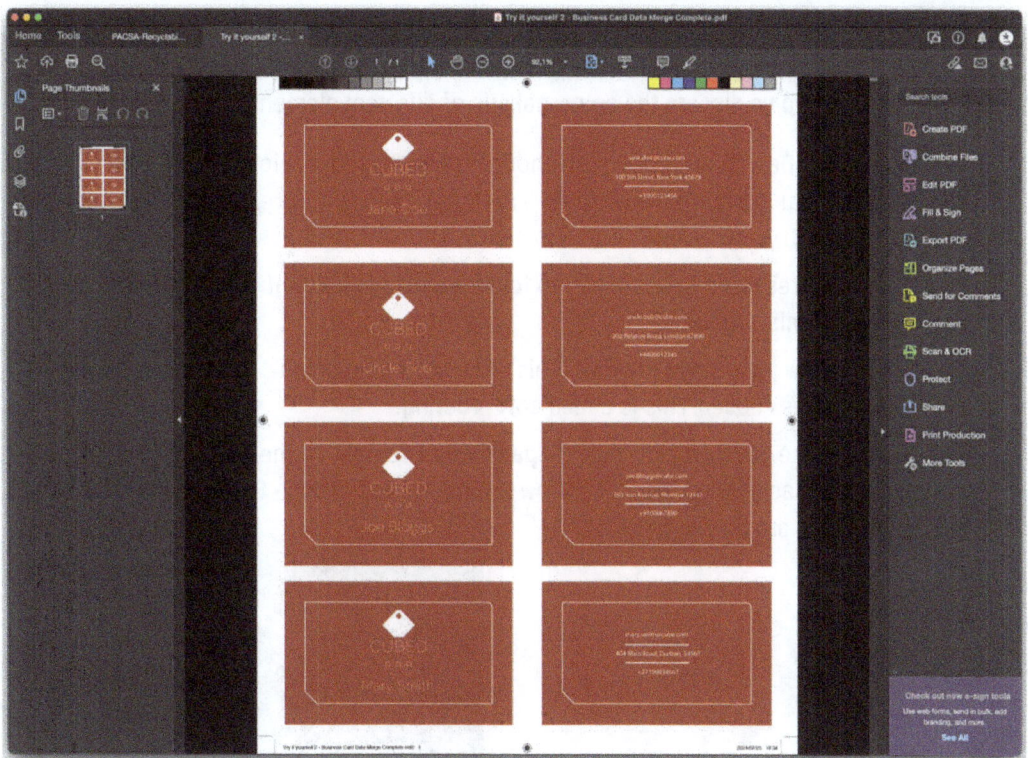

*Figure 10.13: The exported PDF file ready for print production
(The image is intended as a visual reference; the textual information is not essential.)*

That wraps up our conversation on exporting to standards-based PDF export for high-end printing. The document is now ready to continue its way through the prepress and print production processes. In the next section of this chapter, we will look at color separations and how to preview printing plates on-screen.

Color separations

Separations Preview in InDesign is a valuable tool that allows designers to preview and analyze color separations within their documents before printing. By simulating how colors will separate onto different printing plates, including CMYK and spot colors, you can identify any potential overprint, trapping, or missing color issues.

For this segment, we'll work on the menu design we worked on in *Chapter 9, Advanced Typography*. It has a good balance of images, graphic elements, and typography. We'll look at individual print separations that will help us discern the color makeup of different elements in the design.

1. Open the InDesign project file by choosing **File** | **Open**, navigate to the Chapter 10 Professional Print Example Files | Try it yourself - 3 Prepress folder, and open the file named Try it yourself - 3 Prepress.indd.

2. If you are presented with a missing fonts warning, click **Activate**, and InDesign will install any missing fonts.

3. Choose **View** | **Overprint Preview**. This will imitate your press conditions based on the color profiles chosen. This is called **soft proofing**.

4. Next, choose **Window** | **Output** | **Separations Preview**. In the **Separations Preview** panel that has opened, click the **View** dropdown and choose **Separations**. The color separations are now active.

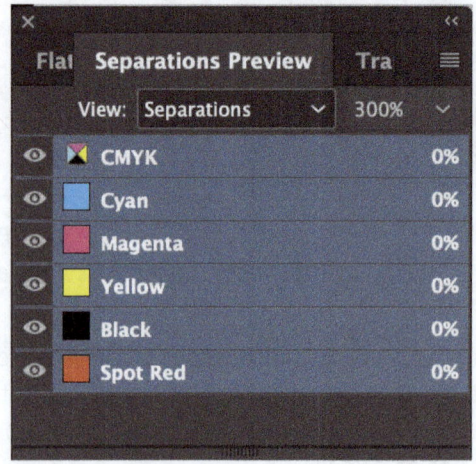

Figure 10.14: The Separations Preview panel showing the various printing separations

5. Click the eyeball icon to the left of **Black** to hide that color.

6. What remains on the page is the image and the red element of the logo. Click the eyeball alongside **Spot Red**. The red logo element toward the bottom-right of the design should disappear from view. This acts as a confirmation that the red line that forms part of the logo on the **Spot Red** separation (See *Figure 10.15*).

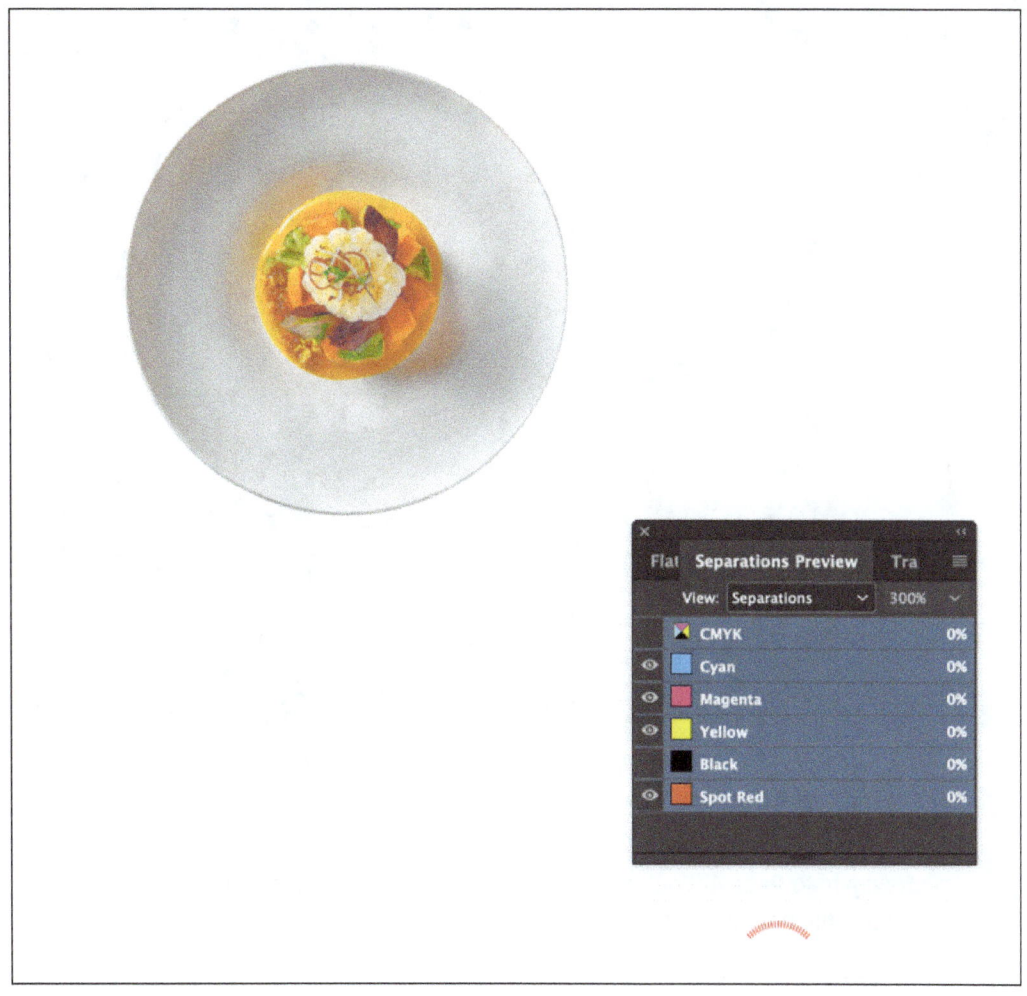

Figure 10.15: Separations Preview with the Black separation hidden from view

7. Navigate to the pages 2-3 spread. Notice that the black panel on the right of **Page 3** is made up of a rich black color. This means that the black color of the background is made up of a mix of cyan, magenta, yellow, and black. We'll need to rectify this as it will pose a registration problem for the type that sits on top of it when printed.

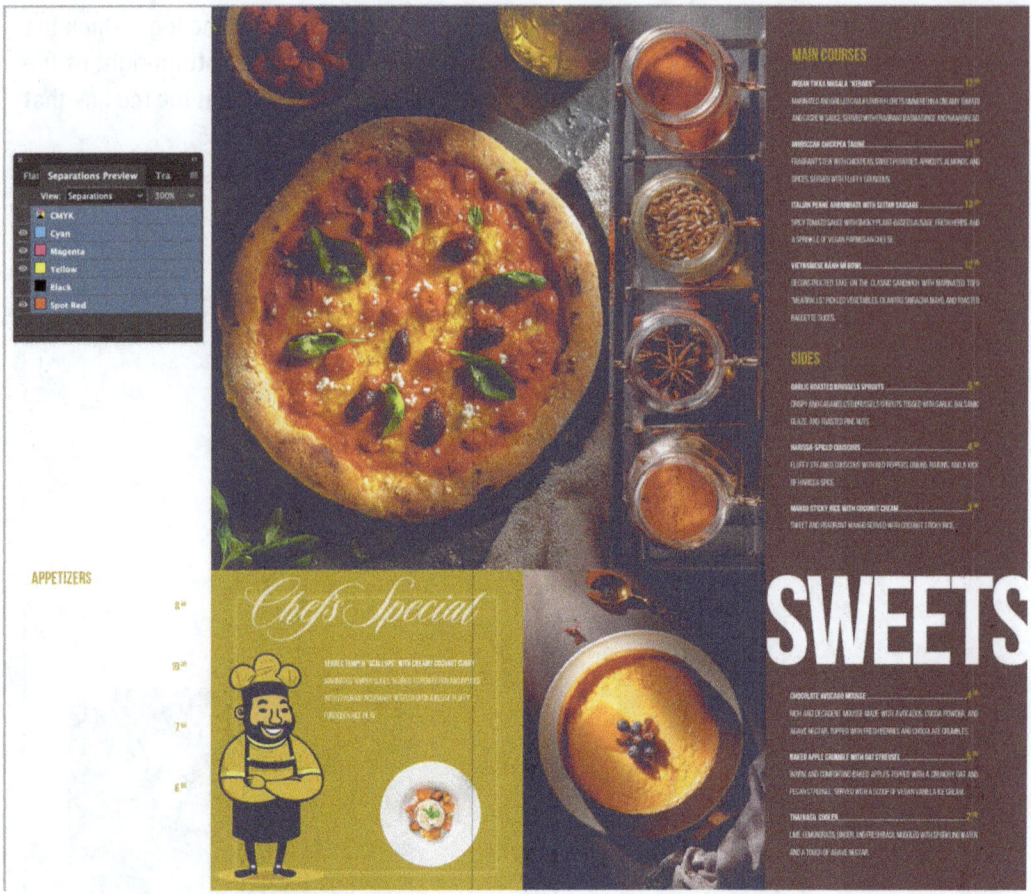

Figure 10.16: Pages 3 and 4 with the rich black design element to the right (The image is intended as a visual reference; the textual information is not essential.)

8. Navigate to **Page 4**. You can see that we have a repeat of the **Spot Red** color in the logo at the bottom of the design.

9. As you navigate across multiple spreads, click on the visibility icons for various separations. When you are done exploring ensure that all separations are visible.

As you can see from our exploration, identifying color plates and how elements will be color-separated is invaluable. We'll look at how to correct an object's color mix next so that it is optimized for print output.

Correcting a color mix

Being able to identify potential problems allows us to easily fix them. We'll choose the rich black color we identified on **Page 3** with the help of InDesign's **Separations Preview** panel. Follow the next steps:

1. Navigate to **Page 3** and choose the rich black object on the right.
2. Then, click on the **Fill** swatch under the **Appearance** subset on the **Properties** panel.
3. The color is currently **c65m73y69k90**. Click **[Black]** toward the top of the list to change the color:

Figure 10.17: Correcting color in the Swatches panel with the help of Separations Preview

As you can see, we can use the **Separations Preview** panel to view various separations and identify potential problems in our print jobs quickly and effectively. This feature, together with the **Overprint Preview** command, is invaluable in any print production and design environment.

In the next section, we will look at how preflighting helps us identify and rectify potential problems in a design.

Preflighting

Preflighting in InDesign is a quality control inspector that uses a built-in panel to automatically scan your document for potential errors before sending it to print or when sharing it digitally. Preflighting checks for issues such as missing fonts, low-resolution images, overflowing text frames, and incorrect color settings. By addressing such problems beforehand, you can avoid costly errors and reprints, ensuring your final project goes smoothly and meets professional standards.

We will continue working on the menu design. We'll cover some of the salient must-know features in this section. This will stand you in good stead as you adjust preflight profiles to accommodate the needs of your workflow. We'll use the menu design to unpack InDesign's preflight functionality. With Try it yourself - 3 Prepress.indd open, choose **Window | Output | Preflight**.

1. Let's import a preflight profile that was pre-created for this task. Click the **Preflight** panel menu and choose **Define Profiles**. You'll see that there are two existing profiles named **[Basic]** and **Digital Publishing**.

2. Click the **Preflight** panel menu icon ![icon] and choose **Load Profile**. Navigate to the Chapter 10 Professional Print Example Files | Try it yourself - 3 Prepress | Links folder and select the InDesign Masterclass Preflight Profile.idpp file. This action will add our profile to the list of available profiles. Click **OK** to close the dialog.

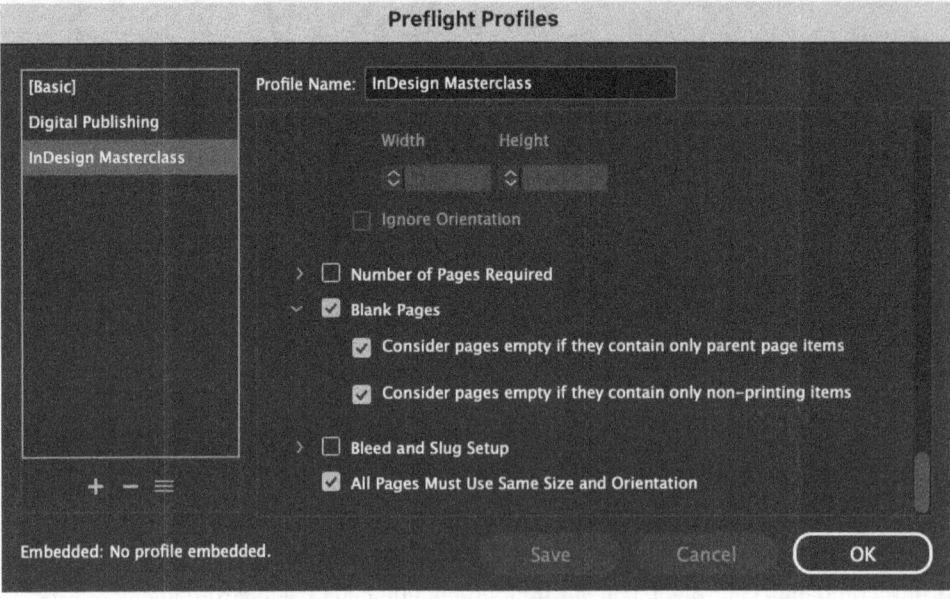

Figure 10.18: The InDesign Masterclass profile loaded into the project

3. Go to the **Preflight** panel, click the **Profile** drop-down list, and choose **InDesign Masterclass**. Several preflight errors will be listed under the error section of the panel. Click the twirl-down arrow alongside **Info**. This option gives more information about problem objects and offers potential solutions to resolve them:

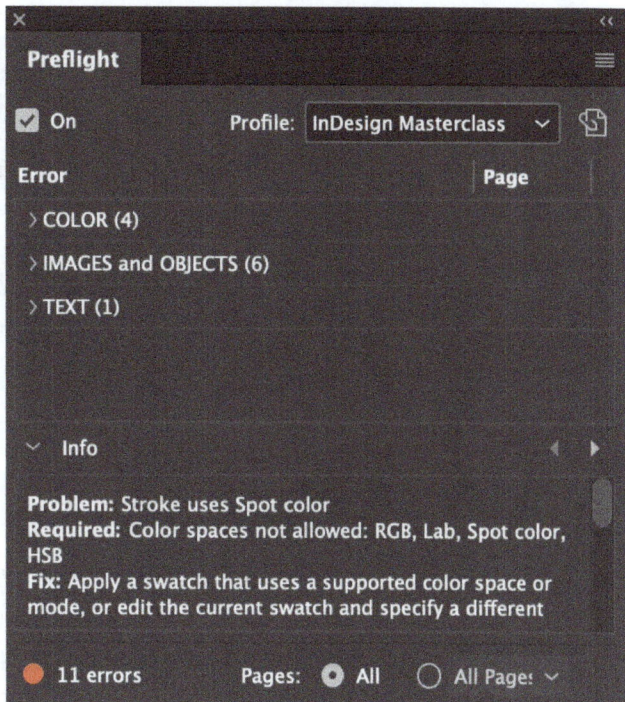

Figure 10.19: The Preflight panel showing 11 potential errors based on our chosen profile

4. Click the arrow alongside **COLOR**. This will show all objects that do not meet the preflight rules of the **InDesign Masterclass** preflight profile.

5. Double-click the object named path in the **Preflight** dialog. InDesign will take you to the object and select it for you on the page. The object has a spot color applied to its stroke. As you are aware, this will result in the generation of an additional printing plate. We'll resolve this by changing the swatch to **CMYK** as this design is a CMYK color print job.

6. Ensure no objects are selected. Click **Window | Color | Swatches**, then double-click the **Spot Red** swatch. In the resultant **Swatch Options** dialog, change **Swatch Name** to **Red** and **Color Type** to **Process**. Click **OK**. Because we updated the color swatch, this resolved the issue on pages 1 and 4 simultaneously.

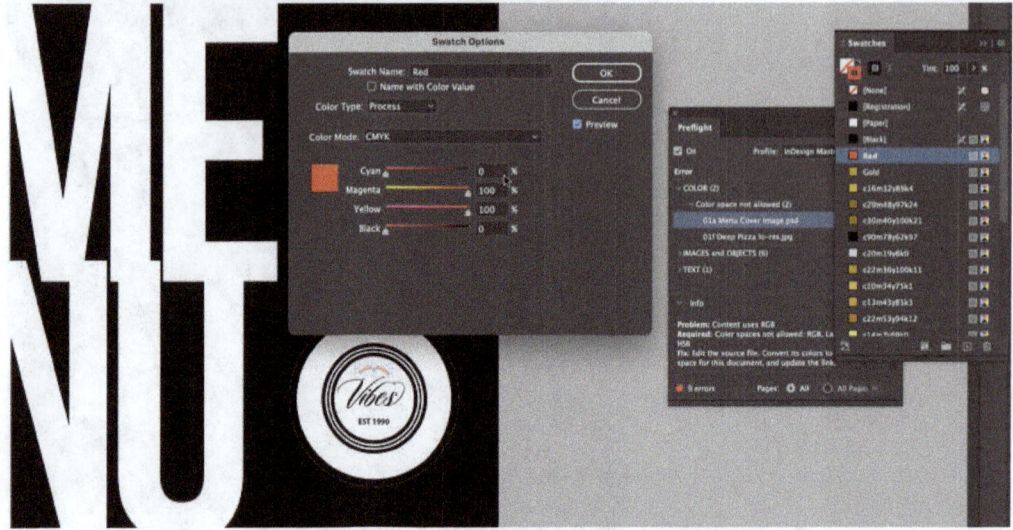

Figure 10.20: The Swatch Options, Preflight, and Swatches panels in view

7. Click the arrows alongside **IMAGES and OBJECTS** and **TEXT** so that identified objects that don't meet the preflight rules become visible too.

8. We'll deal with each of the flagged objects, starting with 01a Menu Cover Image.psd, which is RGB. Double-click the object in the **Preflight** panel to take us to its location in the document. Right-click the highlighted object on the page and choose **Edit with | Adobe Photoshop**.

9. When the image opens in Photoshop, choose **Image | Mode | CMYK Color**. Save and close the file in Photoshop and return to InDesign. Observe that the image now meets the preflight rules and is no longer listed as a potential problem. If you don't have Photoshop, you can ignore this step.

Figure 10.21: Converting the image color mode to CMYK in Photoshop

10. To resolve the remaining three images, we will replace them using the **Links** panel which you can open by choosing **Window | Links**.

11. Click 01f Deep Pizza lo-res.jpg on the **Links** panel. Click the **Relink** icon and choose 01f Deep Pizza Hi Res.jpg from the **Links** folder.

12. Repeat the process, relinking 01g Spices.jpg **to** 01g Spices Hi. Res.jpg, **and** 01e Cuppacino.jpg **with** 01e Cuppacino Hi Res.jpg.
13. Staying with the **IMAGES and OBJECTS** category, we have a circle that has a hairline stroke. This is too fine and will fill in when printing. Double-click to go to the object in the design and have it highlighted.
14. Change the object stroke width to **1pt** on the **Properties** panel.
15. There are occasions where we may want to keep an override to the preflight rules. The example we have in this design is the bullets found in the text at the bottom of **Page 4**. We'll ignore that flag.

This concludes the chapter. As you can see, the InDesign preflight offers a powerful array of tools to help you identify and fix potential problems before committing the design to a PDF or printing plate. It's worth noting that this subject is broad and deep. We're hopeful that the steps covered here help you to get started and open up the possibility of you exploring additional options that may be relevant to your specific workflow.

Summary

The print and prepress tools in InDesign provide designers and print professionals with essential features to prepare documents for high-quality printing, offering precise control over layout, color accuracy, and output settings for various printing processes, resulting in superior print quality. In this chapter, we tackled a range of tasks to ensure professional-quality print output. We set up documents with appropriate print specifications and leveraged InDesign's scripting capabilities to create personalized variable data printed materials. To guarantee accuracy, we preflighted documents, identifying and resolving any potential issues. Finally, we previewed color separations and created print-ready standards-based PDF/X files that adhere to industry standards. In the next chapter, we will look at how to create interactive documents for on-screen deployment and artificial intelligence in InDesign.

Level: Advanced

Multimedia, Interactivity, and AI

In the previous chapter, we looked at how to prepare content for print. This chapter sycnhorinizes perfectly with with the last chapter. We will explore how to create and export interactive documents. It's worth noting that the multimedia and interactional capabilities of InDesign allow you to easily create digital designs for on-screen consumption while enabling hassle-free, code-free interactivity, responsiveness, and navigation. We'll design and export a project to popular formats, including Publish Online, ePUB, interactive PDF, and **artificial intelligence** (**AI**). We'll also include navigation controls that viewers can interact with for an optimized viewer experience.

We will create a five-page portfolio with various interactive elements. Take note that InDesign's ability to export interactive elements reliably is dependent on the format you choose to export. For example, if you choose to export as an interactive PDF, animation does not export at all. Object states, as well as video and audio media don't translate too well either. Interactive forms on the other hand, are quite robust in PDF exports. We will explore two of the export options that offer the most robust interactive functionality: fixed-layout ePUB and Publish Online.

The main topics we will cover in this chapter are as follows:

- Creating hyperlinks
- Working with interactive elements
- Working with navigation controls
- Animating elements in InDesign
- Adding multimedia to your project
- Creating interactive multi-state objects
- Exporting interactive documents
- AI Features in InDesign

You can find the relevant projects/examples for this chapter here: https://packt.link/a19oQ

Exploring the exported project

The project we will be working on for this chapter is an interactive five-page portfolio for a fictitious creative studio called **Cubei**. As we always do in this book, we'll start by looking at the completed project. After our exploration, we'll close the completed project file and explore the interactive functionality in InDesign step-by-step. You can follow along by downloading the files referred to in this project. These files can be downloaded from https://packt.link/a19oQ.

We'll kick off our exploration of the completed project by looking at two exports we've pre-prepared for you. The first is **Publish Online**. The second is fixed layout ePUB. Follow the next steps:

1. In your browser, open this link: https://indd.adobe.com/view/53cba27d-12af-4087-959d-8ed3f201e266. This is the final project we will create. It uses InDesign's **Publish Online** feature.

2. Explore the following interactive elements from the link above. See the following labeled screenshot:

    A. The Cubei logo and **PORTFOLIO** text animations

    B. The navigation controls at the bottom of the design

    C. The contact icons such as email, social, and so on at the bottom-left of the design

    D. The web URL off the bottom-right of the page

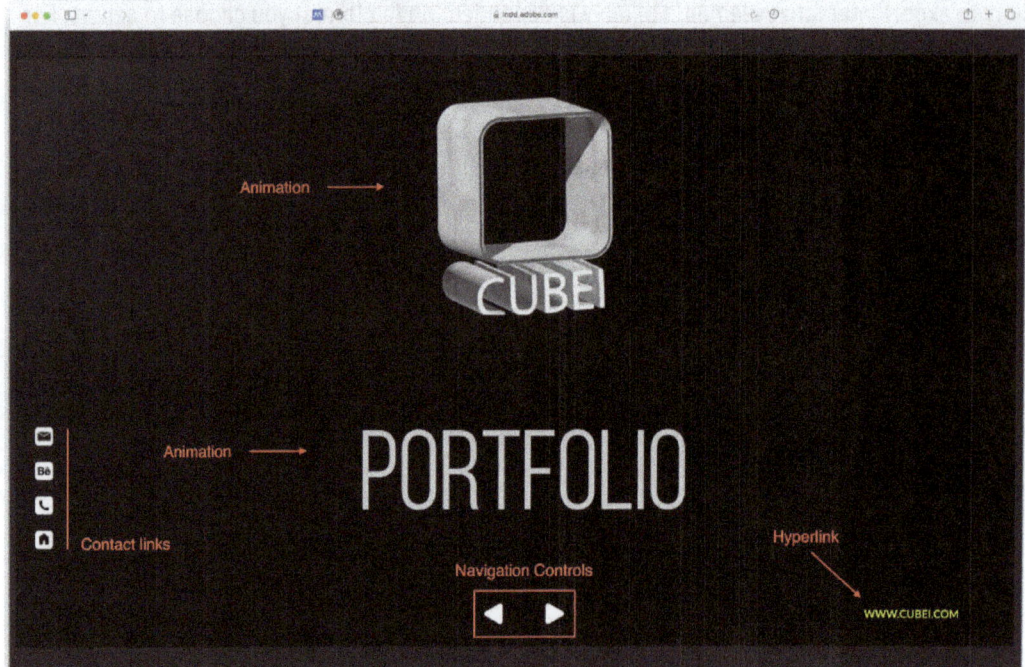

Figure 11.1: The portfolio design cover page with labeled interactive elements

3. Feel free to navigate through the document by exploring the various navigation options. We'll point out the elements per page (see the following screenshots):

    A. **Page 2** has four images that become visible sequentially
    B. **Page 3** has a video element together with a playback control
    C. **Page 4** has an interactive portfolio of work
    D. **Page 5** is a thank-you page with animations that complements the first page

Figure 11.2: The inner pages of the document, showing unique interactive elements (The image is intended as a visual reference; the textual information is not essential.)

We've included an ePUB version in the example files folder for you to view and explore offline. A good example is this book. It is available in printed format as well as an online ePUB or PDF version.

4. *[Optional step]* **To access the ePUB version, navigate to the** Chapter 11 Multimedia, Interactivity and AI Example Files **| folder. Open the file named** 01a Try it yourself 1a - Portfolio Complete.epub.

If you view the document on a Mac, iPad, or iPhone, the file will open in **iBooks**, which is an excellent ePUB reader. On Windows, it should open in the **Microsoft Edge** browser by default. If you prefer a dedicated ePUB reader, we found Thorium to be quite robust. It can be downloaded from the Windows store. Android users can download the app named **EPUB Reader** app from the Google Play store. Since the experience is pretty much identical, we won't waste valuable time to repeat what has already been explored. Now that we have a sense of the interactive document we're going to build, we'll fire up InDesign in the next segment and get to work on creating interactive design elements.

You're probably chomping at the bit. We'll open a document that has been prepared for you and add interactivity to it so that you have an opportunity to fully explore the options InDesign has to offer.

Getting started with interactive documents

Having explored the finished, exported document, you should have a good sense of the completed project. For this segment, we'll open a predesigned document, customize our workspace, and save it for future use. Let's begin:

1. We're now ready to work in InDesign. Close any browser windows or ePUB reader apps. Launch Adobe InDesign and open the file named 01 Try it yourself 1 - Portfolio Start.indd from the Chapter 11 Multimedia, Interactivity and AI Example Files | 02 Try it yourself 1 - Portfolio Start Folder.

2. If you are presented with a missing fonts warning, please click **Activate**. InDesign will automatically install any missing fonts.

3. Let's explore the project. Open the **Pages** panel and click through the five pages of the document to orient ourselves with the project. When you are done, return to the first page of the document:

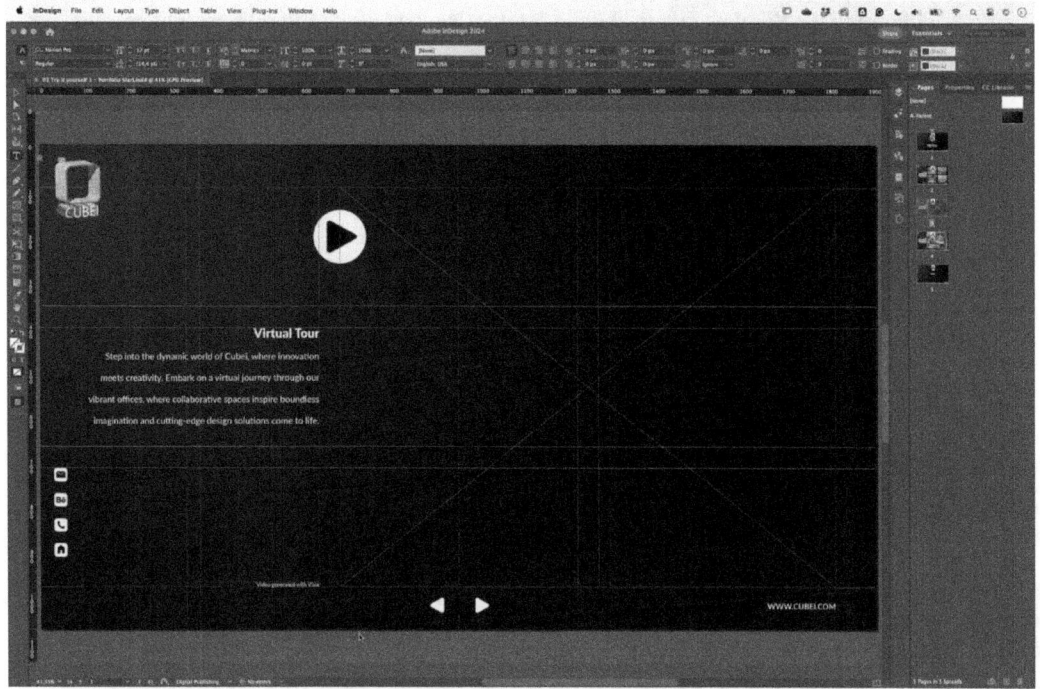

Figure 11.3: The project file showing Page 3
(The image is intended as a visual reference; the textual information is not essential.)

Now that you're familiar and comfortable with the design, let's set up our user interface in the next set of steps so that we have all the relevant panels within reach as we're working.

Customizing the workspace

InDesign offers a number of different panel and interface arrangements called workspaces. We will start with the **Essentials** workspace and scaffold on top of that:

1. Choose the **Window** menu and ensure that **[Essentials]** is checked. Then, choose the **Window** menu again and select **Reset Essentials**.

2. From the **Window** menu, open the following additional panels:

   A. **Control**

   B. **Layers**

   Dock the **Layers** panel to the right of the interface.

3. Return to the **Window** menu, choose **Interactive**, and make the following panels visible:

    A. **Animation**
    B. **Buttons and Forms**
    C. **Hyperlinks**
    D. **Media**
    E. **Object States**
    F. **Timing**

    Dock these panels to the right of the interface below **Layers** as has been done in *Figure 11.4* below.

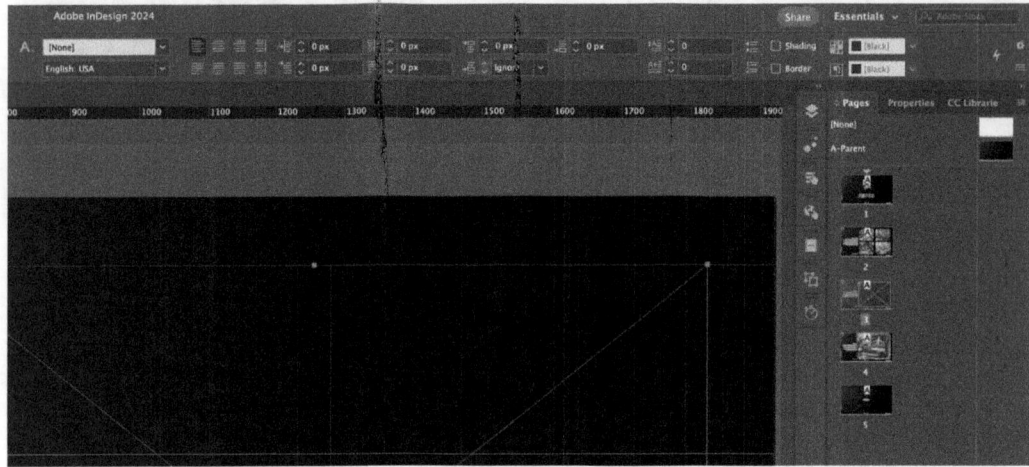

Figure 11.4: A zoomed-in view showing the control bar and panel arrangement

4. We'll now save our interface arrangement. To do that, choose **Window | Workspace | New Workspace**.

5. Name the custom workspace in the **New Workspace IDMC Interactive**.

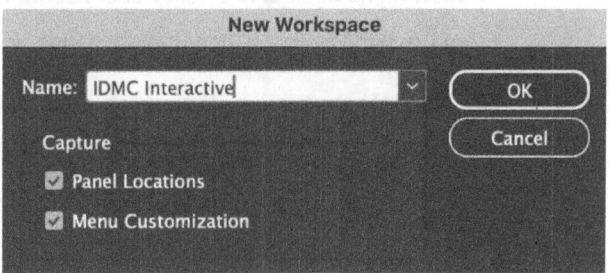

Figure 11.5: Saving the custom workspace

We're done setting up our interactive environment. Remember, with the custom workspace now set up, you can make any changes to the panel arrangement. If you need to revert to the workspace we just saved, choose **Window** | **Workspace** | **Reset IDMC Interactive**. We'll start our design on the parent page and enable all the social elements, hyperlinks, and navigation controls thereafter.

Creating hyperlinks

We'll explore the hyperlink options available to us in InDesign. Hyperlinks are the easiest form of interactive functionality as they are super easy to create. There is a URL that appears on all pages of the document. This element appears on a parent page. We'll apply our hyperlink there. Follow these steps:

1. Choose the **A-Parent** page from the pages by double-clicking it. A double-click is imperative to ensure that it is active.
2. Choose the www.cubei.com URL with the **Selection** tool.
3. Open the **Hyperlinks** panel. Since we're working on a fictitious project, we'll direct the link to the Packt website.
4. In the URL text field at the top of the **Hyperlinks** panel, type https://www.packtpub.com/ and hit *Return*.
5. You'll see a green circle to the right of the object name (see *Figure 11.6*). This indicates that InDesign has tested and validated that the link is live.
6. Observe the blue dotted frame around the text object on the page. This is a visual indicator that the text object is a hyperlink.
7. Click the green circle icon to be taken to the URL. This is a quick and easy way for you to validate links.

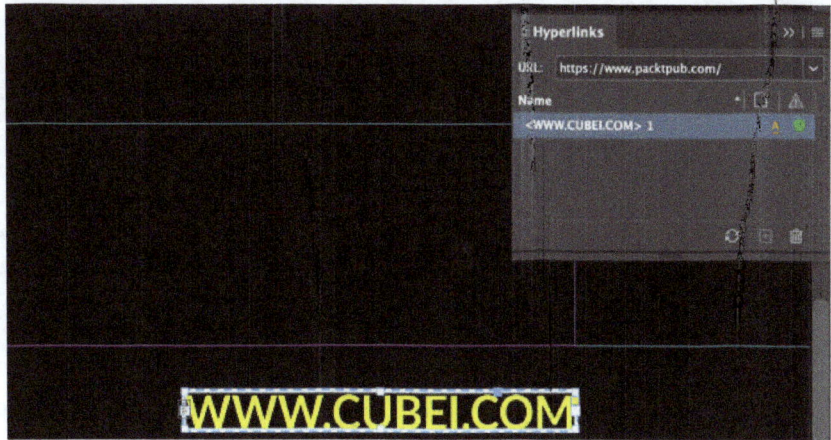

Figure 11.6: The Hyperlinks panel displaying the verified link and the hyperlinked object on the page

8. We'll now turn our attention to the set of four icons to the left of the page. We'll set them up as hyperlinks too. To do that, choose **View** menu | **Fit Page in Window**.

9. Click the **Email** icon ✉ with the **Selection** tool ▶.

10. Click the **Create new hyperlink** icon 🔳 off the bottom of the **Hyperlinks** panel.

11. In the **New Hyperlink** dialog box that appears, make the following changes:

    A. From the **Link to** drop-down list, choose **Email**.

    B. Type an email address. We used this fictitious one in our example: me@myemail.doesnotexist

    C. Let's add a Portfolio Query subject line.

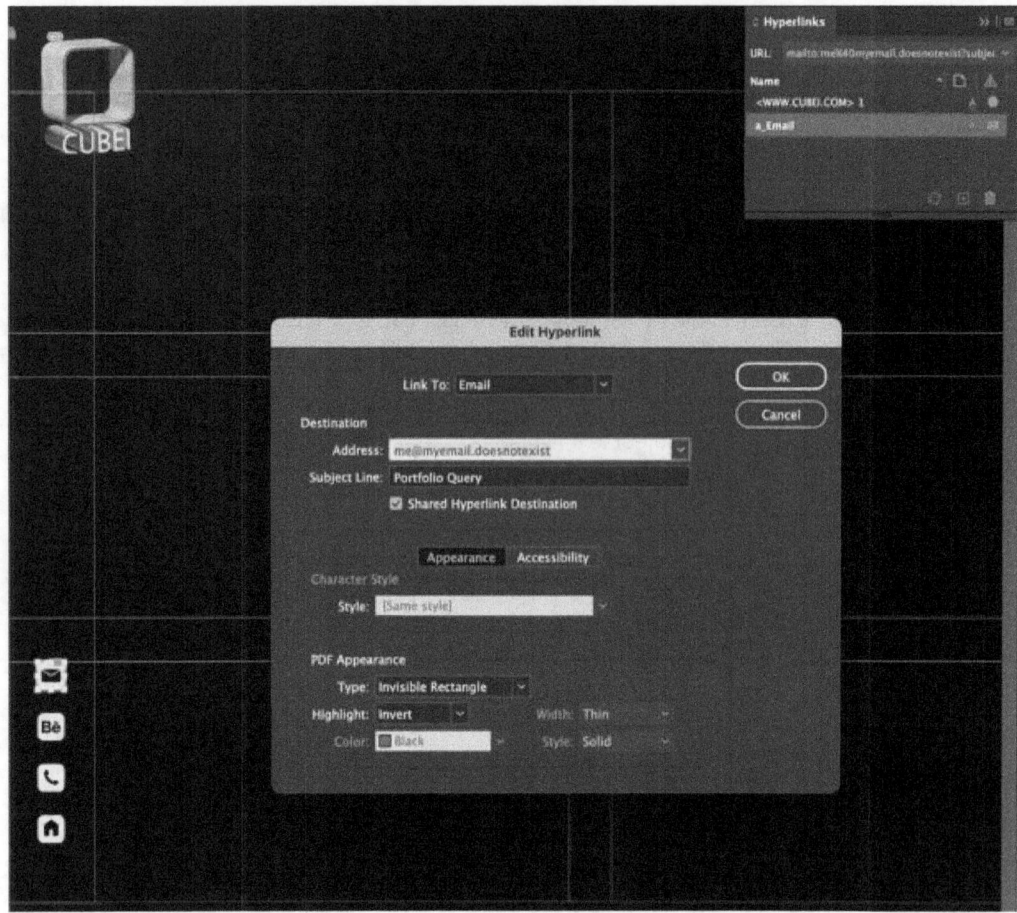

Figure 11.7: The Email element, the Hyperlinks dialog and panel

12. Observe the **envelope** icon to the right of our email link on the **Hyperlinks** panel. Click on it to test the interactivity. Your email client will open with the recipient and subject fields pre-populated. Delete the message and return to InDesign.

13. We'll set up the three remaining icons as follows:

    A. Select the **Behance** icon and click the **Create new hyperlink** icon on the **Hyperlinks** panel. Set the destination URL to https://behance.net in the **New Hyperlink** dialog. Click **OK**.

    B. Choose the **Telephone** icon and click **Create new hyperlink** on the **Hyperlinks** panel. In the **New Hyperlink** dialog, delete the https:// text and type tel:+01234567890. Note that the status icon to its right is red because InDesign is unable to validate telephone numbers. This is perfectly fine. Click **OK**.

    C. Now, select the **Home** icon and click **Create new hyperlink** on the **Hyperlinks** panel. In the **New Hyperlink** dialog, select **Page** from the **Link to** drop-down list. Under **Document**, ensure that 01 Try it yourself 1 - Portfolio Start.indd is selected. Set the **Page** value to 1, and **Zoom Setting** to **Fit in Window**. Click **OK**.

Awesome! That takes care of our hyperlinks. Let's recap real quick. We set up four hyperlinks. An email, telephone, web URL, and page location hyperlink. We now need to test our links. We'll do this directly in InDesign.

Testing interactive elements

InDesign offers nifty tools for testing interactive elements without having to export the document first. This allows you to determine whether the document behaves as you expect it to. It is a great time saver.

> **Note**
> You cannot preview content from a parent page. If you attempt to do so, InDesign will warn you of this fact. There is no negative outcome should you do this in error.

InDesign offers a quick and easy way to test interactive elements through its interactive preview panel. We'll look at how we can leverage this panel to predict how elements will behave in the final export:

1. Double-click **Page 1** on the **Pages** panel.
2. Choose **Window | Interactive | EPUB Interactive Preview**.

3. Make this panel to be as large as possible. Position the panel toward the top of the document window. Then, drag the bottom-right edge out as far as InDesign will allow.

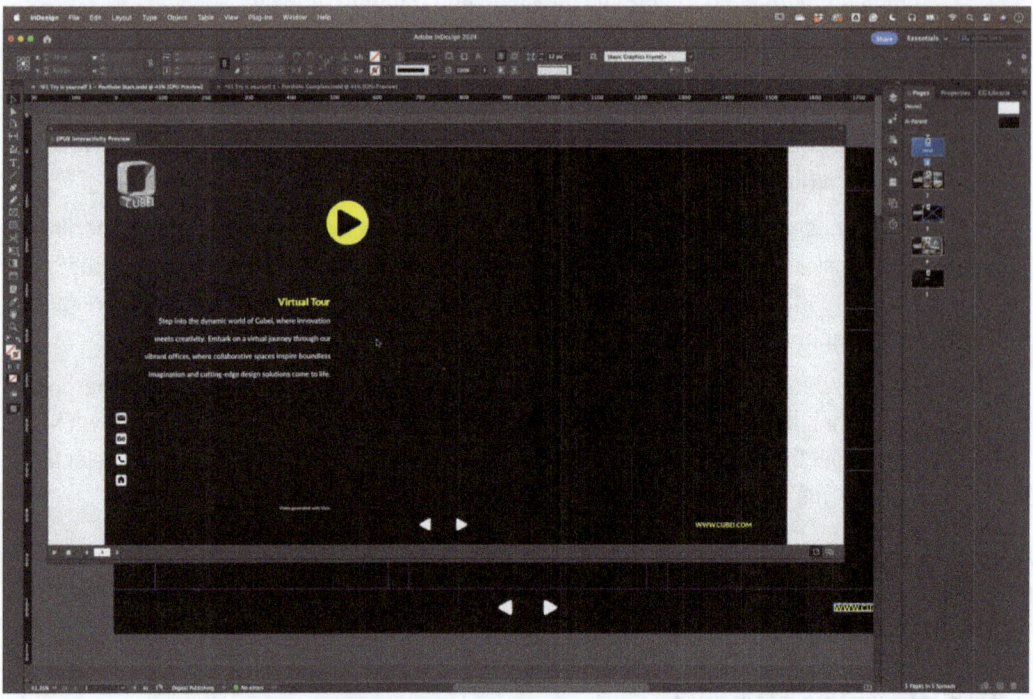

Figure 11.8: The resized ePUB Interactivity Preview panel with its controls at the bottom (The image is intended as a visual reference; the textual information is not essential.)

4. Click the **Play** icon ▶ off the bottom left of the panel to generate a preview.

5. Click on each of the hyperlinks we created to test their interactivity. The telephone hyperlink can't be tested in InDesign.

6. To test the **Home** hyperlink, we need to generate a preview for the entire document. To save on resources and time, InDesign generates a preview for just the page you initiate the preview on – in our case, **Page 1**.

7. Click the **Set Preview Document Mode** icon on the far-right bottom of the ePUB preview panel. Then, hit the **Play** icon to generate a fresh preview of the entire document.

Figure 11.9: The Set Preview Document Mode icon on the right bottom of the ePUB preview panel

8. Navigate to a page other than **Page 1** by clicking the **Go to Next Page** icon on the bottom left of the panel. Clicking the **Home** icon will take you back to **Page 1**.
9. Click the **X** icon on the top left of the ePUB preview panel to close it.

This brings setting up and testing hyperlinks to a close. We looked at four different types of hyperlinks to get you acquainted with the possibilities. We'll make the navigation arrows live in the next segment.

Working with buttons

Buttons allow for additional interactivity with the possibility of setting attributes for various states such as **hover** and **on click**. In this section of the chapter, we will look at how to take static geometric shapes and turn them into rich interactive buttons. We will enable the back and forward buttons found on the parent page.

Let's begin:

1. Double-click **A-Parent** on the **Pages** panel.
2. Select the forward arrow object at the bottom of the page.

3. Open the **Buttons and Forms** panel and make the following changes:

   A. Under **Type**, choose **Button**.
   B. Change the name to `Btn_Fwd`.
   C. Leave **Event** set to **On release or tap**.
   D. Under **Actions**, click the **+** icon and choose **Go To Next Page**.
   E. Leave **Zoom** as **Inherit Zoom**.
   F. Click on the **Rollover** state under **Appearance**.

4. Head to the **Properties** panel and make the following changes under the **Appearance** subset:

   A. Click **Fill swatch** and set it to **None**.
   B. Click **Stroke swatch** and choose **[Paper]**.
   C. Change **Stroke weight** to **3pt**.

5. With the object still selected, choose the **Click** state from the **Buttons and Forms** panel.

6. Return to the **Properties** panel and make the following changes under **Appearance**:

   A. Click **Fill swatch** and choose **[Black]**.
   B. Set **Tint** to **30%**.

7. Return to the **Buttons and Forms** panel and select **Normal** under **Appearance**. This is an important last step since the state that is chosen here will become the button's default state.

8. Let's test the button's functionality by choosing **Window | Interactive | EPUB Interactivity Preview**. The panel will open in its expanded state.

9. Click the **Set Preview Document Mode** icon on the bottom-right of the panel and click the **Play** icon on the bottom left of the panel to generate a preview of the document.

10. Test the button by clicking it.

Figure 11.10: The ePUB preview panel and the Buttons and Forms panel showing the button configuration (The image is intended as a visual reference; the textual information is not essential.)

With the forward button neatly buttoned up, we'll do the same for the back button. We'll revisit the steps we covered for the **page forward** button. If this is new to you, it is good practice.

> **Note**
> As with everything in InDesign, there are multiple ways to get to the same solution. You can copy the **page forward** button, reposition it, and tweak its properties so that it goes back by one page when clicked or tapped.

11. Ensure that you are on the **A-Parent** page by double-clicking it on the **Pages** panel.
12. Select the forward arrow object found at the bottom of the page.
13. Open the **Buttons and Forms** panel and make the following changes:

    A. Under **Type**, choose **Button**.
    B. Change the name to `Btn_Back`.
    C. Leave **Event** set to **On release or tap**.

D. Under **Actions**, click the **+** icon and choose **Go To Previous Page**.

E. Leave **Zoom** as **Inherit Zoom**.

F. Click on the **Rollover** state under **Appearance**.

14. Repeat *Steps 4* to *7*.
15. You are welcome to test the back button by using the **EPUB Interactivity Preview** panel. Remember to choose the **Preview Document Mode** icon on the bottom right and click the **Play** icon on the bottom left of the panel to preview the entire document.
16. As a final step, ensure that you select the buttons one at a time and ensure that **Normal** is chosen under **Appearance** to set their default state.

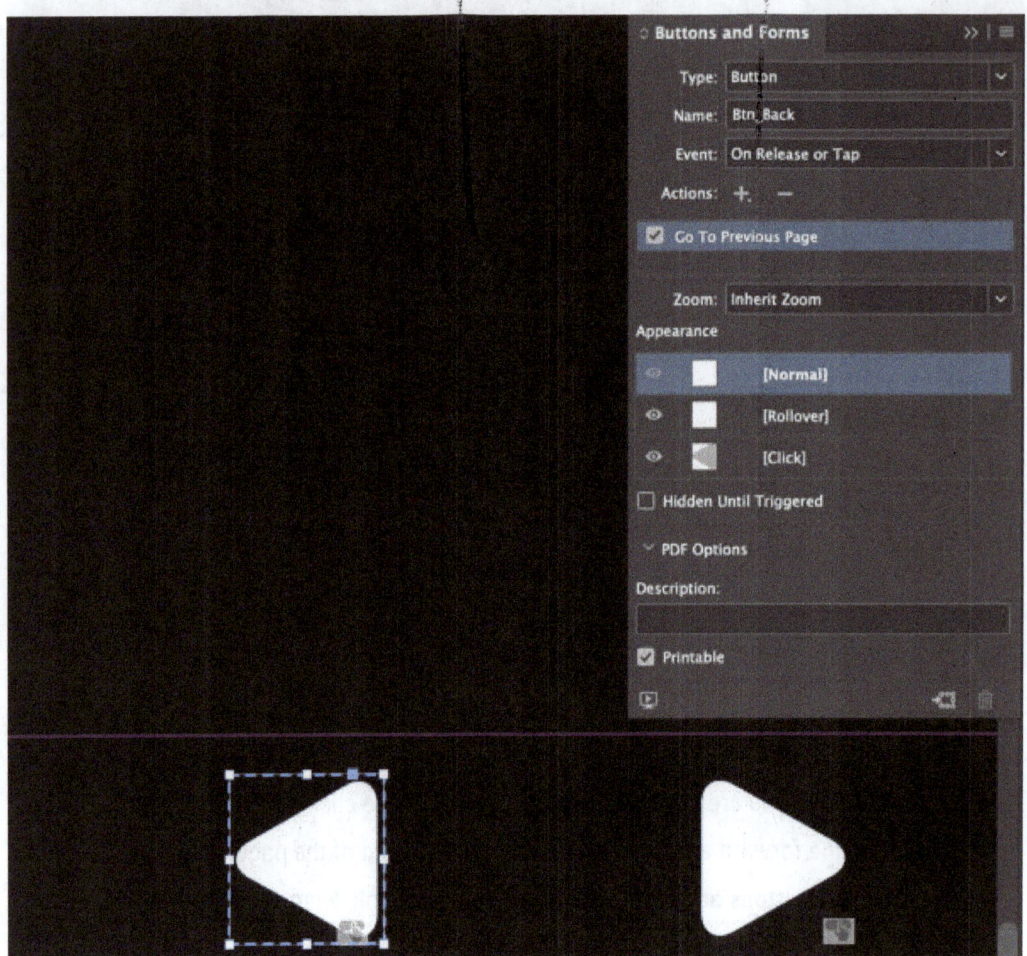

Figure 11.11: The completed navigation buttons with the Buttons and Forms panel visible

Having completed the navigation controls by enabling them as buttons, we are done with all of the required tasks on the parent page. We can move on to exploring interactive options for content on the document pages, starting with animation.

Animating elements in InDesign

InDesign offers animation options that allow users to enhance digital publications by adding dynamic movement and interactivity to elements such as text, images, and graphics. In this section, we will create animations for the cover page of our document. Let's do that now:

1. Double-click **Page 1** on the **Pages** panel.

2. Select the *Cubei* logo on the page. The logo was created using the 3D effect in Adobe Illustrator.

3. Open the **Animation** panel, click the **Preset** dropdown and choose **Fly in from Top**.

   A butterfly proxy shows a preview of the animation in the top half of the **Animation** panel. The vertical green line is the animation path of the object.

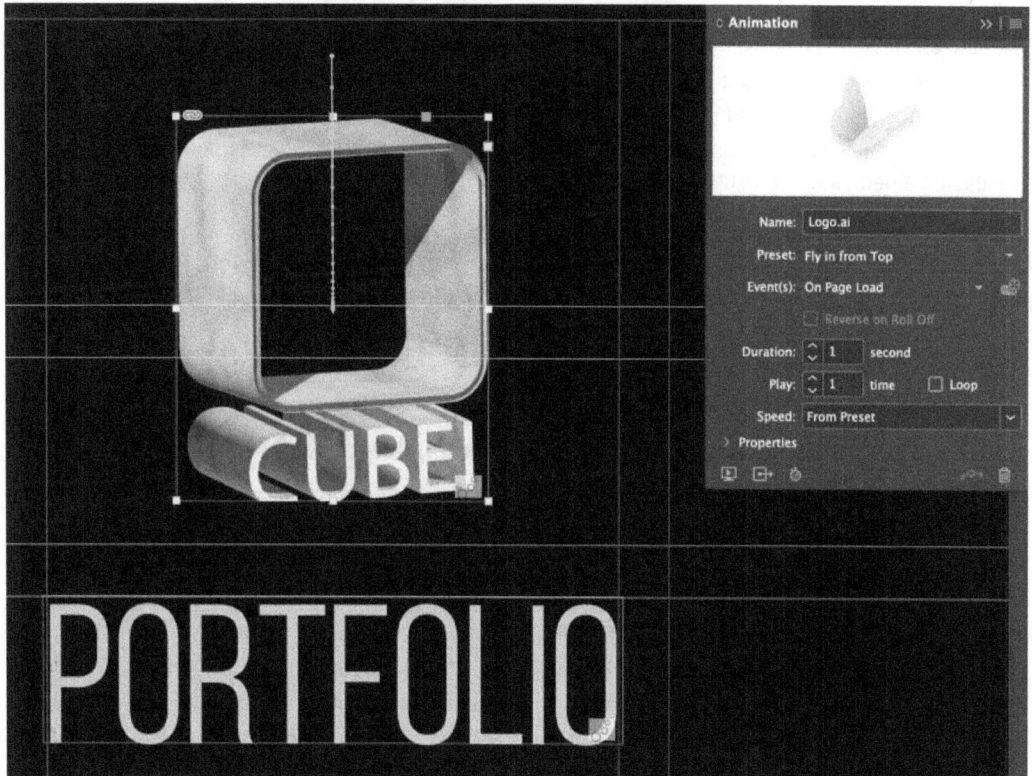

Figure 11.12: The animated Cubei logo with the Animation panel open

4. Now, choose the **PORTFOLIO** text with the **Selection** tool and choose **Appear** from the **Preset** drop-down list.

5. Click the **Preview Spread** icon off the bottom left of the **Animation** panel so that we can see our edits. This is another way to access the **ePUB Interactivity Preview** panel.

6. Close the **ePUB Interactivity Preview** panel.

As you can see, animation is relatively straightforward in InDesign. We'll explore some additional animation options, such as timing, next.

Timing animated objects

Timing allows for the precise moment when various design elements appear, disappear, or transition in InDesign digital publications. We'll implement timing on multiple elements on **Page 2** of our document. The images used were generated using Microsoft Designer, an **AI** powered graphic design app that helps you create professional-looking visuals in a snap. Visit https://designer.microsoft.com/image-creator to explore it on your own. The Cubei logo on the wallpaper in the bottom-right image was applied using Adobe Photoshop using the **Generative Fill** feature.

> **A note on AI**
> The assets used in this chapter were created using various AI generation engines to give you a sense of how you can use AI to enhance your InDesign projects. We will also look at the latest AI features available in InDesign at the time of the writing of this book. Packt Publishing will be releasing a dedicated book on AI for creatives soon.

We'll explore the slew of animation and timing controls relevant to our design. Remember that animations do not work in the interactive PDF format. Follow the next steps:

1. Move to **Page 2** on the **Pages** panel.
2. Select the four images on the page.
3. Open the **Animation** panel, click the **Preset** dropdown, and choose **Appear**.
4. Open the **Timing** panel. You will see the four image names listed in the order they animate into view on the page.
5. On the **Timing** panel, do the following:

    A. Double-click the top-left image by clicking its name, 02 Cubei Brainstorm.jpeg. InDesign will highlight it on the page for you. Ensure that it is the first object on the list of animated elements. This determines the order in which elements appear on the page. If it is not the first object, drag it to the top of the list. Set the delay to 0 seconds.

B. Choose the second image on the list, named Cubei Meeting Cubicle.jpg, **by double-clicking it. Set its delay to** 0.1 **seconds.**

C. Select the image on the list named Cubei Meeting.jpeg **and set its delay to** 0.2 **seconds.**

D. Finally, select the fourth and final image entry on the list, named Cubei Studio.jpeg, **and set its delay to** 0.3 **seconds.**

Figure 11.13: The Timing panel showing the delay for a selected element

6. Click the **Preview Spread** icon ▶ off the bottom left of the **Timing** panel so that we can preview the animation flow on the page.
7. Close the **ePUB Interactivity Preview** panel when done.

The timing controls complement the animation functionality harmoniously. With you having gained an understanding of animation and timing, we can move on to working with video assets.

Adding multimedia elements to InDesign files

The **Media** panel in InDesign provides a convenient interface for managing multimedia elements such as audio and video files. In this section, we will bring in an AI-generated video made in AI tool Visla. It offers text-to-video on a freemium model. Visit https://www.visla.us/ to sign up for Visla and explore it.

We'll look at how to add multimedia content, how to set up a custom poster for our content, and how to trigger content to play using buttons.

Figure 11.14: The video container frame and Play button on Page 3 (The image is intended as a visual reference; the textual information is not essential.)

Placing media elements in InDesign is no different from how we placed other types of assets in previous chapters. We do have additional multimedia controls we can tweak, which is what we will look at now.

1. Double-click on **Page 3** on the **Pages** panel.
2. Select an empty frame and choose **File | Place**.
3. **Navigate to** Chapter 11 Multimedia, Interactivity and AI Example Files | 02 Try it yourself 1 - Portfolio Start Folder | Links. **Select the file named** Inside Cubei_ A Creative Journey Through Design Excellence.mp4 **and click Open/Place** to import it into the container frame.

   The container will be filled with light blue cross-hatching to indicate that a multimedia element is present.

4. Open the **Media** panel.
5. Click the **Play** button to preview the video.
6. We'll replace the blue cross-hatching with a poster from the video. Use the scrubbing control below the video preview to scrub through the video timeline. Somewhere around the **00:20** mark is perfect.

Figure 11.15: Adjusting the video controls in the Media panel

We are now able to activate the button to have it play the video when clicked.

7. Select the **Play** button on the page with the **Selection** tool .
8. Open the **Buttons and Forms** panel and make the following changes:

    A. Under **Type**, choose **Button**.
    B. Change the name to Btn_Play.
    C. **Event** should be set to **On release or tap**.

D. Under **Actions**, click the **+** icon and choose **Video**. The video on our page will automatically be selected.

E. Confirm that **Play** is enabled under the **Options** category.

9. Let's preview the page by clicking the **Preview Spread** icon off the bottom left of the **Media** panel.

10. Once you are done with testing the button and confirming the video quality, close the **ePUB Interactivity Preview** panel.

Well done. We just looked at how to import video content, set a poster frame, and enable a button to trigger a play command. In the next segment, we will look at how to work with multi-state objects.

Creating interactive multi-state objects

InDesign's object states feature allows you to design multiple appearances for a single object, enabling the showcasing of design variations in a dynamic and interactive way. The content in this segment is AI-generated with Adobe Firefly. Visit https://firefly.adobe.com/ to explore Adobe's AI offering.

We'll use the generated images that we created in Adobe Firefly to build an image stack. We'll then use buttons to allow users to interact with and navigate through the image stack using object states. Follow the next steps:

1. Double-click on **Page 4** to make it visible in the viewport.
2. There are four overlapping images. Select them by holding *Shift* and clicking them. Ensure that only these four elements are selected. This can be done on the page and in the **Layers** panel.
3. On the **Control** panel, choose the **Align to** option and choose **Align to Selection**.
4. Click the **Align right edges** and **Align bottom edges** icons to create an image stack.

Exploring the exported project | 351

Figure 11.16: The image stack aligned perfectly using the alignment controls highlighted at the top of the screenshot

5. With the images still selected, open the **Object States** panel.
6. Convert the selection to a new object state by clicking the **New** icon off the bottom right of the panel.

   A new object state is presented in the panel with the four images we just aligned allocated to their own state.

7. In the **Object States** panel, change **Object Name** to **Portfolio** and hit *Enter* to confirm.

Figure 11.17: The Portfolio multi-state object with the Object States panel showing its parameters

We'll need a mechanism to allow viewers to interact with the multi-state portfolio. Buttons have been pre-created for this task. They were hidden from view to make it easier for us to work and reduce screen clutter. We'll make them visible now and make them interactive to allow users to click through the multi-state portfolio.

8. Open the **Layers** panel and activate the visibility switch represented by an **eye** icon for the `Btn_Next` and `Btn_Back` objects.

Figure 11.18: The artwork with the navigation buttons made visible on the Layers panel

9. Select the forward button object named Btn_Next on the right edge of the portfolio multi-state object.

10. Open the **Buttons and Forms** panel and set the following options:

    A. Alongside **Actions**, click the **+** icon and choose **Go to Next State** from the list of options.

    B. For **Object**, ensure that **Portfolio** is chosen.

    C. Check the **Stop at Last State** checkbox.

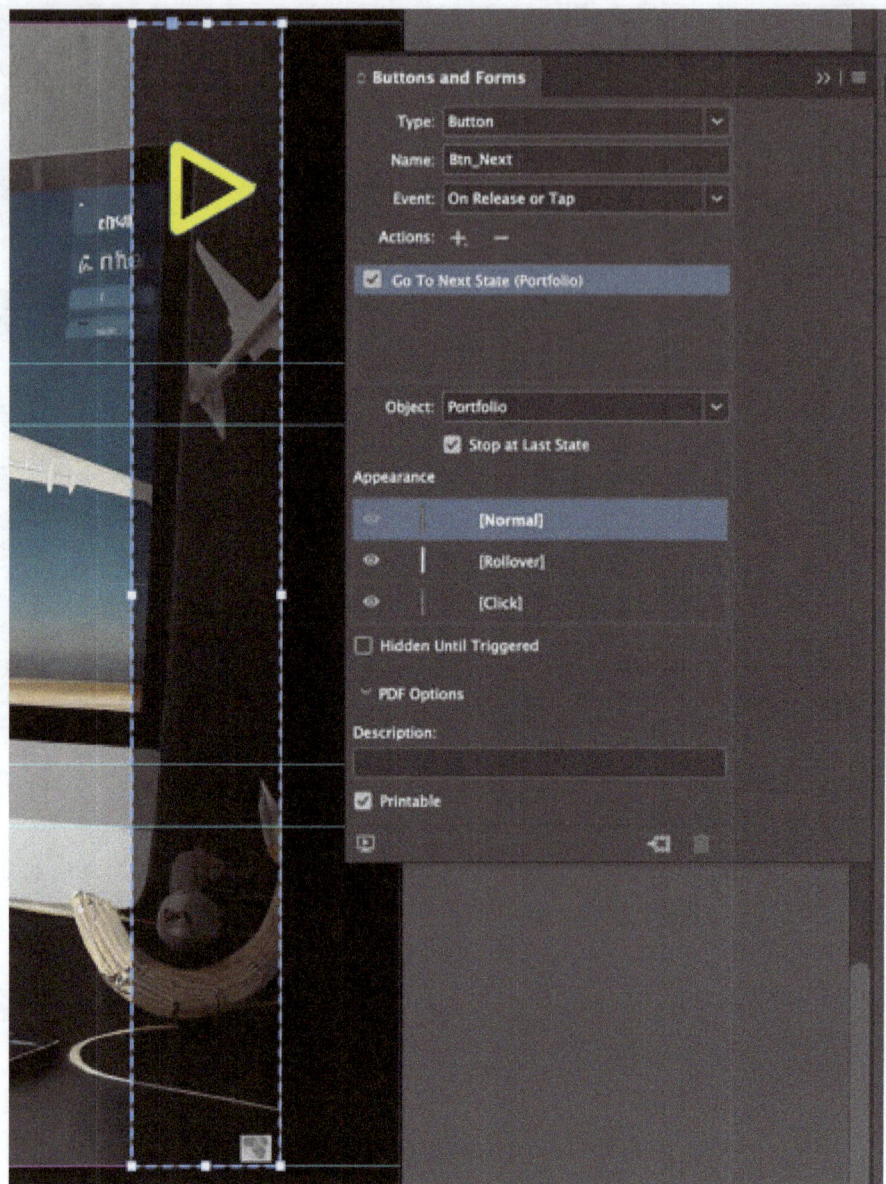

Figure 11.19: The button with its properties visible in the Buttons and Forms panel

11. Repeat the process for the back button by selecting it from the left edge of the portfolio multi-state object.
12. Open the **Buttons and Forms** panel and set the following options:
    A. Under **Actions**, click the **+** icon and choose **Go to Previous State** from the list of options.
    B. For **Object**, ensure that **Portfolio** is chosen.
    C. Enable the **Stop at First State** checkbox.
13. Click the **Preview Spread** icon to test the functionality and click through the portfolio using the buttons we made interactive just now.

As you've just observed, multi-state objects allow you to neatly package layered images and then eloquently presenting them with the clever use of buttons. We'll close out this section by applying animations to elements on the back cover.

Animating elements

In this sub-section, we will mimic the animations we applied to elements of the cover page as a unifying mechanism between the first and the last page of the document – an important principle of design.

We'll use the **Animation** panel once again to achieve our goal:

1. Double-click **Page 4** on the **Pages** panel.
2. Select the *Cubei* logo on the page.
3. Open the **Animation** panel, click the **Preset** dropdown, and choose **Fly in from Top**.
4. Next, choose the **THANK YOU** text with the **Selection** tool and choose **Appear from the Preset** from the drop-down list.
5. Click the **Preview Spread** icon off the bottom left of the **Animation** panel to preview the edits.
6. Close the **ePUB Interactivity Preview** panel when done.

With all of the interactivity in the document complete, we have one last task left – exporting the document in appropriate formats for consumption by your target audience.

Exporting interactive documents

InDesign offers a few options for exporting interactive documents. Two options stand out to us for the number of features that export correctly. These are Publish Online and fixed layout ePUB.

Publish Online

Publish Online enables easy sharing and viewing across various devices through web browsers. Follow the next steps to publish the document online:

1. With the document open in InDesign, choose **File** menu | **Publish Online**.
2. Make the following updates in the resultant dialog:

    A. Under the **General** tab, ensure that the **Publish New Document** radio button is selected.

    B. Under **Title**, name your export. We'll call it **Cubei Portfolio**.

    C. Optionally, you can add a description. We've typed: We're excited to share the latest Cubei portfolio.

    D. **Pages** should be set to **All**.

    E. Set **Export As** to **Single**.

    F. You then have password protection controls which we will leave disabled. The settings you choose will be unique to your workflow. For the project we're working on though, click the **Advanced** tab and check the second option, hide the **Share** and **Embed** options in the published document, which hides sharing by your audience. This checkbox can be found towards the bottom of the dialog.

3. We'll leave the **Analytics** tab as is.

4. Click the **Publish** button to generate an online document.

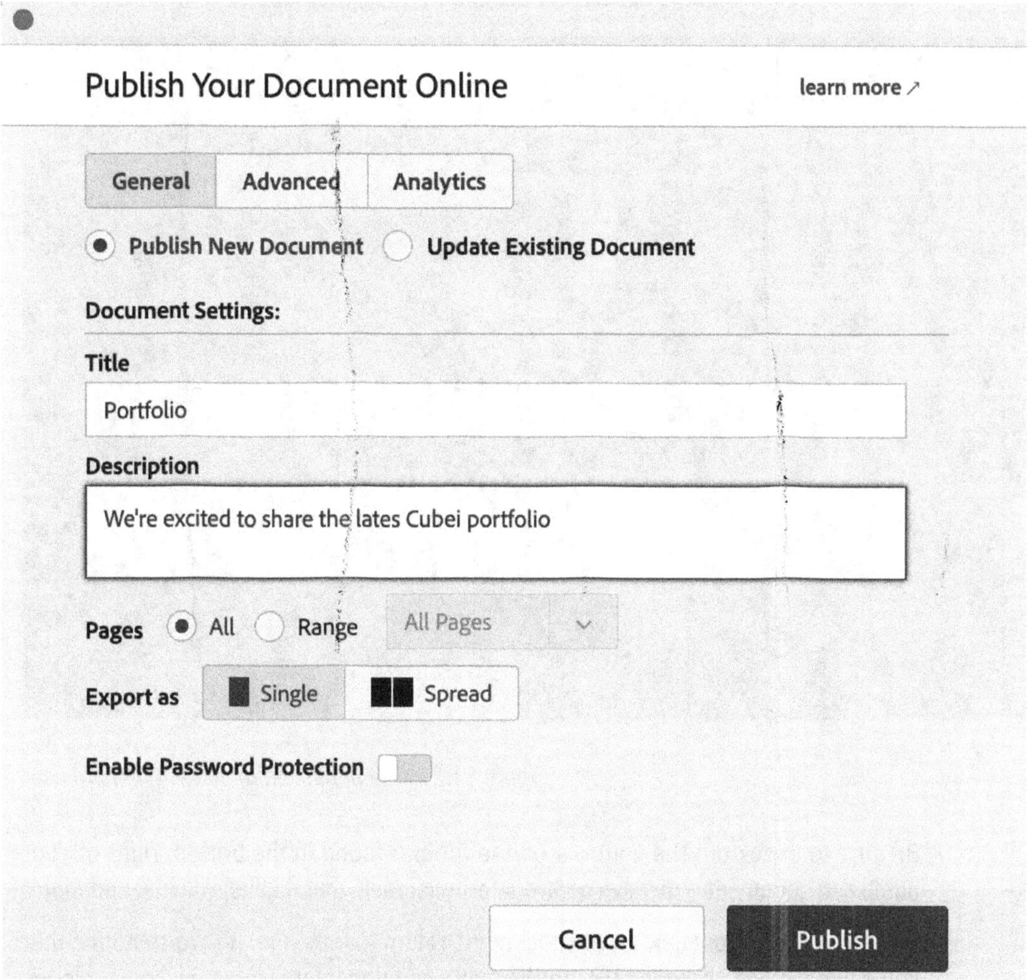

Figure 11.20: The Publish Online settings for our document

5. When the publishing process is successfully completed, click the **View Document** button to view the online export and see the fruits of your labor.

Figure 11.21: The published document in a browser

Be sure to check out the controls on the toolbar found in the bottom right of your published document. You have controls for fullscreen, thumbnails, volume, and more.

6. When you're done previewing the document, return to InDesign. It's worth noting that you can copy and share the URL to the published document via email, social media, or a direct copy and paste. Click the **Close** button to dismiss the dialog.

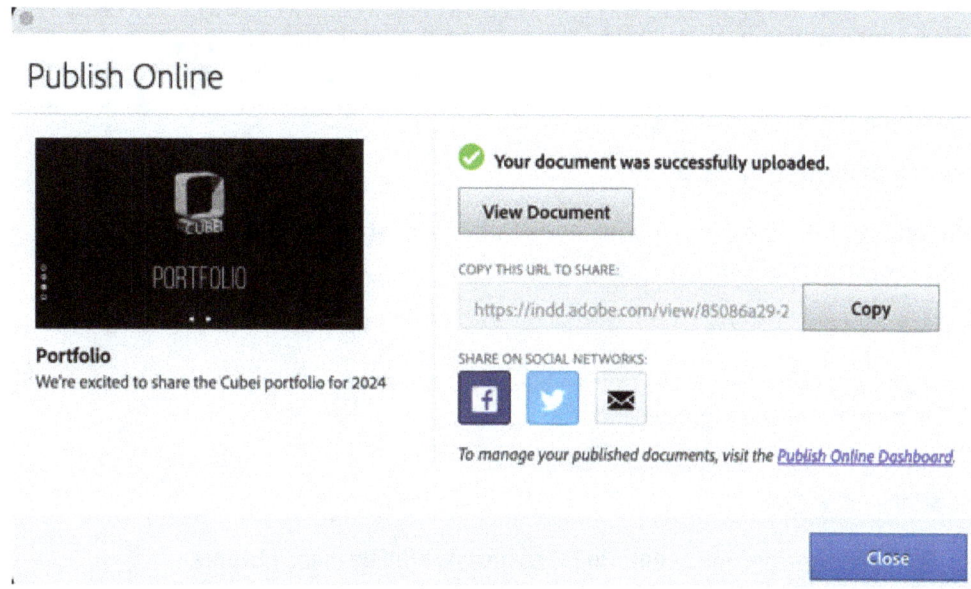

Figure 11.22: The sharing options on successful upload of your document

7. InDesign also sports a handy Publish Online dashboard. Choose **File** menu | **Publish Online Dashboard**:

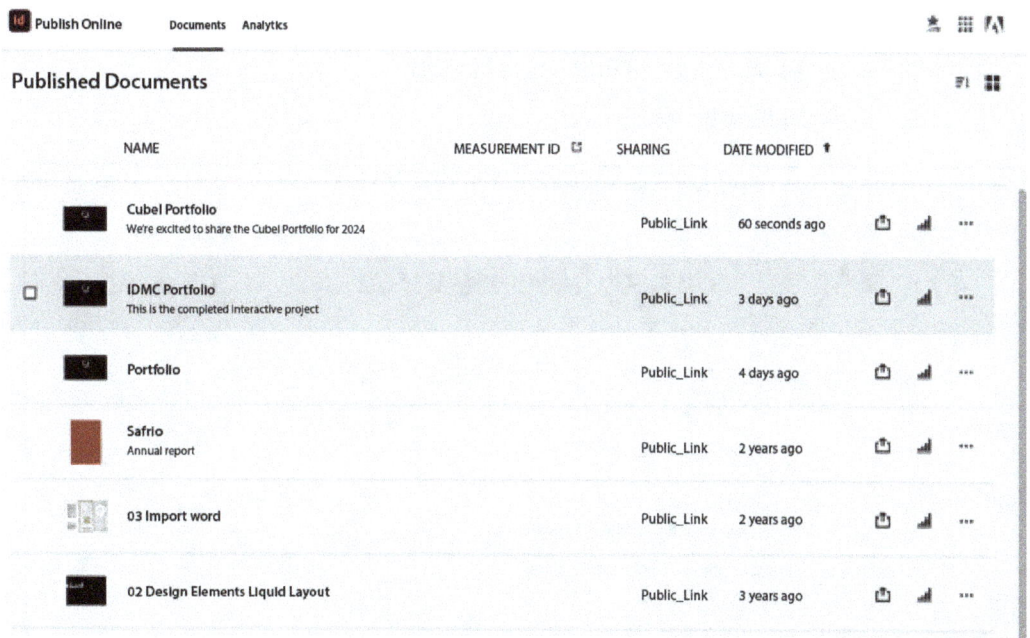

*Figure 11.23: A snapshot of the Publish Online dashboard
(The image is intended as a visual reference; the textual information is not essential.)*

That's us done with Publish Online. As you can see, it offers a rich smorgasbord of options for designers to explore without having to write a single line of code. We'll look at exporting in the ePUB format next.

Exporting to fixed layout ePUB

Fixed layout ePUB is ideal for exporting to e-readers and tablets while preserving the layout. This is a great option for offline and intranet sharing.

> **Note**
> InDesign allows for responsive (reflowable) ePUB export as well. This is good for academic papers and text-intensive documents.

Follow the next steps:

1. With the document open in InDesign, choose **File** menu | **Export**.
2. In the **Save As** dialog that opens, make the following changes:

    A. Uncheck the **Use InDesign Document Name as the Output Name** checkbox.

    B. Change the filename to Cubei Portfolio.

    C. Choose a location on your computer. For this purpose, we'll save it in the 02 Try it yourself 1 - Portfolio Start folder.

    D. Under **Format**, choose **EPUB (Fixed Layout)**.

    E. Click the **Save** button.

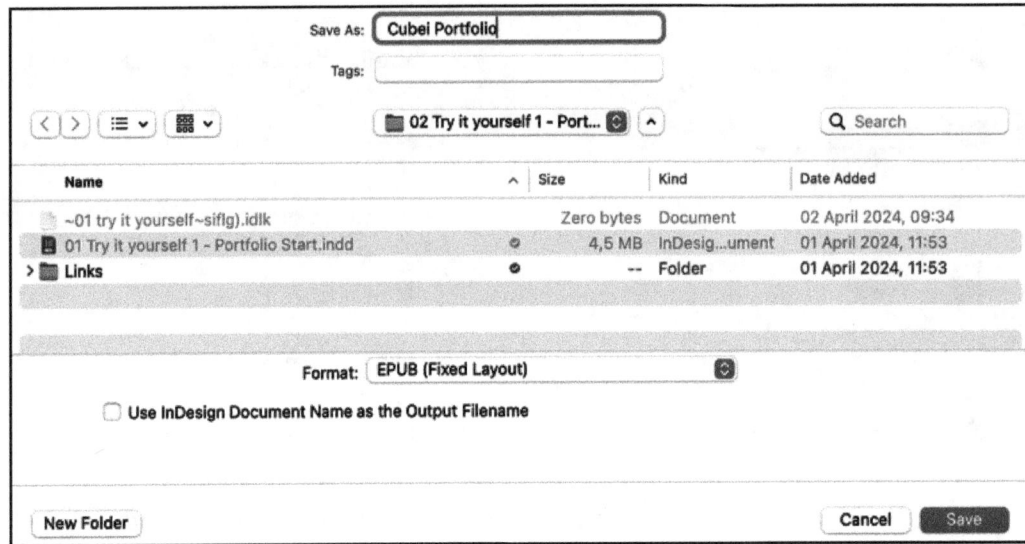

Figure 11.24: The ePUB Save As settings and location

3. You will be presented with the **ePUB - Fixed Layout Export Options** dialog. The numerous options extend well beyond the purview of this book. Our focus is on good design outcomes. So, we'll leave the options at their default settings. Click the **OK** button to generate the export.

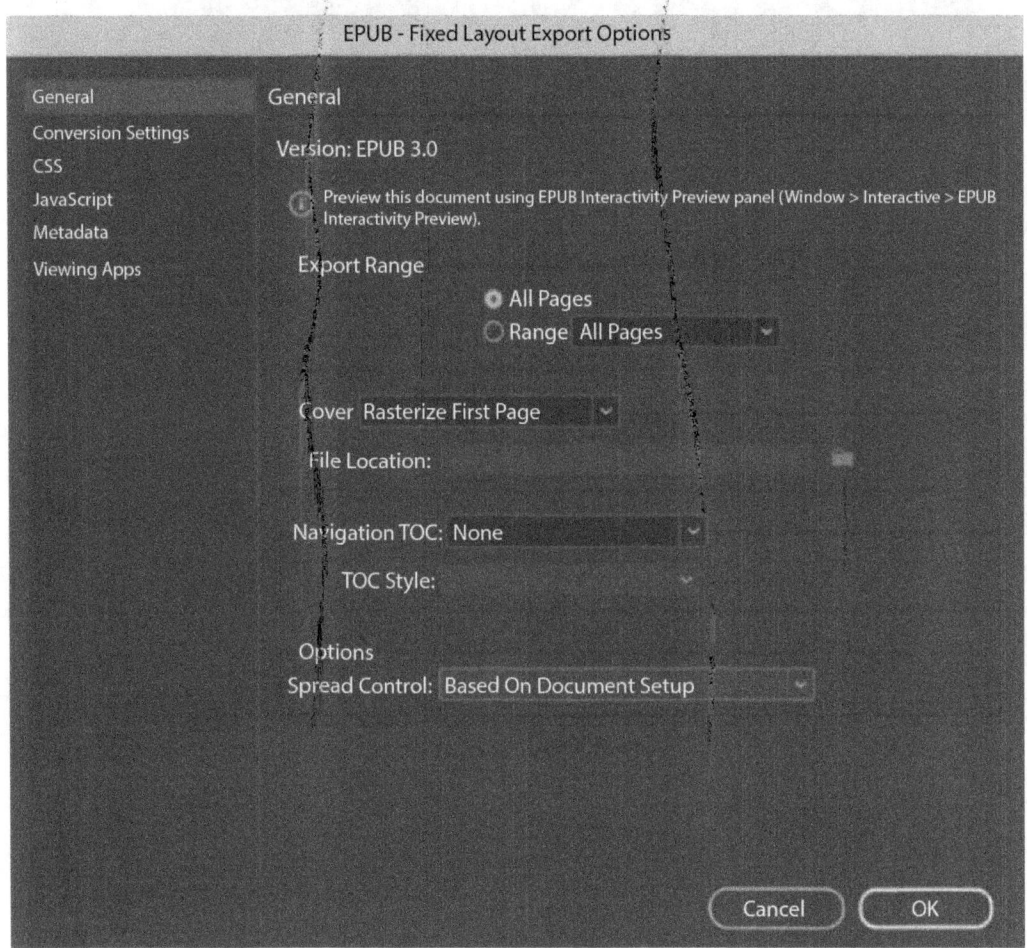

Figure 11.25: The ePUB - Fixed Layout Export Options dialog

4. If you are presented with an **ePUB Export Warnings** dialog, it is a warning for overlapping grouped .jpg files. Since we have none, click **OK**.

5. On a successful export, depending on your individual computer settings, the document should open in the default ePUB reader. Peruse the document to ensure that it meets your creative intention.

Figure 11.26: The exported ePUB in the iBooks app

We trust that you now have the necessary skills to export to ePUB with confidence. We have looked at how to export to ePUB and the rich export options available to you in InDesign. Since ePUB is a format that has many nuances, see the Packt library at https://www.packtpub.com for titles that are dedicated to this topic. From a design perspective, I trust that you agree that it looks good. Please close the current document in preparation for the next section, where we will explore the most poignant AI features available in InDesign today.

AI in InDesign

Adobe is consistently incorporating new AI features across its creative tools. InDesign is no exception. This helps streamline the design process, enhancing both efficiency and creativity for you and me. Some of its standout AI features that we'll explore in this section are content-aware image fitting, applying compelling text styling and pairing with **Auto Style**, generating AI images in your design with the **Text to Image** command, and extending an image to fill empty parts of a frame seamlessly.

Content-Aware Fit

Content-Aware Fit in InDesign intelligently adjusts and positions images within a frame, ensuring the focal point of the image is displayed relevant to the frame size and dimensions.

1. [*Optional step*] To explore the completed project, navigate to the folder named Chapter 11 Multimedia, Interactivity and AI Example Files | 03a Try it yourself - AI Complete. Open the file named 03 Ocean Worlds AI Complete.indd. **The under-sea images have been generated with the Text to Image feature directly in InDesign. The text was styled using the Auto Style command. Close the document when you are done exploring.**

Figure 11.27: A view of the completed project
(The image is intended as a visual reference; the textual information is not essential.)

2. Let's open the working file by navigating to the folder named Chapter 11 Multimedia, Interactivity and AI Example Files | 03b Try it yourself - AI Start. Open the file titled 03b Ocean Worlds AI Start.indd. **You can see that the file is partially completed.**

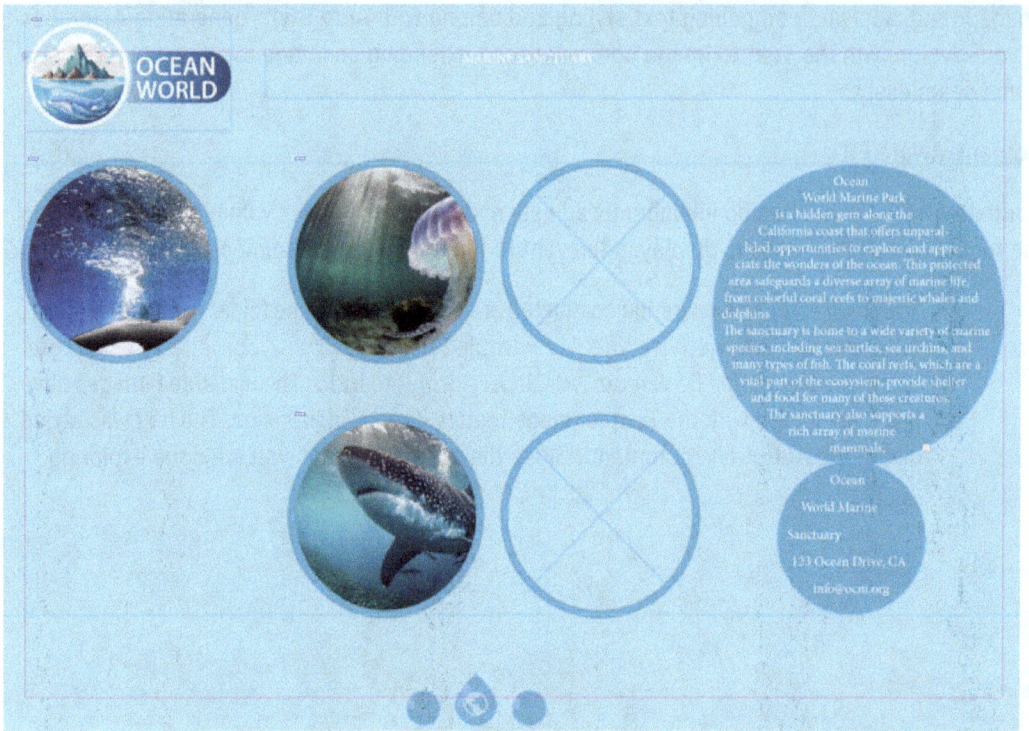

Figure 11.28: The partially finished working file
(The image is intended as a visual reference; the textual information is not essential.)

3. We'll start by using **Content-Aware Fit** to better place the jellyfish in its frame. Select the frame containing the jellyfish by clicking it with the **Selection** tool (V/Esc).

4. Head to the **Properties** panel. Under the **Frame Fitting Options** category, click the **Content-Aware Fit** icon. InDesign will reposition the image to achieve a better composition.

5. Since InDesign uses AI to achieve this, it is a best guess and you may not be satisfied with its proposed composition. You are still able to move the image in the frame using either the **Direct Selection** tool ▶ or the **Content Grabber**.

Figure 11.29: A snapshot showing the original composition (left) and content-aware fit (right) (The image is intended as a visual reference; the textual information is not essential.)

That was fairly straightforward. We'll look at generating our own images in the next step.

Text-to-image generation

In this segment, we'll add two images to the empty frames in the artwork using the power of Adobe's Firefly AI engine directly in InDesign. You can generate images using the **Text to Image** panel or the contextual taskbar. We'll look at both options:

1. Choose the top empty frame with the **Selection** tool ▶.

2. A contextual **Text to Image** taskbar appears below the selected frame. We'll type Coral Reef into it. You can type any prompt you'd like. Then click the **Generate** button.

Figure 11.30: The selected frame with contextual taskbar containing our prompt

3. InDesign will generate three variations of the prompt for you to choose from. Click on the arrows on the taskbar to navigate between the generated results.

Figure 11.31: The updated frame with the generated image and the contextual bar showing the chosen variation

4. Let's now select the second empty frame and generate images using the **Text to Image** panel.

5. Choose **Window Menu Text to Image (Beta)**. You can also click on the ellipsis on the contextual bar to access the panel from there.

6. You'll see that you have more controls on the panel. Input the following parameters:

    A. For **Prompt**, type Shoal of sardines.

    B. Choose **Photo** from the **Content Type** dropdown.

    C. Select **Square (1:1)** from the **Aspect Ratio** drop-down list.

7. Click the **Generate** button and allow InDesign to process the prompt.

8. Twirl open the **Variations** option. Choose the generated image you prefer from the three options presented to you.

That was a fun exploration of generating images in InDesign. In the next section, we will have a look at an allied feature, **Generative Expand**.

Generative Expand

The **Generative Expand** feature in InDesign uses AI to expand images beyond their original boundaries intelligently. It seamlessly fills in missing areas with contextually appropriate content, ensuring a visually appealing composition. We'll use it as follows:

1. Choose the frame with the orcas just below the logo with the **Selection** tool .

2. While pressing the *Shift* key, drag the bottom right control point of the frame to the guide at the bottom of the artwork. Use the drawn guides as an aid. See *Figure 11.32*.

Figure 11.32: The resized frame with the image no longer fitting in it

3. Before we generate our prompt, we'll center our image in the frame. This guides InDesign to generate content around the orcas.

4. Choose the **Properties** panel. Click the **Center content** icon under the **Frame Fitting** options.

5. Choose **Window Menu Text to Image (Beta)** to access the panel.

6. Set the following parameters in the panel:

    A. Ensure that the **Generative Expand (Beta)** command is active.

    B. For the prompt, type Orcas in the middle of composition, ocean extending out.

7. Click the **Generate** button and wait for InDesign to process the prompt.

8. Choose the generated image you think is best from **Variations**.

9. To place the newly generated expanded image more optimally in the frame, click the **Fill frame proportionally** icon . It is found on the **Properties** panel, under the **Frame fitting** subsection.

Figure 11.33: The resized frame with the newly generated expand

This brings our AI image explorations to a close. In the next section, we will use AI to assist in formatting text.

Auto Style

The **Auto Style** feature uses AI to apply consistent paragraph and character styles to text automatically. You can easily transform unformatted content into a beautifully formatted design with a single click. To do that:

1. Click the **Selection** tool in the toolbox.
2. Hold the *Shift* key and click each of the three text elements in the design to select their frames.

*Figure 11.34: The three pre-formatted text frames are selected
(The image is intended as a visual reference; the textual information is not essential.)*

3. Open the **Paragraph Styles** panel by choosing **Window** menu | **Styles** | **Paragraph Styles**.
4. Click the **View Style Packs** icon from the bottom of the **Paragraph Styles** panel.
5. Choose the **Tuxedo** style pack from the list. We encourage you to experiment by choosing different style packs.
6. You can now tweak the text for a better final result.
7. Select the **MARINE SANCTUARY** text with the **Type** tool.

8. Make the following changes on the **Properties** panel:

    A. Under **Character**, change the size from 22 to 36 pt.

    B. Under **Paragraph**, change the alignment to **Align center**.

9. Click inside the descriptor text in the larger circle using the **Type** tool.
10. Choose **Edit** menu | **Select all** to highlight all of the text in the frame.
11. Under **Character** on the **Properties** panel, change the size from 10 to 9 pt.
12. Click inside the smaller text circle that has the company contact information using the **Type** tool once more.
13. Choose **Edit** menu | **Select all** to highlight all of the text in that frame.
14. Under **Paragraph** on the **Properties** panel, choose **Align center**.
15. Let's look at the completed design. Choose **View** menu | **Fit Page in Window**.
16. Return to the **View** menu and select **Screen Mode | Preview**.

Figure 11.35: The completed design with the text styled and tweaked to fit our needs (The image is intended as a visual reference; the textual information is not essential.)

This concludes our tour of the AI tools in InDesign. We're hopeful that your understanding of these tools gives you both a creative edge and the ability to turn out projects more quickly and efficiently. This is such a vast and ever-evolving topic, so be sure to experiment and settle on tools that meet your workflow needs.

Summary

By working through the designs in this chapter, we gained a comprehensive understanding of creating interactive and engaging digital content using InDesign. We learned how to incorporate interactivity into our designs using hyperlinks, navigation controls, bookmarks, and buttons, allowing for seamless user navigation and enhanced user experiences. Additionally, we looked at how to animate elements and embed movies, adding dynamic visual elements to captivate audiences. Working with object states enabled us to define different appearances and behaviors for interactive elements. Furthermore, we mastered the process of publishing documents online and exporting to fixed layout ePUB. Thereby ensuring that our designs are accessible across various platforms while maintaining their integrity and functionality. Overall, these skills have equipped us to create compelling and interactive digital publications that effectively communicate our ideas to a wider audience. We wrapped up our exploration using the latest AI features available in InDesign. There's definitely more to come in future editions.

Sadly, this brings us to the end of this book. We hope you had as much fun reading it as we had in putting it together for you. The next chapter is the help and troubleshooting chapter. It covers a curated set of shortcuts we felt would be valuable to designers. It also has an index and other helpful resources.

Level: All

Help and Troubleshooting

In the previous chapter, we explored interactivity and AI in InDesign – an appropriate way to conclude this book. We're hopeful that our project-based, real-world, hands-on approach to sharing information was of value to you. No book can capture every aspect of a given topic, especially one as broad as InDesign. We therefore would love to hear from you. Tell us what you liked, what we can improve on, and what you would like us to write about next. You can do this by registering a personalized Packt account. This chapter is a collection of useful resources, including a curated list of default shortcuts we think would be of value to you, and where to find help.

The main topics we will cover in this chapter are the following:

- Registering your Packt account
- Keyboard shortcuts
- Helpful resources

Registering your Packt account

Registering for your personalized Packt account is super easy. Unlock extras, articles, discounted offers, and much more by registering here: https://www.packtpub.com/register

Keyboard shortcuts

We've curated the most useful default InDesign keyboard shortcuts for quick and easy reference. You can access a full list of shortcuts and customize them too. InDesign presents keyboard shortcuts alongside menu options for commands that have assigned shortcuts. To view these, follow the next steps:

> **Note**
> This is the most up-to-date keyboard shortcut list at the time of going to press.

1. Choose **Edit** menu | **Keyboard Shortcuts**.
2. Select the shortcut set you wish to see from the **Product Area** dropdown:

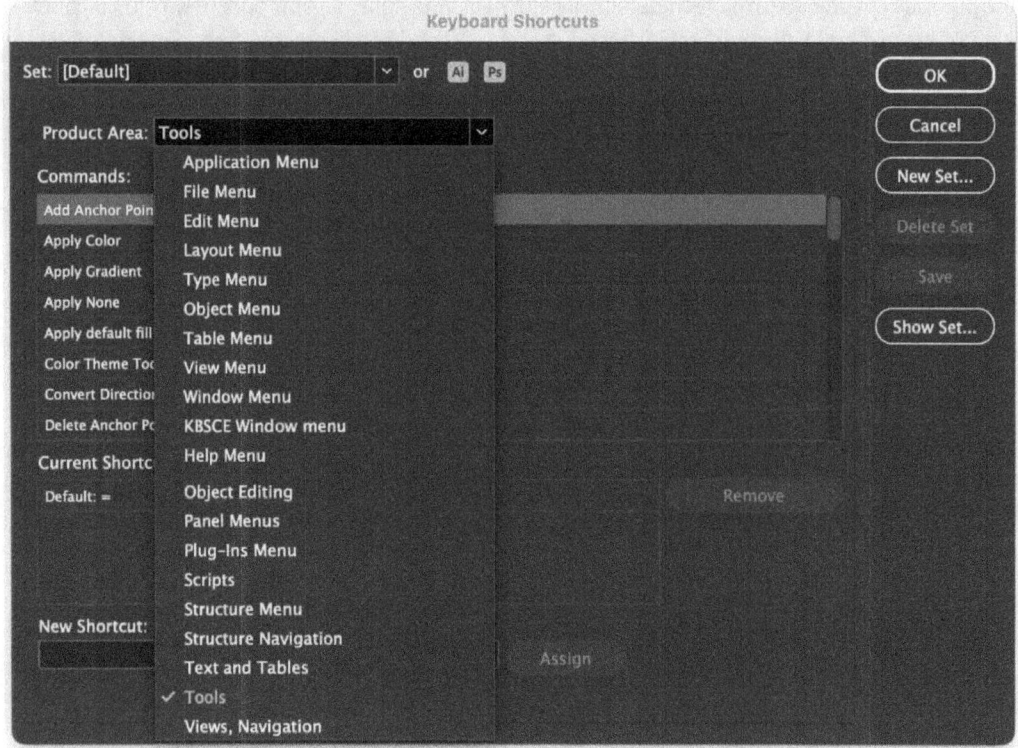

Figure 12.1: The InDesign Keyboard Shortcuts dialog box

You can create custom shortcuts to align with your preferred workflow in InDesign, as shown in *Figure 12.1*.

Shortcuts for tools

InDesign offers a plethora of shortcuts. While there are just too many for us to mention here, we've curated what we believe to be the most important shortcuts for you in the following table.

Tool	Windows	macOS
Selection tool	*V/Esc*	*V/Esc*
Direct Selection tool	*A*	*A*
Toggle Selection and Direct Selection tool	*Ctrl + Tab*	*Command + Control + Tab*
Page tool	*Shift + P*	*Shift + P*
Gap tool	*U*	*U*
Pen tool	*P*	*P*
Add Anchor Point tool	*=*	*=*
Delete Anchor Point tool	*-*	*-*
Convert Direction Point tool	*Shift + C*	*Shift + C*
Type tool	*T*	*T*
Type On A Path tool	*Shift + T*	*Shift + T*
Pencil tool (Note tool)	*N*	*N*
Line tool	**	**
Rectangle Frame tool	*F*	*F*
Rectangle tool	*M*	*M*
Ellipse tool	*L*	*L*
Rotate tool	*R*	*R*
Scale tool	*S*	*S*
Shear tool	*O*	*O*
Free Transform tool	*E*	*E*
Eyedropper tool	*I*	*I*
Measure tool	*K*	*K*
Gradient tool	*G*	*G*
Scissors tool	*C*	*C*

Tool	Windows	macOS
Hand tool	H	H
Zoom tool	Z	Z
Toggle Fill and Stroke	X	X
Swap Fill and Stroke	Shift + X	Shift + X
Toggle between Formatting Container and Text	J	J
Apply Color	,	,
Apply Gradient	.	.
Remove Color	/	/
Toggle between Normal view and Preview	W	W
Frame Grid tool (horizontal)	Y	Y
Frame Grid tool (vertical)	Q	Q
Gradient Feather tool	Shift + G	Shift + G

Table 12.1: Default shortcuts for tools

Next, we'll look at shortcuts for working with text.

Shortcuts for working with text

InDesign is a typographic powerhouse. We'd be remiss if we did not add a curated list of the most important text shortcuts. We hope you get value from this table of text shortcuts.

Command	Windows	macOS
Bold	Shift + Ctrl + B	Shift + Command + B
Italic	Shift + Ctrl + I	Shift + Command + I
Normal	Shift + Ctrl + Y	Shift + Command + Y
Underline	Shift + Ctrl + U	Shift + Command + U
Strikethrough	Shift + Ctrl + /	Control + Shift + Command + /
Toggle all caps	Shift + Ctrl + K	Shift + Command + K
Toggle Small caps	Shift + Ctrl + H	Shift + Command + H
Superscript	Shift + Ctrl + +	Shift + Command + +

Command	Windows	macOS
Subscript	Shift + Alt + Ctrl + +	Shift + Option + Command + +
Align left, right, or center	Shift + Ctrl + L, R, or C	Shift + Command + L, R, or C
Justify all lines	Shift + Ctrl + F	Shift + Command + F
Increase or decrease point size	Shift + Ctrl + > or <	Shift + Command + > or <
Increase or decrease point size x 5	Shift + Ctrl + Alt + > or <	Shift + Command + Option + > or <
Increase or decrease leading	Alt + Up Arrow/Alt + Down Arrow	Option + Up Arrow/Option + Down Arrow
Increase or decrease leading x 5	Alt + Ctrl + Up Arrow/Alt + Ctrl + Down Arrow	Option + Command + Up Arrow/ Option + Command + Down Arrow
Auto leading	Shift + Alt + Ctrl + A	Shift + Option + Command + A
Toggle align to grid	Shift + Alt + Ctrl + G	Shift + Option + Command + G
Toggle Auto-hyphenation	Shift + Alt + Ctrl +H	Shift + Option + Command + H
Increase or decrease kerning and tracking	Alt + Left Arrow/Alt + Right Arrow	Option + Left Arrow/Option + Right Arrow
Increase kerning between words	Alt + Ctrl + \	Option + Command + \
Decrease kerning between words	Alt + Ctrl + Backspace	Option + Command + Delete
Clear all manual kerning and tracking	Alt + Ctrl + Q	Option + Command + Q
Increase or decrease baseline shift	Shift + Alt +Up Arrow/Shift + Alt + Down Arrow	Shift + Option +Up Arrow/Shift + Option + Down Arrow
Increase or decrease baseline shift x 5	Shift + Alt + Ctrl +Up Arrow/Shift + Alt + Ctrl + Down Arrow	Shift + Option + Command + Up Arrow/Shift + Option + Command + Down Arrow
Automatically flow story	Shift-click loaded text icon	Shift-click loaded text icon
Semi-auto flow story	Alt-click loaded text icon	Option-click loaded text icon

Command	Windows	macOS
Recompose all stories	Alt + Ctrl + /	Option + Command + /
Insert current page number	Shift + Alt + Ctrl + N	Shift + Option + Command + N

Table 12.2: Text shortcuts

This is by no means a comprehensive shortcut list. That would be too cumbersome and of little value to you. It is a curated shortcut list that we believe will get you to work speedily and accurately in InDesign.

If you encounter problems with InDesign, you can access help by going to the help and support page for InDesign using this URL: https://helpx.adobe.com/support/indesign.html

You can get help with all sorts of topics, ranging from installing the software through to specific troubleshooting. There is also a vibrant user community. Visit https://community.adobe.com/t5/indesign/ct-p/ct-indesign to join hands with folks there. If you need help from us here at Packt Publishing, visit https://support.packtpub.com/en/

Summary

Thank you for purchasing this book. We trust you had an enjoyable time working through the various projects and topics. A reminder that this chapter covered how to sign up for your personalized Packt account, a curated list of keyboard shortcuts, how to access support, and how to engage with the online InDesign community. Take care and keep InDesigning!

Index

A

Adobe Firefly
  URL 350
AI in InDesign 363
  Auto Style 370, 371
  Content-Aware Fit 363-365
  text-to-image generation 365-369
animations
  animated objects, timing 346, 347
arrowheads
  applying, to strokes 250-252

B

background
  blend modes, applying 197, 198
  coloring 193
  creating 193
  drawing 193
  duplicate copy, creating 195
  objects rearranging 197, 198
  satin effect, applying 196, 197
bleed 20
borders
  creating 218, 219
  Eyedropper tool, using 220, 221
business card, designing
  basic shapes, drawing 29-32
  basic shapes properties, changing 29-32
  files, opening 26-29
  final design, previewing 56
  logo, creating 33-40
  objects, arranging 45-52
  rear of business card, designing 54-56
  resources, accessing 26-29
  text, working with 40-44
buttons 341
  working with 341-345

C

chart objects
  placing 173-177
CMYK color 131, 132
color models
  CMYK color 131, 132
  understanding 130
  RGB color 132, 133
  spot colors 134-136

Index

color separations 321-324
  color mix, correcting 325
Color Tools 15
completed project
  buttons and notch, preparing 144-147
  exploring 141-144
content, for social media posts
  completed project and resources 62, 63
  social media document, creating 63-65
control handles 95
corner earth graphic
  placing 255, 256
cropping 68
Cubed business card design 25, 26
Cubei 332

D

Dainippon Ink and Chemicals (DIC) collection 135
Data Merge 314, 315
  data source, preparing 315-317
  merged document, creating 317, 318
design elements
  using 261
dingbats 291
document
  guides and grids, setting up 190, 191
  midpoint guides, setting up 191, 192
  setting up 19-24, 189, 190
Drawing and Type Tools 15

E

effects
  applying, to text 224-232
  applying, to text frames 230-232
  applying, to type 226-229
  headline 224, 225
elements
  animating 345-355
  combining 221-223
exported document
  exploring 332-334
Eyedropper tool
  using 220, 221

F

Find/Change command
  using 240-242
fixed layout ePUB 360-362
floating panels 16
four-page tabloid-sized menu design 271
  exploring 272
frame 68

G

Generalised Regular Expression Print (GREP) styles 269
gradients 15
graphics
  formatting properties 150-152
  importing 149, 150
  object layer options, adjusting 154
  Photoshop image, importing 153, 154
  transparency and blending mode options 155, 156

H

headline 224, 225
help and support page
  reference link 378

hyperlinks
creating 337-339

I

imposition 271
InDesign 3
core layout concepts 19
workflow 19
InDesign libraries
working with 200, 201
InDesign toolbox 13
Color Tools 15
Drawing and Type Tools 15
Modification and Navigation Tools 15
Selection Tools 15
Transformation Tools 15
Viewing Modes 15
InDesign workspace
Control Bar 6
Document Window 6
exploring 5-13
Menu Bar 5
Panels 6
Toolbox 6
inline graphics 178-184
interactive documents
exporting 356
exporting, Publish Online used 356-359
exporting, to fixed layout ePUB 360, 362
working with 334, 335
interactive elements
testing 339-341
interactive multi-state objects
creating 350-355

K

keyboard shortcuts 374
for tools 375, 376
for working with text 376, 378

L

Layers panel
objects, selecting from 236

M

main sequence labels
placing 253, 254
Master Pages 12
menu design 273
OpenType 275-277
paragraph styles 274, 275
Microsoft Excel tables
importing 115, 116
Microsoft Word
style mapping, from 278
text, importing from 103-106
Microsoft Word styles, mapping to InDesign styles 282
custom bullets, adding to list 293, 294
defined style properties, customizing 288-291
glyphs, using 291, 292
styles, exploring in Word 282, 283
styles setup, exploring in InDesign 284
vertical justification, modifying 297, 298
Word styles, importing and mapping 285-288
Modification and Navigation Tools 15
multimedia elements
adding, to InDesign files 348-350

Index

multiple images
   importing in to InDesign 96
   importing into InDesign 97-100

O

object position
   adjusting, from Properties panel 238-240
objects
   selecting, from Layers panel 236, 237
object style
   applying 233
   saving 233
object stylesheet
   applying, to unformatted design element 233, 234
OpenType 269, 275
   exploring 275-277
outer glows
   creating 234-236
overset text 242

P

page elements, duplicating 157, 158
   color, applying to objects 167, 168
   Direct Selection tool, working with 159
   frame content, assigning 161
   libraries, working with 164, 165
   multi-frame grid, drawing 165-167
   multiple files, importing 169, 170
   navigation bar, creating 163, 164
   object hierarchy 170-173
   object layer options, adjusting 160
   status bar, creating 162
panel menus
   exploring 18

panels 16
   collapsed - icons only 17
   collapsed with labels 17
   expanded with labels 16
   floating 17
   floating panels 16
   panel group 16
   stacked 16
   working with 16, 17
paragraph style
   applying 233, 274, 275
   saving 233
pasteboard 19
Pathfinder commands
   using 256-260
pixels 62
place gun icon 97
placeholder frames 90
   creating 91-96
preflighting 326-330
presentation document
   guides, adding 88-90
   setting up 86-88
primary user interface graphic
   border elements, creating 206, 207
   creating 198
   element properties, adjusting 208, 209
   element properties, duplicating 208
   elements, moving between groups and subgroups 213, 214
   multiple feather effects, applying to elements 209-211
   object styles, working with 203
   Outer Glow effect, adding 201, 202
   ovals, working with 214-216
   polygons, working with 214-216
   stroke styles, varying 211, 212

world map, formatting 204, 205
world map, placing 204, 205
print-ready PDF files
   creating 319-321
print service provider (PSP) 318
Properties panel
   object position, adjusting from 238-240
Publish Online feature 356-359

R

rapid-fire styles 270
reverse type 74
   creating 74-78
RGB color 132, 133

S

Selection Tools 15
social media post document
   creating 63-65
   guides, adding 65
   images, cropping 68
   images, importing into InDesign 66, 67
   multiple objects, placing 81, 82
   objects, locking 69
   QR codes, generating 82, 83
   reverse type, creating 74-78
   rounded corner rectangles, creating 70, 71
   type, working with 71-74
   vector graphics, importing 80
soft proofing 322
solar system graphic
   placing 254, 255
spot colors 134-136
Start workspace 4
Step and Repeat command 243-245
   using 245-249

Step and Repeat function
   artwork, preparing for print 308, 309
   document setup, adjusting 311, 312
   scripts, using 309-311
   setting up 306, 307
   using 312-314
strokes
   arrowheads, applying to 250-252
style mapping, from Microsoft Word 278
   local overrides 301, 302
   paragraph and character styles,
      combining 295-297
   QR codes, generating 302, 303
   text frames, threading 278-282
   Type on a Path feature, applying 298, 299
   variable fonts 300, 301
   Word styles, mapping to InDesign styles 282
styles
   applying selectively 111-113
   imported Word styles, removing 110
   working with 108, 109
stylistic sets 275

T

tables
   alternating fills, applying 126, 127
   cell, changing 123
   cell spacing, adjusting 122
   cell strokes, changing 124, 125
   cell text colors, changing 123
   font and weight properties, adjusting 124
   formatting 118-120
   header and footer rows 121
templates 19
text
   attributes, formatting 107
   effects, applying to 224

formatting 100-102
formatting, for perfect fit 114, 115
importing, from MS Word
    documents 103-106
typing 100-102
wrapping, around objects 117, 118
threading process 278
Transformation Tools 15
troubleshooting 378
Type on a Path tool
using 298

U

unformatted design element
object stylesheet, applying to 233, 234

V

Viewing Modes 15
Visla
URL 348

W

white on black (WOB) 74
workspace
customizing 335-337
wrap object 117

Z

zooming 11

Packtpub.com

Subscribe to our online digital library for full access to over 7,000 books and videos, as well as industry leading tools to help you plan your personal development and advance your career. For more information, please visit our website.

Why subscribe?

- Spend less time learning and more time coding with practical eBooks and Videos from over 4,000 industry professionals
- Improve your learning with Skill Plans built especially for you
- Get a free eBook or video every month
- Fully searchable for easy access to vital information
- Copy and paste, print, and bookmark content

Did you know that Packt offers eBook versions of every book published, with PDF and ePub files available? You can upgrade to the eBook version at packtpub.com and as a print book customer, you are entitled to a discount on the eBook copy. Get in touch with us at customercare@packtpub.com for more details.

At www.packtpub.com, you can also read a collection of free technical articles, sign up for a range of free newsletters, and receive exclusive discounts and offers on Packt books and eBooks.

Other Books You May Enjoy

If you enjoyed this book, you may be interested in these other books by Packt:

Mastering Adobe Photoshop 2024

Gary Bradley

ISBN: 978-1-83882-201-9

- Discover new ways of working with familiar tools, enhancing your existing knowledge of Photoshop
- Master time-saving retouching techniques, ensuring flexibility for repeated edits without compromising on quality
- Create precise image cut-outs and seamless montages with advanced masking tools
- Make Photoshop your go-to application for social media content
- Automate repetitive tasks with actions and scripts that batch-process hundreds of images in seconds
- Integrate vector assets, type styles, and brand colors from other CC applications

Creative Motion Mastery with Adobe After Effects

Vishu Aggarwal

ISBN: 978-1-80461-728-1

- Create and customize text layers, including text animations, using shape layers
- Enhance projects with audio elements and apply audio effects to shape layers
- Develop editable motion graphics templates for Premiere Pro
- Implement color correction and grading techniques to enhance footage in projects
- Use rotoscoping to remove and mask objects seamlessly
- Generate realistic effects such as rain, fire, and smoke using particle simulations
- Master the art of compositing through Chroma Keying
- Get to grips with 2D and 3D tracking for seamless element integratio

Packt is searching for authors like you

If you're interested in becoming an author for Packt, please visit authors.packtpub.com and apply today. We have worked with thousands of developers and tech professionals, just like you, to help them share their insight with the global tech community. You can make a general application, apply for a specific hot topic that we are recruiting an author for, or submit your own idea.

Hi!

I am Mohammed Jogie, author of *Adobe InDesign Masterclass*. I really hope you enjoyed reading this book and found it useful for increasing your productivity and efficiency.

It would really help me (and other potential readers!) if you could leave a review on Amazon sharing your thoughts on this book.

Go to the link below or scan the QR code to leave your review:

https://packt.link/r/1803247444

Your review will help us to understand what's worked well in this book, and what could be improved upon for future editions, so it really is appreciated.

Best wishes,

Mohammed Jogie

Download a free PDF copy of this book

Thanks for purchasing this book!

Do you like to read on the go but are unable to carry your print books everywhere?

Is your eBook purchase not compatible with the device of your choice?

Don't worry, now with every Packt book you get a DRM-free PDF version of that book at no cost.

Read anywhere, any place, on any device. Search, copy, and paste code from your favorite technical books directly into your application.

The perks don't stop there, you can get exclusive access to discounts, newsletters, and great free content in your inbox daily

Follow these simple steps to get the benefits:

1. Scan the QR code or visit the link below

https://packt.link/free-ebook/978-1-80324-744-1

2. Submit your proof of purchase
3. That's it! We'll send your free PDF and other benefits to your email directly